e-Plan Your Wedding

How to Save Time and Money with Today's Best Online Resources

Crystal and Jason Melendez

Mediasoft Press

Mediasoft Press
San Jose, California

e-Plan Your Wedding
How to Save Time and Money with Today's Best Online Resources
by Crystal and Jason Melendez

Published by:
Mediasoft Press
Post Office Box 610487
San Jose, CA 95161-0487 U.S.A.

orders@mediasoftpress.com
www.mediasoftpress.com
SAN 256-5366

Library of Congress Cataloging-in-Publication Data

Melendez, Crystal.
   E-plan your wedding : how to save time and money with today's best
online resources / Crystal and Jason Melendez.
     p. cm.
   Supplemented by a companion website.
   Includes bibliographical references.
   ISBN 1-933457-00-7 (paperbook)
   1. Weddings—Planning. 2. Weddings—Planning—Computer network
resources. 3. Wedding etiquette.   I. Melendez, Jason. II. Title.
HQ745.M55 2006
395.2'2028546—dc22

                                 2006001321

Cover design, graphic design, and illustrations by Peter Estaniel

Exclusive Wedding Website Offer!

Purchase this book and receive a valuable discount on a complete wedding website package at top wedding website provider WedShare.com!

Your package includes:

- Your own domain name (www.yourname.com)
- Email addresses (you@yourname.com)
- Unlimited photo albums
- An interactive guestbook
- Helpful events calendar
- Complete suite of wedding planning tools
- Customized Flash® intro
- Online RSVP
- Countdowns, music, videos, maps, gift registries, and much more!

Just go to:
www.wedshare.com/bookspecial.html

or visit this book's website:
www.eplanyourwedding.com

Contents

Acknowledgments

A great big thank you to everyone who was there for us during this project, especially through our months of self-imposed isolation. Words can't fully express our gratitude to our family and friends for providing never-ending encouragement and support. To our parents and families: thanks for never once losing faith in us. You've been there to keep us going from day one, and our accomplishments are yours. To our friends: you've let us vent, bounce ideas, and have given us invaluable advice and assistance throughout. This project wouldn't be possible without you. To our graphic designer Peter Estaniel, who burned the midnight oil more than once with us: without your creativity and tireless dedication to the project, this would just be "another book". To all the wedding professionals, vendors, wedding websites and couples we've had the honor and pleasure to work with: our deepest gratitude for your time, assistance and contributions.

- Crystal and Jason

Chapter 1

Introduction

- What Will This Book Do for You?
- How to Use This Book
- Your First e-Resource: This Book's Website
- Contact Us

Welcome to the convenient world of e-planning! You're holding a valuable asset: a complete step-by-step guidebook to navigating the wedding planning journey from start to finish. It's also the most comprehensive reference you'll find; we cover some incredibly convenient resources available today that every couple should know about, as well as all the traditions, etiquette, and sage advice you'd expect from a solid wedding planner. The following introduction will give you some quick pointers you may find helpful before getting started.

What Will This Book Do for You?

This book will guide you along as you start your planning, from solidifying your wedding vision and nailing down your priorities to creating a smart, flexible budget and payment system. As you continue along the planning journey, we'll help you stay on track with the million-and-one details you need to manage, and will show you easy ways to stay organized. Along the way, you'll take advantage of great time- and money-saving resources like wedding websites, online RSVP's, guest lists that build and update themselves, online gown and flower discounters, eBay wedding bargains, and lots more! From engagement ring to honeymoon bliss, it's all inside.

How to Use This Book

Is This Just for "Computer People"?

No. You DO NOT need to be a hardcore technophile to make use of this book. In fact, you don't even need to own a computer, although some of the shortcuts and bargains you'll read about may make you want to go out and buy one. This book is designed to help you take every possible advantage of those online shortcuts or bargains (we call them e-Resources), but we also cover all the traditional and non-technical ways of approaching the various steps involved in planning your wedding. Deciding to make use of a suggested e-Resource is your call, and the worksheets included with each chapter can substitute for the essential information gathering and management.

That said, readers with access to a computer and the Internet will benefit most by leveraging on all kinds of fun and timesaving ways to make your planning easier, as well saving some bucks. As long as you have somewhere you can go to jump onto the Internet periodically, you'll be able to reap the e-planning rewards.

Our Planning Strategy

In a nutshell: to preserve your time, money, and sanity with smart preparations and by taking advantage of everything available to you. Chapter 2, "The Big Picture", gives you a great big list of all sorts of things to do between now and the big day. Although your eyes might glaze over when you first see it, don't worry...most of it is just a lot of reminders. The idea is to follow along with the checklist a group at a time. We give recommendations for how long before your wedding each group should be completed. The checklist will help guide you along by cueing you on items you should be thinking about, taking action on, or verifying. It will always refer you to the chapter that relates to each item for more help.

Chapter 3, "The Journey Begins", is the real start of the yellow brick road. It gets you going with the initial considerations and decisions you need to start thinking about. Subsequent chapters guide you through priorities, budgets, finding your locations, and finally dealing with all the vendors and other details you need to take care of. And don't worry if you're already in the middle of your wedding planning by the time you find this book. Just skim what you've already taken care of to make sure you're not missing anything, and go from there.

Your First e-Resource: This Book's Website

Find updated chapters, useful links, new tips and other goodies at the book's companion website: www.eplanyourwedding.com. If you need extra copies of the chapter worksheets, you can download and print them from here, too. And don't miss the exclusive wedding website offer! The password to access the bonus material is: MYEPLANNER.

Contact Us

Got feedback? Suggestions? We'd love to hear from you! Let us know how this book worked for you and your planning, and give us the scoop on how your day went. Send your notes, stories and feedback to: authors@eplanyourwedding.com. You just might find your story in another edition of this book!

Chapter 2

The Big Picture–Your Complete Wedding Checklist

- 12 or More Months Before (Starting ASAP!)
- 8 to 10 Months Before
- 6 to 8 Months Before
- 4 to 6 Months Before
- 3 Months Before
- 2 Months Before
- 1 Month Before
- 2 Weeks Before
- 1 Week Before
- 2 to 3 Days Before
- The Day Before (Rehearsal Day)
- Your Wedding Day
- After the Wedding

The most common planning question from the newly engaged is "where do we start?" The following checklist is a bird's-eye view of your planning journey, while each referenced chapter is an up-close and detailed survival guide. Following the checklist will remind you of things you need to start shopping for or start considering and will prompt you to send or request information from vendors at the appropriate times. It provides a recommended order in which to proceed with your planning, and—perhaps most important—where to get started.

If you've got less time than the assumed 12+ months, don't panic! Weddings have been planned in four or five months (sometimes less)…it just means you'll need to cut back on some of the details and shrink your time windows to fit. Start at the beginning of the checklist and do what you can, moving forward at a good pace until you catch up. If you've already been planning for a while, go back and make sure you haven't missed anything.

12 or More Months Before (Starting ASAP!)

Date:_____

☐ If the engagement ring has not already been purchased, select it now (Chapter 3).

☐ Announce your engagement to friends and family. Traditionally, parents of the bride are notified first (Chapter 3).

☐ Arrange for both of your parents to get together.

☐ Start thinking about possible wedding styles and preferences such as formal/informal, theme, color scheme, and number of guests (Chapter 3).

☐ Select a few possible wedding dates if you're not already sure (Chapter 3).

☐ Get a wedding website and set it up as a public announcement for now (Chapter 4). You may also choose to announce your engagement in the newspaper (Chapter 3).

☐ Get a separate email address for your wedding planning purposes (Chapter 6).

☐ Buy a calendar to jot down important events and deadlines as they come up. Use your online calendar in the place of—or in addition to—the paper calendar (online calendars are covered in Chapter 21).

☐ Determine your overall wedding budget, and divide it into flexible expense categories. Decide who pays for what (Chapter 5).

☐ Start a wedding binder with your preferences, budget, and seperate folders for each wedding vendor (Chapter 5).

☐ Start a record-keeping system for payments, deposits, and due dates. Add it to your wedding binder, and keep every vendor's financial paperwork in the appropriate folder (Chapter 5).

☐ Using your budget, finalize your wedding vision: decide on a formality level, theme, color scheme, number of guests, and wedding date (Chapter 6).

☐ Send save-the-date cards if your wedding falls near a holiday or if you're planning a destination wedding (Chapter 20).

☐ Select your attendants, maid of honor, and best man (Chapter 7).

☐ Select your ring bearer, flower girl, and train bearer, if you'll be having them (Chapter 7).

☐ Get familiar with your wedding website as an information storage tool (Chapter 4). Keep all your printed paperwork—such as receipts and ideas—in your wedding binder.

☐ Plan and throw an engagement party if you'd like (Chapter 3). You may want to register for gifts prior to the party, but this is not necessary (gifts are covered in Chapter 15).

☐ Begin building your guest list. Start gathering contact information manually or using a self-building address book online. Get a rough head count (Chapter 7).

☐ If you plan on using a wedding consultant or coordinator, select and hire one now (Chapter 6).

☐ Start shopping for the wedding gown (Chapter 10).

☐ Start looking at ceremony and reception locations. These go fast, so book something you really love if it's available on your date (Chapter 8, 9).

☐ Begin looking for a ceremony officiant (Chapter 8).

☐ Considering a wedding insurance policy to protect your deposits (Chapter 23).

☐ Book your ceremony location (Chapter 8).

☐ Book your reception location (Chapter 9).

☐ Book your ceremony officiant (Chapter 8).

☐ If you are having a home ceremony or reception, plan for any house and/or garden improvements (Chapter 8).

☐ If your reception location offers a catering service, arrange to check the facilities.

☐ If your reception location does not offer a catering service, begin researching and meeting with caterers for interviews and tastings (Chapter 11).

☐ Begin researching and meeting with photographers (Chapter 12).

☐ Begin researching and meeting with videographers. Request sample tapes (Chapter 13).

☐ Start thinking about your ceremony, cocktail hour, and reception music preferences (Chapter 14).

☐ Begin researching and meeting with DJs, bands, and musicians. Request demo tapes (Chapter 14).

☐ Begin researching flowers and florists. Start meeting with florists and viewing samples of their work (Chapter 17).

8 to 10 Months Before

Date:_____

☐ Finalize any ceremony details: make sure contract is signed and deposit is paid.

☐ As a couple, meet with your officiant and discuss any premarital requirements, such as counseling.

☐ Make sure your reception location contract is signed and the deposit made.

☐ Finalize your guest list. Use your online guest database (Chapter 7).

☐ Book your caterer (Chapter 11).

☐ Book your photographer (Chapter 12).

☐ Book your videographer (Chapter 13).

☐ Book your entertainment, including a DJ and/or musicians (Chapter 14).

☐ Book your florist (Chapter 17).

☐ Select and order the wedding gown (Chapter 10).

☐ Schedule your first gown fitting (Chapter 10).

☐ Gather the bridesmaids' measurements and begin investigating bridesmaids' dress ideas (Chapter 16).

☐ Start a gift registry at your selected store(s). Create a gift registry page at your wedding website for all your guests to access easily (Chapter 15).

☐ Reserve accommodations for your out-of-town guests at a hotel local to your reception location (Chapter 7).

☐ Take into consideration rental items that may be required for your ceremony or reception, such as a tent, outdoor lighting, chairs, tables, and so forth. Start contacting and discussing options with rental companies (Chapter 9).

☐ Sign up for dance lessons.

☐ Begin shopping around at various stationers and start thinking about the invitation style and wording you would prefer (Chapter 20).

6 to 8 Months Before

Date:_____

☐ Begin researching honeymoon spots (Chapter 24).

☐ Obtain or update your passports if you'll be traveling out of the country for your honeymoon. Investigate any vaccination requirements (Chapter 24).

☐ Decide on your wedding stationery and order invitations, announcements, thank-you cards, and any other stationery (Chapter 20).

☐ Purchase the bridal accessories: shoes, veil, stockings, lingerie, and jewelry (Chapter 10).

☐ Select the bridesmaids' dresses, their shoes and any accessories (Chapter 16).

☐ Select attire for the flower girl, ring bearer, and train bearer (Chapter 16).

☐ Provide your bridesmaids and the parents of your child attendants with information to order attire and arrange for fittings.

☐ Make sure mothers are aware of your style and formality level to plan their attire appropriately (Chapter 16).

☐ The groom should begin researching formal wear styles and ideas for himself and his groomsmen (Chapter 16).

☐ Begin considering cake ideas and meeting with bakeries. Set up tasting appointments (Chapter 18).

☐ Work over your menu details with your caterer and come to an agreement on a final menu (Chapter 11).

☐ Plan your beverage and alcohol needs with your caterer or reception coordinator. If they're not handling alcohol, arrange for an outside vendor to provide (Chapter 11).

☐ Start thinking about your wedding day transportation options. Begin researching car companies (Chapter 19).

☐ If you'll be renting items that may be required for your ceremony or reception, such as a tent, outdoor lighting, chairs, tables, and so forth, finalize the reservations and make any deposits to the rental company you choose to go with (Chapter 9).

☐ Let your attendants know which special responsibilities you'll be giving them (Chapter 21).

☐ Check your state's requirements for a marriage license, and make any necessary appointment for a physical exam (Chapter 23).

4 to 6 Months Before

Date:_____

☐ The groom should rent or purchase his formal wear and reserve the groomsmen attire (Chapter 16).

☐ Verify that you've ordered all your bridal attire (Chapter 10).

☐ Select a bakery and order your wedding cake and/or other desserts (Chapter 18).

☐ Book your wedding day transportation (Chapter 19).

☐ Finalize your guest list (Chapter 7).

☐ Make sure you've collected all addresses and contact information: export them from your guest database as a formalized list (Chapter 20).

☐ Hire a calligrapher or obtain a calligraphic font online (Chapter 20).

☐ Start addressing your invitations (Chapter 20).

☐ Confirm the delivery date for you gown and your bridesmaids' dresses (Chapter 16).

☐ Book hairstylist and makeup artist for the day of your wedding (Chapter 10).

☐ Start discussing your plans for a rehearsal dinner time and place (Chapter 22).

☐ Start shopping for your wedding rings (Chapter 15).

☐ Make or purchase your wedding favors, welcome baskets, and other decorative items (Chapter 15).

☐ Finalize the details of your wedding flowers and arrangements with the florist (Chapter 17).

☐ Start building your music list for the ceremony and reception (Chapter 14).

☐ Arrange for guests' transportation needs to/from your location, as well as valet parking if necessary (Chapter 19).

☐ Check that your bridal attendants have attended their first fitting.

☐ Verify the accommodations for your out-of-town guests (Chapter 7).

☐ Book your honeymoon location (Chapter 24).

3 Months Before

Date:_____

☐ Finalize details with your main vendors, such as caterer, photographer, videographer, and so forth.

☐ If you haven't already, book someone to do you hair, makeup, and nails on your wedding day. Set appointments for trial runs to try different looks (Chapter 10).

☐ Make appointment for a bridal portrait session with your photographer so you'll have it available for a newspaper announcement, your wedding website, and/or the wedding day (Chapter 12).

☐ Book your rehearsal dinner location and finalize a guest list. This can be done using an online RSVP-capable event manager such as the one your wedding website may have (Chapter 22).

☐ Start making plans for the pre-wedding events like showers or bachelor/ette parties. You may want to discuss these with the best man and maid of honor and provide them with guest lists (Chapter 22).

☐ Consider legal options like a will or prenuptial agreement (Chapter 23).

☐ If required or preferred, attend a pre-wedding counseling session or program (Chapter 21).

☐ Obtain your marriage license and request certified copies (Chapter 23).

☐ If necessary, make appointments for blood tests.

☐ Get necessary name change forms (Chapter 23).

☐ Book your wedding night accommodations.

2 Months Before

Date:_____

☐ Send out your invitations 6 to 8 weeks before the wedding (Chapter 20).

☐ Mail out the invitations for your rehearsal dinner.

☐ If your reception is seated, start creating a seating chart and start creating your place cards (Chapter 21).

☐ Start putting together a timeline for your wedding day details: when the bride will be getting there, who will drive her, when the ceremony ends and cocktail hour begins, when photos will be taken, and so on (Chapter 21).

☐ Take care of any necessary wedding gown alterations (Chapter 10).

☐ Meet with your hair stylist and makeup artist for a trial run of your wedding day makeup and hair, with your hairpiece (Chapter 10).

☐ If you're publishing an announcement in the newspaper, contact the paper and get information.

☐ RSVPs may be starting to arrive in the mail and online. Add the mailed RSVP information to your guest database; the online RSVPs will be added automatically and require no special attention (Chapter 20).

☐ Gifts may have started arriving already. Start recording gifts as you receive them, using your online guest database. Write thank-you notes as they come in to keep pace (Chapter 15).

☐ Write your wedding vows if you plan to do so and finalize other ceremony details. Meet with your officiant to go over all the details if you need to (Chapter 8).

☐ Pick speakers for your reception (Chapter 7).

☐ Order your ceremony programs, or design and print them yourself (Chapter 20).

☐ Plan your bridesmaids' luncheon (or dinner), and start thinking about what gifts you'd like to give them during the luncheon (Chapter 22). The groom should start thinking about groomsmen gifts to give at the rehearsal dinner.

☐ Attend showers and bachelor/ette parties (Chapter 22).

☐ Have your bridal portrait done (Chapter 12).

☐ Begin shopping for gifts for each other (Chapter 15).

☐ Begin shopping for your accessories, such as toasting glasses, ring pillow, guestbook and pen, candles, and so forth (Chapter 21).

☐ Gather "something old, new, borrowed and blue" (Chapter 10).

☐ Begin shopping for your trousseau.

1 Month Before

Date:_____

☐ Pick up your wedding rings and verify the fit. Resize them if necessary (Chapter 15).

☐ Verify accommodations for out-of-town guests.

☐ Compile information packages for out-of-town guests, including hotel information and things to do. This is best done with your wedding website's out-of-town guests page (Chapter 7).

☐ Order out-of-town welcome baskets or start collecting what you'll need to create them yourself… fruit, chocolates, other goodies, along with extra maps to the ceremony and reception locations (Chapter 15).

☐ Have your final wedding gown fitting; it's a good idea for the maid of honor to accompany you so she learns how to bustle your gown. Get the gown pressed and bring home (Chapter 10).

☐ Verify with your bridesmaids that they have been fitted and have taken care of any necessary alterations or are in the process of getting it done. They should have their shoes as well (Chapter 16).

☐ Have your florist provide you a sample of your centerpiece and be sure you're happy with the style and colors. Make any changes or adjustments now (Chapter 17).

☐ Finalize your photography preferences, such as must-have shots and a time when formal portraits should be taken (before / after ceremony). Get all the information to your photographer, including who will be in the formal portraits (Chapter 12).

☐ Finalize your music preferences, such as a must-play song list, a banned song list, and other notes. Get all the information to your DJ or bandleader (Chapter 14).

☐ If necessary, finalize your videography preferences, such as getting-ready sequences, or must-have shots. Get all the information to your videographer (Chapter 13).

☐ Make sure you have finished purchasing all your wedding accessories, such as toasting glasses, ring pillow, guestbook and pen, candles, and so forth (Chapter 21).

2 Weeks Before

Date:_____

☐ Review Chapter 21, "Countdown Considerations", and highlight points you'll want to keep in mind over the next couple weeks.

☐ Contact your officiant and take care of any unfinished details.

☐ Check your online guest database and do a search for all guests who haven't sent in a wedding RSVP. Call them and get their responses over the phone in order to finalize your headcount (Chapter 20).

☐ Finalize your reception seating chart and place cards (Chapter 21).

☐ If you want to form a receiving line, determine when and where to line up.

☐ If the bride and/or groom are moving, fill out change-of-address forms with the post office and optionally arrange to have them hold your mail while on your honeymoon.

☐ Submit an announcement to the newspaper(s) if you like (Chapter 3).

☐ Shop for your honeymoon, Make sure you have adequate luggage and are stocked up on supplies.

☐ Get the last pre-wedding haircut and/or color touchup.

☐ Break in your bridal shoes by wearing them around the house.

1 Week Before

Date:_____

☐ Complete the detailed timeline for your wedding day. Provide vendor-specific timelines along with an emergency cell phone number in information packets to all your vendors, service providers, and site managers. Include location directions and maps for vendors who will be traveling. Get the info out by hand, e-mail, or fax (Chapter 21).

☐ Along with the detailed timeline, give your caterer the final headcount.

☐ Confirm addresses and pickup times with your transportation providers.

☐ Make sure that you've taken care of all final vendor payments. Use your online payment manager (Chapter 5).

☐ Call everyone in your wedding party and touch bases, making sure everyone has the right date and time as well as directions.

☐ Verify with your site managers that your vendors will have access during the times they need to set up. You may want to provide site managers with contact phone numbers and delivery times for the appropriate vendors and service providers. Refer them to your wedding website's Vendor Contact page (Chapter 11).

☐ Touch bases with your photographer and confirm starting time, date, and location as well as the photo lists you provided earlier.

☐ Touch bases with your videographer and confirm starting time, date, and location.

☐ Touch bases with your DJ, band, or musicians and confirm starting time, date, and location.

☐ Touch bases with your baker and confirm cake size, delivery time, date and location.

☐ Touch bases with your florist and confirm the arrangement count, details, delivery time, date and location(s). Keep in mind there may be more than one delivery location (reception flowers, ceremony flowers, and personal items like bouquets, boutonnières, and so on).

☐ Confirm the reservations for your honeymoon and wedding night. Print out your itinerary and buy travelers' checks if necessary.

2 to 3 Days Before

☐ The groom should take care of the final fitting and pick up formal wear.

☐ Have the best man make sure all the groomsmen pick up their attire.

☐ Prepare toasts for the rehearsal dinner and reception.

☐ Make sure you're all packed up for your honeymoon.

☐ Prepare for your rehearsal by finalizing details such the order of the bridal party's reception. Make copies of the detailed wedding timeline for all attendants.

☐ Deliver items to the caterer to pass out or arrange on the tables, such as table numbers, favors, disposable cameras, and so forth. Provide detailed instructions on how you want items arranged.

☐ Coordinate pickups for guests arriving by airport without a rental car. You can enlist friends and family to help out.

☐ Make arrangements for dress cleaning and bouquet preservation.

☐ If you plan to have anyone in addition to your attendants run errands for you on your wedding day, make the arrangements with them now.

☐ Assemble the out-of-town guests' welcome baskets and have your attendants help place them in the hotel(s) where your guests will be staying.

☐ Touch bases with your beauty contacts and confirm your wedding day hair and makeup appointments.

☐ Spend an evening relaxing. The bride should pamper herself and get a manicure and pedicure.

The Day Before (Rehearsal Day)

☐ Make sure your travel plans are in order.

☐ Prepare final payments for all vendors that need to be paid after the reception and make arrangements for the payments to be made by their due dates. If due at the end of the reception, put them in carefully labeled envelopes for distribution by a responsible individual at the rehearsal.

☐ Calculate vendor tips (Chapter 5). Put tips into carefully labeled envelopes for distribution by a responsible individual, customarily the best man.

☐ The bride should get the wedding gown, shoes, and all accessories together. Put an emergency-kit together (Chapter 21).

☐ Bring all your ceremony accessories (aisle runner, candles, yarmulkes, and so forth) to the ceremony location when you go for your rehearsal, saving you the hassle of dealing with it the following day.

☐ Meet your attendants, readers, officiant, and immediate family at the ceremony location to rehearse (Chapter 22).

☐ Distribute copies of the detailed wedding timeline and contact lists to your attendants.

☐ Attend your rehearsal dinner, spend time with friends and family, and enjoy yourself! Present the attendants with their gifts, as well as other family and friends you'd like to thank (Chapter 15).

☐ Give the best man an envelope containing the officiant's fee with instructions to hand it off after the ceremony. Distribute other vendors' payment and tip envelopes to the appropriate individual(s) or to the best man as well.

☐ If you plan on having wedding announcements mailed, arrange for someone to mail them the day after the wedding.

☐ Make plans for someone to return any rental items the first weekday after the wedding.

☐ Make plans for someone to get the bride's dress to the dry cleaner and the groom's tux back to the rental store the first weekday after the wedding.

☐ Get a good night's sleep!

Your Wedding Day

☐ Eat something for breakfast, even if it's light.

☐ Just follow your detailed timeline and let everyone else that you've entrusted with duties take care of the details and handle any issues that might arise.

☐ Have someone put your luggage into the going away car if you'll be leaving from the reception.

☐ Give the groom's ring to the maid of honor and the bride's ring to the best man.

☐ Relax and enjoy your wedding!

After the Wedding

☐ If you were pleased with your vendors and service providers, send them thank-you notes along with photos of the two of you, preferably with their work visible in the photos.

☐ Record gifts and their senders, using your online guest database. Write thank-you notes and send them off (Chapter 15).

☐ Post photos and video clips of your wedding and honeymoon on your wedding website.

☐ Convert your wedding website to a family or travel site.

☐ Contact us and let us know all about your big planning experience and the big day! (See Chapter 1) What stands out, and what would you have done differently?

☐ Take care of each other!

Notes:

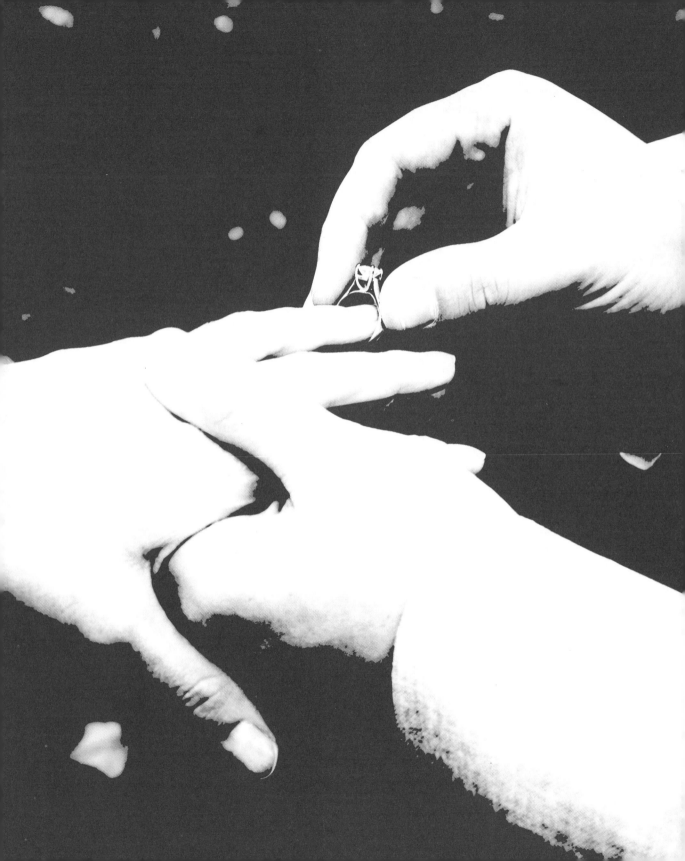

Chapter 3

"Will You...?"–The Journey Begins

- Announcing the Engagement

- The Engagement Ring

- Some Initial Decisions

- e-Plan It! Use Your e-Resources:

  Wedding Announcements on the Web
  Online Jewelry Bargains and Diamond Tutorials

- Worksheets:

  Considerations Worksheet: Engagement Ring
  Comparison Forms: Engagement Ring
  Considerations Worksheet: Initial Engagement Decisions

Congratulations on your upcoming wedding! This chapter serves as a starting point for the newly engaged; whether it's help with the ring, the date, or spilling the beans, we've got you covered.

Announcing the Engagement

So it begins! A new engagement is an exciting and emotional time for a couple. It's a time of happy announcements, warm congratulations, parties, family get-togethers, and lots of planning for the big day. There's plenty to do, and it will be intense at times, but you'll hopefully be enjoying yourself throughout, and having fun as you work together to make your wedding day vision a reality. The first few weeks are great, because you've got this wonderful secret to tell and it's fun letting everyone in on it, whether you do it a few people at a time or all at once in a big bash!

Timing and Technique

How and when you announce your pending nuptials are entirely up to you. Tradition dictates that the bride's parents are the first that should get the happy news, followed by the groom's. Even if the groom has already spoken to his parents about the proposal, they should receive the "formal" announcement afterwards. We'll discuss the traditional order of announcements a bit later on.

<CROSS-REFERENCE>
We'll give you the full scoop on putting a wedding website to work for you in the next chapter.
</CROSS-REFERENCE>

It goes without saying that the preferable way to spill the beans is in person, complete with happy hugs, joyful tears, and clinking glasses of champagne. But if it's just not possible and you're dying to let the word out, a phone call will do just fine—hopefully with a follow-up visit soon after! And unless special circumstances dictate (see the sidebar), the announcement should be made to your parents with both of you present.

Once your close family and friends have been notified, it will be time to let the rest of the world in on the news. This is traditionally done with a formal announcement in the newspaper (more on this later) on your behalf by the bride's parents or someone else close to you, though couples often initiate this task themselves. Today, the latest and greatest method is to announce over the Internet with your own wedding website, so family and friends all over the world can read your stories, see your pictures, access your gift registry and more.

The time to announce a new engagement is almost always right away; or at least as soon as your feet come down from the clouds (you want to give yourself plenty of time to absorb it all yourself and to enjoy the moment). When you do plan on letting the word out, just remember to be sensitive to others and time your announcements so that they don't clash with another big event. You don't want to steal anyone's thunder, or vice versa. Keep in mind what the current situation is for those you're announcing to, and consider whether or not to waiting for a better moment might best allow you both to enjoy the news. A final word on timing: you'll find that great expectation accompanies an announced engagement. Specifically, that expectation is for you to start your planning! Be prepared for the questions on all the details: When? Where? How? If yours is an "indefinite engagement" (defined: no date, no expectation of a specific date anytime soon) and if budgets, vendors, and checklists are not what you're in the mood for yet, you may want to hold off on the announcements until you're better prepared. Above all, remember to do what you feel is right...no rules of thumb or etiquette pointers are going to suit everyone.

Telling Your Family and Friends

You're no doubt looking forward to letting those close to you in on the news. But who to tell first? There are no hard and fast rules, and your own preferences and situation are the ultimate authority. For some additional guidance, the following list displays the order that is generally accepted as "etiquette-safe":

Your Children

If you have kids, remember that they come first. This news can impact them the most, and it's important to be sensitive to the fact that they may not be too happy with the addition to their family. If your spouse-to-be has kids as well, the dynamics are even tougher. It's best to prepare kids for the idea of the engagement as soon as you think it might be a possibility, and to assure them that their place in your heart is not being taken away by any means.

<TIP>

While it's generally accepted that parents are best informed by you and your sweetheart together, feel free to break the news by yourself if you feel it would better suit your own unique situation. You may want to go it alone if your parents:

- have a general problem with or negative attitude towards your spouse-to-be
- have witnessed you go through a difficult divorce
- are overly protective
- have problems with the religion or culture of your spouse-to-be
- are generally opposed for any other reason to the idea of you getting married

Additionally, if you know that your parents are going to have a problem with your plans to get married, consider telling others first—those you know will be happy for you—and letting your parents in on it only *after* you've been given the positive, strengthening boost.

</TIP>

Your Parents

Whether or not the groom has asked for the bride's hand in marriage (not as common these days as in those of yore), it's long been a tradition to formally announce the engagement to the bride's parents first, and then to the groom's. Whether you follow tradition or do otherwise is completely up to you, but you usually want to announce to both sets of parents separately. There's no need to add the awkwardness of hugging and congratulating complete strangers who have suddenly become almost-family to the pressure of the engagement news. Meet with your parents in person and together with your sweetheart. If distance or situation is a problem, by all means give them a call and arrange a visit or get-together as well. For divorced parents, take extra time and see each side separately. Lastly, if you and your folks don't see eye-to-eye, a handwritten letter can be a polite and appropriate alternative.

Your Grandparents, Siblings, and Close Relatives

This list could very well be steep. In considering who to tell first (unless you're sharing the news with all or most of them at once), think about who has the most potential to have their feelings hurt by not being told sooner. Family dinners and get-togethers are great opportunities to tell everyone at once…just make sure you're not breaking your news during another important event.

Your Close Friends

This can be done over the phone, in a group e-mail, or by gathering them together and surprising them all at once.

Your Late Spouse's Family

If this applies to you, don't forget to let this part of your family in on the news.

Your Ex-spouse

If you and your ex-spouse have children together, this is not just a thoughtful gesture; it's necessary. Even if you don't, a phone call or polite letter in the mail is a gracious consideration that will usually be appreciated quite a bit more than hearing the news through the grapevine later on.

Everyone Else!

To let the rest of the world in on your engagement, use all outlets you'd like! Websites, a mass e-mail to coworkers, local newspapers, church bulletins, your old school and hometown newspapers, mailed announcements…anything and everything you wish. Engagement news is happy news, and well received virtually anywhere. See the following discussion on the formalities of posting some of the more traditional public engagement announcements, as well as newer online methods that are quickly becoming popular today.

Public Engagement Announcements

e-Resource

Wedding Announcements on the Web

The number of individuals connected and using the Internet for communication, business and pleasure is an ever-increasing phenomenon, and it will continue to increase as time and technology moves on. A major focus of this book is how to use this powerful tool to your advantage throughout the process of planning your wedding, and the engagement announcement is one of the many items that can be souped up to your—and your guests'—advantage.

We cover wedding websites in detail in the next chapter, so feel free to jump ahead and skim it a bit for a sneak peek. Wedding websites and online tools are going to save you a ton of time and hassle, and this is our first look at one of the many useful conveniences they can provide for us.

Imagine an interactive engagement announcement on the Internet with a website address (also called a "domain name") made up of your own names, like christyandsteve.com. It's easy for everyone to remember and can be printed on your paper announcements or sent via e-mail. A wedding website allows all your family and friends throughout the world to read your stories, hear your wedding music, browse photos and video clips of the two of you, and sign a guestbook. Eventually you can set up features like an online gift registry and a place for your guests to RSVP over the web instantly. These are just a few of the convenient features available to you, and you can grow your website at your own pace. For now, you can be content to post a one-page announcement with some photos and maybe a guestbook—something you can easily do in five minutes or so with the latest wedding website services. It's hip, fun, and totally covered in Chapter 4.

Newspapers and Other Printed Media

To post an announcement in newspapers, printed bulletins, and other such outlets, first get the number of the publication's editorial department and contact them for guidelines and fees. Many publications offer this service for free, but they usually have their own writer's guidelines and follow their own protocols. Some can include color photos, some black-and-white, and others will only run text. Request any required forms and ask if you can obtain them online or via e-mail.

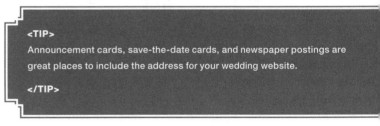

<TIP>
Announcement cards, save-the-date cards, and newspaper postings are great places to include the address for your wedding website.

</TIP>

See if you have to mail the information in, or if you can e-mail it. If e-mailing, scan in your photo at 300 dpi or send it from your digital camera. If mailing, make sure you write your name on the back of the photo, and include a self-addressed, stamped envelope if you'd like it returned.

Newspapers can take anywhere from one to six months to run an engagement notice, so get it done in advance and ask the publications you contact what their typical lead time is. You can specify a date you'd like the notice to be run, although they will usually not be able to guarantee it. You'll probably have to search through the publication's announcement section a few minutes every day until you find yours.

Newspapers may give you strict guidelines as to your announcement's wording. If not, you can go traditional or blaze your own trail. Traditionally, etiquette states that announcements are made by the bride's family, never the groom's, and by someone other than the bride and groom if possible (a close aunt and uncle, for example). The wording traditionally mentions your careers, your parents' names and their city/state of residence, as well as your educational credits if space permits. Never put a specific date in your announcement...you don't want to give potential burglars a tip-off. Check out some examples below, but remember that in the end, the choice of wording is yours.

The bride's family (standard):

Mr. and Mrs. Raymond Gutierrez of San Francisco announce the engagement of their daughter, Amanda Marie, to Robert Lomas, son of Samuel and Lisa Lomas of Houston, Texas. Ms. Gutierrez graduated with honors from San Francisco State University and is a research associate with Brown Pharmaceuticals in South San Francisco. Mr. Lomas graduated from St. Thomas University and is a real estate agent with Land Real Estate in San Jose. A June wedding is planned. (alternatively: No date has yet been set for the wedding)

Single parent sponsoring the wedding:

Ms. Sylvia Allen announces the engagement of her daughter, Patricia Smith to Ruben Lancaster, the son of Albert and Margaret Lancaster of Chicago, Illinois... (You may add an optional closing line: "Ms. Allen is also the daughter of Paul Smith of Miami, Florida.")

One parent deceased:

Ms. Linda Myers announces the engagement of her daughter, Rebecca Myers to Randal Johnson, son of Gordon and Alicia Johnson of Anderson, Indiana. Ms. Miner, also the daughter of the late Peter Myers, graduated from the University of Wisconsin and is a technical writer with Verias Systems, Inc...

Divorced parents:

Mr. Richard Jones, of San Diego, and Ms. Lisa Jones, of Los Angeles, announce the engagement of their daughter, Denise Jones...

Remarried parent sponsoring with new spouse:

Ms. Laura Carols and Mr. Michael Carols announce the engagement of Ms. Carol's daughter, Angelina Faucett...

By another family member:

Gloria Randall announces the engagement of her sister, Janet Randall, to John Rice, son of...The bride is the daughter of (the late) Alan and Marie Randall of Portland, Oregon.

Bride and groom announce themselves:

Ruby Smith, a graduate of Santa Clara University, is to be married to Vincent Lief, a graduate of Sacramento State University. Ms. Smith, the daughter of (the late) Thomas and Gale Smith, owns the Leisure Café in Sunnyvale. Mr. Lief is a software engineer for OneUp Systems in Fremont.

Mailed Announcements

It was once a tradition for the mother of the bride to mail out handwritten notices to friends and family in order to spread the news of her daughter's engagement. These days, such announcements are not common and generally not advised, the main problem being that you'll need to generate your guest list and compile addresses far too long in advance. Some recipients mistake the announcements for invitations. In general, there are easier and more efficient ways to spread the news.

> **<CROSS-REFERENCE>**
> Save-the-date cards and other wedding stationery are covered in Chapter 20.
> **</CROSS-REFERENCE>**

Regardless, some couples like the idea of a mailed card announcing their engagement, and stationery stores contain a wide assortment of beautiful styles and designs of correspondence just for the purpose. The wording is customarily similar to that of newspaper announcements, and can be sent on your behalf by a family member or by yourselves (example: "Ms. Victoria Nelson and Mr. Scott Carlson are pleased to announce their engagement"). The wording can also be nontraditional, so include whatever message you feel works best for the two of you. If you're also planning to send out save-the-date cards, you can have your announcement card double as such just by adding your wedding date.

Should You Throw an Engagement Party?

Engagement parties are a great way to get family and close friends together in celebration of your newly engaged status. Some couples even keep the reason for their party a secret and use the occasion to hit their friends and family with one big surprise announcement. However, you're by no means obligated to have an engagement party at all, and many couples choose not to.

Why wouldn't you take advantage of this opportunity to party with the people you love? First of all, an engagement party has to be planned and paid for, and your overall wedding planning already has its fair share of that. Second, anyone you invite to the engagement party will be expecting to be invited to your wedding, so you're going to need at least an initial sense of your guest list, which you may not have at this point. Also, if your engagement is a short one (say less than six months), it may seem a bit awkward to have the party so close to your wedding.

Etiquette and Issues

The style of the party is all up to you. Champagne and hors d'oeuvres at your friend's home on the lake? Dinner at a fancy local restaurant? Casual buffet at your sister's? Barbecue at your parents? How about cake and coffee at your apartment? It's all good. It really depends on your budget and what would make you most comfortable.

Is this engagement party going to serve as the first-time introduction of your two families? You might want to consider a fun group activity or two to serve as an ice-breaker to warm things up. Make sure that everyone is introduced and made to feel welcome. Another idea if your parents have never met each other is to have a separate get together *before* the engagement party with just them and the two of you present…it's an excellent, even more intimate way of getting them acquainted outside of the party environment and will make them feel more involved in the engagement. This is traditionally initiated by the bride's mother, but feel free to take control and set the meeting up yourself if mom doesn't. Like the engagement party, this can be as casual as sandwiches in the backyard or as formal as a dinner at an upscale restaurant.

One last thing to keep in mind: guests are typically not expected to bring gifts to an engagement party, although some of them will inevitably do so. If you send out engagement party invitations, don't include any gift registry information on them. If guests do bring you something, thank them and then place the gifts out of sight to be opened after the party or in private with the gift-giver. And don't forget to send thank-you notes!

Engagement Party Invitations

The invitations can be as informal as a phone call, or you may want to send something in the mail. For traditional printed invitations, have the wording state that the party is being held in your honor, as in the examples below. There's no need to explain that the party is to celebrate an engagement, as that is generally assumed.

Mr. and Mrs. Jonathan Stewart
request the pleasure of your company
at a dinner in honor of
Miss Elaine Stewart and Mr. Robert Tenant
on
the twelfth of June, two thousand six
at
four o'clock PM,
1555 Summerfield Court
San Bernardino, California 95123
RSVP

Miss Elaine Stewart and Mr. Robert Tenant
request the pleasure of your company
at a party in their honor
on
the twelfth of June, two thousand six
at
four o'clock PM,
1555 Summerfield Court
San Bernardino, California 95123
RSVP

The Engagement Ring

Since ancient times, a lady whose hand was sought in marriage was given symbolic gifts by her suitors as tokens of their love and devotion. Gold coins were given by Egyptian hopefuls, and the Romans gave the objects of their affection plain bands of gold. The symbol of a circle, with its never-ending connotation, remains even today in our own contemporary engagement and wedding rings. Today's sought-after princesses are customarily given a ring topped by a precious stone, usually a "timeless" diamond, at the start of their engagement.

Some Words on the Engagement Ring Tradition

While the multi-billion dollar diamond industry quite happily backs the notion that "a diamond is for-ever" in addition to being "a girl's best friend", don't get caught up in all the hype. The diamond solitaire is the most common form of symbolizing an engagement, but the decision is completely up to you. You might consider one of the many gorgeous and equally beautiful gemstones available, such as rubies, sapphires, or aquamarine. She may appreciate the more personal nature of a ring set with her birth-stone or favorite color gem rather than the more traditional diamond. It's also a common practice to save money by combining the wedding ring and engagement ring into one single piece, an option your jeweler will be happy to discuss with you. Other couples shun the engagement ring altogether and opt instead for their own unique gifts to give one another, symbolizing the promise of their engagement in their own special way.

If a diamond is in your future however, make sure you do your homework and take advantage of every resource available to you. By educating yourself, shopping carefully, and following solid, trusted advice you will be better able to choose the right stone for your budget. You will know how to avoid overspend-ing on status qualities nobody will notice. In the end you will present her with a gorgeous diamond you both can be proud of and whose exceptional quality is assured. With the insight you'll gain by educat-ing yourself and shopping carefully, you're sure to appreciate your diamond as a unique, fascinating treasure and quite a bit more than just an "expensive rock".

The Element of Surprise

Admittedly, there is little we can think of more romantic in engagement lore than the Surprise Proposal: him down on one knee, her overcome with unexpected joy, him taking that gleaming ring and sliding it perfectly onto her finger at the voice of her consent…

Romantic, yes, but just keep in mind a few warnings and some careful advice before taking such a bold leap of faith:

First, be sure you're very confident in her tastes and preferences. We know that most couples are at this point in their relationship, but an engagement ring is not only a very emotional symbol, but one meant to be on her hand for life. She usually knows pretty much what she wants (and doesn't want) and probably has thought about it more than once in the past. For one thing, as we have already mentioned, she may not want a diamond in the first place. If she does, in what shape would she pre-fer it were cut…circular, square, heart, or something unique? Would she like it better clear or slightly colored? On a low setting or raised? With smaller accompanying gems? How big? (Contrary to the general assumption that "bigger is better", many women find large rings uncomfortable or inconvenient, or prefer the subtlety of a smaller stone). Maybe she's not quite sure what she wants and would like to shop for one together.

Even if you feel reasonably confident about her taste in diamond type, you may find it almost impossible to divine her band and setting preference, only because there is so much variety to choose from. Gold or platinum is just a start: there are countless styles and types of settings, ranging from classic to contemporary to some really far-out pieces. Luckily, most good jewelers will let you return or exchange what you purchase, so a good surprise strategy is to buy a more conservative, classic band with your diamond and then return together after you pop the question to let her pick a different band and setting.

These days, engagement proposals are not commonly something that comes out of left field unexpectedly, so you'll probably discuss her likes and dislikes together, which is perfectly acceptable. Get her input before shopping for the ring; you can still keep the date you plan to pop the question a secret, but at least you'll be confident that your choice of engagement ring will be something she'll love (she'll be wearing it for life, after all). Some couples even enjoy shopping for the ring together, and it's not unheard of for both him and her to split the bill.

That said, if your heart and mind are set on a surprise proposal, we wish you the best of luck and hope you'll write to us and tell us all about the outcome! (See our contact info in Chapter 1). To make the best selection possible, consider the following tips: First, pay attention to the jewelry she wears now. What kind of metal is it? Is it more flashy, or subtle? Ask her mom, sister, or friend(s) what they think she would prefer. If she's very active or athletic, consider a setting that will protect the diamond from getting scratched or nicked, such as the cathedral or contour settings.

The Anatomy of a Diamond

A diamond is actually a very unique and remarkable fusion of art and optical science. It takes a great deal of skill and talent to cut a raw or "rough" stone to the precise, mathematical and geometric proportions that become a quality finished piece. Every facet of an ideally cut diamond is aligned in precisely the right way so that virtually all light entering the stone is bounced about and reflected directly back at the viewer in a gleaming dance of brilliance known as the diamond's "fire". Like a prism, light is bent and separated into its component colors as it enters and leaves the body of the diamond, giving the fire its characteristic sparkle.

In order to understand what makes a quality diamond, one must familiarize themselves with the famous "Four C's": Cut, Color, Clarity, and Carat weight. Cut, color, and clarity determine a diamonds quality, and each can be given a specific score, called a "grade". Well-respected laboratories like the Gemological Institute of America (GIA) have adopted a standardized method of measuring these quality grades and you'll be taking advantage of these standards as you compare different diamond samples. Carat weight is a measure of how heavy (or big, as most of us would say) a particular diamond is. We suggest a strategy of exploring quality (cut, color, and clarity) first, and deciding what quality grades you'd be willing to accept before thinking about size (carat weight). After determining your preferred quality, you will obtain a price-per-carat for this quality and will then be able to decide how much diamond your budget will allow.

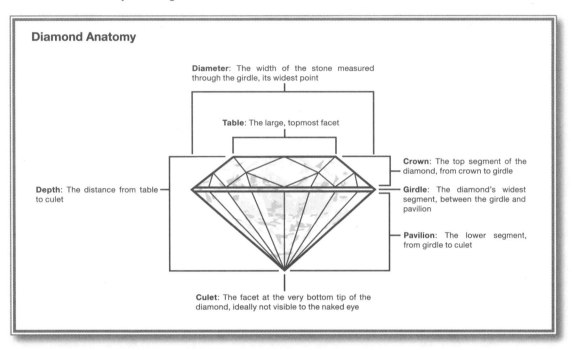

Diamond Anatomy

Diameter: The width of the stone measured through the girdle, its widest point

Table: The large, topmost facet

Crown: The top segment of the diamond, from crown to girdle

Depth: The distance from table to culet

Girdle: The diamond's widest segment, between the girdle and pavilion

Pavilion: The lower segment, from girdle to culet

Culet: The facet at the very bottom tip of the diamond, ideally not visible to the naked eye

The Cut

Most gemologists will agree that the most important aspect of a diamond specimen that contributes to quality is its cut. It takes skill and sacrifice to cut a diamond properly to an ideal symmetry; skill because the facets have to be created to just the right geometric precision and sacrifice because more of the raw stone is usually lost when cutting a diamond to such exact dimensions.

Diamonds with a cut of ideal proportions are more rare, more sought after, and thus more expensive and valuable. Placed next to a diamond of inferior cut, they will always appear more "lit up", with more of a brilliant sparkle and fire.

If a diamond is cut too shallow, some light will be lost, or "leaked", out the bottom of the stone. A cut too deep will cause light to leak out the sides. In either case, the diamond will lose brilliance and appear darker, or dull. Other geometric inferiorities are possible as well, all with the end result of a darker, less brilliant diamond.

Polish, Symmetry, and How to Verify a Diamond's Cut

Jewelers speak about cut in terms of *polish*, meaning how smooth the diamond's facets are, and *symmetry*, meaning how precisely aligned and proportioned the facets are. Both polish and symmetry have specific grades ranging from excellent (EX), to very good (VG), good (G), fair (F), and poor (P). Ask each jeweler you visit to only show you stones with a symmetry and polish of good or better. You want to avoid diamonds with cut grades of fair and poor, because these diamonds will have light leaks that greatly diminish their brilliance and fire. As you will read later in our "Tips for Selecting Your Stone", the only diamonds you should consider are those graded by a respected, independent laboratory like the Gemological Institute of America (GIA). The grade report will include values for polish and symmetry. Review a diamond's grade report before purchase and verify that these scores are "good" or better.

Cut Shapes

While the brilliant round cut is by far the most common shape purchased today, there are many other shapes to choose from, and each has a completely different personality. Some jewelers even carry their own "exclusive" cut shapes offered nowhere else. You may be interested in one of these unique alternatives.

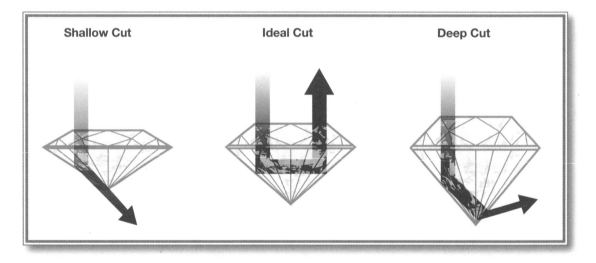

Shallow Cut   **Ideal Cut**   **Deep Cut**

The Color

Most diamonds that are found are slightly yellow or brown in color due to their own unique composition. The clearer a diamond is, the more visible light the finished stone will reflect and the more brilliant it will appear. Since most diamonds naturally exhibit some body color, clear diamonds are found much less often and so these rare stones are considered more valuable. As is the case with cut, diamond color is given a specific grade based on its color (or lack of color). The grade ranges from colorless (D) to light yellow (Z), with the price of D grade diamonds being the highest and Z grade diamonds being the lowest.

So for the money, how much color is too much?

First of all, unless you're a purist, you probably don't want to buy in the colorless (D - F) range. Diamonds in the near colorless range (G - H) are virtually indistinguishable from those in the D - F range and are far less expensive. Even color in diamonds of grades I - J are very difficult to notice; they are still very rare and considered to be of exceptionally high quality. Don't spend money on status that neither you nor anyone else is going to be able to detect. Your best values are specimens of grades H or I. These diamonds are just as brilliant and colorless as the D - F grade diamonds for all practical purposes, and your money will go a lot farther.

On the other hand, diamonds worse than grade J should usually be avoided unless you prefer the colored quality of the light yellow specimens (and there are many people who do).

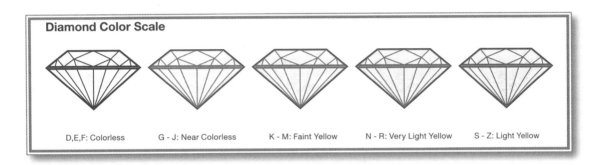

Diamond Color Scale

| D,E,F: Colorless | G - J: Near Colorless | K - M: Faint Yellow | N - R: Very Light Yellow | S - Z: Light Yellow |

The Clarity

When diamonds are mined, they are found embedded and mixed in with rocks, minerals, and all sorts of other stuff. Finished pieces usually still contain some tiny bits of mineral, scratches, or other imperfections that are known in the jewelry world as "inclusions". As you might expect, diamonds with fewer inclusions are more rare and therefore considered more valuable. Diamonds that are absolutely clear, meaning that they have no visible inclusions at a 10X magnification, have a clarity grade of flawless (FL) and are the most valuable of all. They're also the most expensive.

But hold on before plunking down big bucks on a "flawless" diamond. Let's first correct the jewelers' terminology: technically, no diamond is flawless. Every diamond contains imperfections; that's just nature. Diamonds of clarity grade FL may still have inclusions, but they're just not visible at 10X magnification. Likewise, diamonds of clarity grades VVS1 to VS2 have inclusions, but they're not visible to the *naked eye*. Who cares if they're visible at 10X magnification? Nobody's going to be peering at your diamond with a magnifying lens but an appraiser, and even then the inclusions are often difficult to detect.

<NOTE>

"Fancy" Colored Diamonds

Even more rare than colorless diamonds are so-called "fancy" diamonds that come in a variety of deep, intense colors. Yellow fancy diamonds, for example, are a deep yellow color that is darker than Z grade stones. Since these diamonds are so rare, they are considered more valuable; they command a higher price tag than similar colorless (white) diamonds and are graded on a separate color scale.

</NOTE>

Bottom line: opt for an "eye-clean" diamond. Diamonds of clarity grades VS1 and VS2 are your best deals, as they're far less expensive than grades FL - VVS2, yet do not have any visible imperfections that would detract from the diamond's beauty or brilliance. Even SI1 and SI2 specimens are often just as gorgeous, and should be compared alongside VS grade specimens to see if you can even detect a difference. If you're considering purchasing an SI grade diamond online (more on this later), call the company and speak to a consultant who can review the specimen for you and ensure that there are no visible inclusions. Also, as with all jewelers, make sure that you can return the diamond for a refund if you're not satisfied with it after purchase.

Generally, diamonds of clarity grades worse than SI2 should be avoided, as their inclusions will likely be visible to the eye and may detract from the diamond's brilliance.

Diamond Clarity Scale

Clarity	Description
FL	**Flawless:** No internal or external finish flaws.
IF	**Internally Flawless:** No internal flaws.
VVS1/VVS2	**Very very slightly included:** Very difficult to see inclusions under 10x magnification.
VS1/VS2	**Very slightly included:** Difficult to see inclusions under 10x magnification, typically unable to see inclusions with unaided eye
SI1/SI2	**Slightly included:** Easy to see inclusions under 10x magnification, may not be able to see inclusions with unaided eye.

Not All Inclusions Are Created Equal

As products of nature, diamonds exhibit all sorts of unique characteristics that are considered in the jewelry world to be imperfections. These inclusions can range from something like a colorless, nearly-invisible scratch to a small, dark fleck of mineral that's more noticeable. Most inclusions are difficult enough to see under a magnifying glass, let alone with the naked eye, but there are some more notice-able ones that should be avoided. Dark inclusions, or inclusions that appear in the center of the crown or some other conspicuous location may detract from the diamond. When you visit your jeweler, ask them to show you diamonds with clarity grades ranging from VVSI to VSI to SI and to let you use a 10X magnifier to inspect the inclusions. Ask for help in locating an inclusion if you're having trouble (which you very likely will, especially with VVSI). This is a fun, insightful exercise that will give you a solid feel for how inclusions show up in various clarity grades.

You may notice some darker and some lighter inclusions. If you are trying to decide between two or more diamonds of similar quality, inspecting them with a magnifier in this way can help you determine the specimen whose inclusions appear lighter or less obvious. Having the experience and know-how to examine diamonds like this can save you money, since you'll be able to purchase a specimen of lower clarity grade but with inclusions that are acceptable to you as minor or undetectable for practical purposes.

The Carat Weight

It's understandable that when it comes to diamonds, most people feel "bigger is better". Size is what people ask about first when discussing a diamond, and it's usually the only real measurement that people know to apply. There's nothing wrong with wanting and buying a big diamond…as long as the quality is acceptable. By now you should understand what one might be giving up if they focus primarily on size and ignore quality.

A big diamond whose cut is inferior, for example, is less valuable than a slightly smaller diamond with all else being equal. The smaller higher quality diamond, when placed next to the larger inferior one, will always outshine. It will appear more brilliant and sparkle with more fire because it is better crafted to capture and reflect light. Most people, when shown these two specimens, will choose the smaller, more quality diamond. This is another reason why it's so important to compare diamonds side-by-side when shopping.

The weight of diamonds is measured in *carats*. Each carat is equal to .20 grams. In nature, there are a lot of small diamonds found but very few large ones. Because of this, large diamonds are exponentially more expensive than smaller stones, meaning that a two-carat diamond is actually more expensive that two one-carat diamonds of the same quality.

The best recommendation when shopping for diamonds, as we've mentioned before, is to first settle on what grade of cut, color, and clarity you like. From this specific combination of quality grades, you can obtain a price-per-carat. Use the price-per-carat to decide how big of a diamond you can buy within your budget. Keeping the quality the highest priority in this way, you will be sure to get *your* best diamond: it will have the quality you want at the largest size you can afford.

If size is your priority but you're working in a tight budget, consider going with a diamond of good cut, a clarity grade of SI1 or SI2, and a color grade of I or J.

A couple things to keep in mind when contemplating size: remember that some ladies prefer smaller diamonds or feel uncomfortable with large jewelry. By now, you should know if your lady is the flashy type or not, so select accordingly. Also, consider the size of the recipient's finger: a one-carat diamond will look bigger on a size 4 finger than on a size 8.

Tips for Selecting Your Stone

We can't emphasize enough the importance of educating yourself before starting to shop for a diamond. This applies to anything you anticipate spending money on and is just good common sense. You've got a lot of wedding planning to do and a lot of vendor and product selection to make. Arming yourself with knowledge before opening the checkbook is something you'll find will consistently give you an advantage. There are going to be a lot of people ready to help themselves to their share of your wedding funds, and you need to protect yourself from those unscrupulous few that won't mind taking advantage of you if you let them.

So, study up! The previous section, Anatomy of a Diamond, is a good place to start, and you should visit the e-Resources provided in the next section if you feel you need more info. Above all, take your time and never, ever let yourself get pressured into making a purchase when you're not ready.

The following guide should serve you well in your diamond hunt:

First, decide on a budget for the ring. You may hear people suggest two months' salary as a rule of thumb, but it's entirely up to you. The amount you set aside to spend on a diamond depends on your own unique situation and how your overall budget looks. Remember, a big expensive rock doesn't mean a better marriage, and a new marriage has enough pressure on it without also starting out mired in debt.

<TIP>

Jewelers come in a wide variety of quality, helpfulness and reputability. Here's a list of what to look for in a jeweler...the good ones should have most or all of the following traits:

• In business for a long time
• Don't pressure you to buy on the spot
• No charge for sizing
• No charge for engraving
• Lifetime cleaning policy
• Refund or exchange guarantee
• Offer grading reports by the GIA, the AGSL, or the EGL
• Offer outside appraisals
• Have a licensed gemologist on staff

</TIP>

Once you're comfortable with a solid amount, locate reputable jewelers in your area. Try asking around and getting good recommendations from friends and family and other people you trust. Log onto the American Gem Society's website (www.ags.org) to obtain a list of recommended jewelers in your area. Create a list of jewelers to visit from these contacts, and feel free to check them out online or over the phone. Make sure they've been in business for a while. You can even contact the Better Business Bureau in your area to verify that they don't have complaints or claims of fraud filed against them.

Visit the jewelers on your list and take note of their selection and willingness to help. A good jeweler will recognize your diamond knowledge and desire to learn, and will be happy to expand upon your education. If they're pushy or are pressuring you to buy on the spot, politely thank them and leave; you don't want to deal with these kinds of businesses. Ask the jewelers you visit to let you see several different sized specimens of varying cut, color, and clarity grades side-by-side. Take a pen and notepad so that you can jot down the quality grades and how much the specimens cost, as well as any impressions you have. It's also a good idea to ask the jewelers for a 10X magnifying lens so that you can examine the inclusions. While you're at each store, ask about settings as well and take notes on the cost of the ones you're interested in. Take your time, and remember you are in information gathering mode now, not in spending mode.

When you know what you want in the way of cut, color, and clarity, you can determine the cost-per-carat for diamonds of your preferred quality at the various jewelers you've visited. Using this cost-per-carat value, decide how big of a diamond you can buy given the budget you set for yourself earlier. For example, if the cost-per-carat for diamonds of my preferred quality is $4,500 and I have $3,000 budgeted for the ring, I will probably settle on a half-carat (0.5c) diamond, which will cost me about $2,250 (4500 x 0.5) and leave me around $500 for the setting after tax.

This is also a good time to check online jewelers (more about this in the following e-Resource). Knowing the specific cut, color, and clarity grades and the general carat weight of the diamond you're looking for, you may find a better deal online than at the local jewelers. Of course, you'll need to make sure that the online business is just as reputable as the local jewelers you've visited and that they have a guarantee policy allowing you to return the diamond for a refund if you're not satisfied. A couple perks of online buying is that shipping is often free for big ticket items like diamonds, and you may not have to pay tax if the business is based out of state.

When you're ready to buy your diamond, whether online or off, you'll want to check the jewelers' policies and verify that they offer reputable grading reports for all their samples by one of the following respected outside labs: the Gemological Institute of America (GIA) - www.gia.edu, the American Gem Society Laboratories (AGSL) - www.agslab.com, or the European Gemological Laboratory (EGL) - www.eglusa.com. Make sure the jeweler you select offers a refund or exchange for a period of time after purchase so that you can bring the ring or setting back if the bride doesn't approve. This is especially important for Internet purchases! An outside appraisal should be provided. Make sure all these things are noted on your contract or receipt: get it all in writing before you pay!

e-Resource

Online Jewelry Bargains and Diamond Tutorials

We are invariably asked the same question when discussing online jewelers: is it safe to buy a diamond online? In considering an answer for this question, we have to ask another: is it safe to buy a diamond *off*line? The answer to both questions is the same: Sometimes, but not always. Remember that discussion on reputable jewelers? The same issues apply to Internet stores: there are unscrupulous vendors out there, to be certain, and you need to be sure of the reputability of your online jeweler just as you would with the old-fashioned brick and mortar ones. Run them by the same checklist you would for a local vendor, and make sure that they offer a guarantee allowing you to return the diamond for a full refund if you are not satisfied. As always, only purchase a diamond with a legitimate grade report from a respected, third party laboratory.

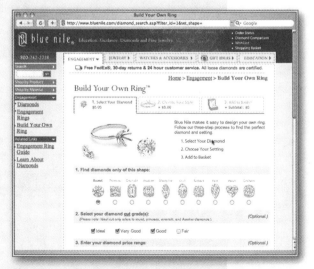

You will be best served by online jewelers once you've done some visiting to local stores, examined diamonds first-hand, and are sure of the cut, color, and clarity grades that you are looking for as well as size. Find comparable stones and compare the prices. It's just another way of increasing your choices, and you can often find some great deals at good online jewelry stores.

And online jewelers don't just have diamonds. Most have a wide selection of quality gems as well, in addition to various setting styles and bands. Even if you plan on

Blue Nile's step-by-step engagement ring builder.

DiamondGrading.com offers a wealth of informative articles and tutorials.

buying ultimately from a local jeweler, browsing the online catalogs can be an invaluable educational tool and a great way to get ideas.

Other resources available on these sites are diamond tutorials, guides and great selection tips. Anyone who sets off to diamond shop without fully investigating these resources is truly missing out on a great deal of knowledge. The following businesses all have online tutorials packed with great diamond knowledge available for you to browse at your convenience.

Blue Nile (www.bluenile.com)

Blue Nile is one of the best online jewelry stores we've seen. They have a large selection of quality diamonds, a step-by-step engagement ring builder, and a solid reputation. But their best asset is the extensive diamond education section, a very helpful resource whether or not you decide to make a purchase online.

Diamond Cutters (www.diamondcutters.com)

A New York based family-owned business that hand-selects, cuts, and polishes certified diamonds to sell directly online at discounts prices.

DiamondGrading.com (www.diamondgrading.com)

Their website's design isn't the best, but DiamondGrading.com has some great articles, tutorials, and how-to's for diamond shoppers.

Some Initial Decisions

Close your eyes and picture yourself on your wedding day, holding your sweetheart's hand as you exchange vows. Where are you? Are you in a church, or on a grassy field overlooking the ocean? A chapel in Vegas, perhaps? Are your bridesmaids wearing a particular color? How many guests are there...do you see practically everyone you know, or is it just an intimate group? Now imagine you're at your reception, sitting at your head table...then cutting your cake...then having your first dance...then grooving to your favorite tunes. Are you indoors or outdoors? Under a white tent lit up with twinkling lights or in a hall under a big chandelier? What's the mood like?

Both of you should do this exercise. Try to imagine what your ideal wedding day would look like barring expenses and then discuss it together. Take notes. You're bound to have some conflicts; work out a compromise...you don't need details, just some general ideas. None of this is set in stone, and will almost certainly change as you set your budget and nail down the detailed decisions, but you need a place to start. Here's some key decisions you need to begin thinking about relatively soon after the start of your engagement:

The diamond-finder interface available at diamondcutters.com

- *Length of engagement: How long until the big day?* This could be influenced by how much time you need to save funds; when working out your budget you may end up deciding to increase the engagement period. You also want to give yourself plenty of planning time to avoid drowning in detail frenzy. Another consideration to make is the season of you wedding. Do you have a specific preference? If you're flexible on the season, consider a fall or winter wedding. Popular months (primarily June, August, and September) book early and vendors are usually busier at these times. You may get less attention and will probably end up paying more if you plan your day to fall during peak wedding season. We'll get into this more in Chapter 6.

- *How many guests?* Some couples envision a great big wedding with everyone they know there to celebrate their union together, while others prefer a very intimate affair with just immediate family and the closest of friends. Just keep in mind that, in general, as the guest count goes up so does your wedding's price tag. Of course, you can spend the same amount of money with less guests as you would with a larger group by opting for higher quality food, entertainment, location, and so forth.

> **<CROSS-REFERENCE>**
> Managing guests and building your guest list is covered in Chapter 7. You'll finalize your ceremony and reception decisions in Chapters 8 and 9.
> **</CROSS-REFERENCE>**

- *How formal?* Whether you envision a tuxedo-clad black or white tie wedding or would rather have a big bash on the beach in sandals and shorts, it's your day and you make the rules. Your wedding's formality is a function of your combined personalities and will set the tone and atmosphere of everything from the invitations to the food. Take note of your initial thoughts now, and we'll dig deeper into how budget and formality relate to one another in later chapters.

- *What kind of ceremony and reception locations?* This is important to start thinking of now because churches, wineries, and other sites tend to book up quickly, especially the really popular ones. You want to start looking for these as soon as possible. Go back to your ideal wedding fantasy and picture your surroundings. Is your ceremony indoors or outdoors? At a place of worship or somewhere special at the reception site? Your reception might be in a fancy hall, hotel, winery, garden, country club or your own backyard. If it's outdoors, would you like the party held under a dramatic white canopy tent? What kind of decoration do you envision?

- *Consider whether you'd like your wedding to have a particular theme.* This is easier for some couples to decide on than for others. Some have an obvious shared hobby, profession, or historical point of interest that makes for a good theme. A couple who loves to surf might have a beach theme, for example. Like everything else, theme—if you choose to have one—is just something to start considering at this point. It will make those final decisions on color scheme, wedding favors, and location that much easier.

Considerations Worksheet: Engagement Ring

Engagement Ring Budget: $ _____

Cut Shapes

☐ Round
☐ Princess
☐ Emerald
☐ Asscher
☐ Marquise
☐ Square
☐ Radiant
☐ Oval
☐ Pear
☐ Heart

Carat Weight

☐ 1/4
☐ 1/3
☐ 1/2
☐ 3/4
☐ 1
☐ 1 1/2
☐ 2
☐ 3
☐ 4
☐ 5

Color Grades

☐ D – F (colorless)
☐ G – H (near colorless)
☐ I – J (near colorless, color slightly detectable)
☐ Fancy (deep colored diamonds)

Clarity

☐ FL, IF Diamonds (flawless, internally flawless)
☐ VVS1, VVS2 Diamonds (very, very slightly included)
☐ VS1, VS2 Diamonds (very slightly included)
☐ SI1, SI2 Diamonds (slightly included)

Engagement Ring Metal

☐ Platinum
☐ White Gold
☐ Yellow Gold

Notes: _____
_____
_____
_____
_____
_____
_____
_____
_____
_____
_____
_____
_____
_____
_____
_____

Comparison Forms: Engagement Ring

Appointment Date: Time:

Jeweler: Years in Business:

Address:

Contact:

Email: Phone: Fax:

Website: Recommended by:

Cut Shape(s):   Carat Weight:

Color Grades: Clarity:

Metal Type:

Payment Policy:

Return Policy:

Additional Fees: $

Total Estimated Cost: $

Appointment Date: Time:

Jeweler: Years in Business:

Address:

Contact:

Email: Phone: Fax:

Website: Recommended by:

Cut Shape(s):   Carat Weight:

Color Grades: Clarity:

Metal Type:

Payment Policy:

Return Policy:

Additional Fees: $

Total Estimated Cost: $

Considerations Worksheet: Initial Engagement Decisions

Here's a very useful mental exercise to define your starting priorities and preferences. Close your eyes and picture yourself on your wedding day, from reciting your vows at the ceremony to celebrating at the reception. What's special or unique about the ceremony and reception locations? Are you indoors or outdoors? What's the season? How many guests are with you...is it an intimate gathering or an all-out bash? How formal? Is there a particular theme or color?

Have the bride write down her thoughts on the length of engagement, guest count, formality, season, theme, and location:

_____

_____

_____

_____

_____

_____

_____

_____

_____

Have the groom do the same:

_____

_____

_____

_____

_____

_____

_____

_____

Where do you conflict? List points that you need to resolve here. Discuss and compromise:

_____

_____

_____

_____

_____

_____

_____

_____

_____

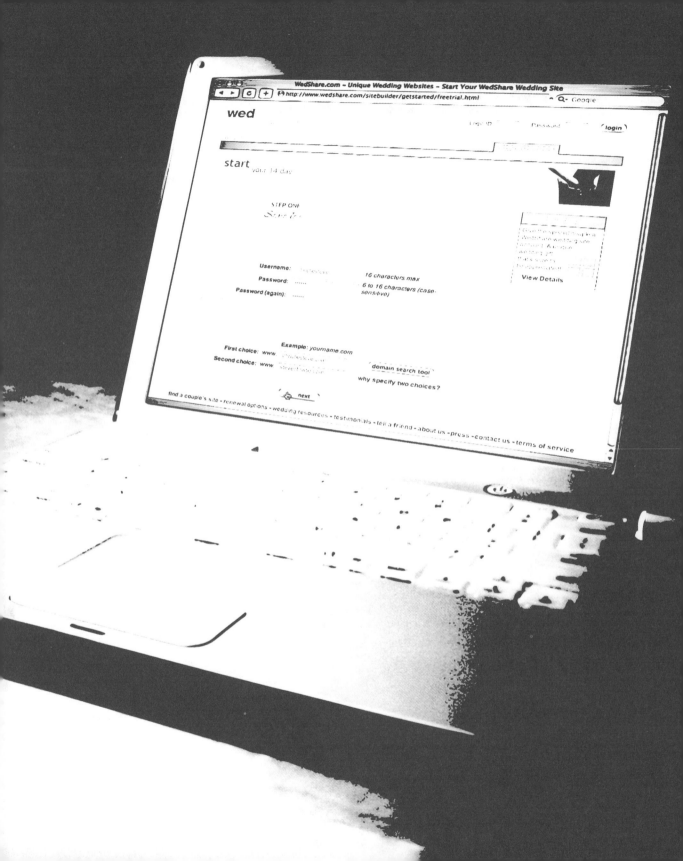

Chapter 4

Get a Wedding Website, Your Communication and Planning Home Base

- Why Have a Wedding Website?

- Wedding Website Services

- Where to Get Your Website and How to Start It

- e-Plan It! Use Your e-Resources:

  Wedding Website Service Directories
  A Wedding Website Service Startup Example
  Free Website Services

- Worksheets:

  Considerations Worksheet: Wedding Website Services
  Comparison Forms: Wedding Website Services

Who says traditions can't be brand spanking new? One of today's biggest and best trends is one that will be an immense help to your planning efforts: your personal wedding website. More and more couples today are making this an essential component of their wedding planning, and for good reason. In this chapter, we'll discuss the how, why, and where of setting yours up, and we'll be making use of it throughout the rest of this book.

Why Have a Wedding Website?

So, what makes a wedding website anyway, and do you really need one? You may be of the opinion that even if you do get a fun kick out of it, the time and money you put towards some online collection of bells and whistles could be better spent elsewhere...like planning your wedding. Well, we're going to show you how a wedding website can be one of the most helpful assets you can have when planning your big day, and why it's a major cornerstone in our e-Planning strategy. And for those of you

who think your options are limited to cheesy templates, expensive custom jobs, or time consuming build-it-yourself-from-scratch projects, think again. Today's wedding websites are slick, beautiful, and powerful services, and you can have yours up and live on the web in just minutes, for little or no cost at all. The sooner you get yours going, the more of a benefit you'll get, so put this convenient and time-saving e-Resource to work for you right away.

What It Is

Your personal wedding website will be a lot more than just a quick splash-screen with your wedding date and a picture of your smiling mugs bordered with flowers or hearts. A good wedding site is professional, just as customized and beautiful as the rest of your wedding details, and packed with convenient features. Your guests will get instant, 24/7 access to your gift registries, RSVP manager, maps and directions, photo albums, video clips and event calendar. Your website will be a centralized source of information for your checklists, guest database, address book, budget manager and payment tracker. And, you'll be able to manage it from anywhere you have Internet access.

continued from page 47

Informative Pages

Post maps, directions, notes and photos to inform your visitors. Some of the more common pages couples set up are listed below.

- Home Page: your welcome mat. Greet your visitors and provide any important notices. A countdown to the big day is often included here.

- Your Story: from both the bride's and groom's perspectives! How did you meet? How did he propose?

- Introducing the Bride and Groom: introduce yourselves...or each other!

- Introducing the Wedding Party: present your entourage, along with photos and bios if you like.

- Your Family and Friends: introduce those closest to you.

- The Ceremony: you can include maps, directions, photos, and anecdotes on why you chose the spot.

- The Reception: if the reception is in a separate location, give your guests the 411 here.

- For the Out-of-Towners: provide info on hotel reservations, local dining and entertainment.

- Games, Polls and Quizzes: an entertaining way for visitors to get to know you better. These can be for your benefit as well (a poll on menu or music choices, for example).

- Vendors Page: keep all your vendor information and contacts in one place.

- Thank-You's: let everyone know how much the help and guidance of special individuals mean to you.

- The Honeymoon: give the scoop on your chosen hot spot. Invite guests back after the wedding to get an update on how things are in paradise.

Planning Tools

Your website will provide tools for you to organize guests, manage headcounts, and track RSVP information, gifts, and thank-you cards. Specialized applications to manage your budget, keep track of payments and due dates, and even build your invitation content are provided by most good wedding website services. Communicate with your guests using e-mail broadcasts and send save-the-date e-cards with an easy click.

Complete Privacy Control

From password protection to visitor identification to a complete registration system, a secure website will give you the ability to restrict access to those you want and keep others out. If you're curious, visitor traffic and usage logs will let you see who's visiting, when they're visiting, and which pages or features they access when they do.

</NOTE>

<NOTE>

Wedding Website Features

The following are some features available with today's best professional wedding websites.

Your Own Domain Name

It's easy for your friends and family to remember your website address when it's as simple as your own names: christyandsteve.com, for example.

Customized E-mail Addresses

Correspond with family, friends and wedding vendors with a personal e-mail address like christy@christyandsteve.com.

Multimedia Gallery

Upload photos and video clips and organize them into separate albums. Some services even allow you to let your guests post comments and rate individual pics.

RSVP Send and Update

Guests can submit RSVP information for your wedding and other events (such as the rehearsal dinner). They may even be able to make changes to their previously submitted information as circumstances change. You'll be blessed with instant reports and real-time changes to your guest list and headcount.

Gift Registries

Placing gift registry information in your wedding invitation is generally considered a bad practice, but including your wedding website's address is always acceptable.

Event Calendar

Keep your notes, dates, and deadlines organized and conveniently available from wherever you have Internet access. Events you designate as public allow friends, family, and vendors to know when they can and can't reach you.

Address Book

A self-building address book collects contact info from your guests and updates your online guest database automatically. A good service will allow you to approve some or all changes depending on your security preferences.

Guestbook and Bulletin/Message Board

A Guestbook allows your website's visitors to leave their mark. Some services give you the capability to let your guests include photos or images with their messages, and to respond to other guests on various topics. What better way to get everyone's opinions on those tough-to-make decisions?

Bride and Groom Contact

Lets your visitors send correspondence to one or both of you. Secure services will present your visitors with a contact form and hide your actual e-mail addresses to guard against spammers (senders of unsolicited e-mail).

continued on page 48

What It Can Do for You

A wedding website can be a tremendous help during your planning and a fun way to manage all the details together. The other beneficiary of this technological convenience? Your guests! Here are a few examples of the benefits your own website will afford you:

Keep in Touch

Is your guest list or bridal party scattered across the country or even the world? No problem. Forget the costly long distance bills: a wedding website is a globally accessible place to exchange ideas, provide information, share photos, and discuss plans for the big day. Got any big announcements, changes in plans, or news on upcoming events? Let everyone know by including the info on your website.

Inform Your Guests

As the wedding day draws near, the questions will start rolling in. "How do I get to the church?"…"Can I change my dinner choice from fish to beef?"…"What's the hotel reservation block number again?"…you get the idea. Without a wedding website, expect your phone to be ringing off the hook, along with your sanity. Having a resource to point everyone towards is going to save you more than a few gray hairs as you scramble to take care of last minute details. Plus, it just makes it easy and more convenient for your guests to have an informative spot to pull maps, directions, reservation info, and more. As an example, the online RSVP update is a hassle-free way for them to inform you of changes in meal choice or number attending without having to track you down by phone.

Manage and Organize Your Planning

Information organization and management are areas a computer is especially good at helping out with, so it only makes sense that you can leverage this processing power to offload some of your wedding planning burden. Most professional website services include planning tools that are integrated with your site. In the next chapter, for ex-

> **<CROSS-REFERENCE>**
> You'll use your website's tools to create a smart budget and payment system in Chapter 5, and to manage guests and attendants in Chapter 7.
> **</CROSS-REFERENCE>**

ample, we'll take a look at your website's budget planning and payment tracking tools to create a smart budget and payment system. In chapter 7, "Manage Your Guests and Attendants", we'll use a database to store guests for easy search and retrieval. We'll group them into categories and enable them to RSVP or update contact info online. We'll even discuss an export feature that formalizes your guests' names and creates a list for easy addressing of your invitations (Peter and Jenny Martin, with two kids becomes "Mr. and Mrs. Peter Martin and Family", for example). There are so many times we'll use the planning tools available with your wedding website, in fact, that we call the wedding website your planning "home base".

Centralize Your Information

Building your guest list online—or creating it offline and importing it—results in a conveniently search-able database of contact information, as we'll see in Chapter 7. It also keeps their RSVP information, gift records, birthdays, correspondence history and more, all in one place. With the self-building address book in place that we'll also introduce in Chapter 7, your guests can even update their contact information for you as it changes. No need to hunt through notes or make phone calls to get the latest scoop on your guests; it's all available in one easy spot. Even after the wedding is long over, having such a dynamic and convenient directory of information for all your friends and relatives is something you can continue to use to send and track thank-you notes, holiday cards or arrange future events and get-togethers. But your guest information isn't the only thing you'll have in one place here. Your website is also an organized source of vendor contacts, events and deadlines, payment schedules, music lists, photo collections...and more. Consolidating it all to a single location that can be accessed 24/7 from anywhere you have an Internet connection is a convenient, headache-saving asset you'll come to love and appreciate. And when you need to have your info to go, most features allow you to generate reports and other printer-friendly take-alongs.

Involve the Groom

While the groom-to-be may not be thrilled about selecting bridesmaids' dress colors or choosing the right floral centerpieces, building a wedding website together is a fun way for you both to be involved in the planning process. He can add his own version of how the two of you met and enter bios for the groomsmen and his family. If he's more technically inclined than his bride-to-be, the groom can take charge scanning (or uploading) the photos, maps, and other additions. We know of couples who, for various reasons, were geographically separated throughout much of the planning period and their wedding website was the primary way for both to keep abreast of the details the other was managing.

Preserve the Memories

In Chapter 12, "Find a Photographer to Match Your Style", we discuss creating your "planning album", a collection of photos that will preserve this exciting and emotional time in your life for years to come. Your wedding website, in fact, is a great place to display this album online. But the website itself is more of a keepsake of your wedding and your planning days than any album could be. With all its photos, guestbook entries, message boards, notes, informative pages and lists, it's a detailed scrapbook that captures all facets of your wedding planning journey. In fact, many couples choose to "evolve" their wedding website into a family, baby, or travel website after their wedding. Others opt to save it away on a CD. Whatever you choose, your wedding website can live on as a great keepsake long after the big day.

Wedding Website Services

In the next section we'll discuss the various ways you can get your own wedding website. As you'll see, one way is to make use of a wedding website service. These all-inclusive companies provide everything to you in a package, including the website-building tools, planning tools, and hosting. Whether you opt to go for such a ready-made service, take the time to do it yourself from scratch, or hire a friend or design company is a decision we'll help you out with in the following section. Let's make that decision an informed one by first investigating wedding website services and what they can do for you.

What They Are

Wedding website services typically charge an annual or semiannual subscription fee to get your spot reserved on the web and often provide easy-to-use tools to get a website up fairly quickly (we're talking minutes here). You don't need to have any web development or coding skills to use such a service, although some services offer advanced site-building interfaces to those who have the know-how and desire to customize their websites even more. Good wedding website services will include the features and tools discussed in the previous section as well as the ability to easily tailor a sleek, professional website that matches your wedding theme and preferences.

The real advantage of using a wedding website service, and why we recommend them to couples planning their own weddings, is the convenience they afford you. Let's face it, you're doing this website thing to save time and offload some of your planning burden, not to gain another to-do task. A wedding website service will get you up and running in minutes, and will bring with it a whole treasure chest full of wedding planning tools that you can start using right away.

For the Tech Newbies: Wedding Websites and Domain Name Basics

Before we go any further, let's quickly bring those less technical couples up to speed on some geeky aspects of websites you should be familiar with. If you already know what a domain name registrar is, what a web hosting company does, and are familiar with the concept of a server, feel free to skip over this discussion.

What's in a Website?

To get a website up on the Internet, there are a few things that have to happen before you can be "live". First, you need to own a domain name. The domain name is what you or your friends will pop into the web browser's address field to get to your website (an example is www.mediasoftpress.com, the domain name for this book's publisher). You may also hear a domain name referred to as a URL (for Uniform Resource Locator). Purchasing your own domain name can cost anywhere from under $10 to over $25 a year, depending on the company you use. Companies who sell domain names are called "domain name registrars".

Next, you need to secure hosting space for your website. This is space on a computer somewhere in Internet-land where all the digital photos, designs, and data for your website will actually reside. The computer is called a server, and the company who owns it will charge you a fee to rent space for your website. This web hosting fee is typically around $90 to $120 a year if you purchase it on your own.

Once you get a domain name and sign on with a hosting company, you've got the digital equivalent of an empty real estate lot. You have an address (your domain name) and you have lot space (the hosting company's server), but you need to build something there for your visitors to actually see and use. If you know how to design a website, you could build and transfer the files yourself to the server. Or, you could hire someone else to do it for you.

What a Wedding Website Service Gets You

What a good wedding website service does is provide an entire package to you: domain name, hosting, and the website itself with an easy-to-use interface to customize, modify and maintain it at your leisure. You don't have to worry about securing the domain name or hosting, and pay only one annual or semi-annual subscription fee to the wedding service provider. This fee can be as little as $70 or so for the whole package for a year, and is often even cheaper than that to extend for additional months or years. And for those of you who believe firmly in the idea that all services on the Internet should be free, don't let a little $70 fee turn you away. There's free wedding website services, too, which we'll discuss towards the end of the chapter. Such freebies will give you the basics, as long as you don't mind some advertisements here and there and some trimmed-down functionality. Instead of your own domain, as in "www.christyandsteve.com", free services will give you a domain name which is an extension of theirs, like "www.someservice.com/christyandsteve", or "christyandsteve.someservice.com". This name sharing may or may not matter to you, and it's something we'll discuss more in the next section.

What to Look for in a Wedding Website Service

If you decide to use a wedding website service, you probably won't be surprised to find that, like everything else, such services are not created equal. Some provide fewer features, more restrictive editing, or designs that have a less-professional, cookie-cutter template feel. Others really excel in the packages they offer and include a lot of extras that aren't even advertised. Let's take a look at some of the features that should be present in a good service, and in the next section we'll show you how to find one.

Security

First and foremost, how secure is the service? The idea of your baby pictures floating around on the web is probably not appealing. Can you password protect your website, and do you have the ability to check your visitation logs? And how about content protection…are visitors of your wedding website able to highlight and copy your web content or drag your images off to save on their computer? A good service will disable as much of this as is technically possible. Make sure your administrative interface (the place you log in to enter information and edit your site) is secure and password-protected as well. If you don't want to go so far as password restricting your website but want to capture the e-mail addresses or names of your visitors, does your service provide such variable security levels? You might want to enforce visitor registration, for example, in which case your website would send confirmation e-mails to first-time visitors before allowing them onto the site. This would ensure that your visitors have valid e-mail accounts that can be logged for you, usually a good deterrent against solicitors and potential troublemakers. Such a registration service should be automatically handled by your website, and should provide the ability to block specific individuals and unwanted visitors.

Free Trial

Most wedding website services provide a no-risk free trial period, usually one to two weeks in duration. You shouldn't have to give up any credit card or payment information to get your free trial, either. The trial period is plenty of time to evaluate the service and decide whether or not it works for you. You should be able to do basically everything you could do with a paid subscription, although you probably won't be given your domain name until you purchase. If the service doesn't offer a free trial or if their trial blocks you from trying out major functionality, move on.

Professionalism

Some wedding website services out there are downright amateurish, and the websites these quick-n-dirty services produce are substandard at best. Such stinkers can almost always be sniffed out just by browsing through their own website. Is it clean, informative, and professional, or does it look cheesy and childish? If their website doesn't provide the answers to your questions, contact the company and request more information. Are your questions answered in a timely and professional manner? Start a free trial with the service you're considering and get a feel for the administrative interface. Is it clumsy or difficult to use? You've got your hands full planning your wedding, and you don't need to spend a week figuring out how to use your wedding website service.

Design Variety

The service's website should have a catalog or gallery where you can browse the available theme designs and color combinations. They represent a starting point that you can customize and build on. Generally, the more variation the better, but pay attention to the variety of the designs, not their sheer number. Some services will boast a wide range of designs to choose from but when you compare them all, they're really more or less the same look with different color schemes or slightly modified imagery. Don't fall for it. Go with a service whose designs are creative, varied and attractive, with more than one that catches your eye as a potential for your own wedding website. The website produced should be as sharp, clean, and professional as anything else you'd expect to buy for your wedding.

Customization

It should go without saying: the more customizable your website is, the better. The overall design, color, and imagery of your website should be changeable. The content should be easy to enter and edit. Look for a slick editor interface that lets you change the font, size, color, and style of text like a modern word processor. The website title, menu order, menu options, page names, page layouts and everything else should be easy to change whenever and however you like. And once you choose your website's design and color scheme, you shouldn't be stuck with it. Make sure you can easily swap designs and colors as many times as you want. A good design that is fully customizable will enable you to quickly and easily produce a website that ties into your wedding theme and says "You". If you've got some design experience, does the website service allow you to add your own HTML code when editing your website? Good services will provide an editor interface that allows you to flip back-and-forth from basic text to advanced HTML design views, satisfying the technical newbies and experienced pros alike.

Price

An annual subscription for a good service will cost around $70 to $100 per year. Don't subscribe on price alone: the most expensive services are not necessarily the best. Make sure you give the one you're considering a solid test drive using the free trial.

Full Featured

Go over the list of features we discussed in the previous section. Of those listed, are any that you especially would like to have absent from the service you're considering? If you're not sure, send them an e-mail and ask. Be sure the service offers everything you're looking for before you subscribe. Will you be provided with a full suite of planning tools? You should have a good budget manager, payment tracker, and guest database, for starters. An address book for guests to enter and update contact info, online RSVP functionality (with the capability to handle multiple events), and the ability to quickly e-mail all guests or specific categories of your guests are helpful as well.

Details

Consider the quality of each service's features, and don't forget those little extras. We've already discussed a few: the ability to add your own HTML, for instance, or a professional editor interface set up like a word processor that lets you change your text's font, style, color, and so forth. How about a photo lab so you can crop, adjust, and modify the photos you upload? Or a visitor registration system that e-mails first-time visitors and allows you to manage their accounts? You may want a smooth, animated Flash® introductory sequence that you can customize yourself as a bit of additional flair to an already beautiful presentation. Another extra detail is the domain name itself: some services will give you a website address that is really just an extension of their own (like "christyandsteve.someservice.com") instead of your own domain name ("www.christyandsteve.com"). Some services will charge an additional fee for this perk. A detail you won't often find is a service offering your own email addresses, like christy@christyandsteve.com. These extras add a lot of value, and should be considered when looking at any potential wedding website service.

Compare the quality of the planning tools and features. Sign up for free trials at more than one service, and compare them all. One service's photo album might display a single photo collection in a plain, one-picture at a time view, for example, while another could offer a slick, easy-to-navigate interface, including the ability to add comments, view stats (like most frequently viewed pics), post video clips, and create an unlimited number of albums.

Where to Get Your Website and How to Start It

So where's the best place to get your own wedding website? First of all, you need to make a choice as to whether you'll be going with a wedding website service, building it yourself from scratch, or hiring a friend or professional. The choice is yours, but our recommendation is to go with a good, all-inclusive service. It's inexpensive, quick, keeps the control in your hands, and gives you instant access to a wealth of planning tools and features we'll be taking advantage of throughout this book.

Not convinced? Here are a few common scenarios:

"My fiancé is a professional web designer. Why can't he do our website?"

Some technical or design-oriented couples would rather design their own wedding website from the ground up (similar to creative do-it-yourselfer couples who prefer to craft their own invitations) and it's a perfectly reasonable alternative in this sense. But there's no real cost-saving or practical advantage to doing it yourself from scratch. It's one more time consuming to-do task you'll have, rather than getting the website up now and moving on to something else that needs to get done. Unless you're hosting the site on your own server, the hosting and domain registration fees combined will probably be more expensive than subscribing to a service, and you won't be getting all the integrated planning tools (online RSVP, guest database, budget manager, and so forth). Plus, a good service will offer a highly customizable website and will even let you edit your content on the HTML level, anyway; you'll get plenty of that do-it-yourself pride and satisfaction. Another consideration: if you want to change the entire look and feel of your website after it's completed, you can do so with a single click using a wedding website service. This isn't really an option for those embarking on a from-scratch job.

"I'm letting a friend design our website for us. She's a real web guru and isn't charging anything."

While this at first seems like a great opportunity, it's most likely the worst choice. You still need to pay for hosting and domain name registration, and you still won't get the integrated planning tools and features that make a wedding website so valuable. Plus, any changes, additions, or notices you want to add may have to go through your friend—a major hassle—and your website can quickly fall out of date. If you just want a splash screen with your names, some basic info, and nothing more, this can be a way to go. But browse through the features list at the beginning of this chapter and see what you'll be missing.

"I found a company to custom design my website. Their fees are very reasonable."

The problem here is that, once again, you're putting the control into the hands of a designer rather than yourselves. Changes or modifications may have to go through them, and you may or may not be blessed with helpful integrated features and planning tools (it depends on whether or not your designer specializes in wedding sites). You'll also still have to pay extra domain name and hosting fees. You can bet that the overall cost is going to exceed a wedding website service.

e-Resource

Wedding Website Service Directories

If you do decide to go with a wedding website service, where do you find them? Here are a couple great sources to start your search from.

WeddingWebsites.com

This directory lists some of the top wedding website services and gives you the ability to compare cost, features, number of designs and more, to get a good at-a-glance take on each. They

WeddingWebsites.com is a great starting point for beginning your wedding website service search.

Select the "Website Design Service" category from TeamWedding's main page to see a list of providers.

also feature customer reviews to let you know what other couples thought of their service; the sites are currently ranked by the power of their reviews, not by advertising dollars. It's a brand-new directory (they launched in late 2005) so you'll likely find the number of reviews to be on the slim side for a while. As convenient as the service is, though, we expect its popularity to continually increase as it becomes more established.

TeamWedding (www.topweddingsites.com)

This portal can put you in touch with a variety of online resources, including wedding website services. Unlike the big corporate portals (The Knot and WeddingChannel.com), companies don't have to pay to be listed here. They're ranked based on the amount of traffic TeamWedding gets from each of the company's websites. This doesn't mean that the top listed sites are any better than the bottom listed ones, so the ranking is of little importance to you. To get a list of wedding website services, go to TeamWedding's home page and select "Website Design Service" from their Category dropdown menu.

A Wedding Website Service Startup Example

So how does one actually start using a wedding website service? We'll run through a step-by-step guided example using WedShare.com, a service the authors pioneered and one which includes all the features, details and perks we covered in the previous sections (yes, we know we're biased). As for choosing your own service, you'll be best served to search for one that suits your individual needs and tastes. The directories listed in the previous e-Resource are great impartial locations to start your research. Most professional services will be similar to the example we cover below.

Five-Minute Quick Start

To start with, the initial objective is to get your wedding website live on the Internet with as little fuss as possible, and you can make it happen in a matter of minutes. You'll be able to add to it later at your own pace, but for now we'll just get the basics up as an online wedding announcement. You'll have a welcome page announcing your coming nuptials, a guestbook that your visitors can sign, a contact page so that guests can get ahold of you via your website, and an animated Flash® introductory sequence. All in five minutes or less! The rest of your website's features can be explored, customized and activated at your leisure.

Log into www.wedshare.com and click the "Start Free Trial" button. You'll be taken to Step One in WedShare. com's three-step start-up process. Pick a username and password; you'll use this information when you want to make changes to your website or to access your planning tools. You're also given the opportunity here to select a website address, or domain name (yoursite.com). Your domain name will be reserved for you when you purchase, and in the meantime you'll be able to access your website using a temporary web address. Upon subscription, your website will become accessible from both your chosen domain name and the temporary address.

In the next step, enter in a contact e-mail address, the bride's and groom's names, and your wedding date. This information will be used to tailor your website's initial title and content, which you can change later. If you'll be using WedShare.com as your website service, make sure you also enter in the promotional code here as described in the exclusive offer at the beginning of this book (as a reader you're entitled to a discount, which will be applied if you decide to purchase your website subscription).

Your account has now been created, and your website will appear live at the temporary address given. Open a new window and browse to your temporary address to see your newborn wedding website, which is presented in your selected design and color scheme. See? We told you it was easy! Of course, you'll want to further customize your content, active pages, design, and theme, which we'll do next. Click the "Go to Control Panel" button to move on.

Starting your wedding website with a website service is as simple as filling out a quick form. Your website is online in minutes!

Your wedding website's control panel lets you build and edit your website, activate features, and access your planning tools.

Pick the general look and feel of your website in the SiteBuilder Theme and Color Scheme tab.

Your Control Panel

When you first start your wedding website, and any time you log in with your username and password, you'll arrive at your control panel. It's the one-screen starting point for doing just about anything, from building your website to activating features to accessing your guest information and planning tools.

Your control panel is divided into four panes, each covering a specific activity type. The account details pane, for example, lets you access your payment history and administrative info, such as a contact e-mail and password choice. The e-mail manager pane is what you'll use to create your own personal e-mail accounts after you subscribe, and the pane for planning tools contains helpful applications to alleviate some of the wedding planning burden. The SiteBuilder pane lists all the resources you'll use to build and manage your website, and it's where we'll go next. Go ahead and click the "Website Designs" link in the SiteBuilder pane.

You'll see that the SiteBuilder submenu appears in the upper left hand of the page, and that all four panes are minimized as tabs at the top. You can always click the "Control Panel" tab to return to the expanded control panel view.

In the Website Designs page, you can change the theme and basic color scheme of your website. Each theme has a number of possible color schemes it can be rendered in; click the color swatches to see the associated example thumbnail change to reflect the new scheme. When you're satisfied with a look that you like, click the "Save" button and then either open a new browser window to your website or click the "Open Your Site" button at the bottom of the page. You'll see that your entire website has changed to reflect the new look and feel you selected. You can change your website in this way at any time you like, and as many times as you like.

```
<TIP>

Additional Website Features We Cover in This Book

Wedding Checklists:                     Chapter 2
Manage and Track Your Budget:           Chapter 5
Vendors Page:                           Chapter 5
Guest Manager:                          Chapters 7, 15, and 20
Address Book:                           Chapter 7
Out-of-Town Guests Page:                Chapter 7
Ceremony Page:                          Chapter 8
Reception Page:                         Chapter 9
Vendors Page:                           Chapter 11
Gift Registry:                          Chapter 15
Invitation Workshop:                    Chapter 20
Online RSVP:                            Chapters 20 and 22
Event Calendar:                         Chapter 21
Honeymoon Page:                         Chapter 24

</TIP>
```

Add content to your pages like photos, text, or even fun content blocks containing polls and quizzes. You can access your individual website pages by selecting "Website Pages and Content Blocks" from the Control Panel. Activate or deactivate the pages to determine which ones visitors can see, and click on each page's "edit" link to edit the page layout and add your content. Don't see a web page that you have in mind? Click "Create a New Custom Page" to add it!

<TIP>

Keep in mind that in addition to changing the general theme and color scheme, the layout and content of each individual page can be modified as well. Access the editors for each individual page by clicking the "Website Pages and Content Blocks" tab.

</TIP>

Growing Your Website As You Go

For now, you may want to just add an announcement message to your welcome page and deactivate all other pages but your guestbook and contact form. This will set you up with a wedding website that serves as a great online wedding announcement. There are plenty more pages and features to add, but the great thing is that you can do it at your own pace, activating features and adding new pages as you have time. We'll be covering a lot of them in this book in fact, as outlined in the sidebar, starting with your Budget Manager in the next chapter. Take a sneak peak at this helpful planning resource by clicking the "Budget Manager" tab located in the Planning Tools pane of your control panel (if you're using another wedding website service, a comparable tool should be offered). Happy e-planning!

Spreading the Word

Now that your wedding website's up, spread the word! Once friends and family know your domain name, they can start visiting your website to take advantage of the information and features you've set up for them there. Many will visit on a regular basis to see what's new. Send out an e-mail using your guest list broadcast: invite friends and family to your new website and ask them to provide or update their contact info in your address book. Put your domain name on your invitations, save-the-date cards and any other correspondence. Let people know over the phone. As the questions start rolling in, tell everyone about the online convenience that awaits them!

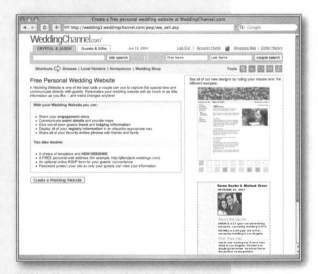

WeddingChannel.com provides a free website as part of their planning tools. Check the next page to read more about free websites.

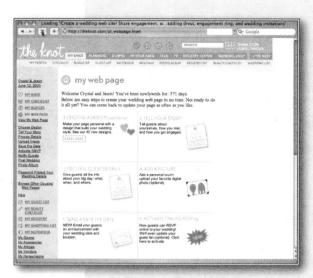

The Knot (www.theknot.com) lets you create a web page for free using the "My Webpage" feature.

<CROSS-REFERENCE>

Learn more about The Knot, WeddingChannel.com, and how these and other big wedding portals can simplify your planning in Chapter 6, Style and Preferences: Capture Your Wedding Vision".

</CROSS-REFERENCE>

Free Website Services

You can't beat free, of course, so we'd be remiss if we didn't mention some no-cost alternatives to a subscription-based wedding website service. A free service might suit you just fine as long as you don't mind the ever-present advertisements and are okay with not having your own domain name. Free sites will also offer fewer features, generally less robust planning tools, and far less customization options. But, hey, who's complaining? It's free! Most of the big wedding portals have options to create a web page or simple website that can convey the basic wedding info, link up to your gift registries, accept online RSVPs and help manage your budget.

WeddingChannel.com

The best free service we found was the wedding website provided by WeddingChannel.com, although we liked the planning tools better at The Knot. WeddingChannel.com's personal website feature has a decent number of designs (even if they are pretty template-ish) and an interface to enter in your story, out-of-town guest resources, registry links, and upload photos. A basic RSVP form is also included. Your web address is tacked on to the domain name "weddings.com", as in "christyandsteve.weddings.com".

The Knot (www.theknot.com)

Clicking on the "My Webpage" link sends you to The Knot's personal web page feature. The best part is that you can link up to their planning tools, like the budget manager and guest list, which are pretty well done. You're limited to a few clip-arty designs and can only upload a single photo onto your page, but it gets the job done. You can provide a basic RSVP page to your guests, and a new feature recently added lets you create an online photo album, too.

Considerations Worksheet: Wedding Website Services

Wedding Website Budget: $ _____

Website Features

☐ Your Own Domain Name
☐ Customized E-mail Addresses
☐ Flash Intros
☐ Your Own Background Music
☐ Multimedia Gallery (photos, videos, mp3s, files)
☐ Online RSVP
☐ Online Gift Registry
☐ Event Calendar
☐ Guestbook and Bulletin/Message Board
☐ Address Book
☐ Contact Form
☐ Privacy Control Options
☐ _____

Informative Pages

☐ Home Page
☐ About the Bride and Groom
☐ Your Story
☐ The Wedding Party
☐ Your Family and Friends
☐ The Ceremony
☐ The Reception
☐ For the Out-of-Towners
☐ Games, Polls and Quizzes
☐ About Your Vendors
☐ Thank-You's
☐ The Honeymoon
☐ _____

Additional Online Planning Tools

☐ Budget Manager and Payment Tracker
☐ Guest Manager
☐ Name Formatter
☐ Address Formatter
☐ Multiple Event Manager
☐ Essential Checklists
☐ Email Broadcasts
☐ Save-the-Date e-Cards
☐ _____

Type of Website

☐ Free Website / Webpage
☐ Wedding Website Service
☐ Custom-Designed Websites
☐ From Scratch

Notes: _____

_____

_____

_____

_____

_____

_____

_____

_____

_____

_____

_____

_____

_____

_____

Comparison Forms: Wedding Website Services 1

Service / Designer: _____

Website: _____

Email: _____ Phone: _____

Free Trial Terms (if any): _____ Recommended by: _____

Type of Service	Service Term	Domain Name Format Available
☐ Free Website / Webpage	☐ 12 Months	☐ http://www.yourname.com
☐ Wedding Website Service	☐ 18 Months	☐ http://yourname.someservice.com
☐ Custom-Designed Website	☐ 24 Months	☐ http://www.someservice.com/yourname

Security Features: _____

Professionalism: _____

Design Variety: _____ Theme(s) You Liked: _____

Customization Level: _____

Features: _____

_____

Planning Tools: _____

_____

Special Details: _____

_____

Payment Policy: _____

Cancellation Policy: _____

Extra cost for your own domain name?   ☐ Yes   ☐ No

If yes, how much? $ _____

Service/Designer Fee: $ _____

Additional Fees: $ _____

_____

Total Estimated Cost: $ _____

_____

Comments: _____

_____

_____

_____

_____

_____

_____

_____

Comparison Forms: Wedding Website Services 2

Service / Designer: _____

Website: _____

Email: _____   Phone: _____

Free Trial Terms (if any): _____   Recommended by: _____

Type of Service	Service Term	Domain Name Format Available
☐ Free Website / Webpage	☐ 12 Months	☐ http://www.yourname.com
☐ Wedding Website Service	☐ 18 Months	☐ http://yourname.someservice.com
☐ Custom-Designed Website	☐ 24 Months	☐ http://www.someservice.com/yourname

Security Features: _____

Professionalism: _____

Design Variety: _____   Theme(s) You Liked: _____

Customization Level: _____

Features: _____
_____

Planning Tools: _____
_____

Special Details: _____
_____

Payment Policy: _____

Cancellation Policy: _____

Extra cost for your own domain name?   ☐ Yes   ☐ No

If yes, how much? $ _____

Service/Designer Fee: $ _____

Additional Fees: $ _____

Total Estimated Cost: $ _____

Comments: _____
_____
_____
_____
_____
_____

Chapter 5

Create a Smart Budget and Payment System

- The Art of Setting a Realistic and Flexible Budget

- The Need for Financial Record-Keeping

- Money-Saving Tips

- Working with Vendors

- e-Plan It! Use Your e-Resources:

  Interactive Budget Manager, Part I: Setting Up Your Budget Categories
  Interactive Budget Manager, Part II: Payment and Due Date Tracker

- Worksheets:

  Worksheet: Starting Budget
  Worksheet: Wedding Budget

B y dealing with your budget properly early on, you can avoid the pitfalls that a lot of other couples wind up struggling with. In this chapter, we'll show you how to discuss straightforward ways to determine your overall budget based on combined savings, salary, and engagement length. Once you have a solid idea of where you stand, we'll discuss using expense categories to maximize your money and emphasize your wedding vision and priorities, all while staying flexible enough to deal with the occasional splurge (it'll happen!). By using some cool online tools, we'll make it as quick and painless as possible. Your budget is the heart of your wedding planning, so work together and take your time with it. The advantages you get back will be well worth it.

The Art of Setting a Realistic and Flexible Budget

Setting up a wedding budget and managing it is usually not one of the more relished aspects of wedding planning. All too often, budgeting is something that's rushed over, put on the backburner, or pretty much ignored altogether. Unfortunately, this lack of good financial planning can often directly result in debt after the wedding (not a good foot to start out on), tension with parents and other family contributors, overspending that spirals out of control, or desperate attempts to compensate for random splurges by over-cheapening other wedding details.

What Are Your Priorities?

One thing you want to remember throughout your wedding planning: you're designing a day for you to enjoy and have fun, a celebration of your love and future together. With this in mind, you should have a good idea of what things matter most to the two of you. Is it a sumptuous meal? Music and dancing that's off the hook? Flowers, decoration, and attire fit for a royal court? What's going to make you enjoy your day most? This should be clear to you as you set out to carve your budget.

Revisiting Your Initial Decisions

At the close of Chapter 3 we discussed some initial decisions that should be made soon after your engagement, in order to get that "wedding day vision" ball rolling. It's time to turn those daydreams into reality now, and the first crucial step is to nail down how everything's going to get paid for. All your initial decisions will be important in setting up a budget to fund the wedding uniquely perfect for you, from the length of your engagement to the level of formality you would like. The reality check here is that dollars—not wishes or daydreams—are going to be the foundation for your big day. That said, a properly managed budget, along with some smart shopping and creative thinking, will allow you to realize your perfect wedding regardless of your budget's size. That's because proper budget management will allow you to be flexible and to emphasize those parts of your day that you feel are most important.

So, start prioritizing now! If you haven't thought about the points discussed at the close of Chapter 3, take some time to do it before going any further. A few of the important things to consider with your sweetheart are how formal you'd like your big bash, how many guests, and how long an engagement period. Would it be an indoor or outdoor affair? Any particular season? What excites you most about the idea of your wedding celebration?

<CROSS-REFERENCE>
We brought up some initial decisions to make at the close of Chapter 3.
</CROSS-REFERENCE>

<CROSS-REFERENCE>
Once you've taken a first cut at your budget, you'll be clarifying your priorities even more in Chapter 6. See our discussion there on "Using Your Budget to Clarify Your Decisions".
</CROSS-REFERENCE>

Who's Paying?

The tradition that the bride's family foots the wedding bill dates back to the ancient custom of fathers providing dowries to attract suitable husbands for their daughters. Nowadays, who pays for what depends solely on your own unique situation. Some couples have families (both on the bride's and groom's sides) that are willing and able to pitch in for most or all of the expenses. Other couples fund their weddings completely on their own, either by preference or necessity. Depending on your situation, you will probably fall somewhere in the middle of these two scenarios.

While it's always nice (and sometimes necessary) to have help, just remember to be gracious and appreciative, never demanding, throughout. Keep in mind, too, that those who provide financial support may have preferences not exactly in line with your own. Everyone knows the Golden Rule: "He who has the gold makes the rules!" and he who hosts the wedding is largely entitled to setting the details as he sees fit. Of course you expect those who provide funds for your wedding to truly want your special day to be everything that makes you happy and respect your wishes…but however well-intentioned, they may not even realize that their own preferences and priorities are clashing with yours. You'll need to be at your diplomatic best to make the most of their contributions while still ensuring that your wedding day is your own.

One strategy, if you're splitting costs between the two of you and family, is to decide which wedding categories you feel are less important to you, relatively speaking (we'll go over categories later), and ask your family to help you with those areas, rather than adding their contributions to one big pot. This allows you to control the areas they have a say in, and keeps the ownership of details most important to you in your own hands. To be courteous, you still should obtain quotes from vendors in those areas you're handing over, to give the family members helping out an up front idea of how much you're expecting it to cost, based on your standards. And remember to be sensitive: if your parents or other family members are going through a tough financial time, consider other ways they can help and still enjoy contributing to your special day. Researching vendors, mailing invitations, creating the wedding fa-

<NOTE>

Traditional Payment Responsibilities

How were expenses traditionally sliced? As you can see from the list below, the bride's family bore the greatest financial burden by far.

Bride

• The groom's wedding ring

• A gift for the groom

• All personal stationery (thank you notes, etc.)

• Accommodations for attendants coming from out of town

• Gifts for the bridesmaids

• Blood test and medical exam, if required

Groom

• The bride's engagement ring and wedding ring

• A gift for the bride

• The bride's bouquet

• The marriage license

• Fee for the ceremony officiant

• The groom's formalwear

• The mothers' corsages

• The fathers' and groomsmen's boutonnieres

• Blood test and medical exam, if required

Bride's Family

• The ceremony and reception costs

• The engagement party, if you have one

• The bridal gown and all accessories

• Wedding transportation

• Flowers and décor for the ceremony and reception

• Bouquets for the bridesmaids

• Wedding invitations and other stationery

• Gift for the bride and groom

Groom's Family

• The rehearsal dinner

• Travel expenses and accommodations for the groom's family members

• Expenses for the honeymoon if not paid by the groom

• Gift for the bride and groom

</NOTE>

vors, or doing your flower arrangements…any of these would be an incredible money- and time-saving help to you.

Even between couples, one often has more to contribute than the other, which might lead to some sticky situations. Communication is key, and it is imperative that the two of you sit down and discuss how you'll be dividing the wedding costs up front. Perhaps one of you has savings and the other does not, or maybe your sweetheart has a sizeable full-time salary but you're working part-time and going to school. Regardless of who is putting in more, make sure you each know which details are most important to the other. This goes back to deciding your priorities early on; you want to discuss this freely and often among each other, and compromise on which areas you're willing to splurge on and which areas you're willing to cut back in. You'll find this vital to staying within your budget while having the wedding you both envision.

Using Expense Categories

Now that you've set your priorities and have a good idea who's paying for what, you need a strategy to determine just how much you actually have, and to make the most of those funds.

<TIP>

$$ Asking family for help with wedding funds $$

What if you're in need of financial aid, but your sweetheart's parents have yet to offer assistance? This can be a very sensitive situation, and you don't want to get started on the wrong foot with your future in-laws. Communication with your spouse-to-be is essential, of course. Is there a known issue? Perhaps they're going through a tough time. Remember that there are a lot of non-monetary ways they can contribute to your wedding, and you might want to consider something aside from cash that they might be able to help out with, such as creating the favors or addressing and mailing the invitations.

It could also be the case that they simply don't realize you need the help. It should be up to your sweetheart to raise the issue with his (or her) own folks, and probably alone, in order for them to be more comfortable discussing a potentially awkward or touchy issue. Rehearse an opening together that is direct but courteous. Try a light opening such as: "You know, I was discussing our wedding budget with Laura and we're coming up a little short. It would be great if you might be able to help us out a bit; we're trying not to have to cut back on inviting some of the guests that would be important for both you and us."

Remember that there may be very good reasons why the parents in question might not be able to help out. Never take the attitude that they're obligated to do so (they're not), and be sensitive to their situation.

</TIP>

We'll show you how to quantify your total budget, slice it up into manageable categories, and how to do it all online…efficiently and conveniently. We'll also discuss how to keep your cool—and keep out of debt—when the urge to splurge kicks in and things in budget-land get hot (hey, we never said this would be easy).

Determine Your Overall Wedding Budget Amount

Okay. So how much money is your wedding going to cost? We're talking total cost here, from the stamps on your invitations to your toasting glasses to your catering bill to your dress. How much?

While the national average for a wedding's total cost is currently just over $26,000 (a 73% increase in the last 15 years), weddings have been planned for as little as $5,000 and for as much as $80,000 (and up!). Ultimately the amount you're going to spend will depend on how much you have, and how much of that you're willing to put towards your wedding.

So let's figure out how much you have first, and we'll go from there. The easiest way to do this is to skip forward to the following e-Resource (Interactive Budget Manager) and figure it out with the help of an online budget calculator. But what's happening under the hood with those calculators is shown below, as well as on the Starting Budget Worksheet at the end of the chapter.

Here's how it works: decide first how much of your combined savings (if any) that you want to use. The online calculators typically suggest 50%, although you'll need to adjust this up or down depending on your other financial pressures (debts, non-wedding expenses, etc.). Add this amount to any funds that your families are contributing. Next, think about how much of your monthly income you and your spouse-to-be will each be able to add to the pot. Here, the online calculators and our worksheet suggest 20%, but this may differ for you. Multiply your combined income contribution by the number of months of your engagement. Add everything up and you should arrive at a solid starting point that you can safely call your total available funds. We know this can be pretty hard to follow in words, so check out the following example:

Savings:

$1,200 in bride's savings, $2,000 in groom's savings (Combined = $3,200)

(3,200 ÷ 2 = $1,600 available)

Income:

Bride's monthly income: $3,000 (3,000 x .20 = $600)

Groom's monthly income: $4,000 (4,000 x .20 = $800)

800 + 600 = $1,400 per month

Engagement length = 12 months

(12 X 1,400 = $16,800 available)

Family Contribution

Bride's family's contribution: $5,000

Groom's family's contribution: $3,000

5,000 + 3,000 = 8,000 available)

Total Available: $26,400

Note that in this example, the engagement was long enough to compensate for the lack of substantial savings the couple had when they were first engaged. Your own example will certainly vary, but you should have a good idea of your overall available funds by working through this calculation exercise. You may even want to adjust your target wedding date if possible, to give you some extra time to save.

From this available money, how much do you want to put towards your wedding? If you were the couple in the example above, you might want to put the entire $26K into the wedding pot, or you might want to split it in half. You could challenge yourself with a limit of, say, $13 or $14K and build your budget to accomplish that, leaving the rest in savings. It's up to you. Just make sure you work through it together, and that the final decision is one you are both comfortable with. The money that you finally agree on to put towards your wedding is going to be your total wedding budget. You'll use it in the next step.

Create Your Categories

Once you've settled on a total wedding budget, it's time to divide and conquer. The concept of dividing your total budget into categories, each with its own budget carved from the overall pie, will allow you to focus on the individual details of your wedding and will help control cost ("I know I have just $1,000 for flowers…that's it, and that's my budget"). That said, you still want to allow your budget to flex and adjust as unexpected splurges or discounts pop up, otherwise you'll fall into the "well, I went over my budget

<NOTE>

Typical Budget Categories and Average Percentages

If you look over the Wedding Budget worksheet at the end of the chapter, you'll notice several recommended categories and the percentages of your overall wedding budget that are suggested as typically used for each category. Some of the major points are listed below. These are not rules or requirements! Your situation will differ, and you'll need to adjust them to suit your own situation and priorities.

Based on your overall budget, a good online budget manager will list recommended expenditures in all subcategories as well (for example, beneath the Music category, suggestions will be provided for ceremony music, cocktail hour music, and reception band or DJ). See the e-Resource section for tips on using this convenient time-saving and money-protecting tool.

Ceremony	2%
Reception	48%
Attire	8%
Photography	6%
Videography	5%
Music	5%
Flowers, Decorations	8%
Stationery	3%
Wedding Rings	5%
Transportation	3%
Prewedding Parties	2.5%
Gifts	2%
Miscellaneous	2.5%

</NOTE>

so many times already, what's a little more?" trap. We'll cover adjustments and the need to "splurge and compensate" a bit later on in the chapter.

So how will you carve up your budget into categories? What will the categories be, and how much should you put into each one? This is where your priorities come into play, as well as unique situations. The Wedding Budget worksheet at the end of this chapter—as well as the online budget managers—will suggest a percentage for you, but it's up to you to decide the actual amount of your total budget that will go into each category. If you add more of your budget to one category, compensate by removing the same amount from other(s). For example, if music and dancing is your big love, and you know your best man is donating his gorgeous ride for your transportation while your maid of honor's dad is doing the videography with his digital camera, remove a couple percentage points each from the transportation and videography categories and add them to music.

This will take some time playing with the figures, but don't give up or be too hasty! Your budget will be supporting your entire planning, and you'll be referring to it again and again, making adjustments as necessary to stay in control of your spending. As you set up your categories, you'll notice that it really does help to work with solid dollar amounts rather than vague percentages. This is where the online budget manager really comes in handy.

e-Resource

The Planning Tools pane of your WedShare control panel gives you access to your suite of planning tools, including the budget manager.

Interactive Budget Manager, Part I: Setting Up Your Budget Categories

When you're tired of pencil sharpening and eraser dust, take your budget-building work online. There are some exceptional wedding budget managers out there that will greatly simplify the tasks we've been discussing, and the good ones suggest how to divide up your funds based on your overall wedding budget. They'll even provide advice on how to cut costs and stretch your money. Like all such tools, your budget manager can be accessed from anywhere you have an Internet connection.

What Can You Do with It?

Get an immediate feel for how your money is spread out across categories; as soon as you plug in your overall wedding budget amount, the budget manager will automatically divide the funds into categories and assign suggested amounts to individual items, which you can then adjust to your liking. Add new items, and move the money around at will. Seeing actual dollar figures next to each wedding cost will make more sense than seeing percentages on paper. An always-present "budget-at-a-glance" window lets you see quickly if you're over or under your total budget amount, and how you're doing on your payments.

Good budget managers will allow you to record deposits, payments, and scheduled installments (many wedding vendors will charge you in installments, with a deposit to hold the date). You can even have your budget manager send you e-mail reminders when deadlines are approaching. Having your information available anywhere you can get online is convenient, but you'll also be able to export the data to a spreadsheet like MS Excel, or print everything out in attractive reports. Take the reports with you for your own reference when you meet with vendors or to discuss with your sweetheart over a lunch break at the cafe.

<TIP>

Features to Look For in a Budget Manager

- The ability to save your information. You should be able to log off and trust that your information will be safely waiting for you whenever you come back
- A starting budget calculator or guide
- Flexible, modifiable expense categories
- Item amounts that pre-populate based on your total budget and suggested cost percentages
- Ability to add new items and categorize them any way you wish
- Information at a glance: total budget, the amount you've allocated to categories, total of all payments made, total amount remaining in your budget, and so forth
- Payment tracking, including the deposit and all installments. Look for the ability to record the due date and amount for each
- Automatic reminder emails for upcoming payment deadlines
- A feature to export to common formats, like MS Excel
- Ability to print your budget, payments, and all other information in an attractive format (not just messy screen shots)

</TIP>

Set Up Yours!

If you set up a wedding website like we discussed in Chapter 4 (it only takes a few minutes) and if you picked a good service provider, you probably already have a budget manager of some sort. Most wedding website services offer a suite of planning tools, although as with everything else, some are better than others. The great thing about utilizing the tools available with your wedding website is that all your information and planning is centralized and located in one place.

<CROSS-REFERENCE>
We showed you how to set up a wedding website as your communications and planning home base in Chapter 4.
</CROSS-REFERENCE>

If you're going the free route, the best free-of-charge budget manager we know of is available at The Knot (www.theknot.com), as long as you don't mind the advertisements and providing some marketing information. To find others, just type "wedding budget" into any search engine, such as Google (www.google.com). You'll get plenty of links for online worksheets, calculators, and advice forums for your number-crunching pleasure. Make sure your budget manager has the features we mentioned in order to get the most out of it.

For our examples, we'll use the tool suite from the wedding website service WedShare.com, since we outlined it in Chapter 4. However, our directions will apply to any good budget manager.

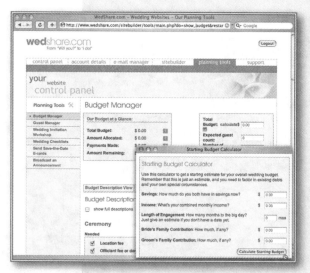

Use the handy starting budget wizard to guide you through the process of determining the amount of your overall wedding budget.

The budget manager description view allows you to allocate funds to specific categories, based on your starting budget amount and pre-loaded suggestions.

To get to the WedShare budget manager, log onto your control panel (free trial accounts can be obtained at www. wedshare.com), and click on the "Track Your Budgets and Payments" link in the Planning Tools menu pane.

The first time you access the budget manager, a "Starting Budget" wizard will pop up in a separate window, which you can use to guide you through the process of determining the amount of your overall wedding budget, as we discussed earlier. Plug in the numbers requested, click "Calculate", and the wizard will display the results, as well as the calculations it used. From here, you can click the "Populate to Budget Manager" button to copy the results into your budget manager and close the wizard. You can always re-open the wizard later by clicking the Total Budget calculator icon on your budget manager.

Using The Budget Manager

The WedShare budget manager has two views: a description view, which is where you'll be taken when you first start it up, and a payment view. We'll just use the description view for now and save the payment view for later, when we discuss payment tracking. Most other budget managers will provide information similar to the description view.

At the top right of the screen is your budget generator, which you will use to generate budget amount suggestions. Enter in your overall budget amount in the Total Amount box, or click the calculator icon to pop up the starting budget wizard, as discussed above, which will walk you through the process. Enter in your expected guest count and the number of attendants (don't worry about being exact…just take your best guess. You can always re-generate your budget suggestions later). Click the "Generate Budget Selections" button and your category item amounts will be automatically populated with suggested amounts.

Take a look at the top left of the screen. It contains your budget-at-a-glance panel. This shows you your current numbers as a quick summary: total budget (this is your overall budget amount), amount allocated (how much you've allocated towards your categories), payments made, and amount remaining (your total budget less any payments you've made). As you move money around, make sure that your amount allocated is as close as possible to your total budget amount: if the amount allocated is too high, you're aiming over your budget. If it's too low, you're not putting enough into your categories. Right now the amount allocated is exactly equal to what you have, since the budget manager automatically divvyed up your money in the way it thought was best. You'll be adjusting those assumptions in just a bit to best suit your own situation and priorities.

It's easy to add your own custom items to your budget. The amount you allocate to the item will be integrated into your total budget cost.

Below the budget-at-a-glance panel, there is a small navigational menu letting you switch back and forth from description to payment views. You can also export your budget to MS Excel here, open a printer-friendly report page, and star the whole thing over (If you click on "Start Over", all your information will be wiped clean and the starting budget wizard will pop up again). The "Show Full Descriptions" checkbox allows you to toggle advice and cost-cutting tips on and off for each category item.

All your category groups are listed below the navigational menu. You can modify the amount of money you're allocating to each item as well as decide whether or not you even need it in your budget. Any time you make a change, you'll need to click on one of the "Update" buttons. You can click on any of them; it won't make a difference which.

Let's pretend that your ceremony is taking place at your mother's church, free of any charge. Since you won't need ceremony location in your budget, let's remove it: scroll down to the Ceremony category and uncheck the "Needed" box next to "Ceremony Location". Click on an "Update" button. Notice that in your budget-at-a-glance pane, the Amount Allocated is now less than the Total Budget. This is because the cost of the ceremony location is no longer being counted, since you designated it as not needed.

You can now take the excess money you just freed up and move it anyplace you need it more. For this example, let's first add to the officiant's donation, since they're being so kind as to let you use their location for free. Scroll down to the Ceremony category and find the "Officiant Fee or Donation" item. In that item's "Actual" box, increase the suggested amount by $50 or so. Click Update.

Notice how your Amount Allocated has increased by $50. You may still have excess funds; it's up to you how to allot them. The point is that you can immediately see, at any given time, how your allocated funds compare with your total available budget amount.

If you want to add an item that's not on the budget list, just scroll all the way down to the Add Custom Item pane and fill in the item name, any notes, and an amount to allocate to that item. Choose a category to add it to, and click Update. Now you will be able to see the new item in its proper category, and the Amount Allocated will adjust to include it. The notes you entered for the item, if any, will display when you turn on the "Show Full Descriptions" checkbox. If you want to remove a custom item at any time, just uncheck it's "Needed" checkbox and it will be deleted, freeing up the money you allocated to it.

This is essentially how you would build your own budget: by allocating more funds to items that you feel are higher in priority and removing funds from items where you know or feel that the suggested amounts won't be needed. Throughout the process, keep an eye on your Amount Allocated. Your goal is that, in the end, it should match your Total Budget as much as possible. In this way, you can be sure that you stay within your budget while flexibly and easily moving funds between items to suit your situation and priorities, and also as things change during the course of your planning (see the following discussion on how to "splurge and compensate").

To start building your own budget, just click the "Start Over" icon to get started with a fresh slate. Good luck in your budget planning, and have fun doing it online!

Splurge and Compensate

Okay. Now that your budget is set, you're ready to start making some big wedding decisions, looking at venues, interviewing vendors, getting quotes, and so forth. Everything's all set up reasonably within their categories in your budget, so it's just a matter of staying within your limits now, right?

If only things were that simple! Your budget and your category divisions are going to be an indispensable help, to be sure…that's why it's so important to take your time building them. But, a wedding is a very emotional event, and—let's not kid ourselves—when emotion takes control, logic and reason (and all those oh-so-rational budget categories) just kinda blur out into the background.

Consider finding the perfect dress with a price tag that's far over your budget. Or falling in love with a band at a friend's wedding…and finding that they're available for your day!…yet all you can really afford is a DJ. It's your special day after all, so should you hold back or just go for it?

It's natural to splurge and want the most for your wedding day. And in these matters of the heart, it's unlikely you'll hold back; besides, you shouldn't have to. Remember that you're designing a day for you, and you'll want it to be everything it can be, not something you'll be disappointed in and regret later. However, you can also get into some financial trouble if you let your wishes run wild, and the last thing you want is to start your life together with your finances in the negative column.

So how can you splurge and still protect your budget? The first step you should already have done: you should have prioritized before creating your budget in the first place. Putting more money in categories that were most important to you while compensating in other, less essential areas was a critical component of creating your categories. But for those unexpected splurges, just remember not to abandon your budget. Splurge, but compensate. Return to your budget together and rework it by cutting corners in other areas so that you can make the splurge work. One of the biggest pitfalls couples fall into is that they splurge once (or twice...), and think "well, I've gone over budget already, so what's a little more?" Before they know it, they're in the red so far that they can't help going into debt to pay for everything.

But when you have to remove funds from one or more categories to account for your splurge, how do you make it work for the categories on the short end of the trade? Be smart and creative, and investigate all the ways you can save money without compromising quality; there are a lot of frugal options out there. Take a look at the discussion on "Money Saving Tips" a bit later in this chapter, and scour the web for more. The pitfall you definitely want to avoid is the all-too-common scenario where a couple tries to compensate for a splurge in one area, so they work cheaply in another. Don't hire unprofessional vendors without experience or good referrals just because "the price is right." Is it worth saving a couple hundred bucks on a DJ you're not sure of when he plays the wrong song on your first dance? Or consider the scenario where you hire a caterer who cuts the price, and all the corners, to such a degree that you lack the proper number of waitstaff. This creates a timeline bottleneck causing your entire reception before the meal to be awkward and prolonged, while the rest is hurried and unsatisfying. Better ways to save would be to cut back on your guest count, or to have a simple but classy lunch buffet or cocktails-and-hors-devoires rather than a sit-down meal. Consider having your wedding on Friday or Sunday instead of the over-booked (and more expensive) Saturday. In the "Money Saving Tips" we'll get to in a bit, you'll find more ideas on how to make the most of a tight wedding budget but still have, in the end, what's most important: an enjoyable day tailored just for the two of you, and lots of great memories for you both to share!

Above all, remember that your budget is not set in stone. Stick to your rules when you can, and when you must bend them, do it right: work with your budget to adjust it rather than abandon it. It will be your guide through all the storms!

The Need for Financial Record-Keeping

With a good budget in hand and a commitment to maintaining it, you're already putting yourself at a great advantage over most couples, who tend to "wing it" financially. In order to protect your funds even more, you'll want to be very careful about the records you keep when you start shelling out your hard-earned bucks to vendors. How you organize your invoices, receipts, and contracts can either help you or hurt you should issues or conflicts ever crop up with a particular vendor. Besides, flying blind—with little idea how much of your money has been spent, or which payments have been made— is a dangerous situation to be in. You always want to know exactly how much you've spent, how much you still need to spend, and exactly when you're supposed to spend it. This paves the way to save money, keeps you in control, and prevents unnecessary disasters like late fees, double-payments, or last-minute vendor cancellations.

Tracking Payments

You'll want to set up a wedding binder, with a folder for every vendor (we'll discuss this in our discussion on "Working With Vendors" in just a bit). Every time you make a payment, get a copy of your receipt and add it to the appropriate folder along with the vendor's contract and any invoices they provide. Many wedding vendors charge you in installments, with a deposit up front to hold the date. Every deposit and installment should be recorded and saved together in your folder.

If a vendor doesn't provide an invoice from the beginning (when you provide your deposit), ask them for one. You can draw up your own as well: just get a sheet of paper and write down the date, the vendor name and exactly what they're providing, the deposit amount paid and any installments expected (along with their due dates). Write down the check number or credit card you used to make the payment, too. File the invoice away in the appropriate folder.

A great way to keep everything organized in one place is to manage your deposits and installments online using your budget manager, in addition to keeping the receipts, invoices, and hardcopies in a folder. Refer to the e-Resource below.

Payment Due Dates and Reminders

Since you're going to be juggling several vendors, each with their own deposit and payment schedules, you're going to need an efficient way to keep track of all those deadlines. A great low-tech way to do it is to get a calendar and mark every deadline on it. Big calendars work best. Follow your calendar day by day, or at least week by week, to ensure that you don't miss anything.

An even better solution, especially if you're online a lot, is to use your wedding website's online planning calendar. This will let you put as much info on your calendar as you like, and make it searchable as well. Check out Chapter 21, Countdown Considerations, for more information on this convenient tool.

With all the deadlines you'll have flying around, it's easy to miss one or two, even if you're following a calendar. Wouldn't it be great if someone could send you an e-mail as a reminder when a payment deadline was approaching? Say a few days, a week, or even a month before the due date? Luckily for you, your budget manager may very well have such a feature. Check out the following e-Resource for more on that and other cool online payment help.

e-Resource

Interactive Budget Manager, Part II: Payment and Due Date Tracking

If you followed along with our prior e-Resource exploration, you already have a budget online that's set up to manage your various spending categories. Now we're going to explore a step further and discuss how you can use your budget manager to keep track of your deposits, payment installments, and even receive reminder e-mails. If you didn't read the previous e-Resource, you may want to skim it now to get a general idea of the concept of an online budget manager and how to set up your own.

For those of you using the WedShare.com budget manager (if you're using a different tool, the main concepts will be the same), access your payment details by opening up your budget manager and clicking the "Payment View" button. You'll notice that the payment view is similar to the description view, with the same category listings and items, along with the suggested and actual budget amounts for each. The difference here is that payment information is displayed as well, including a total amount paid and balance due summary for each item.

Notice that for each item you can enter in amounts for the first payment (or deposit), the second payment, and the final payment. Every one of these installments can also be marked as "paid". Once paid, the amount is added to that item's total amount paid summary, as well as to your budget manager's at-a-glance panel, in the Payments Made field.

Let's explore further. Pick a random item and click the "Details" link for one of its payment fields. A payment details view opens up, listing detailed information about the payments of the particular item you selected. You can enter in the payment amount here and whether or not it has been paid, as you could in the previous screen. But you can also enter in more record-keeping info: the due date, the payment date, and even the form of payment (check, credit card, and so forth).

Another very useful feature you'll notice here is the email reminder option. Turning it on will enable your budget manager send you a reminder e-mail when this particular payment's deadline is approaching. You can set the reminder to be sent the day before, a week before, or even a month before the due date.

Tracking your payments and deadlines online may or may not be for you, depending on how comfortable you are with working online versus pencil-and-paper. It certainly will not substitute for your hardcopy and receipt records, but managing your wedding payments here will allow you to save time and have a searchable, printable record of all payment activity and due dates, located in one place that you can access from anywhere. If your budget manager

Your budget manager's payment view allows you to review, enter, and modify payment amounts for each item.

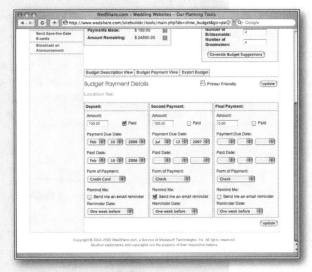

A good budget manager will allow you to enter in detailed payment information for each item's individual installments. E-mail reminders can be set up to remind you of approaching deadlines.

does not offer all these features and you're using a different wedding website provider (or none at all), try the free budget manager available at The Knot (www.theknot.com).

Money-Saving Tips

As you work on solidifying your budget and making important wedding decisions at an early stage, it's essential to know what the main cost factors are likely going to be. If your budget is especially tight, there's no time like now to get a handle on the best ways to save. You're probably still at an early enough place in your planning that you can cut the guest list down, for example, or decide to opt out of hiring certain vendors that may not be important to your priorities, like a fancy limousine or that expensive florist. You might even want to change your wedding date (or set it, if you're still looking) to an off-season month to take advantage of lower costs.

Know Your Biggest Cost Factors

Let's take a look at those things that most directly influence the cost of a wedding. Cutting back or modifying these factors will greatly reduce your overall cost, and should help wrangle an out-of-control wedding price tag to one that's more compatible with your budget. You'll find that most ideas to cut cost (whether they're from this book or any other outside source) will relate to these four basic fund factors. Where you decide to cut and compensate will be a decision you need to both make together, based on your wedding vision and your own individual priorities.

Guest Count

This is arguably the most influential factor. Your overall cost for the biggest ticket items, like catering, are priced on a per-person basis. And, more guests mean more tables, which mean more china, flatware, floral centerpieces, and overall space. A bigger tent, if you're having one. More beverages. You get the idea.

Formality

As you might guess, the more formal the wedding, the more expensive the overall cost. Meals, attire, location, and décor are some of the many details that will require more flow the higher up the formality scale you go.

Timing

First of all, your engagement length can make a big difference (see "Using Expense Categories" at the beginning of this chapter for more on the impact of engagement length) since the longer your engagement, the more time you have to build up funds. Your wedding date itself makes a difference as well, depending on the season and day of the week. During peak wedding months (June, August and September are the busiest, followed closely by May, July, October, and December), vendors are more in demand, and so are wedding locations, which results in higher prices for just about everything. Likewise, since there are only 52 Saturdays a year, the demand for locations and vendors for Saturday weddings are huge. Friday and Sunday weddings typically cost much less.

Elbow Grease

Pretty much anything you can do yourself, or have someone you know do for you, will save money and personalize your wedding even more.

<CROSS-REFERENCE>
For more on narrowing down your wedding preferences, see Chapter 6, "Style and Preferences: Capture Your Wedding Vision".
</CROSS-REFERENCE>

Ideas to Help Cut Cost

Great cost-cutting tips and suggestions abound in every chapter of this book. As you step through your planning, revisit the appropriate references and make use of the time- and money-saving e-Resources whenever possible. The following are some considerations to make right now as you try to design a budget you can afford for the wedding that you and your sweetheart envision.

Remember that no matter what your overall available budget is, you can capture your wedding vision by focusing on your priorities, thinking creatively, and working with a good, categorized budget strategy like the one we describe in this chapter. You'll be compromising in certain areas, but the important factors—the ones that make it your wedding—will be there, just as you envision.

Guest Count

One of the quickest and easiest ways to cut down a wedding's cost, without affecting the quality of any of your services, is to simply limit the number of guests you're inviting. Instead of 150, try for 100. Instead of ten attendants, have four. If you're really strapped for cash and the idea of a big wedding isn't that important to you, consider an intimate gathering of only your immediate families and close circle of friends.

Formality

If formality is not a priority, consider loosening up the affair a bit. Rather than having a sit-down meal, have a pasta bar, casual brunch, or a lunch buffet with the food catered by the platter rather than the plate (this can cut your catering bill by 20 or 30 percent!). Hire a good DJ instead of a band. Less extravagant location and floral arrangements will be easier on the budget as well. Just remember to tone down the formality, not the professionalism. Hire only the most professional and reputable vendors to provide your service, and your wedding will shine regardless of the formality level.

Timing

If you haven't yet set a date, consider a longer engagement to help build up your funds, and start saving now. Unless season is a priority, consider a wedding during the off-season, especially in winter (December is an exception). Vendors will be able to devote more time to you, you'll get better service, and they'll usually charge less. Think about a Friday or Sunday wedding instead of settling on an expensive, over-booked Saturday. If you choose a Saturday wedding, make sure your engagement is long enough to book the best vendors well in advance, at the best rates. And lastly, morning or afternoon receptions can usually be pulled off for less than those held in the evening.

Elbow Grease

Are you or is anyone you know especially creative? Does a friend or family member have professional expertise (a friend who's a florist, or an aunt who bakes cakes, for example)? You might want to consider requesting their assistance; tell them it's their wedding gift to you, and that you're looking for their special, personal touch. It also helps to put some thought into who your attendants will be: recruit those individuals who are going to help out! Think of anything you can do on your own or with others to save on vendor costs: do your own calligraphy or use an elegant computer font and print your own stationery. Buy your own alcohol in bulk at a discount, or purchase your flowers from online wholesalers and have a talented friend or relative help you create your own arrangements.

Just be wary of a couple of pitfalls here: don't take on so much yourself that you drown in planning and details (planning and coordinating everything is a big enough task without also having to do the work). And you don't want to get stuck trying to do something so fast and cheap that you wind up regretting it later. Be smart, creative, and use your resources wisely. You can save a lot of money without compromising quality.

Working with Vendors

Much of your planning will involve working with various wedding professionals that each have the resources and skills to make a particular part of your special day come to life. As with any business (and the wedding industry is big business!) there are the unscrupulous bad apples every so often that require you to shop carefully throughout. Follow our advice on educating yourself, finding reputable leads, and being picky with contracts to give yourself an edge in the world of the wedding pros.

Prepare Yourself

Before contacting a vendor, make sure you've educated yourself on their particular specialization by brushing up on all the main points you should be aware of. Organize yourself to efficiently store information and receipts from each vendor for quick reference at any time. Give yourself every advantage in obtaining the best price and avoiding rip-offs and sub-standard service.

Study Up!

Be aware of the world each vendor lives in before you make contact. Reference the appropriate chapter in this book and make use of the provided e-Resources to bring yourself up to speed fast on the points you need to know and the questions you need to ask. Knowing as much as possible before meeting with the first professional will put you in the best possible position to make a good decision in hiring the right vendor.

Create an Organization System

We touched on this earlier in the chapter when introducing "The Need for Financial Record-Keeping". Pay a visit to your office supply store and buy a binder and an inexpensive pack of manila folders, or a multi-pocket planning folder. Put your folders into the binder and designate one to each vendor. You'll put everything related to that vendor in its appropriate folder. You should also set aside a separate folder for hardcopy printouts of your overall wedding budget and anything else related to your big day. Keep this book together with your wedding binder: you'll be using it often.

For example, as you browse through bridal magazines or online websites, you may see great wedding cake ideas. Clip the magazine images and print out the web pages, and add everything to the "Cake" folder. Share your ideas with your sweetheart by bringing the folder with you during a lunch meeting, or when lounging on the couch in the evening. When your checklist (Chapter 2) notifies you that you need to start shopping for cakes, review Chapter 18, "A Cake to Remember", and make use of the e-Resources. Add more ideas to your folder. As you make tasting appointments with bakeries, add the paperwork for each bakery along with your tasting notes to the folder. Always take your folder with you to each bakery or cake designer, and show them your ideas. When you select a bakery and pay your deposit, add the receipt, contract, and invoice to your folder. When you make an installment payment...you got it...add it to the folder. Everything is always in one place and available for you to take whenever you meet your bakery.

Do this for every vendor. Keep your folders in a safe place and within each folder, organize it by payments, ideas, and notes. All legal and financial information will be easily retrieved at any time, and you'll save a headache or two by avoiding lost notes and paperwork. As the Big Day looms closer, you'll find that every minute saved is a minute earned, and you'll appreciate the timesaving organization that you set up from the beginning.

What You Need to Know About Working with Wedding Professionals

Finding the right ones and avoiding the wrong ones is a careful matter of following trusted recommendations, shopping around, and asking plenty of questions.

Finding Good Leads

The best source for good wedding vendors is from glowing recommendations by trusted sources who have used them before. Ask friends, coworkers, family members, or anyone else you trust who has recently wed who their best (and worst!) experiences were. Put the good ones on your list and make sure to keep away from the bad ones.

Every vendor chapter in this book contains good tips and references for selecting a reputable professional. We make use of online directories, trade organization websites, and other convenient sources of information to help make your search as efficient and convenient as possible.

Attend a bridal show or two. These are great, low-cost events that will let you hunt for deals, meet other brides and grooms, and chat with local wedding professionals.

Shopping Around

Make sure you visit a variety of vendors for each service you shop for, in order to get a good feel for their overall skill, expertise, and style. Get written estimates from them to compare prices. As always, store all this paperwork in the appropriate folder and bring these notes with you every time you meet with another vendor. Ask them plenty of questions (this book will list essential questions you should ask each vendor in the appropriate chapters), and never settle on a vendor unless you feel absolutely comfortable with them and their terms. Feel free to negotiate the price and agreement terms; vendors need your business, especially in the off-season, and would much rather come to an agreement than lose you as a customer.

Get a Contract

Get a contract from every vendor; if they don't offer one, ask for a written agreement of their terms. Make sure the contract is understandable, and that everything you've discussed and agreed upon is written out clearly. Check the fine print, too: what is their cancellation policy? It's fair enough if they charge a fee if you cancel at the last minute, but a policy that states you're liable for 50% of the total cost upon cancellation, even if you've only paid a deposit, might be a red flag. The main point is that you are aware of the agreement you're signing, and that you are comfortable with it. When it comes time to sign the contract, make sure that both you and the vendor sign and that you get a copy. File the contract away in the appropriate folder.

<NOTE>

Items That Should be Included in All Contracts

Critical contract notes will be provided in each vendor chapter, but in general you should always look for the following:

- The date and time of the service (typically your wedding day)
- Detailed list of merchandise ordered. Make sure this is explained down to the smallest possible detail
- Detailed list of services provided. Make sure this is just as detailed
- The entire length of service, including times for set up and break down
- Any dress code required of staff to be compliant with your event's level of formality
- Contact information for both parties
- Schedules for deposit and payment, with exact amounts, including tax. Any possible overtime rates
- The deadline for making any changes
- The cancellation and refund policy
- If you're renting any equipment, make sure it is clearly stated when and how the equipment will be delivered to you and when it needs to get back to the vendor

</NOTE>

Pay Your Deposits with a Credit Card

This is a bit of sage advice that might save you the amount of a deposit if you ever have to tangle with an unscrupulous vendor. It's just a precaution, and hopefully you'll never need to fall back on it, but in the event that you have an issue with a vendor that they refuse to resolve with you, you can file a claim with your credit card company. The card companies are required by law to investigate all such claims, and will remove the funds from the vendor's account (and add it to yours) if you can prove that the vendor was in the wrong. This is another reason to have a good, solid contract and all your paperwork safely stored together. If you've got a card that rewards you with airline miles it's a double bonus, and you can put those miles towards your honeymoon or first big trip together.

Tipping Guide

As you divide up funds in your budget, make sure you account for service tips. Tips can increase your wedding cost by hundreds or even thousands of dollars, depending on the size of your wedding. How do you know who to tip, and how much should you expect to have to fork over?

First of all, remember that tipping a wedding vendor—like any other service tip—is meant to be a way of rewarding those who did a good job, in this case making your wedding dreams a reality. If you feel someone did a poor job or if you are in any way unhappy with their service, you shouldn't feel the obligation to give them anything on top of the already sizable payment you're handing over. On the other hand, if you thought someone did an exceptional job, feel free to give them a little extra.

Take a look at the following suggestions, but remember to follow your own conscience and tip what you feel is deserved based on the service provided. Assign the job of tipping to someone you trust with the task, such as the best man. Place tips in envelopes carefully marked with recipient name and instruct the tipper to give them out upon completion of service, such as the end of the reception. Of course, as your reception progresses, be prepared to let the tipper know not to distribute a tip you feel is not deserved.

<NOTE>

Wedding Insurance

You may want to consider purchasing a wedding insurance policy since you're putting quite a bit of money into this one single event. Such a policy would cover you in the event of vendor mishaps, cancellations forced by natural disasters, injuries to guests, or even in the event that military duty requires the bride or groom to have a last-minute absence. Check into the Fireman's Fund Insurance Company (www.firemansfund.com or 800-ENGAGED) for more information on wedding insurance.

</NOTE>

Caterer

You need to read your contract and be up front with your caterer as to whether or not they are including gratuity in your bill. Usually, an 18%-20% gratuity is added right into your bill and called a "service fee" or "service charge"; the lingo will differ between catering companies. It's your caterer's job to make it clear to you how much of that service fee is actually going to the waitstaff, and if anything additional might be needed. If the service fee is just for the catering company, for example, you may want to tip the waitstaff at least $20 each.

If gratuity is not added into your bill, figure on tipping the waitstaff between 15% - 20% of the cost of the food bill (not including alcohol). Have the best man or host of the wedding provide it to the maitre' d or serving captain for distribution to the servers.

Hotel Maitre' d or Banquet Manager

The standard tip range is 15% - 20% of the reception bill.

Bartender

Expect to tip the bartenders between 15% - 20% of the bar bill. However, make sure that the bartender does not accept tips from your guests. A sign at the bar that reads "No tipping please" should do the trick.

Limo Driver

As long as your contract doesn't include gratuity, the standard tip is 15% - 20% of the limo bill.

Valet and Parking Attendants

They are ordinarily prepaid based on your guest count. Figure on at least $1 per car, and arrange to pay the gratuity as a flat fee before the wedding. Again, check your reception site contract to make sure this isn't already included.

Musicians and DJs

The standard tip is $20-$25 per band member or, for a DJ, 15% of their total bill. If you're going with the ceremony musicians that a house of worship has provided, their tip is normally included in the fee that you paid to rent the church. If this isn't the case, a gratuity of at least $35 would be appropriate.

Florists, Photographers, and Bakers

They are not usually tipped, and won't expect to be.

Worksheet: Starting Budget

Calculate your starting estimate for your overall wedding budget using the guide below. The calculations assume you'll put half of your savings and 20% of your monthly income towards your wedding expenses. This is just an estimate, so adjust the numbers to suit your circumstances.

Information to Collect:

Savings: How much do you both have in savings now? $ _____

Income: What's your combined monthly income? $ _____

Length of Engagement: How many months to the big day?   (months) _____
(Just give an estimate if you don't have a date yet)

Bride's Family Contribution: How much, if any? $ _____

Groom's Family Contribution: How much, if any? $ _____

Your Calculations:

Savings: $ _____   ÷ 2   = $ _____
                      (Combined Savings)   Total Savings Available

Saving Potential: ($ _____ x _____ months) x 0.20 = $ _____
                      Combined Monthly Income   Length of Engagement   Saving Potential

Family Contribution: $ _____   + $ _____   = $ _____
                      Bride's Family   Groom's Family   Total Family Contribution

Add Total Savings + Saving Potential + Total Family Contributions: _____

Total Wedding Budget Available   = $ _____

Worksheet: Wedding Budget

Use the following worksheet to divide your budget up into expense categories and track your payments. If you need to spend more than the suggested percentage of your budget for certain items, compensate by deducting a percentage point or two from other categories to make up the difference. Remember to also consider honeymoon expenses and wedding consultant fees.

Total Wedding Budget Available = $ _____

Ceremony (Typically 2% of budget) $ _____ X 0.02 _____ = $ _____

                                                 Total Budget   Available funds for ceremony

Items	Estimated Cost	Actual Cost	Deposit Payment	Second Payment	Balance Due
Location Fee					
Officiant					
Accessories					
Subtotals:	$	$	$	$	$

Reception (Typically 48% of budget) $ _____ X 0.48 _____ = $ _____

                                                 Total budget   Available funds for reception

Items	Estimated Cost	Actual Cost	Deposit Payment	Second Payment	Balance Due
Location Fee					
Rentals					
Food, Wait Service and Gratuity					
Beverages, Bar Service and Gratuity					
Wedding Cake and Cake Cutting Fee					
Subtotals:	$	$	$	$	$

Worksheet: Wedding Budget (continued)

Attire (Typically 8% of budget) $ _____   X 0.08 _____   = $ _____
                                  Total budget   Available funds for attire

Items	Estimated Cost	Actual Cost	Deposit Payment	Second Payment	Balance Due
Bridal Gown and Alterations					
Headpiece and Veil					
Bridal Accessories					
Bride's Hair and Makeup					
Groom's Formalwear					
Groom's Accessories					
Subtotals:	$	$	$	$	$

Photography (Typically 6% of budget) $ _____   X 0.06 _____   = $ _____
                                      Total budget   Available funds for photography

Items	Estimated Cost	Actual Cost	Deposit Payment	Second Payment	Balance Due
Photographer					
Engagement Session					
Wedding Portrait					
Extra Hours					
Proofs					
Wedding Album					
Extra Prints and Albums					
Disposable Cameras and Developing					
Subtotals:	$	$	$	$	$

Worksheet: Wedding Budget (continued)

Videography (Typically 5% of budget) $_____ X 0.05 = $_____
Total budget   Available funds for videographer

Items	Estimated Cost	Actual Cost	Deposit Payment	Second Payment	Balance Due
Videographer					
Wedding Video					
Extra Hours					
Additional Video Copies					
Subtotals:	$	$	$	$	$

Flowers & Décor (Typically 8% of budget) $_____ X 0.08 = $_____
Total budget   Available funds for flowers

Items	Estimated Cost	Actual Cost	Deposit Payment	Second Payment	Balance Due
Ceremony Flowers and Decorations					
Bridal Bouquet					
Bridesmaids Bouquet					
Groom and Groomsmen Boutonnieres					
Flower Girl(s) Flowers					
Additional Boutonnieres and Corsages					
Reception and Cake Decorations					
Table Centerpieces					
Subtotals:	$	$	$	$	$

Wedding Rings (Typically 5% of budget) $_____ X 0.05 = $_____
Total budget   Available funds for rings

Items	Estimated Cost	Actual Cost	Deposit Payment	Second Payment	Balance Due
Bride's Ring					
Groom's Ring					
Subtotals:	$	$	$	$	$

Worksheet: Wedding Budget (continued)

Music (Typically 5% of budget) $ _____ X 0.05 _____ = $ _____
Total budget   Available funds for music

Items	Estimated Cost	Actual Cost	Deposit Payment	Second Payment	Balance Due
Ceremony Music					
Cocktail Hour Music					
Reception Band or DJ					
Subtotals:	$	$	$	$	$

Stationery (Typically 3% of budget) $ _____ X 0.03 _____ = $ _____
Total budget   Available funds for stationery

Items	Estimated Cost	Actual Cost	Deposit Payment	Second Payment	Balance Due
Invitations and RSVP Cards					
Calligraphy					
Place Cards and Table Numbers					
Monogrammed Napkins, Ribbons, etc.					
Ceremony Programs					
Announcements					
Postage Stamps					
Thank You Notes					
Subtotals:	$	$	$	$	$

Transportation (Typically 3% of budget) $ _____ X 0.03 _____ = $ _____
Total budget   Available funds for transportation

Items	Estimated Cost	Actual Cost	Deposit Payment	Second Payment	Balance Due
Limo or Car Rental					
Guest Shuttle					
Valet Service					
Gratuity					
Subtotals:	$	$	$	$	$

Worksheet: Wedding Budget (continued)

Parties (Typically 2.5% of budget) $ _____ X 0.025 _____ = $ _____

Total budget   Available funds for parties

Items	Estimated Cost	Actual Cost	Deposit Payment	Second Payment	Balance Due
Engagement Party					
Bridesmaids' Luncheon					
Rehearsal Dinner					
Subtotals:	$	$	$	$	$

Gifts (Typically 2% of budget) $ _____ X 0.02 _____ = $ _____

Total budget   Available funds for gifts

Items	Estimated Cost	Actual Cost	Deposit Payment	Second Payment	Balance Due
Favors					
Bridal Party Gifts					
Parents' Gifts					
Bride and Groom's Gifts					
Out-of-Town Welcome Baskets					
Subtotals:	$	$	$	$	$

Miscellaneous (Typically 2.5% of budget) $ _____ X 0.025 _____ = $ _____

Total budget   Available funds for miscellaneous

Items	Estimated Cost	Actual Cost	Deposit Payment	Second Payment	Balance Due
Wedding Website, Planning Software					
Marriage License					
Wedding Night Hotel					
Accessories (Guestbook, Pen, etc.)					
Sales Taxes					
Subtotals:	$	$	$	$	$

Total Wedding Costs: $ _____

Notes:

Chapter 6

Style and Preferences: Capture Your Wedding Vision

- Using Your Budget to Clarify Your Decisions

- Alternative Wedding Ideas

- Using a Wedding Consultant

- e-Plan It! Use Your e-Resources:

  The Online Wedding Portals: Ideas and More Galore

- Worksheets:

  Considerations Worksheet: Wedding Vision
  Contact Sheet: Wedding Consultant

Y ou've got a vision for your wedding and a set budget. Now how do you match the two up? In this chapter, we'll lay out our strategy for capturing your wedding vision on any budget and show you how to bring those daydreams to life!

Using Your Budget to Clarify Your Decisions

After working with Chapter 5, you should have a good budget in place, with flexible categories for each element of your wedding. Before you actually get to the business of searching for locations and vendors, take some time to iron out your preferences, keeping your budget constraints in mind.

Our Strategy for Capturing Your Wedding Vision at Any Cost

We're going to recap your priorities and preferences in order to really forge ahead with identifying your wedding vision. Our goal is to bring a solid approximation of your dream wedding to life no matter what your overall budget may be, so it's essential that you get a firm grasp on what you see as *your* perfect wedding.

What have you done so far to achieve this? Let's take a look at a summary:

- In Chapter 3, you did a little daydreaming. You both fantasized freely and decided what you felt would be most important and special about a Perfect Wedding. After comparing your thoughts and ideas, you agreed on the common points and loosely negotiated the others. These were your starting priorities.

- You started bringing your priorities and preferences more into meaningful focus when we began talking dollar amounts in Chapter 5. You considered what the biggest cost factors are in a wedding like the one you envision, and compromised based on your available budget. You then spent some time breaking up your budget into manageable categories and added or removed funds from each based on your priorities and preferences.

So where do we go from here?

<CROSS-REFERENCE>
You made your initial decisions at the close of Chapter 3.
</CROSS-REFERENCE>

Now that your budget has been given the initial carving and you know pretty much what you have to work with in each category (though it's not set in stone; things can and will change as you go), you'll need to take your initial preferences and build onto them by looking at all your options. Grab ideas and chat with other brides using the big online wedding portals. Solidify what you feel your priorities are and come to a more final agreement on a wedding date and time, guest count, style, formality level, and location type. This will prepare you for the coming tasks of venue hunting and vendor interviewing. And with each qualified vendor that you match to your preferences and book for your date...with each wedding detail you align with your priorities and iron out...with each issue you compromise on and resolve...you come that much closer to a day that will be a realization of your own unique wedding vision.

<CROSS-REFERENCE>

In the last chapter, you created a smart budget and payment system to get your funds under control.

</CROSS-REFERENCE>

If you feel overwhelmed at everything looming up in the horizon, just close your eyes. Breathe. Relax. Wedding planning should be fun (no, really!), and we're going to help you take it one step at a time.

Write Everything Down

Okay, enough pep talk. Let's start getting things done. As you step through the chapter, jot down your notes in your Wedding Vision and Priorities worksheet (located at the end of the chapter) to keep a written record of your thoughts and conclusions. It's best if you both go through the chapter together, although if your sweetheart's attention span won't make it the whole way through, the worksheet provides a good summary to review together over lunch at a downtown cafe or while snuggling on the sofa, after you've filled in your own thoughts.

Pencil in Your Wedding Date and Time

By now you should have a general idea of when you'd like your ideal wedding to take place. Now it's time to settle on a solid date, as well as a time. Without it, you'll have no idea if the vendors you're talking to will even be available when you need them. A good practice is to actually select two or three dates: a first choice and one or two backups. This can be helpful for situations like finding a location that really calls out to you but is booked on your primary date, or even your second. Having more than one option to fall back on is a smart strategy, and flexibility is truly essential during your planning.

Settling on a Day

There are some important questions to consider when identifying the big date. These will all depend on your overall budget and priorities: how much time do you need to prepare and save? Should you consider an off-season month or a day of the week that's in less demand in order to cut cost and broaden your options? Do any of your close friends or family have conflicting plans on the dates you're looking at? Review the discussions below for the points you need assistance in.

How much prep time do you need? The longer your engagement period, the more time you have to save up your wedding funds and space out your planning. Plus, you'll have more lead time to scope out vendors and are more likely to have first pick of the best ones. In our opinion, the ideal planning time is 12 months, which gives you plenty of time to get everything done at an easy pace and usually allows for some adequate fundraising. Are you itchy to get to the altar, or otherwise looking at a shortened timeframe? 8 months is a good compromise, and 6 months is doable (just expect less relaxation, more rushing, and less vendor selection–especially if you're shooting for a popular month). Planning a wedding in less than 6 months is still a human possibility so long as your style is a bit more relaxed, your guest count is small, and you have an available venue. Planning a large, very formal, all-inclusive wedding in less than 6 months is not for the faint of heart; you really want to consider getting some professional assistance if you decide to brave these waters. See our discussion on "Using a Wedding Consultant" later on in the chapter for more information on hiring a professional consultant or coordinator.

Consider avoiding peak months and popular days. June, August, and September are wedding madness months. Not far behind are May, July, October, and festive December. These are the months where weddings skyrocket, and vendors are scrambling to keep up. Your choices of vendors, locations, and timing will be limited during these months and your overall cost will usually be higher due to the increased demand for service. You may also find that hectic, overbooked vendors will have less attention to give to you and your wedding. Couples planning a wedding in November or anytime from January through April will usually enjoy more choices in location and vendors, more attention from those vendors, and lower prices. Of course, your style and location would need to be considered; a garden or beach wedding in winter is not going to fly unless you're tying the knot in the Caribbean. If you're set on marrying in one of the wedding madness months, make sure you have a long enough engagement to do your vendor shopping and venue booking well in advance while the choices are still open.

Which Day of the Week? Just as there are peak wedding months, there are also peak days of the week. The most popular day is Saturday, for obvious reasons: it fits in well by allowing plenty of time for out-of-town guests to arrive on Friday evening, and there's a full 24 hours after the main event to rest and recover before the next work week. Saturday weddings are especially good for late- or all-night bashes. But with only 52 Saturdays per year, they are the first days to book up and will usually be the most expensive, especially during peak months. A Friday or Sunday wedding is something to consider if your budget is tight and you don't mind the missing "kick-back" days that bookend a Saturday wedding. You may also need to look into it if your planning period is short and the services and locations around your target date are booked up. Weddings held during the week aren't common, nor are they advised if you're expecting a lot of out-of-town guests or would like a late-night reception party. On the other hand, you're sure to get a better choice of vendors and will likely be able to cut your costs considerably.

Accommodating family and friends. You can't please everyone, but it's a good idea to find out if your VIP guests (parents, close friends and family, and others your day wouldn't be the same without) have a conflict with the date you're considering. Obvious examples are birthdays, anniversaries, graduations, and so forth. If you're thinking about setting your date during a three-day weekend or other holiday period, remember that it may conflict with vacation plans or other festivities that they're looking forward to. If your heart is set on a wedding date near a holiday, be sure to send out Save-the-Date cards to your guests as soon as possible.

> **<CROSS-REFERENCE>**
> Read all about save-the-date cards in Chapter 20.
> **</CROSS-REFERENCE>**

Commemorating a special date. You might want to have your wedding date (and all your subsequent wedding anniversaries) fall on a date of special significance to the two of you: on the day of your first kiss, for example, the first time you met, or on the anniversary of a close and respected loved one.

Settling on a Time

Once you've settled on a date (with a backup or two for good measure), you'll need to choose a time for your ceremony and reception. For religious ceremonies held in a church, your starting time will more than likely be determined by your church's scheduling; they often have different available time slots per day (10:00 am, 12:00pm, 2:00pm, for example). For other locations, the choice is largely up to you.

Aside from preference, the main budgetary consideration you want to keep in mind when selecting a time is that the earlier you start your reception, the lower it's likely to cost you. A brunch, luncheon, or teatime reception will cost far less than one held in the evening with a full dinner, dessert, and appetizers served.

One way to approach the issue of divining your ceremony and reception start/end times is to decide first a general timeframe when you'd like your reception to take place (morning, midday, or evening) and the type of meal you'll serve, if any (breakfast, brunch, lunch, or dinner). With this in mind, settle on a start and end time for the reception. Then, work your way backwards and estimate a ceremony time. Allow enough time between the end of your ceremony and the start of your reception for guests to be transported from one location to the other (if the sites are separate) and for any portraits you might want to have done at the ceremony location.

> **<TIP>**
>
> **Reception Times and Styles**
>
> The style and atmosphere you want for your reception goes hand in hand with the time you hold it. Here are just a few examples:
>
> - 10:00 a.m. to 12:00 p.m. breakfast following an early ceremony
> - Casual 11:00 a.m. to 1:00 p.m. brunch
> - 1:00 p.m. to 4 p.m. luncheon
> - Relaxing 3:00 p.m. to 5:00 p.m. teatime affair
> - Cocktail hour reception from 4 p.m. to 7 p.m., with hors d'oeuvres
> - 6:00 p.m. to 10:00 p.m. (or later) dinner and dancing event
> - Formal 8 p.m. to 10:00 p.m. evening of drinks and dessert
>
> **</TIP>**

Knowing what times you want for your ceremony and reception, you'll be ready to visit locations and check availability for your specific time slots.

Top off Your Guest Count

We won't sugar-coat it: building your guest list is one of the more stressful tasks you'll be dealing with during your wedding planning. Deciding who's in and who's out is something that will take a lot of time, discussion, compromise, and thought. The next chapter is entirely devoted to it; we've got some great e-Resources up our sleeve that will make things a lot easier to manage.

> **<CROSS-REFERENCE>**
>
> Read more about how time of day and other factors affect your reception style and location in Chapter 9.
>
> **</CROSS-REFERENCE>**

Your first step–the one we're going to take now–is simply a matter of finalizing the overall count, the total number of guests you're going to have share your day with you. This is something you should already have a good idea about after our work making budget decisions in the previous chapter, but we need to more or less solidify it now. Before you can decide who's in, you need to know your cap.

Your main considerations when deciding on a guest count are budget, your style and preferences, and the constraints of your location.

We already know that guest count is one of the most important cost factors; an increased guest count means a higher cost for almost all your expense categories, from catering to beverages to flowers to cake. More people need more stuff, and more stuff means more money.

> **<CROSS-REFERENCE>**
> Once you've settled on a total guest count, you can start building your guest list one group at a time. We discuss some good strategies and online tools to help in Chapter 7, "Manage Your Guests and Attendants".
> **</CROSS-REFERENCE>**

Your preferences are going to influence your choice as well. Do you envision a more intimate affair during which you're able to spend a good deal of one-on-one time with each of your guests, or a big bash with everyone you know–family, friends, coworkers, childhood pals, and everyone in between?

When choosing your location, you'll need to keep your guest count in mind (another reason we're nailing it down now!) Depending on the location, they may or may not be able to accommodate your party size; guest count is one of the first things they'll want to know after date and time. You may already have your heart set on a particular location, however. If so, the capacity of that location will put an upper limit on your total guest count as you make your choice.

> **<CROSS-REFERENCE>**
> If you missed our discussion on the budget consequences of your guest count, take a look at the section in Chapter 5 on "Money-Saving Tips".
> **</CROSS-REFERENCE>**

Discuss the main factors together and decide on a guest count that is a good compromise between budget and preference (if you're lucky, both will be aligned!) and make sure it is compatible with your idea of a location. If you absolutely *must* have a big crowd but you're on a strapped budget, look for all the ways you can cut cost: set your date on an off-peak month or on a Friday or Sunday instead of Saturday. Opt for a buffet style luncheon rather than the more expensive sit-down dinner. If you're going for formal, scratch the meal altogether and consider a classy dessert-and-cocktails affair in the evening; hold it in a formal ballroom with a big band providing the entertainment. Refer to every chapter in this book for ways to save in each category.

What Kind of Style and Formality?

The formality level you choose for your wedding should be consistent and reflected in all elements: the invitations, location, your attire, the guests' dress code...you name it. So it's a good idea to have a solid commitment early on to the level of formality you'd like.

Consider your preferences and budget, and discuss your options together. How formal do you envision your ideal wedding? Remember that, in general, the more formal the wedding, the more costly your services and the higher your reception tab will be. That said however, you can be creative and have a black tie bash on a low budget with some thought and creativity: there's the late night cocktail hour that we previously mentioned, and by considering your other major cost factors, try coming up with ways to cut less important corners to maintain the formality level if it's important to you.

Extremely Formal

No etiquette detail is missed: Invitations are engraved, floral centerpieces grace every table, and the meal is usually a large and elaborate multi-course feast with entertainment and dancing provided by a big band or orchestra. The location is typically held in a church, a temple, or synagogue if it is religious. The bride dons a classic long gown and train, while the groom is attired in a tail coat and white tie. The guests appear in evening gowns and tuxes, and the attendants are comprised of four to twelve brides-maids and groomsmen. There is a maid or matron of honor, best man, an usher for every 50 guests, flowergirls, and ring-bearer.

Formal

Similar to extremely formal weddings, but classic etiquette rules are not as strictly followed, and the ceremony location might just as likely be at a private home or overlooking the ocean as in a place of worship. Most traditional elements of the bridal gown, floral, invitations, and attendants are present. Guests wear formal attire but are not expected to be in tuxes or evening gowns. Music is provided by a band, trio, or DJ, and a meal is usually served. Formal weddings are very popular, retaining the charm and traditional feel of extremely formal weddings while allowing the flexibility to include more of your own personalization.

Semiformal

The overall style is less traditional and has more of a personal, individual touch. There are usually fewer attendants, and the wedding attire might be a suit for the groom and a stylish skirt or dress for the bride. Guests Invitations are engraved, but don't necessarily contain RSVP cards.

Informal

Almost anything goes with an informal wedding. Whether they are a day of sun and sand on the beach or a garden party, informal weddings are just as special and memorable as the most expensive and formal affairs, so long as everything is done in good taste. Invitations might be as simple and personal as handwritten notes, and floral decorations might not even be incorporated at all. It goes without say-ing that wedding attire and guests' dress is completely up to you; a beach wedding could even warrant attire as informal as shorts and sandals.

<NOTE>

Formality, Defined

Just for clarification: wedding formality is not a measure of how pompous the event is. It is really a measure of how classic the style, and how closely the traditional etiquette and customs are followed. A formal East Asian wedding, for example–with its own etiquette rules and traditions–is very different from a formal western-style wedding.

</NOTE>

Theme and Colors

While you're at it, make some final decisions on your theme, if any, and the color scheme you'll be using throughout your wedding. Like formality, your theme and colors should be used in every element of your wedding planning: from the invitations to the decor to the look of your wedding website.

Your Location Type

While considering a wedding date, guest count, and formality, you can't help but take into account the location type, even if it's still just a general idea at this point. If an outdoor wedding is important to you, that will influence your wedding date (a winter wedding would be out, for example). If your heart's already set on that charming winery with the view but whose capacity can only hold 150, you'll need to be aware of that upper limit on your guest count. And if a beach wedding is your thing, you'll likely be looking at an informal affair, since sun, sand, tuxedos and suits don't usually go together.

> **<CROSS-REFERENCE>**
>
> In Chapter 8, "Determine Your Ceremony Details and Location" and Chapter 9, "Plan the Party: Find a Reception Location and Lay Out the Details", we delve deeper into the search for the right ceremony and reception spots.
>
> **</CROSS-REFERENCE>**

What City?

Decide first where the wedding will be held. Will it be in the bride's hometown, according to tradition? In your current city of residence? In one of your parents' hometowns? Or perhaps a special place of significance to the two of you? Think about where the majority of your guests will be coming from, and choose the most logical locale. Some couples choose to marry at their honeymoon destination, and still others plan a multi-site wedding spanning separate cities and even states, to incorporate all of their far-flung friends and families. We discuss these options more in the upcoming section on "Alternative Wedding Ideas".

Are You In or Out?

If you're planning a wedding during a warm date, do you envision your ceremony and/or reception taking place in the great outdoors? An outdoor affair can be beautiful and dramatic, although it usually comes with a bigger price tag. You'll have some extra details to consider such as lighting, rental equipment, accessibility and compatibility on the part of your vendors. You'll also need to come up with a backup plan in case the weather decides to throw you a curve ball on the day of.

Mother nature certainly has a way of adding a powerful aesthetic addition to a wedding, wether it's saying "I do" under a blue sky or in a serene redwood grove, or partying the night away on a dance floor under the stars. Outdoor venues can be used for the ceremony, the reception, or both. You might have a religious exchange of vows in your mother's church, for example, and then hold your reception party at a local winery. Or you might keep the entire affair outdoors, holding the ceremony on a grassy knoll overlooking the ocean, just a short walk from a tented reception party.

As for the specifics of your outdoor location, you'll narrow your options down more when you actually start searching for that perfect spot, and we'll help you along in Chapters 8 and 9. For now, just deciding on being "in or out" is the key. To get your juices flowing, keep some of the following possibilities in mind: a home or garden wedding, with the ceremony under a majestic tree or under a gazebo that overlooks a breathtaking view. An old, historic winery with beautiful, rustic grounds and an elegant tasting room could lend the perfect touch. Parks, beaches, and other natural settings provide count-less possibilities for a unique, memorable event.

e-Resource

The Online Wedding Portals: Ideas and More Galore

With all these possibilities, options and decisions to make, where do you go for further inspiration? For advice on your specific questions? For examples on the items you're interested in?

Enter the online wedding portals. The wedding portals are all-purpose wedding websites that ca-ter completely to all things wedding. They're each loaded with articles, frequently asked questions and photo galleries of cakes, gowns, flowers and lots more. They provide directories for finding local vendors, planning tools like budget managers (we discussed these in Chapter 5) and online gift registries.

We'll be hitting these and other information sources up for help throughout the book. In fact, we already snuck in a few previews: we checked out their free website services in Chapter 4, and tried our hand at their budget managers in Chapter 5. Each time we turn to the big portals for help, though, make sure to stay focused on the topic at hand unless you're just browsing them for gen-eral information. It's easy to get sidetracked and distracted with everything being thrown at you.

<NOTE>

What's a Portal?

In tech terms, a portal (also called a web portal) is a website designed to be a starting-off point for your web-browsing session. Think of it as a gateway to other websites and online resources.

In the case of wedding portals, the big ones are stocked with helpful articles, advice forums, directories and links to online vendors, wedding planning tools, message boards, and more. They aim to be a "one stop shop" for your wedding planning and the place to start searching for other vendors and services, who usually pay to be included in the portals' directories.

Remember that while the portals are a great source of ideas and information, not all vendors are listed with them, especially local businesses. Try using a search engine like Google (local.google.com)to perform local vendor searches and to get information on weddings as well. Never rely on just one single resource.

</NOTE>

Things to Watch Out For

The online resources we cover in this section provide a wealth of information. They are rich with ideas, suggestions, and advice and can put you in contact with local vendors, other brides, and professional wedding consultants. But there are a few sharks beneath the appealing waters of convenient knowledge, and it's important to know what they are and how to handle them before jumping in.

Spam

Ah, yes, the thorn in many a technophile's side. Unsolicited e-mail advertisements from businesses and organizations, collectively known as "spam", are an unfortunately well-known issue to anyone who has spent any moderate degree of time with an e-mail address. Many online sites providing free resources ask you to sign up, or "register" to use their services. They harvest your demographic information as well as your e-mail address and use it as an advertising channel for their sponsors. Sign up for a few and you'll begin getting bombarded with unsolicited ads, "notices" and "great deals" in very short order.

What's the solution? Set up a separate wedding-specific e-mail address, one you'll only use for wedding planning purposes and will discard afterwards. The best place to go is Yahoo! Mail (www.yahoomail.com) or Hotmail (www.hotmail.com) and sign up for a free web-based mail account. The sign-up will take just a few minutes, and then you can start giving out this public planning-specific e-mail address to all the websites, surveys, and planning resources you like without fear of inundating your personal mailbox with wedding advertisement garbage.

Advertising Overload

Free websites and online services need to derive their income in some way, and that way is usually advertising. Pop-up windows, banner ads, and sponsor links abound on most portal sites, in addition to the aforementioned spam. Consider using a pop-up blocker for those pesky pop-up ads, and don't confuse the advertisements with real advice—it's a technique we like to call "marketing camouflage". Real advice will give you unbiased tips, pointers, and useful information. Advertised "advice" will will provide tips and suggestions that also try and push a particular service or product.

Privacy Issues

Be very, very stingy in giving out personal information. In fact, don't do it. Whether you're registering for a site or posting messages on a website's bulletin board, train yourself to hold back on personal details like your full name, mailing address, wedding date, or anything else identifiable. Only use the public planning-specific e-mail address you created earlier. You don't want to start receiving more junk mail at your personal e-mail account or in your physical mailbox, nor do you want to tip off potential burglars that you'll be out of the house during a specific date. When it comes to security and privacy online, you can never be too paranoid.

Introducing Our Top Three

Without further ado, allow us to introduce you to our top picks for the best wedding portals out there today. In the world of online wedding websites, these are the heavy-hitters, containing everything from advice, articles, planning tools, to vendor directories. You may have already used their services in one way or another and will continue using these helpful resource gateways often as you proceed with your planning efforts. They are an indispensable wealth of ideas and information to mine whenever you

<TIP>

Staying Focused

Right now we're discussing the decisions you need to make regarding wedding dates, guest counts, formality, themes, colors, and location types. Sticking to these topics, try using the portals to get more info on any questions you may have, or advice you might need. Use the Search function (all the portals have them) to narrow down the information available to just what you're looking for at a given moment.

</TIP>

start looking into virtually any aspect of your wedding (cakes, photographers, florists, and so on). They usually also offer newsletters that you can subscribe to in order to receive periodic wedding articles, advice, and deals from their sponsors in your e-mail box. If you subscribe to the newsletters, make sure you use your wedding-specific public e-mail address, and feel free to unsubscribe to any newsletter you later decide you don't want to receive anymore.

The following are a few of the most popular wedding portals, and our personal favorites: use them now to help solidify your wedding preferences and to obtain ideas and creative starting points.

The Knot (www.theknot.com)

The Knot was started in 1996 and has grown to be one of the largest wedding portals to date with over two million visitors every month, and over 3,600 new members joining every day. The home page–typical to many portal sites–has a lot on it and can come off as busy, but you get used to it after browsing a bit. There are links here for advice, planning tools, featured articles, local vendor resources, and galleries for gowns, cakes, and more.

We'll be returning to The Knot and our other portal favorites as we cover subsequent chapters (wedding gowns, for instance: The Knot has an extensive gown database that can be searched by price, designer, and even silhouette or neckline). For now, browse their links for Ideas and Advice, Message Boards, and Special Features. Try to approach each with questions you have about the top-

The Knot's home page is a gateway to a wealth of wedding information and resources.

From the home page of WeddingChannel.com, you can springboard into their extensive assortment of advice, articles, planning tools, and more.

Modern Bride offers a stylish portal to content from their magazine articles as well as vendor directories and message boards.

ics we've covered in this chapter (wedding date, guest count, formality, and location types). We mentioned this before, but we'll say it again: beware of information overload and don't try to take it all in at once. Just look for what you're interested in at the time and ignore the rest; you can come back later when you need info or ideas on something else.

WeddingChannel.com

WeddingChannel.com was launched in July of 1997 and, has grown to be one of the largest online wedding resources currently at your disposal. It also boasts over 2.5 million unique visitors every month, with more than 3,000 users joining daily. It offers similar services, although you'll find their starting home page layout a bit more condensed—which you may or may not prefer. In the end, you'll decide which you prefer and stick more to the portal that makes you feel more comfortable. Pay them all a visit, though: you may find that you like one website for a certain feature and a different website for another.

Like The Knot, WeddingChannel.com's home page is a gateway to a wealth of information. You'll notice links to local vendors, planning tools, and wedding planning resources, among others..

The planning page offers a great interface to access ideas (using online photo galleries), noted designers, and articles on each element of your wedding. Browse around for ideas that pertain to your overall wedding vision.

Note: In 2006, The Knot announced a merger with WeddingChannel.com. Time will tell if this results in better services or less diversity between the two sites.

Modern Bride (www.modernbride.com)

Though not as extensive as The Knot or The Wedding Channel, Modern Bride Magazine's website is a rich source of information, articles, and local vendor directories. Being an outlet of a publishing group, the site feels more like a magazine, and you might prefer that.

From the home page, check out the Photo Flipbooks, which link to a rich offering of photo galleries from which to draw ideas on all your wedding categories. You can also click the "Wedding Planning" link to access their online planning resources, advice database, and message boards.

Message Boards: Exchange Notes with Fellow Brides

One of the great things about wedding tradeshows is that they're full of people who are in the same boat as you: other brides and couples planning their own weddings. And nobody knows the duality of pain and excitement you're going through like another bride who's going through it, too. Chatting with other brides is a great way to vent, to get advice about vendors and wedding ideas, and to get some empathy for what issues you may be dealing with.

Want to enjoy the interaction while at home in pajamas? Just tap into the virtual community created by most portal websites. Their online message boards aim to capture that community feel by allowing brides and couples to post and respond to messages on everything from planning problems to reception ideas to getting in shape for the big day.

If you're about to settle on a vendor, for example, you could always post a message in a local forum asking other brides who may have used that vendor what their own experiences were.

Alternative Wedding Ideas

After all that talk about traditions and customs, let's break (or at least bend) the rules a bit and think about ways to personalize your wedding to your situation even more!

The Weekend Wedding

Why limit your wedding to a single day? Expand it out to include an entire weekend, and make it a memorable activity-filled gathering for everybody. Weekend weddings can be a lot of fun, and don't necessarily have to be much more expensive. It mostly constitutes a little more organization and getting the information out to all your guests. And since you're e-planning, you have a great medium for publishing all this information: your wedding website.

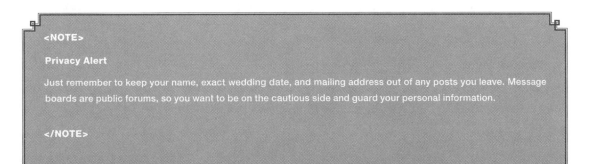

<NOTE>

Privacy Alert

Just remember to keep your name, exact wedding date, and mailing address out of any posts you leave. Message boards are public forums, so you want to be on the cautious side and guard your personal information.

</NOTE>

On Friday night, Saturday morning, and Sunday, plan dinners, get-togethers, and activities that your out-of-town guests are invited to. Keep it optional; you don't want to be too pushy for those guests that just want to chill out at the hotel, the pool, or venture off on their own. Make sure the itinerary is available ahead of time so that everyone can adequately prepare. You'll also want to provide maps, lists of local attractions and resources, and information about any transportation you may have arranged. This is a great candidate for an addition to your wedding website. In the next chapter we'll discuss more about your website's page for out-of-town guests; the weekend wedding information would fit right in. Make sure you have an alternate way of notifying those guests who aren't connected to the Internet.

<TIP>

Ideas for a Weekend Wedding

These are just some ideas. Take your own situation and guests into consideration, and come up with your own scheduled get-together!

Friday

You might want to include the out-of-town guests at your rehearsal dinner and have it double as a welcoming party.

Saturday

Have a friend or relative host a breakfast get-together or luncheon. Depending on the time of your ceremony, you might invite everyone to an outdoor picnic at a local beach or park. Consider a game of softball, volleyball, or golf as a fun prelude to an evening wedding and reception.

Sunday

Have your guests invited to a post-wedding breakfast or brunch. The bride and groom might say their goodbyes and leave for their honeymoon, giving the guests a chance to finish visiting family and leave at their leisure.

</TIP>

The Progressive Wedding

An interesting wedding idea you may have heard of is the progressive wedding, which takes a wedding and spaces it out across not just days, but locations as well.

Perhaps you have family in different parts of the country but they all don't have the financial means to travel to your location for a single-site wedding. Or maybe there are divorced parents involved who don't want to attend the same event together. A progressive wedding would move from one location to another, bringing the wedding to your guests instead of your guests to the wedding!

As an example, perhaps the bride's parents live in Boston, and the groom's family all live around Denver. But you and your sweetheart live in San Diego, along with your friends. You might decide to hold the ceremony and a reception hosted by the bride's parents in Boston. After a grand exit, you could then fly over to Denver and celebrate with a reception that the groom's parents host. To wrap it up, you'd return home and throw a late night reception bash for you and all your friends. Each reception following the original could vary in formality or could maintain the same style as the first. Some couples even repeat their ceremony, or bring along photos of the original to each location.

The Destination Wedding

Does your wedding vision include white sands and palm trees, but you happen to live in Minnesota? Perhaps circumstances are such that you need to marry this winter, but your dream is an outdoor affair.

Consider the destination wedding, in which you invite your guests to share a romantic location (typically your honeymoon destination).

The location can be anywhere you like: southern California, Hawaii, Mexico, the Caribbean, Jamaica...you name the spot! Your guests will fly out for a weekend of vacation fun and attend your ceremony and reception. The bride and groom typically remain at the location after the guests leave and enjoy their honeymoon, or they might travel to yet another spot.

Destination weddings tend to be smaller and more intimate. Since all your guests pay their own airfare and accommodations–with the exception of children and older parents who might not be able to afford it–the guests are typically limited to close friends and family, which is a reason many couples choose the option.

<TIP>

Destination Weddings

- If you're expecting a large guest count, check in with airlines and hotels for group discounts.

- Prepare the extra paperwork for marrying abroad, and check with the location's requirements. You'll likely need proof of citizenship, proof that you're not currently married (including divorce or death certificates if they apply), and perhaps blood test results. If you want to avoid the paperwork, consider a legal marriage at home just before heading out to your destination, where you'll have the ceremony and reception performed.

- If you're thinking about a country and not a specific resort, contact the Tourism Offices Worldwide (www.towd.com) for more information on your destination.

</TIP>

In addition, destination weddings are usually relatively inexpensive and require less of a planning effort. The guest count is small, which cuts cost, and many resorts offer package deals for your ceremony, reception, and honeymoon. The package deals often include an on-site coordinator that takes care of most of your planning burdens by recommending and booking vendors, hiring an officiant, and even walking you through legal requirements for tying the knot in their country. Plus, extravagant decoration is usually not needed; the dramatic beauty of the location is often an enchanting enough backdrop.

Using a Wedding Consultant

Maybe you and your family don't have the time to plan, manage, and coordinate an entire wedding. Maybe you don't want to. Or, maybe you just prefer (and can afford) to have some professional assistance. A wedding consultant can save you stress and do some or all of the dirty work–depending on how much you want him or her involved–by setting up a realistic budget, recommending vendors, negotiating contracts, managing all the sticky details, and hopefully saving you money in the process.

What Can a Consultant Do for You?

Wedding consultants eat and breathe weddings. They're active in the industry, so they know people who know people, and they use those connections to put you in contact with good vendors and to save you money. They'll answer your questions, provide recommendations, and offer tips on the latest trends. Depending on how long they've been in the game, they have probably seen it all once or even twice, so they know how to handle last-minute emergencies and other situations that would cause the average bride and groom to sprout a few grey hairs. A wedding coordinator will draw up a timeline for you similar to your checklist in Chapter 2, and they'll help you stick to it. They'll create a wedding binder for you that includes your vision details, budget, and vendor paperwork (as we show you to do in Chapter 5). For the wedding day, they can coordinate all the minute-by-minute events and keep everyone communicating, working together properly and on schedule.

A wedding consultant can be hired to work with you full time (from determining your overall vision to booking your honeymoon), part-time (getting your planning started and then handing it off to you), or they can simply be hired to coordinate the wedding day itself.

Full-Time Consultant: From Starting Vision to Honeymoon

For the "full-service package", your wedding consultant will pretty much do everything we show you how to do for yourself in this book. She'll meet with you to lay out your preferences and overall wedding vision. Using this information, she'll help you create a realistic budget to capture your vision, and will put you in contact with appropriate vendors. She'll help you negotiate contracts and tie up all the loose ends to make sure everything's a go for the big day. On the wedding day of itself, she'll help you create a timeline and coordinate with all your vendors to take the burden and stress off of your shoulders.

Expect to shell out 10% to 15% of your overall wedding budget for this service. For example, if your overall budget is $20,000, then $2,000 would be a fair price to pay.

Part-Time: Set It Up and Hand It Off to You

In this case, your consultant will do all the prep work: she'll meet with you at the beginning of your planning, answer questions, and provide recommendations. She'll help you identify your overall vision, set up your budget, create your wedding binder, lay out a wedding day timeline, and draw up lists of recommended vendors. Then, she'll hand the whole thing over to you to take over from there.

"Day Of" Coordination

You'll meet with a wedding coordinator a couple times before the big day so that she'll have ample time to prepare. On the day of your wedding, she'll direct events and coordinate your vendors to make sure that everything happens at the appropriate time and that everyone is doing their job. If emergencies arise, she'll take care of them, as well as handle anything else to ensure that your day comes off without a hitch.

Looking for a Consultant

Start off with referrals from those you trust, as always. You can also check for consultants in your area by contacting the Association of Bridal Consultants (860-355-0464, www.bridalassn.com), the Association of Certified Professional Wedding Consultants (www.acpwc.com), and the Association for Wedding Professionals International (www.afwpi.com).

It's important that you have a good chemistry with the person you select, so chat with them on the phone first. If you're not comfortable talking to them on the phone, don't waste time with an appointment. Do make appointments with as many consultants as you have time for; you want to shop around as much as possible. We give you a list of questions and discussion points to bring up with each one below.

Check everyone's credentials and select one that you feel the most comfortable with, someone who shares your tastes and preferences. Also, make sure to keep in mind that you're hiring someone to realize your wedding vision, not theirs. If they won't listen or keep pushing their own ideas of what an ideal wedding is, don't hire them.

Questions to Ask Wedding Consultants

- How long have you been in business?

- Are you a registered business?

- Do you do wedding consulting full time or do you have another job? (It's okay if they have another job, but if they're full time they may be easier to contact and better able to talk to vendors during business hours)

- What consulting course did you take? Do you have a certificate / diploma?

- Do you charge as a percentage of total wedding cost, by the hour, or a flat fee?

- What is your cost estimate for the services we need? What deposit do you require?

- How often will we meet? How long will the meetings be?

- Can you help us choose vendors and go over our contracts with them?

- If there's an emergency and you can't be there at our wedding, do you have a backup?

- Will you be with us during our rehearsal? Will there be an extra charge for this?

- We have a venue in mind. Have you worked there before?

- We have some vendors in mind. Have you worked with them before?

- Do you have a preferred vendors list?

- On our wedding day, at what times will you arrive and leave?

- Will you handle payments to our vendors if we provide the funds to you?

Get It in Writing: The Consultant Contract

Make sure the following is in ink: How the consultant charges and what the cost will be for the service she's providing to you, along with a description of what that service is. Your contract should also contain a cancellation policy and a no-show policy that outlines what happens if the consultant can't make it to your event in the case of an emergency. Make sure that your wedding date is given, and that both you and the consultant sign the contract.

Considerations Worksheet: Wedding Vision

As you solidify your wedding vision, jot down your notes and conclusions here.

Item	Your Thoughts
☐ Wedding Budget	
☐ Engagement Length	
☐ Accommodating Family and Friends	
☐ Wedding Season	
☐ Wedding Day of the Week	
☐ Wedding Time of Day	
☐ Wedding Date Option 1	
☐ Wedding Date Option 2	
☐ Wedding Date Option 3	
☐ Wedding Location (City, State)	
☐ Indoor or Outdoor	
☐ Approximate Number of Guests	
☐ Adults Only Reception?	
☐ Wedding Formality	
☐ Wedding Theme and Color Scheme	
☐ Wedding Consultant/Coordinator	

Notes:

Contact Sheet: Wedding Consultant

Date Booked: _____

Consultant/Coordinator: _____

Address: _____

_____

Assistant: _____

Email: _____

Phone: _____

Fax: _____

Website: _____

Years of Experience: _____

Staple Business Card

Type of Service Provided

☐ Full-Time Consultant: From Starting Vision to Honeymoon _____

☐ Part-Time: Set It Up and Hand It Off to You _____

☐ "Day-Of" Wedding Coordination _____

Service Description: _____

Meeting	Schedule Date	Time	Meeting	Schedule Date	Time
1.			5.		
2.			6.		
3.			7.		
4.			8.		

Professional Credentials: _____

Payment Policy: _____

Cancellation Policy: _____

Payment Options

☐ % of Total Budget: $ _____   ☐ Hourly Rate: $ _____   ☐ Flat Rate: $ _____

Additional Fees: $ _____

Total Cost: $

Deposit: $ _____   Date Paid: _____

Balance: $ _____   Date Due: _____

Mr. Robert Jones

Table 5

Chapter 7
Manage Your Guests and Attendants

- Wedding Party Roles

- Building Your Guest List

- Out-of-Town Guests

- e-Plan It! Use Your e-Resources:

  A Flexible Guest Database
  A Self-Building Address Book
  Your Website's Out-of-Town Guests Page

- Worksheets:

  Guest List: The Wedding
  Guest List: Wedding Party / Attendants

A big part of your day will be all those friends and loved ones getting together to show their support and help you celebrate! From selecting your overall group to identifying those special VIP's for your bridal party entourage, this chapter will guide you through all the necessary people tasks. And with resources like a guest database that automatically maintains your headcount and an address book that updates itself, we'll show you how to do it all more conveniently, easier, and in less time than ever before.

Wedding Party Roles

Your wedding party will be there to support you on the big day and throughout the planning adventure. The number of attendants is up to you, but make sure that it's not too crowded; a huge number of attendants might make finding a sizeable enough ceremony location more difficult. Keep your budget in mind, too...more attendants mean more thank-you gifts, more of a bill for the bridal luncheon and rehearsal dinner, and more wedding day flowers (bouquets and boutonnieres). Some couples go all out and have a dozen or more attendants, while others stick to just the best man and maid of honor. Generally, a large wedding party is indicative of a more elaborate, formal affair.

> **<TIP>**
>
> **Special Roles for Special Folks**
>
> Not everyone has to stand beside you at the altar. There are plenty of other special roles those close to you can fill: singers, ceremony readers, candle lighters, speakers at the reception, and more
>
> **</TIP>**

It's up to you if you'd like the number of your bridesmaids to exactly match the number of your groomsmen. It's not required, and with a little creative shuffling of the procession and recession (one groomsman for every two bridesmaids, for example), your ceremony can easily accommodate unequal attendant counts.

Can't decide who to pick as your honor attendant between your sister and best friend? Why not both? It's totally acceptable to have two maids of honor, as long as you clearly divide up duties between the two. And don't be afraid to gender-bend: the bride may prefer a close male friend as her honor attendant while the groom may have a great female chum willing to be the "best maid" (don't worry, she doesn't have to be involved in potentially awkward male-specific roles like planning the bachelor party). Remember that every situation is unique, so feel free to bend the "rules" to accommodate yours.

The Maid of Honor (Honor Attendant)

The maid of honor (or matron of honor, if she's married) is often a sister or close friend of the bride, although it could be anyone you like: a mother, older daughter, or even a brother or close male friend. Your honor attendant traditionally:

- Hosts / cohosts your bridal shower

- Assists you with prewedding duties like addressing invitations and making favors

- Joins you in your gown and bridesmaids' dress shopping (she purchases her own attire)

- Plans or coplans your bachelorette bash

- Attends the rehearsal and rehearsal dinner

- Assists you at the ceremony by adjusting your train and veil, holding your bouquet and carrying the groom's ring until you need it

- Signs the marriage certificate as a witness

- Gives a toast at the reception

- Helps the bride bustle her gown before the reception and change into her getaway clothes afterwards

- Sees that the gown makes it home safe

Bridesmaids

Your bridal entourage will back you up on the big day and can also assist with planning tasks. Choose trustworthy maids that can be counted on to help out when needed; it will be to your sanity saving advantage! Your girls traditionally:

- Attend your prewedding parties

- Assist with your planning tasks as needed, such as helping out with the favors or running bridal errands

- Attend and may coplan parties like the bridal shower and bachelorette bash

- Often join you in at least one bridesmaids' dress shopping trip (she each purchases her own attire)

- Attend the rehearsal and rehearsal dinner

The Best Man

He's the groom's trusted right-hand man, dependable valet, personal aide and toastmaster. It's usually a best friend, brother, dad or an older son. In this day and age, it might even be a close gal pal. Make sure you select someone tustworthy who isn't too busy to provide the help and support you'll need. Your top guy traditionally:

- Plans or coplans your bachelor party

- May help shop for the formalwear (he purchases or rents his own attire)

- Attends the rehearsal and rehearsal dinner

- Gets the groom to the ceremony on time, and makes sure nothing's forgotten (marriage license, rings and so forth)

- Carries the bride's ring until you need it

- Signs the marriage certificate as a witness

- Drives you from ceremony to reception unless you arrange other transportation

- Starts off the toasts at the reception

- Distributes tips and final payments to the officiant and vendors

- May handle transportation of you and your luggage to first night accommodations or airport after the reception

- Organizes the return of rented formalwear

Groomsmen / Ushers

Those loyal and responsible friends who have been there for you through all the good (and bad!) times will be the ones to provide the same trusted support on your big day. They traditionally:

- Attend and may help coplan the bachelor party

- Purchase or rent their own attire

- Attend the rehearsal and rehearsal dinner

- Assist guests in ceremony seating and hand out ceremony programs

- Ensure that guests have directions to the reception location after the ceremony

- Decorate the getaway vehicle

Child Attendants

Kids can be adorable, but also unpredictable! Keep your tots at four years of age or older, and leave the more important roles to the grown-ups. Here are some roles to give the wee ones:

Flowergirls - They traditionally come down the aisle just before the bride, scattering rose petals or handing out long-stemmed roses as they go. They can carry a decorated basket, little bouquet or pomander ball and wear dresses that have a hint of the bridesmaids' dress color.

Ring bearer - Usually a boy carrying a satin pillow on which symbolic replicas of the wedding rings are sewn or tied. The real rings will usually be safely in the hands of the best man and maid of honor. These little gents are often donned in a suit or tux with a mini boutonniere on the left lapel.

Pages (train bearers) - In a very formal ceremony, you might have a pair of youngsters follow behind you to help carry an especially lengthy train. These are traditionally boys, but it's fine to ask girls, too.

Candle lighters - In a Christian ceremony, preteen kids (nine to twelve years of age) from each family could be asked to light altar candles just before the mother of the bride is seated.

Special Roles

Give others important to you a chance to be a part of your wedding, too. Younger relatives can be asked to pass out ceremony programs or yarmulkes, or oversee the guestbook at the reception.

Ushers are in charge of seating the guests and, sometimes, rolling out the aisle runner. The groomsmen often double as ushers, but you might want to separate the duty if you have other men you'd like to include.

Ask that close friends or family members read scripture passages, poems, or other meaningful words during your ceremony. If you know of anyone with musical talent, they might be up for singing or playing an instrument.

Your Parents' Roles

Traditionally, the father of the bride footed the wedding bill and mom did all the work planning the big day. Today, especially with more couples handling the bill and planning themselves, parental involvement depends more on the closeness of your relationship, their availability and how much extra help you need.

Parents can assist in any area of your wedding planning they (and you) feel comfortable with. Mom can help you shop for the wedding dress, for example, and join you at the florist to give her opinion on the colors and styles. Parents also often assist in gathering contact information and compiling your guest list. Dads will usually give toasts and speeches at the reception and rehearsal dinner, and the father of the bride is often her escort down the aisle. If you have a receiving line, mom and dad will normally line up with you to greet your guests.

Building Your Guest List

After the budget discussion in Chapter 5 and the wedding vision notes in Chapter 6, you should have a general idea as to the upper limit of guests you'll want at your wedding. The main consideration factors in coming to this decision, you'll remember, were your overall budget (guest count is a major money factor) and the desired mood of your affair (intimate gathering versus big bash). Space constraints of your location will come into play, too, although it's generally best to settle on a guest count first and then look into ceremony and reception sites afterwards.

Deciding Who's In and Who's Out

This can be tough, especially if you're shooting for a more conservative guest count. Split the guest count (usually in half, but it's up to you and your individual needs): one amount for the groom and one for the bride. Or, if your parents will be more involved in the guest picks, you can ration the guest count into thirds: a third for you two and a third for each family. Once everyone has their allowed limit, you should then get to work creating your lists; you'll combine them into a "master list" later.

Ways to Keep the List Under Control

Got the potential for a beefy guest list and need to drop a few pounds? It can be done, though it will require diplomacy and plenty of communication to ensure that all your guests understand the situation. Start by eliminating specific categories (coworkers, social groups, general acquaintances and so forth). Remember that imposing limits on who attends works only if you don't make exceptions. Once you bend the rules for one person and not another, feelings are bound to get hurt. Here are some other areas to get stingy on:

Kids - It's your choice. They can be charming and priceless but they're also the epitome of chaos, and your theme might be more of an adult one (late evening cocktails and dancing, for example). Pulling the little guys from your list will cut your guest count and save you money. If you decide to go without young kids (say, by only inviting guests age thirteen or above), address invitations to parents and older children only. Have your attendants and family pass along the discreet word as well. A possible compromise is to allow children at the ceremony and have a sitter watch the out-of-town guests' youngsters at the hotel, a child-friendly home of a family member, or in an adjoining room at the reception location (arrange for toys, coloring books, and perhaps a couple DVDs of kiddie flicks).

Guests of guests - Feel free to cut down on who your guests can bring with them. If you're inviting groups of people like coworkers or your yoga partners, invite them without significant others. Send unmarried friends and family members who aren't in serious relation-

<TIP>

Factor in the Regrets

Unless your guest list contains just an intimate group of family and friends, expect around 20% of your invitees to decline your invitation. As they send in their regrets, you may be able to invite some individuals you had to cut originally. It's okay to send such last-minute invites up to three weeks before the wedding. After this point, invite those on your "wish-list" in person or over the phone.

</TIP>

ships solo invites as well. You can let folks know that your guest count is tight and you're having trouble fitting both families in under the cap.

Consolidate the Master List

When you (and your parents, if applicable) have settled on your individual lists, go over them and elimi-nate any duplicates. Combine them into a single master list that includes full names (including children, if invited), the number of reserved seats and their contact information. At the very least, accurate mail-ing addresses and zip codes should be noted. Such information management is ideally suited for the following e-Resource, which can save you an incredible amount of time and hassle right now and in the long run.

e-Resource

A Flexible Guest Database

Keeping your guest info in the digital world gives you immediate time-saving advantages. It can be sorted, searched, categorized, and edited with ease. If it's online, it's accessible anywhere you have Internet access. It can be exported to lists (for placecards and so forth), address sheets (for invitations and other mailed correspondence) and printed reports. If you have guests' e-mail addresses, you can send group broadcasts to everyone or to spe-cific categories of guests (rehearsal dinner invitees, for example, or your bridal party).

Of further advantage is a guest database that is integrated with your wedding website. Why? Because now you can activate an online RSVP page to track guests' responses automatically and to update your headcount in real-time. Or have guests update their contact information them-selves in an address book that builds itself (we'll cover this more in a bit). Get the guests into your database as soon as possible in order to begin taking advantage of all the online conveniences right away.

Your wedding website service should have a guest data-base as part of its built-in planning tools suite. If you're using the WedShare.com service, click on "Guest Man-ager" in the Planning Tools pane of your Control Panel.

WedShare.com's data record for a guest. Information can be entered a guest at a time, in bulk, or as a data import from a text file or spreadsheet.

Capture Necessary Information

A good guest database will let you easily enter information for each guest, including address, contact info, and spouse or other accompanying individual. You'll be able to group them into categories and assign guests a number of reserved seats. Guest records will allow you to track RSVP information too, like number of adults/children attending and so forth. If you enable online RSVP from your website, this information will be updated for you automatically as guests log in to respond!

<CROSS-REFERENCE>
Learn all about online RSVPs in Chapter 20, "Send Invitations and Manage Your Responses". You can even use your guest list and online RSVP for other events like pre-wedding parties! Get the scoop in Chapter 22, "Enjoy the Pre-Wedding Parties".
</CROSS-REFERENCE>

Quick Summaries and Convenient Headcount Tracking

A summary page gives you an at-a-glance snapshot of how many people are on your list, your current headcount, the number of guests that have accepted and the number that have declined. You should also be able to perform searches (by name or category, for example) and list guests by criteria: out of town guests, guests of the bride, guests of the groom, guests who have or haven't sent in an RSVP, guests who've sent a gift, and so forth.

Future Convenience

The convenience of your guest database will live on after the wedding, too. Use it to manage your gifts and thank-you correspondence. Stay on top of everyone's current contact info by letting your address book update itself. Remember birthdays, anniversaries, and other important dates, and track holiday cards you give and receive.

Missing or Changing Contact Information

Getting all the contact info you need to send out invitations and other mailed correspondence like save-the-date cards can take a lot of time and work, especially for those with larger guest counts. And then staying on top of those individuals that move or change phone numbers before the wedding only adds to the pressure. Wouldn't it be great if your address book could just...build and update itself?

A Self-Building Address Book

With e-Planning, your wish is granted! With your wedding website's Address Book feature, guests can provide their contact information when they visit your website, including mailing address, e-mail and phone numbers. They can even correct possible planning hiccups like last-name misspellings (woops...how embarrassing!) or incorrect titles (I prefer Dr., thank you). And if they move or change phone numbers, just ask that they update it for you the next time they visit your website.

Such additions and updates are automatically reflected in your guest database, which you're already using to manage all your guest information.

How It Works

First, build your guest database. Just use what you've got; at a minimum, enter their names. Not sure of the spelling? (is it Crystal or Chrystal? McWhorter or McWorter?) Just take your best guess…they'll be able to change it later.

<TIP>

Don't Forget the Anti-Tech Guests

The blessed advantages of your online address book won't apply for those old school guests who haven't yet made the evolutionary leap to the digital age. You'll still need to get contact info from technophobes the old-fashioned way.

</TIP>

Once you've got most everybody in (if you're missing a few, you can always add them to your guest database later) activate your website's Address Book feature. If you have a WedShare.com wedding site, just click on "Available Features" in your Control Panel's SiteBuilder pane and select to activate your Address Book. Edit your Address Book's preferences to make sure the security level is satisfactory. A good security scenario in most cases is to allow any new information to automatically go to your guest database and require that any updates be approved by you first.

When you let the word out about your website, mention that you'd like everyone to use the address book page to assist you in maintaining updated contact info. Mention it on your home page. If you set it up, they will come.

Guests can access their address book entry easily using their name or part of their name. If it's misspelled, a good address book should be smart enough to figure it out in most cases and let them update their name along with their contact info (using the security setting we advise above, you'd need to approve the name change).

Now all you have to do is sit back and let the contact information roll right into your guest list…without you lifting a finger! And since your guests are familiar with it, it's easy for them to quickly update if they move or switch phone numbers. Check in with your Control Panel to approve any such updates whenever you like. It's a great way to let your guests save you some much needed time for your planning and to maintain a more accurate guest list.

A guest reviewing their address book entry in a couple's wedding website.

Out-of-Town Guests

Don't forget to go the extra mile for those guests that are traveling potentially many miles to be at your wedding. How will they get around? Where will they stay? Make sure accommodations are arranged for: reserve a block of rooms at a nearby hotel and find out if any relatives are willing to host family members coming from afar.

Inform Them

Make sure your travelers have maps, contact numbers, hotel reservation info, and the dates and times of any activities you're planning that they're invited to. You can stuff it into their invitations, mail or e-mail it, or use the following e-Resource to let your wedding website handle the work and provide them with a convenient way to get all the 411.

<CROSS-REFERENCE>
For more on wedding day wheels, check out Chapter 19, "Arrange Transportation".
</CROSS-REFERENCE>

Move Them

Guests flying in will need to get from the airport to the hotel. A nice gesture is to have a friend or family member pick them up and transport them over unless they're renting a car. Check to see if the hotel provides a free shuttle service.

<CROSS-REFERENCE>
We discuss welcome baskets and other gifts in Chapter 15, "To Give and to Receive".
</CROSS-REFERENCE>

Welcome Them

Your guests have come a long way, so show them some love! Invite them to the rehearsal dinner or to another get-together especially for them. A welcome basket filled with goodies waiting for them at their room is a nice, classy touch that will be greatly appreciated.

e-Resource

Your Website's Out-of-Town Guests Page

You can include all the extra information like maps, hotel, and local entertainment in the invitations of those guests who are coming a distance...if you can fit it. But the most efficient way to provide all this need-to-know stuff is to create an out-of-town guests' page that encompasses it all on your wedding website.

Post everything they'll need on a page just for them. Include links to the hotel, local restaurants you recommend, sightseeing spots and even the local weather report.

Guest List: The Wedding

Photocopy this page for your guest list or download and print it out from this book's website, www.eplanyourwedding.com.

☐ **Bride's Guest**　　　　　　　☐ **Groom's Guest**

Name(s): _____

Address: _____

Email: _____　Phone: _____

Sent	Date Sent	R.S.V.P.	Number Reserved	Number Attending
☐ Save-the-Date:				
☐ Wedding Invitation:		☐ Yes　☐ No		
☐ Announcement:				
☐ Thank-You Note:				

Gift Received: _____

Date Received: _____　Store: _____

☐ **Bride's Guest**　　　　　　　☐ **Groom's Guest**

Name(s): _____

Address: _____

Email: _____　Phone: _____

Sent	Date Sent	R.S.V.P.	Number Reserved	Number Attending
☐ Save-the-Date:				
☐ Wedding Invitation:		☐ Yes　☐ No		
☐ Announcement:				
☐ Thank-You Note:				

Gift Received: _____

Date Received: _____　Store: _____

☐ **Bride's Guest**　　　　　　　☐ **Groom's Guest**

Name(s): _____

Address: _____

Email: _____　Phone: _____

Sent	Date Sent	R.S.V.P.	Number Reserved	Number Attending
☐ Save-the-Date:				
☐ Wedding Invitation:		☐ Yes　☐ No		
☐ Announcement:				
☐ Thank-You Note:				

Gift Received: _____

Date Received: _____　Store: _____

Guest List: The Wedding (continued)

☐ **Bride's Guest**   ☐ **Groom's Guest**

Name(s): _____

Address: _____

Email: _____ Phone: _____

Sent	Date Sent	R.S.V.P.	Number Reserved	Number Attending

☐ Save-the-Date: _____

☐ Wedding Invitation: _____ ☐ Yes   ☐ No _____

☐ Announcement: _____

☐ Thank-You Note: _____

Gift Received: _____

Date Received: _____ Store: _____

☐ **Bride's Guest**   ☐ **Groom's Guest**

Name(s): _____

Address: _____

Email: _____ Phone: _____

Sent	Date Sent	R.S.V.P.	Number Reserved	Number Attending

☐ Save-the-Date: _____

☐ Wedding Invitation: _____ ☐ Yes   ☐ No _____

☐ Announcement: _____

☐ Thank-You Note: _____

Gift Received: _____

Date Received: _____ Store: _____

☐ **Bride's Guest**   ☐ **Groom's Guest**

Name(s): _____

Address: _____

Email: _____ Phone: _____

Sent	Date Sent	R.S.V.P.	Number Reserved	Number Attending

☐ Save-the-Date: _____

☐ Wedding Invitation: _____ ☐ Yes   ☐ No _____

☐ Announcement: _____

☐ Thank-You Note: _____

Gift Received: _____

Date Received: _____ Store: _____

Guest List: Wedding Party / Attendants

If you need more space for your attendants, photocopy this page or download and print it out from this book's website, www.eplanyourwedding.com.

Name: _____ Title: _____
Email: _____ Phone: _____
Cell: _____ Work: _____

Name: _____ Title: _____
Email: _____ Phone: _____
Cell: _____ Work: _____

Name: _____ Title: _____
Email: _____ Phone: _____
Cell: _____ Work: _____

Name: _____ Title: _____
Email: _____ Phone: _____
Cell: _____ Work: _____

Name: _____ Title: _____
Email: _____ Phone: _____
Cell: _____ Work: _____

Name: _____ Title: _____
Email: _____ Phone: _____
Cell: _____ Work: _____

Name: _____ Title: _____
Email: _____ Phone: _____
Cell: _____ Work: _____

Name: _____ Title: _____
Email: _____ Phone: _____
Cell: _____ Work: _____

Chapter 8
Determine Your Ceremony Details and Location

- What Type of Ceremony?

- Finding Your Location and Officiant

- Share It! Informing Your Guests

- Planning Your Ceremony

- e-Plan it! Use Your e-Resources:

  Online Location Searches
  Your Website's Ceremony Page

- Worksheets:

  Considerations Worksheet: The Wedding Ceremony
  Comparison Forms: Ceremony Location
  Comparison Forms: Officiant
  Contact Sheet: Ceremony Location
  Contact Sheet: Officiant

Your ceremony defines your wedding. It's the big, anticipated event that joins you as husband and wife before the eyes of those most important to you. Your wedding vision, along with your personal beliefs, will be a major part of what fashions and shapes this historical moment in your lives. In this chapter, we'll guide you through all the decisions, considerations, and resources involved to ensure that your ceremony is everything it should be.

What Type of Ceremony?

Before you can start location hunting, make sure you have a good idea of exactly what type of ceremony you envision. Researching and visiting venues is time consuming, so don't fall into the trap of leaping into it before doing your homework. The first point to consider–which may already be a given for you based on your personal beliefs–is whether your ceremony will be overseen by a religious officiant according to the customs and traditions of a particular faith, or presided over by a legal official with a more flexible ceremony format. Your options for location type, formality, and style will be based on where your beliefs and preferences direct you.

Religious or Civil?

Let's start building the foundation for your wedding ceremony with this all-important question, and discuss just what it means to have a *religious* ceremony as opposed to a *civil* one.

<TIP>

If you believe in God but not in an organized religion, you may want to consider a non-denominational officiant (such as a Unitarian minister), or an officiant whose faith is open to your beliefs. Referrals for non-denominational officiants can be obtained from the American Ethical Union: (212) 873-6500.

</TIP>

Religious Ceremonies

For many couples, their faith is an important part of their lives and background. Having your church or congregation–in addition to the state–recognize your union is a necessary requirement for some and a nice touch for others. For some very religious couples or those with especially religious families, it is *the* binding force of their marriage. Perhaps you're not exactly a member of a particular religion, but feel a certain connection to one (it may be your parents' religion, for example) and you might like to make the values and traditions of that faith an integral part of your wedding ceremony. Or perhaps you've always wanted to get more involved with a particular religion and have decided to make your wedding part of your embracing of it.

Whether it's your religion or whether you'd like to show respect for that of your parents or sweetheart, a particular faith will have its own traditions, customs, and requirements for marriage beyond that of the state. Religious ceremonies are presided over by an officiant of that faith, and usually have a very specific format. The details may vary from one congregation to another, or from church to church, but the basic elements will be the same. Most religious ceremonies are performed in a place of worship: a church, temple, or synagogue.

If you both are of different faiths, don't let this become a barrier for you. Appreciate the fact that you have more than one source of tradition and customs to draw upon! Many religions welcome interfaith marriages (see the section on this topic later in the chapter), and there are several options for including both of your beliefs in your ceremony. For some, the easiest way to include both of their religions is actually to have a civil ceremony (more on this paradox in a bit).

Some (but not all) religious officiants will agree to perform the ceremony in a non-religious site of your choosing. You'll need to check up on this when deciding on an officiant and a location; most Roman Catholic clergy members, for example, will only perform a wedding ceremony in a Catholic church.

Civil Ceremonies

No, this isn't just for couples who want to take the Vegas route or say a quick "I do" at the county court-house. While you're welcome to tie the knot those ways, you can also opt for a ceremony every bit as detailed, symbolic, and traditional as a religious one performed in a house of worship.

A civil ceremony is simply one that is presided over by a legal officiant rather than a religious one. This officiant may be a judge, county clerk, magistrate, justice of the peace, mayor or notary public. They'll often travel to a location of your choosing, and are usually flexible in terms of ceremony format, additions, and details—meaning that you can customize as you please. You may be able to add certain customized elements that a religious officiant might not allow, for example, while including enough religious and traditional additions to satisfy your family and personal beliefs.

Civil ceremonies are the option to go with if neither of you is religious, or if you just aren't comfortable with a religious ceremony in general. You may want the ceremony held at a non-religious location and are having trouble finding an officiant of your religion willing to oversee the ceremony in a place other than a church.

Another reason you might opt for a civil ceremony is if you are both of different faiths, having trouble settling on the appropriate place of worship, and unable to find a religious officiant who is open enough to include both faiths to the extent you'd like (see the section on interfaith ceremonies later in this chapter for more options within this topic). In this case, you could find a location of your own that suits you and have a civil officiant—one who would allow you to bring in the rituals and traditions as you see fit—oversee the ceremony.

<CROSS-REFERENCE>
For more on wedding rehearsals, skip over to Chapter 22,
"Enjoy Those Pre-Wedding Parties".
</CROSS-REFERENCE>

Length and Formality

Both religious and civil ceremonies are fairly open when it comes to duration. You can have a full-length, symbolic, tradition-filled ritual that lasts for an hour or more, or keep the whole thing short and sweet in less than fifteen minutes. It's a balance you'll need to decide between the two of you. While your guests will appreciate a short, concise ceremony that isn't drawn-out or overly lengthy, you don't want to rush such an important moment in your life. Make sure that every detail significant to you is included, and work with your officiant to get the timing down to something that you'll be comfortable with. You'll have plenty of practice with this during your rehearsal; just make sure at this point that the officiant you choose will be open to your suggestions.

<CROSS-REFERENCE>
Review our notes on solidifying your wedding vision,
including style and formality, in Chapter 6, "Style and
Preferences: Capture Your Wedding Vision".
</CROSS-REFERENCE>

As far as formality goes, you'll want your ceremony to be as formal or informal as your reception. Keep in mind that religious ceremonies are, as a general rule, more formal and you'll be subject to the dress code of the particular religion (usually nothing too revealing). With civil ceremonies, dress code won't be an issue at all. If your wedding vision is a barefoot beach affair, for example, your best bet would probably be a civil ceremony.

Finding Your Location and Officiant

Your wedding's location is the backdrop for your day. The setting for your ceremony will create the overall atmosphere and should reflect the formality you have chosen. In addition, the individual officiating your ceremony is as important as a conductor is to a symphony, and will play a major role. In this section, we'll discuss how to go about finding and settling on both.

Decide on Your Setting

After deciding whether you'll be having a civil or religious ceremony, your next decision to make is the setting. Where is your ceremony going to take place?

You have four basic options as to the location of your wedding ceremony and reception. We discuss them below; take a moment to consider all your options. If you have a solid wedding vision in mind it'll be easier to narrow your choices down. You'll notice that the first and last option we give describe having your ceremony and reception at the same location. Because these events are usually priced together as a package they will usually be easier on your budget, although you'll need to be twice as careful when choosing a location that will serve as your ceremony *and* reception site. Look over the next chapter for things to keep in mind regarding reception sites.

Hold Ceremony and Reception at a Place of Worship

Many churches and temples have adjoining meeting halls or event centers that can be used for receptions. Ask about any restrictions on alcohol and music that might be enforced there.

Hold Ceremony at a Place of Worship and Reception Elsewhere

Your ceremony will take place at your chosen place of worship, and then you will move the party to a separate reception location (an event hall, country club, winery, or other site). You'll need to make sure there is adequate travel time for your guests between both events, and that everyone has clear directions on getting from one location to the other. Many couples add this information to their ceremony programs (skip over to Chapter 20 for more on programs) and you should definitely put the details of both locations on your wedding website, as we'll discuss in the next section.

Hold Ceremony and Reception at Two Separate Non-Religious Sites

Similar to the option above, except that you won't be marrying in a place of worship. You might have a minister or legal officiant marry you against the gorgeous backdrop of a cliff overlooking the ocean, for example, and move your reception to a nearby event hall. As with the previous option, you'll need to make sure that everyone's informed as to getting from one location to another. Look for an officiant willing to travel to the ceremony location; if your ceremony is a religious one, make sure that the officiant will perform your ceremony at a non-religious site.

Hold Ceremony in a Location at Your Reception Site

You might want to combine both locations at a non-religious reception site. Be it an event hall, winery, old mansion, garden location, or nearly anywhere else, you can usually select a special spot at the site to tie the knot and have everyone already gathered in the right place to kick off the reception party. Many reception sites have areas specifically set aside for the ceremony; check with the site managers as you browse reception sites (covered in the next chapter) if this is the option you're leaning towards.

Search for Locations and Make Appointments

When you've decided where to hold your ceremony, it's time to start location hunting! Remember that the best places book up fast, so you want to get on top of this as soon as possible. Ask around for references, check with other wedding professionals and coordinators, and look up local venues online and in local editions of bridal magazines. Contact the tourism board or chamber of commerce in the area you intend to hold your wedding; these are usually top sources for good venues.

<CROSS-REFERENCE>
For a discussion on finding great reception sites, take a peek at the next chapter. Places we'll consider: event and banquet halls, hotels, country clubs, restaurants, wineries, beaches, parks, gardens, mansions, private homes, museums, schools, and more.
</CROSS-REFERENCE>

Start building a list of potential ceremony locations and contact the person in charge of coordinating weddings at each site (the person may also be the officiant). Go over some initial questions—we suggest some questions to ask at the end of this section—and eliminate sites from your list that are unavailable on your date (and backup dates) or those you don't feel would meet your needs. When you've called them all or checked out their websites and scratched off the ones that don't make the cut, set up appointments with each of the remaining potentials. Visit the location, do a walk-through, and discuss the details with the site manager and officiant.

e-Resource

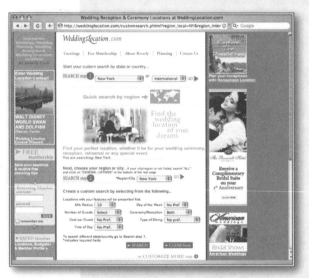

WeddingLocation.com's search criteria include location, guest count, meal type (if the location will also be used for your reception) and more.

Online Location Searches

Location hunting can be incredibly time-consuming. Even after narrowing down your search with phone calls, you still need to see the place. The good news is that most wedding venues have websites that are informative and chock full of photos. While you'll still need to visit the actual locations before making a final decision, checking out the website for each potential venue is a fast way to eliminate even more locations that aren't up to par with your preferences. You'll get a better feel for each location by viewing pictures of other weddings held there, and it's a lot faster to grab initial information off the websites than to ask for it over the phone.

Another convenient and time-saving set of resources are the online directories that you can search. Find venues in your area, link directly to their websites, and add those that catch your eye to your list of potentials. Use the web to get your homework done and give yourself the most options possible in the quickest amount of time.

Venue Search Services

WeddingLocation.com is a service provided by wedding guru Beverly Clark that is similar to the portal websites' venue search features. This service allows you to submit more detailed search criteria to obtain results narrowed down by location, guest number, cost, time of day, and so forth.

<CROSS-REFERENCE>

Learn more about the big wedding portal websites from our discussion on "The Online Wedding Portals: Ideas and More Galore" in Chapter 6.

</CROSS-REFERENCE>

If you're considering having both wedding and reception in the same spot, check out Country Club Receptions (www.countryclubreceptions.com) which provides a detailed list of country clubs in your area as a comparison chart of amenities and features.

If you're tying the knot in California, don't miss the online resources provided by the publishers of the book and magazine "Here Comes the Guide". Their website, www.herecomestheguide.com, is a great source for finding some of the best venues and vendors in the golden state.

The Wedding Portal Sites: An Introduction to Local Directories

The big wedding website portals like The Knot, The Wedding Channel, and Modern Bride (www.theknot.com, www.weddingchannel.com, www.modernbride.com) all have local vendor directories where you can search for wedding professionals in your area that provide services on everything from cakes to flowers to gowns. You can also use them to search for ceremony and reception sites.

Keep in mind when browsing these directories that they are far from being a complete list of vendors and sites in your area. Businesses, in fact, pay big bucks to be on the top of these lists. Some of the very best vendors and locations may not advertise this way at all, getting plenty of business by word of mouth. On the other hand, businesses depending on a quick turnaround who may not offer the highest quality of work may need to pay the most to ensure their spot in these directories for a steady stream of clients. The take home message: local directories on the portal sites are great to browse, get ideas, link to vendor and location websites. And while many good, reputable wedding professionals can be found on them, don't restrict your search to the portal directories exclusively.

Try running a search on ceremony sites in your area on each of the big portals and see what comes up. Check out the websites for those venues that interest you and seem to fit with your wedding vision. Keep in mind that since the venues listed are businesses who pay to be in these directories, they'll most likely be hotels, country clubs, and restaurants. Don't expect to find any places of worship here.

Country Club Reception (www.countryclubreceptions.com) lists the amenities provided by each local facility in a comparison chart.

Couples in California can find great locations using www.herecomestheguide.com.

The Wedding Channel (www.weddingchannel. com), like the other portal websites, provides a search directory for local ceremony sites. Thumbnails of each venue are provided, with links to their websites.

Online search engines are a great way to quickly search for local wedding venues and services.

The Search Engines

Using online search engines like Google and Yahoo (www. google.com, www.yahoo.com) is always a great source of leads. Include the city and state of your wedding in your keyword set in order to get more localized results (use keywords like "wedding ceremony locations san francisco ca" for example). Another great way to fish for local results is to use local search engines like CitySearch.com and Google Local (local.google.com). Both allow you to narrow searches down to a specific region, and Google Local will even display your results with markers for each on a slick GUI map. Try it with your city and state and add to your list any potentials that you find.

Find and Meet Your Officiant

Your officiant plays a major role in your wedding ceremony, and has a lot to do with shaping, directing, and conducting the event. You want to make sure that the individual you select is someone you like and trust. It's necessary that your officiant be open to your views, beliefs, and wedding vision.

If you have an officiant in mind, check for his or her availability on your wedding date (or one of your backup days). Schedule a meeting between the three of you to discuss your options, wedding vision, and whether or not he or she would be open to including any additional elements that you may be looking for. Ask if you can obtain an outline of the officiant's standard ceremony and customize it. We'll give you a list of questions to ask towards the end of this section.

If you don't have an officiant in mind, start hunting now. If you're tying the knot in a place of worship, your officiant will come with the location; so you should meet and discuss your options with the officiant before booking the site. Otherwise, check with family members and friends first to get trusted recommendations. Call your city hall for civic referrals. Check with your church, your parents' church, or that of a friend. Ask around with other wedding professionals: your photographer, florist, wedding consultant, or the coordinator of your venue.

e-Resource

You can do your officiant hunting on the web, too. Go to a search engine like Google and use the keywords "wedding officiant <city> <state>" for a list of local resources and contacts.

Questions for Site Managers and Officiants

Before meeting with officiants or site managers, make sure that the officiant and location will be available on your wedding date or on one of your backup dates. Then set up an appointment to go over the details; ask what documents and information you should bring along. When meeting, make sure that you're completely comfortable with the officiant. You should like and respect the person who will be directing your wedding, and they should feel the same about you. When looking at potential ceremony locations, make a note of the seating capacity, layout, and wheelchair accessibility if this will be an issue. The location shouldn't be too big or too small with respect to your anticipated guest count.

Questions for Site Managers

• What is the fee for the location? Is there a deposit? What is the payment policy?

• What is the maximum number of guests for this site?

• Are there any accessories provided (such as an aisle runner, flower vases, candles, and so forth)?

• Do you have a dress code?

• Will my photographer and videographer be able to take pictures at the site? Do you allow flash photography?

• Are there any restrictions regarding rice or flower-petal tossing?

<NOTE>

Prewedding Counseling

If you're selecting a religious officiant, you'll usually be required to attend some number of prewedding counseling sessions. It's a good opportunity for all three of you to get to know each other better (yes, even you and your sweetheart!), and to discuss your views and beliefs regarding marriage and faith. You'll want to find out what the schedule is and what options are available to you. The Catholic Church, for example, has a program called "Catholic Engaged Encounter" (www.engagedencounter.org) where couples sign up for prewedding counseling that takes place as a weekend group retreat with other engaged couples. Schedule your prewedding counseling now so that it doesn't slip between the cracks later on as your planning starts to get busy.

</NOTE>

- What kind of floral decorations will be provided and allowed?

- What kind of musical instruments are available and allowed?

- Do you have enough parking for my anticipated guest count?

- Will we need to rent any equipment? (we cover rentals in the next chapter)

Questions for Officiants

- Do you have a standard ceremony format that you typically use? Would we be able to get a copy of it and make changes for our ceremony?

- How open are you in allowing us to select readings, music, and other personalized additions to the ceremony?

- Will we need to participate in prewedding counseling?

- Can we write our own vows? Would you be able to provide guidance or suggestions in writing our vows or selecting our readings?

- In the case of a civil ceremony, can we add certain religious symbolism and rituals?

- If we have a location in mind, will you be willing to travel there?

- Can you recommend any locations for us?

- Is there a ceremony fee required?

- When should the rehearsal take place? Will you be there?

- When will the marriage license need to be signed (before or after the ceremony)?

Share It! Informing Your Guests

Some couples include a map card in their invitations to assist their guests in finding the location (check out Chapter 20 for more on invitations), but you're still going to get plenty of phone calls requesting directions and information. Your friends and family will want you to describe the lovely place you've selected to exchange your vows. Save yourself the repetitive dialogue and give your guests all the information they need with your wedding website's ceremony page. Posting photos, maps, directions, and informative side-notes in a universally accessible place like your website will let your guests in on where the big event's going to take place, and will make them feel more a part of it. It also ensures that everyone knows where they're going and how to get there without you having to reiterate anything beyond your website address.

Your Website's Ceremony Page

Your wedding website service should provide an interface that allows you to customize a page for your ceremony. Start by filling in the necessary information that your guests will be needing (time, address, and so forth) and add information to the page as you have time. If your ceremony spot has a website, add the link. Post photos, maps, directions...anything you think would help your guests out. If you're getting a lot of the same questions from friends and family, add it to your page and start referring everyone to the website for pictures and information.

You'll be setting up another page for your wedding reception in the next chapter. Your guests will definitely appreciate having all of this information available to them, and in such an accessible way. It will also free you up from the time you'd be otherwise be spending giving directions and location details on your own.

Your wedding website's ceremony page allows you to easily provide all the necessary time and address information to your guests along with photos, maps, and some fun side-notes as well.

If you're having your ceremony in the same location as your reception, you won't need a separate reception page. Just rename the ceremony page and its associated menu link from "Ceremony" to something like "The Location", and include the reception time along with that of the ceremony. Keeping everything in one spot will make it easier for your guests.

Planning Your Ceremony

Your ceremony is truly the most important aspect of your wedding day. Everything else is just celebration and recognition leading up to or following the big moment that you become husband and wife as everyone looks on. It's easy to get caught up in the details of flowers, photos, and cake and neglect what the wedding day is really all about.

Planning the ceremony will start at the time you first begin searching for locations and won't end until you both part after the rehearsal. Don't worry too much about the details now (where you'll stand, who pairs up with who, what readings you'll want, and so forth)...your officiant will help out and you'll have plenty of time to nail everything down during the rehearsal. Once you get the big choices (location, officiant) settled on and booked, you can take your time in considering details like unity rituals, cultural additions, readings, and so forth.

What Makes a Ceremony?

Your wedding ceremony is an outward expression of the love you have for each other, and enables those closest to you to witness and be involved in one of the most special moments in your lives.

The key elements to just about any Western wedding ceremony are pretty much the same, whether the ceremony is religious or not. Certainly religion will add its own traditions and rituals, but the basic elements will still be present. Likewise, if you're having a civil ceremony, you and your officiant will simply plan on a variation of these components (unless you're cutting to the chase and tying the knot in a no-fuss county courthouse appearance). Civil officiants typically provide a basic structure to which you can then add your own preferential details. The extent to which you tailor the basic elements with your own personal touch will make your wedding ceremony truly yours.

Procession

The entrance of the groom, parents, bridal party and the bride is symbolic of the marriage itself: You each enter separately, representing your individual lives leading up to the point where you both meet. In your wedding procession, you meet at the altar or stage, flanked by those closest to you and backed by your family for support, as you merge your lives into one.

During religious ceremonies, the procession of you, your sweetheart, your parents, and your bridal party typically has a prescribed format, although you can certainly add your own touches. For civil ceremonies it's all up to you. You might very well decide to follow one of the familiar religious processions or at least base yours on one.

In a traditional Christian procession, the groom, his best man, and the officiant stand at the altar facing the doors of the church. The groomsmen can either enter together before the procession and stand up at the altar with the groom, or they can enter down the aisle in the procession, each accompanying one of the bridesmaids. The bridesmaids come down the aisle starting with the one who will stand farthest from the bride, followed by the maid or matron of honor, the ring-bearer and flower girl, and finally the bride. The bride walks to the left of her escort, who is traditionally her father (you may choose to be escorted by whoever you wish, however, or even to take the trip solo). Relatives are seated in the front rows of the church, with the bride's family and friends on the left and those of the groom on the right.

A traditional Jewish procession begins with either the Rabbi or cantor (or both), followed by the groom's grandparents, and then by the bride's grandparents. The groomsmen proceed afterwards in pairs, followed by the best man, then the groom with his father to his left and mother to his right. The bridesmaids proceed starting with the one who will stand farthest from the bride and ending with the maid or matron of honor. The ring-bearer and flower girl are next. The bride proceeds to the altar last, traditionally escorted by both of her parents: her father to her left and mother to her right. Family is seated at the front, and the bride's friends and relatives sit on the right, with those of the groom on the left.

Opening

The officiant will begin by announcing the couple and their intent to marry, and by welcoming the guests to participate as witnesses, supporters, and (if the ceremony is a religious one) with their prayers. During the opening, the official will also remind everyone of the importance and solemnity of the ceremony that is about to take place.

Main Body

The nature and meaning of marriage will usually be addressed here by the officiant, including its significance in light of God and the church if the ceremony is a religious one. The importance of the bride and groom's decision to become man and wife is laid out in this context. The officiant will also often include more casual comments on how he or she has gotten to know the couple, their fitness for one another, or even an entertaining story or two, especially if the couple has known the officiant for some time.

At this time, religious or other readings may be given by the officiant and any other individuals who the couple might have asked. For non-religious ceremonies, poems or other text with special meaning to the couple are often read.

Vows

Both the bride and groom face each other, hands held, and individually assert their intentions to marry and their commitment to the other. Some couples choose to use the familiar, time-worn vows that have been repeated by countless couples before them. Many feel that this timeless aspect to traditional vows often lends a greater weight to the words, underscoring their importance. Other couples opt instead to personalize their ceremony even more by writing and reciting their own vows, emphasizing the uniqueness of their relationship and expressing what their future together means for them. If you and your sweetheart decide to write your own vows, you'll usually need to run them by your officiant ahead of time.

After the exchange of their vows, the bride and groom are officially married in the Western Christian tradition.

<NOTE>

Selecting Your Escort(s)

The bride may choose to be escorted by the person or persons she feels most close to as parental or guiding figures. It can be anyone, and as many as you like (as long as the aisle is wide enough!). If your mother has remarried, for example, and you're close to your father, mother, and stepfather, feel free to walk with all three of them (your father on one side, your mother and stepfather on the other). You'll discuss this with everyone ahead of time of course, to make sure there's no objections on anyone's part. And if you feel that you made it to this point in your life on your own, you're welcome to walk down the aisle unescorted to reflect that.

</NOTE>

Exchange of Rings

At the direction of the officiant, the bride and groom each places a ring onto the finger of their betrothed, with an explanation of the action's significance and promise of commitment. The rings, an ancient tradition dating back for centuries, symbolize unity and an everlasting bond.

After the exchange of rings, the bride and groom are officially married in the Western Jewish tradition.

Unity Rituals

While the exchange of wedding rings is one of the most familiar unity rituals to us, many religions or cultures include others, and some couples–whether the ceremony is religious or not–add their own. The unity candle is a popular choice, for example.

Pronouncement of Union

The officiant will announce that the couple is officially wed, and will introduce the newlyweds to the guests. The officiant will also often let the new husband know that he can "kiss the bride" at this point.

Closing Remarks

This is the official wrap-up of the wedding ceremony, and the officiant will end with some closing words and a final prayer or blessing if the ceremony is a religious one.

<NOTE>

How Does the Unity Candle Ritual Work?

The unity candle is not associated with any single culture or religion, and so is often used by couples wether their ceremonies are religious or not. It's a strong symbol of their two lives coming together as one.

The unity candle is a large single candle that is arrange between two smaller tapers and displayed in the area where the ceremony will be performed. The smaller tapers may be lit prior to the ceremony, or a representative of each family (most often the mothers of the bride and groom) can come forward to light a taper after the vows and rings have been exchanged.

After the exchange of vows and rings, the bride and groom come forward towards the unity candle and each take the taper that their family has lit. They bring the two flames of the tapers together in unison and light the single unity candle in the center. Then they extinguish the tapers and place them back in their holders.

Couples often bring out their unity candle and relight it on their wedding anniversary or other special occasions.

</NOTE>

Recession

After the ceremony, the bride, groom, bridal party, and family leave the ceremony location in essentially the reverse order of the procession, except that the bride and groom leave first (hand in hand!) and everyone else follows in turn.

Personalizing Your Ceremony

The moment you say "I do" and become husband and wife is one of the biggest moments in your lives. Make sure how you do it reflects the two of you and your beliefs, in as unique and personal a way as you can.

Interfaith Ceremonies

The wedding ceremony will be the first of many blended rituals and traditions for you if you and your sweetheart are of different faiths. The communication, planning, and patience required will naturally be higher in these cases than others—between the two of you as well as your families. Be prepared for some extra effort in finding the right officiant, and the extra creativity and thoughtfulness you'll need to combine both sets of traditions in a way that won't ruffle any of your family's feathers. But the higher level of understanding and respect in each other's beliefs that results will only bring the two of you closer, and make your ceremony that much more special and unique.

The first step will be to talk to one another and discuss your concerns and preferences openly. Be considerate of each other's beliefs and try to share a genuine interest in both sets of traditions. This is a topic that concerns not only your wedding day but your lives together; make sure you're both clear on how you will integrate each other's faiths in your everyday lives and when raising your children.

When you're at a mutually comfortable point in this dialogue, you'll need to think about who will officiate your wedding. There's a couple different options here: you can look for an open-minded officiant from either of your religions (if the bride has known her parish priest since childhood, for example, you may want to start there) or you could have two officiants, one from each of your faiths. Having co-officiants is a good way to go if you can find willing clergy members on both sides who are receptive to your views and beliefs. They'll be able to work with you in the sometimes complicated task of combining the culture and tradition of each faith into your ceremony in an appropriate way. If you're having trouble with a starting point in locating the right officiants, ask around with those you know and trust: chances are someone else has searched for and found officiants willing to perform interfaith ceremonies, and you can obtain a reference. If officiants turn you down, ask them for references of others that might be more open to an interfaith ceremony.

Work with each other's families. You'll need to be especially patient and understanding, and may encounter resistance. Solicit suggestions from both sides, in order to make everyone feel involved. But above all, remember not to let others exert their own views and tell you what you're doing is wrong. This is between you and your sweetheart, and nobody else. Do what feels right to the two of you. Remember, you've talked about this and worked it out among yourselves ahead of time, and should stand firm on any decision you make.

If you can't find the right officiants to work with you to the extent you wish, consider taking the civil route. You'll be able to fully control what happens during your ceremony, and can pick and choose which traditions and rituals to add from each faith. Finding a civil officiant you like who is open to allowing any number and combination of religious customs that will suit you and your families shouldn't be difficult.

Cultural Additions

Your cultures are an important part of who you are, and they will influence the choices you make when planning your wedding. Discuss your ideas and options with each of your families and make sure your officiant is open to any cultural details and rituals that you may wish to include in your ceremony.

Considerations Worksheet: The Wedding Ceremony

Ceremony Budget: $ _____

Ceremony Date Options

First Option: _____ Season: _____

Second Option: _____ Season: _____

Third Option: _____ Season: _____

Ceremony Setting

☐ Hold Ceremony and Reception at a Place of Worship
☐ Hold Ceremony at a Place of Worship and Reception Elsewhere
☐ Hold Ceremony and Reception at Two Separate Non-Religious Sites
☐ Hold Ceremony in a Location at Your Reception Site

Ceremony Type

☐ Religious
☐ Civil

Vows

☐ Traditional
☐ Your Own

Traditional Elements You Wish to Cover

☐ Procession
☐ Opening
☐ Main Body
☐ Vows
☐ Exchange of Rings
☐ Unity Rituals
☐ Pronouncement of Union
☐ Closing Remarks
☐ Recession
☐ _____

Personalized Ceremony Elements/Rituals You Wish to Add (religious symbolism, cultural and interfaith traditions, etc.)

1. _____
2. _____
3. _____
4. _____
5. _____
6. _____
7. _____
8. _____
9. _____
10. _____

Notes: _____

_____

_____

_____

_____

_____

_____

_____

_____

Comparison Forms: Ceremony Location 1

Appointment Date: _____   Time: _____

Ceremony Location: _____

Address: _____

Site / Event Coordinator: _____   Officiant: _____

Email: _____   Phone: _____   Fax: _____

Website: _____

Date Available: _____   Time Spot(s) Available: _____

Guest Capacity: _____

Parking and Accessibility: _____

Musicians Recommended or Available: _____

_____

_____

Payment Policy: _____

Cancellation Policy: _____

Ceremony Location Fee (if any): $ _____   Donation?   ❑ Yes   ❑ No

Booking Deposit: $ _____   Required by: _____

Additional Fees: $ _____

Total Estimated Cost: $ _____

Comments: _____

_____

_____

_____

_____

_____

_____

_____

_____

_____

_____

_____

Comparison Forms: Ceremony Location 2

Appointment Date: _____ Time: _____

Ceremony Location: _____

Address: _____

Site / Event Coordinator: _____ Officiant: _____

Email: _____ Phone: _____ Fax: _____

Website: _____

Date Available: _____ Time Spot(s) Available: _____

Guest Capacity: _____

Parking and Accessibility: _____

Musicians Recommended or Available: _____

_____

_____

Payment Policy: _____

Cancellation Policy: _____

Ceremony Location Fee (if any): $ _____ Donation? ☐ Yes ☐ No

Booking Deposit: $ _____ Required by: _____

Additional Fees: $ _____

Total Estimated Cost: $ _____

Comments: _____

_____

_____

_____

_____

_____

_____

_____

_____

_____

Comparison Forms: Officiant 1

Appointment Date: _____   Time: _____

Officiant: _____   Years of Experience: _____

Address: _____
_____

Email: _____   Phone: _____   Fax: _____

Website: _____   Recommended by: _____

Date Available: _____   Time Spot(s) Available: _____

Documents Needed: _____
_____
_____
_____

Special Rules or Restrictions: _____
_____
_____

Pre-Wedding Requirements: _____
_____
_____

Payment Policy: _____

Cancellation Policy: _____

Officiant Fee (if any): $ _____   Donation?   ☐ Yes   ☐ No

Booking Deposit:$ _____   Required by: _____

Additional Fees: $ _____

Total Estimated Cost: $ _____

Comments: _____
_____
_____
_____
_____
_____
_____

Comparison Forms: Officiant 2

Appointment Date: _____ Time: _____

Officiant: _____ Years of Experience: _____

Address: _____
_____

Email: _____ Phone: _____ Fax: _____

Website: _____ Recommended by: _____

Date Available: _____ Time Spot(s) Available: _____

Documents Needed: _____
_____
_____
_____

Special Rules or Restrictions: _____
_____
_____
_____

Pre-Wedding Requirements: _____
_____
_____
_____

Payment Policy: _____

Cancellation Policy: _____

Officiant Fee (if any): $ _____ Donation? ☐ Yes ☐ No

Booking Deposit: $ _____ Required by: _____

Additional Fees: $ _____

Total Estimated Cost: $ _____

Comments: _____
_____
_____
_____
_____
_____
_____
_____

Contact Sheet: Ceremony Location

Date Booked: _____

Ceremony Location: _____

Address: _____

_____

Staple Business Card

Site/Event Coordinator: _____

Email: _____

Phone: _____

Fax: _____

Website: _____

Ceremony Date: _____

Exclusive ceremony location reservation time from _____ to _____

Package Description: _____

_____

Special Instructions: _____

_____

_____

Ceremony Requirements

1: _____ Date Due: _____

2: _____ Date Due: _____

3: _____ Date Due: _____

4: _____ Date Due: _____

Total Cost (if any): $ _____

Deposit: $ _____ Date Paid: _____

Balance: $ _____ Date Due: _____

Notes: _____

_____

_____

Contact Sheet: Officiant

Date Booked:

Officiant:

Address:

Email:

Phone:

Fax:

Website:

Ceremony Date:

Time:

Staple Business Card

Special Instructions:

Meetings Schedule

1:                    Date: Time:

2:                    Date: Time:

3:                    Date: Time:

4:                    Date: Time:

Total Cost (if any): $

Deposit: $ Date Paid:

Balance: $ Date Due:

Notes:

Chapter 9

Plan the Party: Find a Reception Location and Lay Out the Details

- What Type of Reception?

- Finding the Right Location

- Share It! Informing Your Guests

- Planning Your Reception

- e-Plan It! Use Your e-Resources:

  Online Location Searches
  Your Website's Reception Page

- Worksheets:

  Considerations Worksheet: The Wedding Reception
  Comparison Forms: Reception Location
  Contact Sheet: Reception Location

The bulk of your wedding planning, and therefore this book, will be devoted towards planning the celebration that follows your ceremony. We'll give you a bird's eye view of what to consider and expect in this chapter, and leave the big decisions and details up to you and your wedding vision. Discuss all your options together, and have fun planning the party!

What Type of Reception?

Your wedding vision and budget will determine what type of post-ceremony bash you plan on having. Most of the details that will guide you in narrowing down your search for the perfect setting should already be fairly well decided: check your notes for Chapter 6, "Style and Preferences: Capture Your Wedding Vision". You'll see that we've already considered topics like guest count, formality, date and time, meal type, and more. So how does this help you in finding the right spot?

<CROSS-REFERENCE>
Review our suggestions for capturing your wedding vision in Chapter 6.
</CROSS-REFERENCE>

Time Plays a Role

The time you hold your wedding will affect the formality and atmosphere of your reception. It will also affect your cost. Holding your reception during an earlier time of day is suited for less formal breakfasts, brunches and luncheons, and will generally cost less than holding your reception in the evening if you plan on serving a dinner. On the other hand, evening cocktail parties or champagne-and-cake affairs can be more on the formal side and still be easier on your budget than a sit-down dinner.

<TIP>

Book the Whole Day

If at all possible, find a location that you can reserve by the day. You don't want to be sandwiched in between other events, or have to worry about wrapping up your reception on time for the next group to take over. Knowing the place is yours for the day will be one less thing on your mind and will ease the timeline burden.

</TIP>

Breakfast or Brunch - Start Between 10 and 11 a.m.

Following an early morning ceremony, breakfast or brunch is provided for your guests. This is a relaxed, more casual affair. Have plenty of fresh fruit, juice, coffee, and tea on hand. Alcohol is optional; you might serve champagne, mimosas, punch, wine, or bloody marys.

Luncheon - Start Between 12 and 2 p.m.

Held after a late morning or noon ceremony, and similar to a brunch reception. Sandwiches, cheeses, salads, and cold cuts can be served in a very inexpensive buffet, or consider a light sit-down meal preceded by a cocktail hour with hors d'oeuvres. An espresso or cappuccino bar is a nice addition to cake-cutting time.

Tea - Start Between 2 and 3 p.m.

Often the least expensive reception you can have, and well-suited for especially large guest counts. Provide coffee, tea and, optionally, wine or champagne—along with plenty of finger foods, tea sand-wiches, and your wedding cake.

Dinner - Start Between 4 and 6 p.m.

The meal for a dinner reception can be sit-down or buffet style, and is often preceded by a cocktail hour that allows guests to chat with friends, go through your receiving line, and mingle. To keep costs down, consider limiting the drinks served to just beer and wine.

Cocktail or Dessert Party - Start Between 5 and 6 p.m.

Similar to a tea party but often more formal. You'd typically serve champagne, wine, and beer along with your wedding cake in a location that reflects your style and formality (a home or garden cocktail party will have a different air than one in a grand ballroom with a jazz orchestra, for example). Depending on your budget, you can also offer an open bar, passed hors d'oeuvres, and even a dessert table in addition to your wedding cake. Like tea receptions, cocktail parties are well suited for a large number of guests and a tighter budget, while still allowing you to have a more formal affair if your wedding vision is so aligned.

Indoors or Outdoors?

Some of the most enchanting locations can be found outdoors. Alfresco possibilities include wineries, beaches, parks, gardens, or the courtyard of a charming old mansion.

You probably have a good idea as to your preference for an outdoor reception after coming out of our discussion "Are You In or Out?" in Chapter 6. A reception party in the big outdoors, whether under a blue sky or under the stars, lends a particularly dramatic and unforgettable touch. Just make sure your wedding date is set for a warm month (no winter beach parties unless you're going to be south of the border!) and that you have a backup plan in case the weather decides to make things complicated. Also, keep in mind that outdoor venues usually end up being more expensive since you'll need to take care of additional items like tents, generators, lighting, rental equipment, and so forth.

When looking at outdoor venues, ask about permits you may need and if there are any amplified music or alcohol restrictions. Will they allow you to stake a tent? What equipment and items do the venue provide, and what will you need to rent? (ask about chairs, tables, lights, and so forth). As with any venue, make sure you *look* at the equipment, too: folding plastic chairs may not suit your formal wedding vision, for example. Check for on-site event rooms or other buildings that can be available to you in case of a chance storm or ill-timed shower. In our upcoming discussion on "Finding the Right Location" we'll give you more tips on things to watch out for.

Sit-down Meal or Buffet?

Depending on your budget and preferences, decide what type of dining (if any) you'll be offering to your guests. Having a good idea of your culinary demands will assist you in knowing what to look for when it comes to searching for the perfect venue and finding a caterer. You'll find that some venues have their own catering services available. Certain styles will lend themselves better to your reception time than others; a stand-up buffet, for example, is particularly suited to tea and cocktail parties. In terms of cost, buffets will be easier on the budget than sit-down meals, and stand-up buffets—with less rentals and equipment to worry about—will be the least costly of all.

Sit-Down

Sit-down receptions are those in which guests are served by waitstaff, and usually—though not always—have more of a formal air. Some feel that this setup limits the interaction of guests and quiets the overall party, although we've been to plenty of lively sit-down affairs. It certainly helps to have a well thought-out seating plan, and many couples include a cocktail hour so that everyone can mingle and socialize before dinner.

Buffet

During a buffet reception, guests help themselves to food and drinks that are set out on buffet tables or stations (see the food stations idea below). Your guests can have set places at their tables, similar to the sit-down style, or may be allowed to choose their own seats. For less formal affairs during which mostly finger foods are served (cheeses, fruits, sandwiches and so forth), you might even opt for a standing buffet style. Standing buffets offer fewer seating areas as it is anticipated that most guests will be milling about and standing while eating.

<CROSS-REFERENCE>
Learn more about catering and your culinary choices in chapter 11, "Choose Your Food, Beverages, and Catering".
</CROSS-REFERENCE>

Food Stations

Your caterer or site manager will be able to best suggest ways to arrange your buffet tables. It will depend on the number of guests and the layout of your site, but keep in mind that the main goals include adding to the overall atmosphere of the location and avoiding long lines for your guests. One fun idea is to have several small buffet tables placed throughout your site, each with their own theme and food type. You might have a fruit station, a pasta station, or a seafood station, for example. Beautifully decorated, they add to the location's décor and offer your guests a fun way to eat with a variety of choices.

Finding the Right Location

Finding the right setting for your big day will take time and a lot of careful consideration. Keep in mind that the best spots book up fast (a year and a half is not too early to reserve your location), so it's important to be as efficient as possible when comparing your options.

Location Types

What type of location suits you? Even with a clearly defined wedding vision you may have many options and favorites to pick from. In order to make the best use of your time, eliminate anything you feel is clearly not compatible with your preferences before looking into and comparing venues. Below are some of the more popular venue choices, but feel free to get creative and choose a spot that's more personalized. Have something cool and unique in mind? Go for it! Regardless where you look, make sure to consider our discussion on "What to Look For" later in this section.

Church Halls

If you're holding your ceremony in a place of worship, ask if they have an adjoining event hall or social room. Church halls can be one of the least expensive venue options, and it's convenient to have the reception at the same location as the ceremony instead of having your guests relocate. As with all locations, make sure you do a thorough walkthrough to verify that the room is suitable for a wedding reception and meets your approval. Ask about any restrictions they might have on music and alcohol.

Hotels, Event Halls, Country Clubs, and Restaurants

These traditional standbys have plenty of wedding experience and offer a wealth of information for you to draw upon. Most such venues will offer an event coordinator, on-site catering (in a restaurant this is a given), bar service, and sometimes even a florist and bakery. The advantage to this package approach is that you'll be working with experience and will be relieved of the burdens of finding and coordinating all the vendors yourself. On the other hand, you'll generally be stuck with the venue's schedules, style, vendors, and often pre-established menu options, which may not match up with your own wedding vision and preferences. It may not be so easy—or downright impossible—to bring in your own flowers, alcohol, or cake. They may charge a steep cake-cutting fee, or a corkage fee for outside alcohol, as a way of persuading you to use their own services. Make sure you ask about what fees are involved if you were to bring in your own vendors.

Even if you'll be using your venue's on-site services for things like catering, decorations, flowers, and so forth, follow the vendor chapters of this book in the same way you would if you were hiring your own vendors separately. Put the facility's catering services to the test by taking into consideration everything discussed in Chapter 11. Request a cake tasting and ask the same questions as described in Chapter 18. If anyone doesn't make the cut, look for an outside vendor.

Sit down with the site coordinator and find out exactly what can and will be provided by the site. Chairs, tables, decorations, china, flatware, votive candles, potted trees, and arches are just some of the items that may be included in the price. If items are not included, ask how much it would cost to add them, and see if you can bring in outside rentals. Compare the facility's price to those of a rental company before adding anything extra to your package.

Wineries

Breathtaking views, charming grounds, historical buildings and, of course, great wine! What's not to love about a winery reception? If you live in or near wine country, you'd be well served to look into this dramatic and flexible option. Most wineries have a number of different locations on site that would serve well for ceremonies or receptions, indoors and outdoors, depending on the effect you're looking for. The ease of moving the party plans outdoors to indoors, from a garden setting to a historical tasting room (or vice versa), will ensure that you have a great setting regardless of the weather.

Most wineries, for obvious reasons, will require that the choice of wine (and champagne, typically) served at your event is exclusively theirs. Ask for a tasting of the winery's goods before settling on the location.

Home

What can be more personal than a home wedding? Imagine tying the knot under the big tree out back where you used to climb as a kid, and then enjoying a catered dinner beneath a beautifully decorated tent beside the pool. If you or your parents own a spacious, beautiful pad, this is an option you may want to consider. With most venues you pay to add personality, but at home the personality is already there…free of charge! Just keep in mind that—as with any outdoor reception—the cost of all those rentals (chairs, tables, dishware, heaters, and so forth) add up quickly, and you'll need a backup plan in case the weather sours. Can everyone be moved inside the house, or can the area be tented? Some other considerations are parking issues, neighbors (let them know what's going on, or invite them over!), and the fact that the entire coordinating burden will be on your shoulders; there's no site coordinator at home, so you may want to hire a professional wedding coordinator to help out. As with any outdoor location, make sure you have adequate kitchen and restroom facilities.

Parks, Beaches, and Gardens

Dramatic and unforgettable, outdoor venues really are spectacular. Whether it's a gorgeous beach setting, lush garden, poolside at a fancy resort, or the breathtaking view of a park…the romantic possibilities abound. Remember that outdoor weddings will generally cost more, considering the added rentals, tenting costs, facilities (portable restrooms and kitchen), and any equipment you'll need: heaters, lighting, a generator, and so forth. Some locations will have all of the above available for you already, while others will require you to bring in everything and the kitchen sink (literally). When checking out different venues, make sure you're comparing apples to apples and considering any extra rental costs you'll need. Some of the cost will depend on what your caterer can provide. Discuss your options at length with a representative of the site itself (be it the parks and recreation office or event manager, depending on your location). Find out what they can and can't offer, as well as any restrictions on music, alcohol, timing, and the like. Will you need any permits? Have a rental company or two send out a representative to meet you at the location so that they can give you an estimate on the electrical, tenting, and facilities items you'll need.

Mansions, Estates, and Historical Buildings

Grand old estates, castles, and mansions are picturesque and charming. They provide a unique and memorable setting for your big day, as well as some fantastic wedding photographs! You'll usually also get the added bonus of beautiful grounds that make for great romantic walks and excursive strolls. Make sure to find out which, if any, parts of the building are off-limits, and whether or not you'll need to provide a security deposit in the case of property damage. The great thing is that with all the visual beauty of the location, you probably won't need to bring in much decoration.

Other Ideas

Consider having your wedding on the move! A yacht, cruise ship, New Orleans trolley, or other mode of transportation can be a romantic way to mirror the two of you "moving forward" in your lives. How about a nightclub, a museum, aquarium, or the zoo? If you're an alumnus of a local university, you might want to check into renting out a picturesque and memorable building there. Many places will have event staff on hand to assist in the coordination of your reception. Some will have catering staff and plenty of equipment available, and others will require you to hire your own and rent (or buy) all your gear. Keep an open mind when considering your venue options, and try to find the location that says *you* more than any other.

> **\<CROSS-REFERENCE\>**
> For a discussion on finding great ceremony sites, take a peek at the previous chapter.
> **\</CROSS-REFERENCE\>**

Where to Start

Whether your reception location is the same as that of your ceremony or not, follow the steps we outlined in the previous chapter for finding ceremony spots. Ask for references from those you trust, look up venues online, and check with your other wedding professionals for suggestions. Build an initial list of potentials and check out their websites or give them a call and speak to each location's event manager, if possible. Eliminate those who are not available on your date, don't meet your needs, or are obviously not on par with your wedding vision. You'll need to visit the locations and do some face time with the management staff to narrow the choices down to the right spot for you; we'll give you some advice on what to look for and some questions to ask towards the end of this section.

e-Resource

Online Location Searches

It's a lot faster checking out the websites of potential venues to collect the preliminary info you need than it is calling each one and trying to catch the appropriate event manager. Browse each location's website and gather all the main facts: can it hold your maximum guest count? Does it provide the specific features you're looking for? How's the parking? What restrictions are there?

Check out photographs of the site online; hopefully they'll have a wedding section with photos of other weddings that have taken place there. How does it look? How much would it cost to book? Are you interested?

Jot down your potentials, and eliminate the ones that don't grab you. You'll need to actually visit the venues to see them firsthand before booking of course, but using the web to eliminate as many as possible now will save you a lot of time and allow you to direct your energy to those best suited to your vision.

Venue Directories

In the previous chapter we introduced these as well. WeddingLocation.com allows you to submit detailed search criteria to obtain results narrowed down by location, guest number, cost, time of day, and more. Country Club Reception (www.countryclubreceptions.com) provides a detailed list of country clubs in your area as a comparison chart of amenities and features. And for those in California, definitely look into the online version of "Here Comes the Guide" (www.herecomes-theguide.com).

The Search Engines

Give local search engines a try as well. Google Local and CitySearch are two services that we mentioned previously. Look up keywords like "wedding reception locations", "banquet facilities", "event halls", "hotels", "historic locations", and so forth. Add your city and state to the keyword list if you need to.

The Wedding Portal Sites

Use the same resources we suggested in the previous chapter when it comes to venue hunting on the web. Check out the local directories offered by the big portal websites (The Knot, WeddingChannel.com, and Modern Bride are three of the biggest).

What to Look For

Just like finding your one true love, an accomplishment you've since mastered, finding the perfect location for your wedding requires that you consider every option until you find the one that fits you like a glove. Go down your list of potential venues and set up an appointment with the management of each to do a thorough walkthrough and to ask plenty of questions. As you're checking out venues, keep the following in mind:

Compatibility with Your Style and Theme

Your location doesn't have to match your color palette exactly, and you'll be adding your own decorations anyway (flowers, candles, and so forth). But watch out for styles that would definitely clash with yours. Check the colors of the carpet, wall, seats, and curtains...are they compatible? For a classic, elegant look, neutral colors or black-and-white work best. For a spring wedding, look for soft, light pastels. Find out if you can put decorations on the walls and ask about what things you can and can't change.

Guest Capacity

This is a big reason we wanted to nail down a guest count before looking at venues: you need to know if the location you're considering is going to be the right size (of course, if you fall completely in love with a spot, you can always work backwards and tailor your guest list to fit it). If it's too small, you're either just plain not going to fit, or you'll feel cramped the whole time and won't have enough dancing room. If your guest list is small and intimate, a location that's too large can make the affair feel awkward and lonely. Consider any columns or pillars, too: will they block the view? If the location is divided up into smaller, disjointed spaces, it could affect the flow of your party as well. Try to imagine how people will be moving around and interacting.

Keep in mind that the place you're looking at might seem huge when it's empty, but after putting in all the tables, chairs, catering stations, dance floor, buffet area, DJ station, and so forth, there's going to be a lot less room. Make sure the space is large enough so that your guests won't be rubbing elbows all the time. Ask to see pictures of the location during a wedding of a comparable size to your own.

Parking and Accessibility

Make sure that the location has adequate parking facilities for your guest count. A lack of good parking at the site itself isn't necessarily a deal-breaker, but you'll have to spend a bit more money in order to arrange valet parking or shuttle service. If the venue is located off a main road or otherwise secluded, make sure you've provided careful directions. You can include this—in addition to giving guests a heads-up regarding valet parking or shuttle service—on your website's reception page, which we'll discuss in a bit.

> **\<CROSS-REFERENCE\>**
> We discussed coming to a decision regarding a maximum guest count in Chapter 6, "Style and Preference". In Chapter 7, "Manage Your Guest List and Attendants", we gave you some tips on building your guest list.
> **\</CROSS-REFERENCE\>**

The View

Sure, it's a given that the practical stuff needs to be addressed, but looks are important too...and the thing most likely to make or break a location for you is going to be the view. Rolling hills, a gorgeous expanse of ocean, breathtaking architecture, or a luxuriously designed interior will lend character to your reception and make it that much more memorable. When you look at photographs of the venue and do your walkthroughs, keep the lighting in mind. Try to see it during the same time of day your reception will be held. A location at night by candlelight will look a lot different than the same spot in the daytime. Darkness will hide imperfections and aged carpets, and the sun flowing in from the windows can transform the entire mood and character of a room.

On-Site Services

Most event halls and hotels will include a full-time event coordinator and services such as on-site catering, bar service, and possibly even a florist. Find out if these are included in the base price or charged at an additional fee. And ask about bringing in your own caterer or professional in case the services they offer don't match up with your style and preferences. Are there any cake-cutting or corkage fees?

As long as you're cool with the services they offer, these combined package deals can make things easier for you; you won't need to hunt down vendors and coordinate them yourselves, for example. Make sure you go through the relative chapters of this book anyway to verify your contact points and stay aware of pitfalls. Don't hesitate to bring in an outside vendor if the one they provide for you doesn't make the cut.

Accommodations and Facilities

It's a much overlooked detail, and compensating for a lack of restrooms or kitchen space will cost you, so make sure you add this to your list of considerations. What condition are the restrooms? Are there enough for your guest amount? You may need to bring in mobile ones, but don't shudder at the thought of those unsightly blue construction site portables. Rental companies offer complete trailers with elegant stone countertop restrooms. If the kitchen facilities aren't sufficient, your caterer might also need to bring in their own setup, which will likely add to the cost.

See if the electrical needs of your DJ and lighting will be met, or if you'll have to bring in a generator. Talk to your site manager about the power available and if you need to, bring in the representative of a local rental company to check things out and get generator quotes. If you're going to be indoors, ask if you have control over the lighting and temperature. You'll want to heat the facility if your wedding date is in the winter months, and air-condition it if it'll be summer. If you're marrying outdoors, see if the facility has space heaters available in case the evening gets chilly. Your rental company should have quotes for these as well.

Questions to Ask Site Managers

When you're looking at venues, make sure you speak with the site manager; don't just go and wander around, and don't settle for talking with anyone other than the person who would be working with you to coordinate your event there. The best thing to do is make appointments. It will save time, ensure that you're speaking to the right person, and allow you to arrange all your visits to fit your schedule.

When talking to the site manager, ask yourself if you like the person. Is he or she enthusiastic about your wedding day and your vision? Remember that you'll be dealing with this person a lot, so make sure the chemistry is there. Does the person seem receptive to your ideas and questions, and do they seem willing to be flexible and compromise to make the day the one you envision? Or, are they rigid in their policies and cold to your ideas, with a "we don't do it that way here" attitude?

Here are some questions to ask:

- Exactly what is included with the venue reservation? Will a caterer, bar, baker or florist be provided? How about a site coordinator?

- Can we bring in our own caterer, baker, or other vendor? Is there a fee for this, such as a cake-cutting fee? How much?

- Can we bring our own alcohol? Is there a corkage fee? How much?

- What sort of items and equipment do you provide? (ask about everything: chairs, tables, linens, china, glasses, flatware) Is there an added fee for any of this? How much?

- Do you offer a discount for certain dates or times?

- If we prefer, can we hold our ceremony at the location as well?

- Will there be other weddings at the location on the same day? (If possible, look for a place that will be yours the whole day; you really don't want to have to worry about starting late or hurrying to wrap up your celebration so the next group can come in)

- Is there a kitchen facility available for our caterer? (You caterer might need to check the facilities to make sure they're adequate. It helps to find a caterer who has experience at the venue you're considering)

- Are there adequate restroom facilities for my guest count? (Make sure you check these out yourself)

- Is there enough heating and lighting if the location is outdoors? Do you offer space heaters, and is there an added fee for this?

- Is there enough power available to run sound equipment, lights and everything else? If we need a generator, do you provide one? How much?

- Do you provide a coat check?

- If the area is outdoors, can we put up a tent? Do you offer one, and can we see photos of it? (Check that the tent is the style you want; there are a lot of styles, and rental companies can show you all your options. You also want to make sure that the tent isn't overly aged or ragged in spots).

- If the area is outdoors, is there an indoor spot we can use as a backup location in case of bad weather? Can we see it?

- Are there any music restrictions? What are they?

- Are there any alcohol restrictions? What are they?

- What kind of room and table decorations are available for us to use? Can we hang decorations up on the walls?

- Do you have enough parking for our guest count? Is there a valet service provided, and if so is this an extra fee? Can we hire and arrange our own valet service?

- Do you have full liability insurance? (You don't want to be held responsible for anything that might happen during your event. If the place isn't fully insured, check out WedSafe at www.wedsafe.com, which will allow you to purchase a very reasonably priced, bulletproof liability policy for wedding day venues)

- What's your payment policy? How much will it cost to book our date? (The deposit will usually be around 10% to 25% of your overall rental cost. If it's more than 50%, look somewhere else)

- What's your cancellation policy? (You need to know this. If you have to cancel, some venues will refund most or all of your deposit as long as you let them know early enough for them to book the date with someone else)

Get It in Writing: Your Venue Contract

Make sure you've done a full walk-through and have spent plenty of face time with the person who will be actually working with you to coordinate your reception. If you both love the place, have done your site inspection, asked your questions, and are cool with everything, it's time to pay the deposit and sign the contract. Congratulations on booking your venue!

Your written contract should include the date and time of your wedding, the name of the representative who will be there to assist and coordinate on your wedding day, as well as the name of a substitute in case of emergency. There should be an itemized account of everything included in your package, as well as the cost for each. This should be everything that the site includes: service providers, tables, glasses, linens...everything. The contract should also include anything that you've orally agreed to. Make absolutely sure it's all in writing. If there is more than one room or location at the site, the contract should specify which location you'll be at (like "Main Ballroom", "Event Hall B", or "Grand Terrace". If you're booking the whole place, the contract should say that, too). The venue's cancellation policy should also be clearly specified.

Share It! Informing Your Guests

In the previous chapter, we covered the advantages of posting your location info on your wedding website, as a central resource for your guests. Cut down on the repetitive venue descriptions and phone directions by making photos, maps, website links, and interesting side-notes available to everyone on your website.

e-Resource

Your Website's Reception Page

Your wedding website service should provide an interface that allows you to customize a page for your reception. Add anything that you feel would be helpful or interesting to your guests: a map, directions, photos, maybe even a side-note on why you selected the spot. As you get questions from friends and family, add the information to your website for everyone's benefit.

Your guests will definitely appreciate having all of this information, as well as the ceremony info you posted in the previous chapter, available to them in such an accessible way. It will also free you up from the time you'd otherwise be spending giving directions and location details on your own.

Your wedding website's reception page allows you to easily provide all the necessary time and address information to your guests, as well as photos, maps, and some fun side-notes.

Planning Your Reception

Even the most spontaneous-seeming wedding reception is the result of a large amount of precise, almost militaristic preparation and planning. From creating your seating chart to setting up a full reception timeline to ensuring that all your vendors are coordinated and know exactly what to do, where to do it, and when...it takes effort, patience, and a lot of organization. Your site's event coordinator will help (and if your venue doesn't offer one, you might want to hire one anyway) but you're the one who will be making the choices so that your big day really does turn out to be the event you envision.

The bulk of your wedding planning will be committed towards preparing for your reception, and most of this book's chapters and resources are devoted to some part of it. Keep your wedding vision clearly in mind as you progress, and remember not to feel like you have to include anything you don't want to. Your day is just that: your day. Include what you want, do it the way you want to, and enjoy yourselves.

What Makes a Reception?

So what makes a wedding reception, anyway? There's plenty of traditions and rituals involved, many of which you've no doubt experienced yourselves as guests at other weddings. Think about the elements of each wedding you've attended that you liked and disliked. Your own wedding reception will be a combination of traditional elements, personal touches, and the influence of your cultures. A basic idea of a typical Western style wedding follows, just to give you an overview of what to expect. You'll tailor your own timeline later on, but you can use the framework here as a starting point.

Example of a Dinner Reception

The order of events will be different depending on the type of reception you'll be having. A typical reception includes dancing and a meal, and may go something like the following:

- Guests arrive at the venue. The bride and groom may choose to greet them in a receiving line.

- Cocktail hour commences as soon as guests begin arriving. Hors d'oeuvres are passed and/or available in stations for guests to graze while they mingle. A band, instrumentalist, or DJ may play background music.

- The site manager, DJ, or band leader notifies guests to take their seats or invites them into the main dining area.

- The bride and groom, along with the bridal party, may be announced.

- Dinner is served or the buffet is opened. Background music may be played.

- Toasts are made.

- As dinner ends, the bride and groom have their first dance, followed by the bride and her father, then the groom and his mother.

- The floor is opened and guests are invited onto the floor.

- The cake is cut by the bride and groom (half an hour or so after dancing begins).

- Cake is served to the guests.

- The bride and groom may choose to toss the bouquet (and garter).

- Open dancing commences.

- The bride and groom stay to the last dance and bid farewell to their guests, or leave beforehand in a getaway vehicle.

Example of a Breakfast, Brunch, or Cake-and-Champagne Reception

If you're having an early breakfast or brunch reception, or if you're planning on an evening cake-and-champagne affair, things might go something like this:

- Guests arrive at the venue. The bride and groom may choose to greet them in a receiving line.

- If cocktails or other beverages are to be served it is done right away, along with any hors d'oeuvres so that guests can sip and munch while they mingle. A band or instrumentalist might perform, or background music may be played by a DJ.

- Breakfast or brunch is served, or the buffet is opened.

- Champagne is served, a blessing may be given, and toasts are made.

- The cake is cut by the bride and groom.

- Cake is served to the guests.

- The bride and groom may choose to toss the bouquet (and garter).

- The bride and groom stay to bid farewell to their guests, or leave beforehand in a getaway vehicle.

Greeting Your Guests

Spending time greeting and accepting the happy congratulations of all your guests is a big part of your reception. You can do this by "making the rounds" during the reception, approaching every table and greeting your guests one group at a time. Your photographer can follow as you do, snapping shots as you greet.

You can also greet your guests in a formal receiving line if you prefer, either during your reception's cocktail hour, or directly following the ceremony. Receiving lines work by lining up outside the ceremony location doors or in the lobby of your reception area along with your parents and, optionally, best man and maid of honor. Greet all your guests as they file by in turn.

Have a guestbook and pen stationed where everyone will see it and be able to sign their best wishes. You may want to enlist the help of a teenage relative to oversee the guestbook table and make sure everyone signs.

The Cocktail Hour

The cocktail hour is a great chance for guests to mingle and chat, especially if the reception is seated with assigned places. It also offers you a chance to steal away and take photographs while guests make their way over from the ceremony. Drinks can be served along with hors d'oeuvres so that people

\<NOTE\>

Receiving Line Order

In a formal receiving line, the bride's parents traditionally stand first—starting with the mother of the bride—followed by the groom's parents, then the bride and groom, and finally the maid of honor and best man. You can always swap and stand before your parents if you're hosting the event yourselves and most of the guests are friends of yours rather than your parents.

\</NOTE\>

have something to sip and munch on. If the reception is held during the summer months (and especially if it is outdoors), consider having a tea and lemonade station as well.

A nice touch during the cocktail hour is to have background "mood" music played by a band, instrumentalist, or your DJ.

Seating Your Guests

Decide if you want to arrange the seating of your guests with a seating chart, or if you'll let them decide for themselves. Seating charts are great for taking the guesswork out of the process and ensuring that everyone has an appropriate spot, in a group they'll be comfortable with. You control who sits closest to your head table (the table where the two of you will be basking in the limelight) and ensure that those you feel would get along the best are grouped together. You can also arrange it so that any guests who might not necessarily be on the best of terms are spaced far apart. Some couples group all the bride's guests in one half of the room and all the groom's in the other, although we like combining everyone together (you're joining the two families, after all).

<TIP>

Don't let the cocktail hour last longer than an hour. Guests will start getting restless, and you don't want people drinking so much before dinner that they're drunk and unruly for the rest of the reception.

</TIP>

For very small or informal weddings a seating chart is not necessary but can be a useful organizational tool for you, whether your reception is a sit-down meal or buffet. It's another way you can control the otherwise chaotic hustle and bustle of your guests on the big day.

Once your guest list is more or less solidified, create placecards for each of your guests. These can be arranged on a table in a location everyone will pass as they arrive; either at the entrance of the main dining area or in some other visible location. Each placecard will have the guest's name and an appropriate table identifier. While the most common identifier is simply a number card placed on each table, feel free to be creative here and add something more personal. Name each table after a favorite location of yours, or tie it into your wedding theme. If your reception follows a travel theme, for example, name each table after a favorite spot you've been to. Add a little descriptor to the table cards so that your guests know why each spot is special for you. It'll be a great conversation piece for them, and it's a way for everyone to learn a little more about the two of you. Have fun with it!

Announcement and Introduction

After everyone takes their seats, the DJ, bandleader, or site coordinator (whoever is acting as the "master of ceremonies" at your event) will normally take the mike and announce each member of your bridal party, often in the order they walked the aisle at your ceremony. The final members of your entourage to be introduced is usually the maid of honor and best man, with the two of you—appearing for the first time as husband and wife—introduced last of all.

Toasts to You

Toasts are often done once the guests have had a go at the buffet, or after the first course has been served if the meal is a sit-down one. It can be scheduled before the food if you like, or during the cocktail hour once everyone has been served a glass of champagne. The best man traditionally takes the mike first (although the bride's father may start off as well). You'll decide ahead of time who you'd like to speak, and whether or not you want it to be an open mike afterwards (discuss this beforehand with your DJ or bandleader). Typical toasters are the maid of honor, close friends, and your parents. The two of you will go last of all: it's your chance to thank everyone for their presence, gifts, and good wishes.

The Meal

Your meal might be a buffet, a three course sit-down experience, finger food stations, or just the cake. You'll work the details out with your caterer; just make sure that they're in the loop regarding your timeline and reception site floor plan. E-mail or fax copies of both and alert them anytime something changes.

> **<CROSS-REFERENCE>**
> We'll discuss all about choosing and working with your caterer in Chapter 11.
> **</CROSS-REFERENCE>**

Your First Dance and the Parents' Dances

It's time to take your first dance as a married couple! Pick a favorite song, one that means something special to you. Feel free to forego this tradition if you'll be anxious or uncomfortable cutting the rug solo while everyone watches. And don't feel the need to dance the entire song; you can always arrange a hand-off (the bride to her father for the father-daughter dance) midway through.

Cake Cutting

The sharing of food as a symbol of your union is an ancient one. The tradition is to serve each other a bit of your celebratory confection, symbolizing the support you'll be providing one another over the coming years. When cutting the cake, the bride holds the cake-cutter and the groom places his hand over hers, and the first piece is carved out to be shared by the two of you. The caterer will then take over, serving the rest of the cake to your guests.

> **<CROSS-REFERENCE>**
> Design a cake to remember in Chapter 18.
> **</CROSS-REFERENCE>**

Bouquet and Garter Toss

During the bouquet toss, all the single ladies get a chance to catch the bride's bouquet. As tradition goes, whoever does so will be the next to wed. You'll probably want to keep your actual bouquet and preserve it, so have your florist create a second, smaller bouquet just for the tossing.

If you're also planning a garter toss, you'll have the single guys group together in the same way for a chance to catch the bride's garter, which is typically removed from the bride's leg by the groom while your guests look on. Most garter sets come in two's: one to keep and a smaller one to toss. If you're

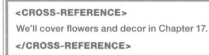

> **<CROSS-REFERENCE>**
> We'll cover flowers and decor in Chapter 17.
> **</CROSS-REFERENCE>**

making your own garter and want to keep it, prepare another one for the tossing.

Remember that these traditions, like all wedding rituals, are completely optional. Don't hesitate to leave them off your agenda if they don't fly with your wedding vision.

Everyone on the Floor!

After your first dance and the parents' dances, the floor will open and the party gets going. A good DJ or band will read your crowd and keep music up that you and your guests want to hear. You'll meet up with your entertainment crew ahead of time to settle on the style and overall type of tunes you prefer, as well as to go over must-play and no-play lists. Some couples are of the opinion that you just *gotta* have the chicken dance, YMCA, and electric slide in your musical arsenal, for example...while others warn their entertainment people to steer clear or else!

Departure Considerations

> **<CROSS-REFERENCE>**
> Get the scoop on your music and entertainment in Chapter 14.
> **</CROSS-REFERENCE>**

Whether you decide to party on with your guests until the last dance, or cut out early in a getaway vehicle, make sure to have a change of clothes stored away. Designate helpers ahead of time to transport your gifts from the reception site, return the groom's tux, and make sure that the bridal gown gets home safe. If you do plan to make a dramatic getaway, have the bridal party or some other creative force decorate your departure vehicle with "Just Married" messages and anything else that suits them (within reason!). Many couples these days decide to stay to the end of the reception—it's their party after all—and spend as much time as possible with their friends and family before heading out for the honeymoon.

Your Reception Timeline

> **<CROSS-REFERENCE>**
> For more on your wedding reception timeline and to see an example, check out Chapter 21, "Countdown Considerations".
> **</CROSS-REFERENCE>**

Most wedding receptions last four to five hours. Between the two of you, your site coordinator, and your caterer, you'll need to come up with a fairly detailed timeline of events for your reception. A copy of this timeline will be given out to all your vendors: caterer, DJ or band, photographer, videographer, and so forth. It will keep everyone on the same page, and ensure that whoever is acting as the master of ceremonies for your affair (typically the DJ or bandleader) keeps things moving on the right schedule.

Suggestions and Cost-saving Tips

Most of the chapters in this book cover some aspect of the reception, and all are geared towards saving you time and money. Here's some food for thought up front.

Buy your own plates, linens and table settings to avoid costly rental fees. It's often less expensive than renting if you buy in bulk online or from a discount retailer, and you'll be able to use them for future parties. Consider eBay (www.ebay.com) for this and other reception party supplies.

Having your wedding in the off-season, in the morning, or on Friday or Sunday will usually save you some bucks on venues and vendor prices.

Flowers make beautiful decorations, but they can get pricey. Think about using realistic silk flowers to mingle in with the fresh ones. You can put these flowers away and use them for other parties and events as well.

Bubble machines add a great touch, and they can be purchased inexpensively from stores like Wal-Mart or online.

Think about ideas for inexpensive centerpieces that you or a creative friend can do yourself. We've seen a simple cake pedestal loaded with fruits and illuminated from beneath by votive candles. The fruity centerpieces work great if you're marrying in an orchard or vineyard. Another idea we've seen are charming porcelain mini-vases that—with some hunting—you can find at a discount or online store and place a few simple but beautiful flowers in each to match your color palette. We've seen it done with orchids, and it worked. A breakaway cluster of these vases at each table is very cute, and the overall cost is low, especially if you purchase your flowers from a wholesaler. You can do this online too, and we have some contacts in Chapter 17.

Buy your own alcohol. This will save you money, but be aware that your venue might not allow it or might impose a corkage fee.

Go for a buffet instead of a sit-down meal. Or, cut down on the passed hors d'oeuvres and consider making them available at small food stations rather than passed by waitstaff.

If you're having a sit-down meal, opt for a single "surf-and-turf" entree, which are plates that have both a meat and a fish serving, as opposed to more than one meal choice, which will drive up your cost. The dual-protein option makes things easier for the caterer, and guests of all food preferences will be satisfied. To this end, it's good practice to have a vegetarian option as well.

A community center or church hall will be easier on your budget than a country club, traditional event hall, or hotel.

Considerations Worksheet: The Wedding Reception

Reception Budget: $ _____

Reception Date Options

First Option: _____   Season: _____

Second Option: _____   Season: _____

Third Option: _____   Season: _____

Reception Type and Time

☐ Breakfast or Brunch – Start Between 10 and 11 a.m.
☐ Luncheon – Start Between 12 and 2 p.m.
☐ Tea – Start Between 2 and 3 p.m.
☐ Dinner – Start Between 4 and 6 p.m.
☐ Cocktail and Dessert Party – Start Between 5 and 6 p.m.

Reception Formality

☐ Extremely Formal
☐ Formal
☐ Semiformal
☐ Informal

Reception Meal Style

☐ Sit-Down
☐ Buffet
☐ Food Stations
☐ Buffet

Reception Style

☐ Indoor
☐ Outdoor

Reception Location

☐ Home
☐ Church Hall
☐ Hotel, Event Hall, Country Clubs, Restaurant
☐ Winery
☐ Park, Beach, Garden
☐ Mansion, Estate, Historical Building
☐ Yacht, Cruise Ship
☐ Nightclub, Museum, Aquarium
☐ _____

Reception Location Considerations

☐ Compatibility with Your Style and Theme
☐ Guest Capacity
☐ Parking and Accessibility
☐ The View
☐ On-Site Services
☐ Accommodations and Facilities
☐ _____

Notes: _____

_____

_____

_____

_____

_____

_____

_____

_____

_____

Comparison Forms: Reception Location 1

Appointment Date: _____   **Time:** _____

Reception Location: _____

Address: _____

_____

Event Managers / Coordinator: _____   Assistant: _____

Email: _____   Phone: _____   Fax: _____

Website: _____   Recommended by: _____

Date Available: _____   Time of Day Available: _____

Compatibility with Your Style & Theme: _____

Guest Capacity: _____

Parking and Accessibility: _____

The View: _____

On-Site Services Available: _____

On-Site Items Available (tent, tables, chairs, etc.): _____

Outside Vendors Welcome? _____

Payment Policy: _____

Cancellation Policy: _____

Reception Location Fee: $ _____

Booking Deposit: $ _____   Required by: _____

Additional Fees: $ _____

Party Extension Fee: $ _____

Total Estimated Cost: $ _____

Comments: _____

_____

_____

_____

_____

_____

_____

_____

_____

Comparison Forms: Reception Location 2

Appointment Date: **Time:**

Reception Location:

Address:

Event Managers / Coordinator: Assistant:

Email: Phone: Fax:

Website: Recommended by:

Date Available: Time of Day Available:

Compatibility with Your Style & Theme:

Guest Capacity:

Parking and Accessibility:

The View:

On-Site Services Available:

On-Site Items Available (tent, tables, chairs, etc.):

Outside Vendors Welcome?

Payment Policy:

Cancellation Policy:

Reception Location Fee: $

Booking Deposit: $ Required by:

Additional Fees: $

Party Extension Fee: $

Total Estimated Cost: $

Comments:

Contact Sheet: Reception Location

Date Booked: _____

Reception Location: _____

_____

Address: _____

_____

Event Manager / Coordinator: _____

_____

Email: _____

Phone: _____

Fax: _____

Website: _____

Reception Date: _____

Exclusive reception location reservation time from _____ to _____

Package Description: _____

_____

Special Instructions: _____

_____

_____

Staple Business Card

On-Site Items Available	Included in Cost	Additional Fee
☐ Tent / Canopy		
☐ Tables / Chairs		
☐ China / Flatware / Stemware		
☐ Linens / Decorations / Candles		
☐ Outdoor Heaters / Band Stage		
☐ Other:		
☐ Other:		

Total Cost: $ _____

Deposit: $ _____   Date Paid: _____

Balance: $ _____   Date Due: _____

Notes: _____

_____

_____

_____

Chapter 10

Play Dress Up: Create Your Wedding Day Look

- All About Bridal Gowns

- How to Find the Dress of Your Dreams (and Afford It!)

- Dressing It Up: Hair, Makeup, Accessories, and More

- Gown Preservation

- e-Plan It! Use Your e-Resources:

  Online Gown Galleries and Catalogs
  Dress Designers' Websites
  Online Gown Bargains

- Worksheets:

  Considerations Worksheet: Bridal Gown
  Checklist: The Bridal Look
  Comparison Forms: Bridal Gowns
  Contact Sheet: Bridal Gown
  Contact Sheet: Gown Alterations

Your glowing bridal look will be a unique reflection of your personality and the atmosphere you envision for your wedding. In this chapter we'll cover the ins and outs of finding a gorgeous, affordable gown tailored just for you, as well as rounding up all the details and accessories that will tie your look together.

All About Bridal Gowns

<TIP>

Gown Timetable

It's going to take you some time to decide what gown style you like and what best complements your figure. Once you make your selection, the gown you order will need to be custom tailored to fit your bod perfectly. The whole process could take a lot longer than you think, so start planning early. You don't want the pressure of a ticking clock hurrying your decision, forcing you to make a choice before you're ready, or robbing you of the fun you should be having.

9 months before or more: Start researching gowns to get ideas. Set up appointments with at least two or three local salons and dress shops.

4 to 6 months before: Settle on your choice of gown. Order it.

2 to 3 months before: Have your first fitting now to leave plenty of time for any necessary alterations. Get the shoes and undergarments you'll be wearing beforehand and bring these with you.

About 6 weeks before: Have your final fitting.

1 week before: You should have your finished dress in hand.

</TIP>

Knowing proper gown-speak will really help you in your quest for finding "The One". The more you know about dress silhouettes, necklines and fabrics, the easier it will be to determine your ideal style and work smoothly with bridal gown salespeople. The right gown will flatter your figure and bring out your best look. So which is the right one for you?

The only way you're really going to get a handle on it is by checking out the dresses themselves, and the next section will take you step-by-step as you go through the gown-hunting process. But before you do, make sure you know your lingo. The anatomy of a gown can be broken down into six main categories: silhouette, neckline, sleeve, train, fabric and color. Let's take a look:

Silhouettes

The silhouette, or cut, is one of the main features of a wedding gown—it dictates the overall shape. Here are some of the silhouettes you may find:

A-line (Princess): Today's most popular—and versatile—style. No matter what your body type, it's hard to go wrong with the A-line silhouette, as it will flatter just about anyone. Depending on the gown's fabric, it can be designed as either backyard-ceremony casual or ballroom formal. It's fitted at the waist and flares out in an "A" shape as it falls, hence the name, and has no waist seam—so it can actually help elongate your torso if you happen to be short-waisted. While it hugs the natural curves of your upper body, it isn't as form-fitting as a sheath, so a wider range of brides are likely to feel comfortable in it. Most designers feature A-line dresses in their catalogs.

Ball Gown: Offers that classic, elegant look (think Cinderella). The ball gown is composed of a form-fitting bodice that leads down to a full, floor-length skirt. It flatters most figures, but is especially good at hiding large hips as it draws the eyes up from the lower body to the bodice. Brides with narrow hips will also benefit, since this style will give you more of a curvy look. If you have a smaller, petite figure you may want to avoid this one, however, as the style's sheer volume may make your gown look as though it's wearing you.

Sheath: Simple, sleek, and elegant, a sheath gown is an example of the less-is-more school of thought. It either falls nearly straight down from shoulders to hem, or hugs the natural curves of your body on its way, sculpting the torso, waist and hips. It's quite flattering on a tall and thin frame, as you'd expect, but also looks great on shorter, more petite brides because it tends to add length to your appearance. If you've got problem areas or larger hips that you're uncomfortable with, you may want to skip this one.

Mermaid: Curvaceous and form-fitting, mermaid gowns hug the body all the way down to the knees, where the silhouette then flares out. These gowns follow and draw the eyes down your waist, hips, and thighs, so they're perfect for brides with great figures who want to show off their curves. On the other hand, if you don't want such a truthful silhouette, consider something else.

Basque Waist: One of the most waist-slimming styles, and thus a popular choice for full-figured brides. Dresses with a Basque waist come down from a natural waist to a "V", elongating the torso and providing a sleek, slim appearance. The full skirt, similar to a ball gown, de-emphasizes the hips and draws the eyes upwards towards the chest. With a sweetheart neckline (we'll discuss necklines in a bit), you've got the perfect match for full-figured or hourglass-shaped brides.

Empire Waist: Gowns with an empire waist have a very small bodice and a high waist that begins just under the bustline and falls with a slight flare to the hem. If you have a thicker waist, an empire dress will minimize it, softly sweeping over your curves in a slimming fashion. However, brides with large hips or a fuller bust will probably want to avoid this one.

Necklines

The neckline of a gown frames your face and neck. Most dress silhouettes are available with a variety of different necklines, so the combination of the right neckline and silhouette will probably mark the winning choice for you. The neckline you choose will depend on the silhouette you're pairing it with, as well as the size of your bust and arms: some necklines work better with fuller upper bodies, and some flatter a smaller bride. Here are some of the necklines you may find:

Strapless: These dresses are usually cut straight across the bustline, and have no sleeves or shoulders. It's a flattering style for most body types and very common with A-line dresses.

Off-the-Shoulder: Sleeves sit just below the shoulders, highlighting your collarbones and giving you the feel of a strapless gown without baring as much skin—which also works well if your house of worship has a problem with bare shoulders. It's flattering with most chest sizes, although especially so with brides more endowed in that area, and the straps will provide added support for larger chests. If your shoulders are on the broad side, though, you'd probably be better off considering a scoop or square neckline.

Spaghetti Strap: The neckline is often cut straight across the top of the bust, with very thin straps supporting the bodice. If you want the look of a strapless with a little added safety and support, you can usually convert most strapless gowns to a spaghetti-strap without much fuss. Like strapless gowns, they're flattering on most figures.

Jewel: A neckline that sits just below the base of the throat. It's slightly rounded, similar to the neckline of a T-shirt. It tends to enhance the bust of those brides who are a bit smaller on top.

Bateau (Sabrina): This neckline gently follows the curve of your collarbone all the way across your chest and nearly to the tips of your shoulders. It's a great choice for brides with small chests as it gives more weight to the bust. Because it draws the eye up and focuses attention on the shoulders, those whose shoulders are especially broad should avoid it.

Halter: Features a halter shape with straps starting low at the top of the bodice and reaching up to wrap around a high neck, leaving the shoulders (and usually the back) bare. It highlights the shoulders, so make sure they're a feature you're proud of. Halter necklines work best for taller brides (5'7" and up) with a more or less athletic build, and are suitable for most bust sizes.

Scoop: Scoop necklines curve down in the shape of a "U". They can be cut high or low, and suit most figures, although especially large-chested brides should be careful with lower cut scoops.

Square: Similar to a scoop neckline, but the neckline falls in a square instead of a rounded "U".

Sweetheart: This neckline is shaped like the top of a heart, with a scintillating yet tasteful glimpse of the décolletage (if you're not comfortable baring too much, you might be able to find a dress with a sheer overlay that rises above the top of the heart shape). If you have a full chest, you'll look great in this neckline. If your cup size is on the small side, you probably want to avoid it.

Sleeves

Whether your arms are a feature you'd like to show off or conceal, there's a sleeve style for you. Keep in mind that you can also wear a shawl, little jacket, or other cover-up if you'd like to conceal your arms more temporarily: say, during the ceremony. Here's some of the sleeves you may find:

Cap: A very small sleeve that just covers your shoulders.

Puff: A short or long sleeve with a pouf at the shoulder, as you'd expect.

Three-quarter: An elegant sleeve that ends midway between your elbow and wrist.

Fitted: A long sleeve that extends to your wrist, fitted tightly all the way. This one is best worn on small, slender arms.

Juliet: A classic renaissance look, fitted tightly on the arm and with a little pouf at the shoulder.

Poet: These long sleeves are tapered at the forearm and then flare out, often with a pleated flare.

Fingertip: This long sleeve sweeps down your arm and covers it all, up to your fingertips.

Bell: A sleeve that starts out fitted to your upper arm and flares out at the wrist.

Trains

This is the part of your gown that sweeps along behind you as you make your way down the aisle, and it lends a very dramatic touch to your overall look. As a general rule, the more formal your wedding is, the longer your train should be...although as always, the rule is yours to break. Some gowns don't even have a train. Others are detachable or made to be "bustled": a process whereby the train is pulled, hooked, or buttoned up so that you can get around at the reception without worrying about it. Trains are named after their length, like so:

Sweep: The smallest type of train, extending a foot or less behind you once it reaches the floor.

Chapel: Extends three and a half to four and a half feet from your waist.

Semicathedral: Extends four and a half to five and a half feet from your waist.

Cathedral: Extends six and a half to seven and a half feet from your waist.

Extended Cathedral: For that real princess look. Extends twelve or more feet from your waist.

Fabrics

The type of fabric your gown is made of will depend on the season (heavier fabrics are better suited for cooler weather), body type (fabrics hang differently depending on their weights, so each may flatter certain body types better), formality (you guessed it: the more formal the wedding, the pricier the fabric), as well as your budget (silk is the most expensive). Just so you know the lingo, here are some fabrics you can expect to find:

Brocade: A heavier, Jacquard-woven fabric that includes raised designs. Due to its weight, it's popular for cooler-weather weddings.

Charmeuse: A soft, lightweight, clingy fabric with a satiny feel and glossy luster. This is one of the more unforgiving fabrics, best for the well-fit.

> **<TIP>**
>
> Which fabrics for which weather? There are really no hard and fast rules, and you should get a gown made of a fabric you love and will feel comfortable in. In general terms, heavier fabrics are often chosen for weddings in cooler weather, and lighter fabrics for warmer times. A few examples:
>
> Warm Weather Fabrics (Spring and Summer Weddings):
>
> Chiffon, linen, lightweight satin, organza and voile
>
> Cool Weather Fabrics (Fall and Winter Weddings):
>
> Brocade, heavy lace, moiré, satins, richer tafettas, and velvet
>
> **</TIP>**

Chiffon: A lightweight, sheer fabric made of silk or rayon that's often used in overskirts and sheer sleeves. It's one of the most delicate and transparent of fabrics.

Crepe: Lightweight, porous, and slightly pebbly in texture, crepe is made of silk or rayon.

Damask: Medium-weight woven fabric; it's a lighter version of brocade.

Duchess Satin: A hybrid fabric of silk and polyester.

Dupioni: Fabric made of thick, coarse silk.

Eyelet: An open-weave, embroidered fabric. Often used to create design details.

Gazar: A four-ply, linen-like organza made of silk in a criss-crossing box weave.

Illusion: A fabric that's similar to organza: thin, finely netted and semitransparent. Often used in sleeves and necklines.

Linen: A light, breathable cloth made of flax. Strong and textured, but easy to wrinkle.

Mikado: Twill-like, crisp silk fabric.

Moiré: A glimmering silk taffeta that reflects light as though it were water.

Organdy: A crisp, sheer fabric made of silk or rayon.

Organza: Similar to tulle but woven tighter, it's a stiff, sheer fabric that can be quite sculptural.

Polyester: An artificial fabric that is often combined with other fabrics or made to mimic another type of material.

Rayon: A fabric similar to but more elastic than polyester.

Shantung: A fabric similar to raw silk, with a rough and nubby texture.

Silk-Faced Satin: Smooth silk that is glossy on one side and flat matte on the other.

Taffeta: A smooth and crisp fabric that has luster and a slight crosswise rib.

Tulle: A fine, sheer netting of silk, rayon, or nylon. It's often used for veils and skirts.

Velvet: Soft, smooth, and dense fabric made of silk, rayon, or nylon. Often used for details at sleeve cuffs and bodices.

Voile: A fine, sheer, easily draped fabric of cotton, silk, or rayon.

Lace

Alencon: A French needlepoint lace with a floral design against a sheer net background.

Belgian: Comprised of machine-made grounds.

Battenburg: A type of renaissance lace with a satin background and often trimmed with sequins, beads, and linen tape. Edges are clean and scalloped.

Chantilly: Elaborate floral lace on a hexagonal mesh ground, with edges that are often scalloped and outlined in heavy silk thread.

Dotted Swiss: Small flocked fabric circles against netting.

French: Machine-made fabric that mimics handmade French lace.

Guipure: Large, often flower- or rose-like geometrical motifs against a coarse mesh background.

Schiffli: A lightweight and intricate embroidered floral pattern against a net background.

Spanish: A flat rose pattern against a net background.

Venise: Heavy damask lace that often has floral or geometrical leaf patterns.

Colors

Think all white is the same? Think again. You'll get different shades of white depending on the fabric you choose, from stark white to eggshell or ivory. Most gowns can be ordered in different types of fabric—and, therefore, different shades of white—and different whites go better with different complexion types and skin tones. While we're on the subject, keep in mind that your dress doesn't have to be white at all; if you're not into the white dress look, feel free to add some color.

Stark White: This is the brightest, whitest white you can get, and it can only be achieved with synthetic fabrics like polyester blends, satins and taffetas. If you've got dark skin, this white will look gorgeous on you, but it tends to wash out those with light complexions.

Natural White: Also called "diamond" or "silk", this is a shade off of stark white, and is the whitest you can get with natural fibers like silk. A lot more flattering to the skin, it looks about the same as stark white in photos, and is wearable by just about anyone.

Ivory: Also called "eggshell", this white has slight yellow undertones that flatter fair skin. Often used to obtain that vintage or antique gown look.

Other Colors: A lot of soft colors can be had, from "champagne"—which has a slight pink undertone but looks nearly all white in photos—to soft lavenders, blues, and so forth. Great for brides who feel their complexion gets washed out by any shade of white.

How to Find the Dress of Your Dreams (and Afford It!)

Now that you know the lingo, it's time to put it to work. The broad range of gown styles available is matched only by the equally broad range in prices. How do you find the right options? Where do you start? We'll show you the way, and as always we'll be taking liberal shortcuts by leveraging on the convenience of several helpful online resources. When you've found the One You're Looking For and it comes time to plunk down the change, keep your options open and see if a discount warehouse or on-line bargain shop might have the same—or a very similar—model for a serious discount. Then, regardless where you buy from, you'll need to take into account timely fittings and necessary alterations.

Where to Start Looking

Start off with your wedding vision, as your formality and location will certainly play a role in the direction you take. How do you picture yourself coming down the aisle? In full princess form, classic Cinderella-like, or do you want to keep it simple? Are you going for retro, a vintage look, traditional, or contemporary? Conservative or more flashy? The choices you make will depend a lot on your personality, so do some good soul-searching.

With your wedding vision in mind, it's time to look through dress examples, and the more the better! Once you start really solidifying an idea of how you want your dress to look, you can start limiting your research to those styles that interest you the most. Bridal magazines are a traditional source of images, and since you probably have a few (or a ton!) already, start making clippings of gown pictures that catch your eye.

e-Resource

Online Gown Galleries and Catalogs

But the real gown idea gold mine? The Internet. Everything in the magazines is online as well, in a searchable format, and with all the info you need right at your fingertips. And, unlike five dollar bridal mags, the online catalogs are free. Search for dress ideas faster, more thoroughly, and easily with online catalogs and dress galleries that you can find at wedding portals like The Knot (www.theknot.com) and WeddingChannel.com.

The Knot's (www.theknot.com) advanced gown search lets you hunt for gowns based on more than ten options: from designers and style numbers to silhouette types to special features like open backs or matching jackets.

The Knot (www.theknot.com)

The Knot's extensive online gallery can be accessed by clicking on the "Gown" menu option from their home page.

You'll be provided with search options and a list of their featured designers. Select up to four search criteria (designer, silhouette, neckline, and price range) and click "Go" to start browsing. Looking for something strapless in an A-line for under $1000? You've got instant results to browse through. If you want to fine-tune your search even more, click the "Advanced Search" link and specify even more details, from style number to embellishments like lace and beadwork, to special features like open backs or matching jackets.

Clicking on any one of the featured designers will bring up all The Knot's results for that designer, which can be useful if you like a specific designer's style. Or, you can simply hop over to that designer's website (we'll talk more about designers' websites in a bit) and see everything they have to offer.

During your browsing, if you see anything that happens to catch your eye, click on the dress you're interested in to get a detailed page on the selected style. The details covered include designer, style number, silhouette, neckline, fabric, train, and a lot more—even the retail price range. Click the "save to my notebook" link to add this gown to your personal Knot notebook for later review. If you want to see stores in your area that carry the dress, select your area from the drop-down menu (for some designers, this feature isn't available) and see if any shops local to you come up. The list of shops include links to their website and a phone number to make locating the dress that much more convenient.

While browsing The Knot's dress catalog, clicking on a dress brings up its detail page. You can see all the style information, available colors, and a list of stores in your area that carry the dress.

WeddingChannel.com

The online dress gallery of WeddingChannel.com is another great browsing point, and a resource you'll want to add to your arsenal. Get to it by navigating to Fashion and Beauty > Dress Search using the left-hand menu.

Wedding Channel.com's Dress Search lets you narrow your search by designer, silhouette, neckline, and price range as does The Knot, and like The Knot they have a list of featured designers you can click on if you want to see dresses by a particular name. Something different that WeddingChannel.com offers is their "Sketch Pad", available by clicking the "Advanced Search" link. It allows you to fine-tune your search even more by specifying a range of gown elements. If you pass your mouse cursor over an element option, you'll see an illustration of the element's style in the sketchpad window, useful for comparisons.

The detail page for each dress is similar to The Knot's, and the larger designers will have a drop-down menu you can use to locate shops in your area that carry their

WeddingChannel.com's advanced gown search features a sketch pad that not only lets you search for gowns based on specific elements like silhouette, neckline, and so forth, but also displays a sketch of the various options as you move your mouse cursor over them.

gowns. If you see items you want to save to consider later, you can add it to your personal WeddingChannel.com scrapbook, similar to The Knot's notebook, and review all your considerations together after you've browsed a bit.

David's Bridal (www.davidsbridal.com)

A popular and economical bridal retailer with hundreds of locations nationwide. Their website is a great resource that shouldn't be missed when doing your online research and gown hunting. Browse their online collection and check out the helpful Style and Fashion Guide, which includes a complete pictorial glossary.

Dress Designers' Websites

If you find a dress or style you like, consider checking out the designer's website for other models that might be up your alley. Most designers' websites will have a store locator so that you can search for stores in your area that carry their products.

Narrowing Your Choices and Trying Them On

Nine or more months before your wedding, you'll want to hit the shops and start actually trying on dresses. Do your research first! After you've read the previous section, "All About Bridal Gowns" and have scoped out the online catalogs and galleries, you should have a good idea of what you like. You may even have some specific dress manufacturers and item numbers you're interested in.

Many shops require appointments, so call ahead to be sure. If you're interested in a specific item number or have been referred to the shop by an online source, let the shop know so you can verify that they'll have the dress(es) you want to see in stock when you go in. When visiting the shops, try to do it on a weekday if you can, and the earlier in the day the better. You'll have more attention and better service, since the shops can get pretty crowded during evenings and especially on weekends.

Who and What to Take

When you embark on your shopping expeditions, bring along a couple trusted supporters to provide input and advice: mom and sis, or maybe a close friend. Try to limit your entourage to three friends or family members at any given trip. You're going to be faced with a lot of options (that's why it's so important to do your research first!) and too much input at once can easily overwhelm you—and your salesperson. If there's more people you'd like to bring along, swap invitees for the next shopping trip.

Bring along all your research info: printouts of dress photos, manufacturer names and style numbers, and any magazine clippings. You'll also want to have a strapless bra to try on a wide range of dress styles, sheer control top panty hose, and shoes with heels approximately the same size as those you'll be wearing for your wedding.

Where to Go

You may already have a list of shops to hit based on your online research. As we mentioned before, most online catalogs and designers' websites have a feature that allows you to search for shops local to you that carry the dress(es) you're interested in.

Salons - Bridal salons are the most traditional source of wedding gowns, and the more boutique-style ones can be found in most upscale urban shopping areas: malls, shopping districts, department stores, and so forth. They're usually pricey, carrying top designers' wares that will be custom ordered for you (expect to pay an average of $2,000). Whether or not you buy from a salon, they're good places to try on plenty of dresses and get some expert advice. Find salons via references from bridal websites or check local search engines like Google Local (local.google.com) using keywords like "bridal shop" or "wedding gowns dresses". Our opinion is that it's far more convenient using search engines like Google Local rather than using the Yellow Pages, and you'll be provided with a map, directions, phone number, reviews by other brides, and links to the shops' websites.

Discount Outlets and Warehouses - These are great spots to check out if you could care less who the designer of your dress is and are more interested in just getting a great price on a traditional style. If you happen to have a discount outlet or two near you, it's worth taking a look. You'll find large rows of dresses on racks, usually designs that have already had a run at the salons, or those made by lesser-known designers. There are great deals to be had here if you don't mind spending the time to browse, and you just never know if your treasure is buried somewhere in those racks. There may or may not be a salesperson to assist you in locating dresses for you; otherwise, you'll need to browse along on your own. You might actually find this more comfortable than dealing one-on-one with a salesperson as you do during salon sessions, or you may feel that it takes far too much time.

Shopping Tips and Things to Expect

The treatment you get at a shop can vary from more of a "do-it-yourself" approach in which you search through dresses on your own (you'll find this at warehouses and outlets, for example) to a "closed stock" service. With a closed stock, you don't get to search for dresses yourself. Rather, a salesperson greets you, consults with you, and brings out dresses to try on that she feels would suit you best. Some boutique shops and designer salons are small and more intimate, whereas others (particularly warehouses and more popular salons) are large, bustling, and—especially on evenings and week-ends—crowded. Some shops specialize more in expensive, higher-end designer gowns, while others offer less expensive, mass-marketed attire or that of lesser-known designers. The key is to try a few different types of stores so you can see which you prefer.

Take advantage of a salon's experience. Most salons and boutique gown shops will take the closed stock approach and have a salesperson (sometimes called a bridal consultant) sit with you to discuss your options. This is your chance to use their expertise to your advantage! The consultant deals with suiting up brides every day, and a good one will be experienced at matching the right dress types with the right figure, budget, and taste preferences. Tell her your price range, formality, colors, and theme if any. Show her clippings or printouts of gowns that you like. You, as an informed consumer (you've studied the "All About Bridal Gowns" section and done your online research, right?), can bounce ideas off the consultant, ask questions, and request to try on specific silhouettes, necklines and even individual style numbers that you're interested in.

Throughout your shopping, keep an open mind. This is important! The only way you'll know for sure what looks great and what doesn't—even after all your preparation and research—is to try the gowns on. If your consultant brings out a dress you think you'll hate, try it on anyway. Remember, something that looks great in a picture might not look so hot on you. On the other hand, a silhouette, neckline, or color you might previously have avoided even considering could wind up looking amazing after you try it on. And never discard an option at first glance. Dresses on the hanger look nothing like they do when they're on a body, so try on everything suggested and don't judge a dress by how it looks on a rack.

Take your time. Start early enough so you won't feel pressured, and make sure you visit plenty of shops—even if you think you find a winner your first day out. You can always come back and buy the first one you tried, but do it *after* you've seen what other shops have to offer. If you find something you really like, don't order it right away. Shop around. You may even want to check online discounters or warehouses for the same dress and see what the difference in price would be (we'll cover online shops a bit later).

Take notes for comparison. For each gown you find that interests you, make sure you write down the name of the manufacturer or designer, the price, the shop you saw it at, and a style number if you can get it. Shops usually won't let you take photos of the dresses and sometimes withhold style numbers as well, but you're buying your wedding dress—potentially a very expensive wedding dress, at that—and you have a right to know at least the name of the designer you're buying. Explain this to the shop, and if they still won't give it to you, look somewhere else. If the shop won't give you the style number, make a note of all the dress' elements: silhouette, neckline, sleeve, hem length, and anything else setting this dress apart. You can compare this price with another shop's or an online source using the information you collect along with the designer's name...or, you can try looking it up at the designer's website to get the style number there.

Don't expect a perfect fit. Most salons carry a large number of dresses in a limited range of sizes. Because of this, the consultant will pin your dress in place or have you try on a similar style that fits to give you a sense of how the gown will look. Another thing you'll notice is that normal dress sizes don't apply in wedding gown land; gowns are usually sized differently than other clothes. In fact, each manufacturer has their own sizing chart, which tends to make things that much more confusing. Your consultant will be able to accurately recommend the proper size for the gown you're interested in once she takes your measurements.

Choosing "The One"

Okay. So you've done your shopping, made your decision, know which gown is the One and which store it's at, and you're ready to lay your claim on it. Your search is over! From here on, it's just a matter of securing your gown and making sure you get the best deal possible, at a price you can afford.

Tips on Gown Ordering

Ask plenty of questions. You're making a major purchase—emotionally and financially. If your questions aren't getting answered in the way you'd like, or you're uncomfortable for any reason, don't hesitate to look someplace else. You should have your dress info (designer name, hopefully a style number, descriptions of the dress elements, and so forth) so you can check for it at other shops you feel more comfortable at, or even online (More on this in the next e-Resource. Checking online is a smart move before you buy anyway; you never know if the same dress can be ordered for 80% off the retail price from an Internet discount source). Find out how long it will take to get the dress once you've ordered it, and if you can work with the same salesperson when you come in to do your fitting or during any follow-up appointments. Also, check to see if the shop sells accessories and headpieces, and if they can be customized to go better with your choice of dress. What deposit do they require, and what is their payment policy? Their cancellation policy?

Work with your budget. If the dress of your dreams is pushing the limits of what you can afford, ask if it's available in a less expensive fabric. If you must splurge, do so within reason...you want the dress you love, by all means. Just make sure you work with your budget to compensate for the added cost by managing your other expense categories to accommodate it (we covered flexible budgets and spending categories in Chapter 5). Don't abandon your budget and get swept away in the romance and excitement of the moment—which is all too easy to do at a time like this—as your financial management will only go downhill from there. And take a serious look at online discounters; you might be able to find the same dress at a price much easier to swallow.

Choose the right size. Order a dress size that will be as close as possible to your largest measurement: if you've got a fairly large bust and a small waist, for example, order a dress in a size that comfortably fits your bust and have the waist taken in. It's a lot easier and cheaper to take a dress in than it is to let it out, so keep that in mind. For this very reason, buy a dress to fit you based on the size you are today. Don't order a dress a size smaller because you plan on losing a lot of weight. If your weight tends to fluctuate or you plan on dieting before the big day, have your last fitting done ten days or so before the wedding (we'll cover fittings a bit later on). If you do lose weight, it'll be easy to have the dress taken in. A dress that's too small, however, cannot be let out a whole size.

<TIP>

A Word on Color

Before you buy a dress, ask to see a clean fabric sample. Because they're handled so much, sample dresses in the shops tend to fade and get dirty, so the dress you receive might actually be a shade brighter. Make sure you're buying the color you intend to.

</TIP>

Minimize expensive alterations. Maybe you adore a dress but feel it would be perfect with a different neckline or sleeve style. Make sure you ask up front how much it would cost to make the change, or if it's even possible. Such design modifications can get very expensive, and you're often better off switching to a similar gown that already has those features from the start.

e-Resource

Online Gown Bargains

As you well know, the Internet is a great place to find some real bargains, and wedding gowns are no exception. Online discount shops slash prices by 20%, 30%, even 50% and sometimes more. You can often find brand-new accessories and gowns from auction sites like eBay (www.ebay.com) at less than half the retail price. An additional perk: if the online business is not in your state, you probably won't even have to pay sales tax. All this adds up to some real savings in your pocket for a normally big-ticket item.

On the down side, you'll need to make arrangements with a seamstress or tailor separately, in order to take care of your alterations (see the discussion on "Dealing With Fittings and Alterations" later in the chapter). And you'll need to try on the same style of dress in a local shop separately to make sure you like the look; buying a wedding gown in blind faith without expert help is a pretty risky move, and one we don't advise. Make sure you know your measurements (hips, bust, etc.) when shopping online, as bridal gown sizes seldom have much in common with ordinary clothing sizes. Check designers' websites for sizing charts, or use the online shops' sizing aids to help out. The money you save can be substantial, and you won't be disappointed as long as your expectations are that your gown will be shipped to you in a small box, wrinkled and in need of pressing.

How do you decide whether or not buying a dress online is for you? Our advice is to leave this decision towards the end unless you're in a *serious* budget crunch and you know for sure you'll be going for an online bargain. Do your research as you would normally, using the online galleries as a helpful starting point (discussed earlier). Make your list of preferences including any designers and style numbers, call local shops to make appointments, and go in for try-ons.

BrideSave.com allows you to search their selection of bridal gowns by a number of criteria, including the style number of a gown you may be interested in.

When you've found "The One", or a few competing potentials, go ahead and check the online sources. See if the online shops offer the dress(es), and what their discounts are. Run the designer and style number through eBay. Any hits in your size? (eBay bargains can be amazing). How much would you be saving by getting it online? Factor in shipping (usually around fifteen dollars), the hassle of finding a seamstress or tailor, and the cost to press your gown when it arrives. Make your decision then whether to go with your local shop or snatch up the online bargain, based on how much you'll save.

The Sites

So where do you find these online discounters? There's plenty of dress sites on the web, but be careful who you're dealing with. Make sure they are authorized dealers of the designs they feature (meaning that they work directly with the manufacturer) and that they accept returns and will refund payments if you're not satisfied for any reason. The following are some of the better bargain sites:

BrideSave.com

BrideSave.com allows you to search gowns by a number of criteria, similar to the portal sites' gown searches. Enter in your search options and click the "Find Dress" button to begin browsing their selection. If you have the item numbers of dresses you may have tried on and liked in a bridal shop, enter each into the keyword search box at top of the page to look for those specific gowns.

Clicking on any dress in the results list will provide all the necessary details of the item, including specific prices for each size range. BrideSave.com also offers a "hold rack", where you can place dresses you're considering for friends and family to log in and browse.

eBay's "Wedding Apparel" Section (www.ebay.com)

eBay can be a source of big savings for many items, including brand new wedding gowns. It's worth it just to run the gown's designer and style number by eBay's bridal apparel search and see if you come up with anything. If you're lucky and find the same dress online in your size, you just might be in for some sweet e-savings.

Find eBay's Wedding Apparel section by selecting the "Clothing, Shoes, & Accessories" category from the home page menu and clicking on "Wedding Apparel" from the list that is presented next. From here you can browse the gowns listed to see the price ranges and designers or search for specific gowns you're interested in. To do a search, just enter in a designer name and item number in the search box provided.

eBay (www.ebay.com) has thousands of brand new bridal gowns up for auction at incredible discounts in their "Wedding Apparel" section.

NetBride (www.netbride.com)

NetBride offers more designers than BrideSave.com (above), but doesn't list their prices in a catalog; you need to request an e-mail quote. Click on "Bridal Gowns" and then "Price Quote" to submit a request for a price quote on a specific gown (you provide the designer and item number). If you've gone into dress shops already, you can compare the quoted price with what your local retailers are giving you to see how much of a discount is available.

Get It in Writing: Your Bridal Gown Contract

Your gown is a big expense—emotionally and financially—and you want to make sure your purchase is protected. Check that all the dress details, including alteration estimates (discussed next) are inked out in your contract. You should see a detailed description of your dress and all its elements, details on required alterations, fitting dates, a promised date of delivery, and a clear cancellation policy. The cancellation policy should specify that if you don't receive your dress in good condition on the date promised, you're entitled to have your deposit refunded.

As with all major wedding purchases, pay with your credit card for extra consumer protection, and verify that both you and your shop sign a copy of the contract. Request your own copy and file it away in your "Attire" folder.

Perfecting It: Dealing with Fittings and Alterations

The dress is yours, but the shape won't be totally *you* until it's been altered to fit your body perfectly. As we mentioned, you'll typically order a gown to fit your largest feature, so parts of it will likely need to be taken in. Get these alteration estimates before you order (they're not typically included in the cost of your dress), and make sure the alterations are detailed in your contract along with your fitting appointments. If you've ordered your dress online, take some time to find a good seamstress or tailor if you haven't already, and make appointments for your fittings with the one you select. You may also have to do this if your shop doesn't do alterations in house (though they can most likely recommend someone). Regardless where you buy your gown, you want to allow about four to six weeks for your alterations, or more if you're making extensive design changes.

<TIP>

Come Prepared

If possible, bring the actual bra, slip, and shoes that you'll wear on your wedding day to your fittings. A different size heel or style of bra can make a big difference when it comes to alterations.

</TIP>

How Do Fittings Work?

If all goes as planned, the dress will reach your store (or home, if you've ordered online) on time, and will be the right style, color, and size. But final alterations will still need to be made to get your dress to fit just perfectly on your own unique shape.

When you ordered your gown, you should have set up an appointment for your first fitting, either with the shop or with an outside seamstress or tailor of your choice. You'll need to try on your gown, and the seamstress will take measurements, make notes, and then get to work on the necessary alterations. These can be as simple as taking in the waist and raising the hem or as extensive as adding beading or lacework, or even changing the basic style elements. You'll come in for a follow-up fitting once the alterations have been completed, and if things look good at that point, the dress will finally be yours! If changes still need to be made, you'll come in again later on. Depending on the extent of changes that need to be done, the whole alteration process could eat up a lot of time. So remember to allot at least four to six weeks for alterations when you're setting your first appointment.

Dressing It Up: Hair, Makeup, Accessories, and More

Your gown is only one component of your total bridal look. You'll also need to add accessories like shoes, lingerie and headpiece, most of which you can obtain at the same shop you purchase your gown. But don't limit your cost-saving options there...online bridal shops and auction sites like eBay (www.ebay.com) are great sources to find really gorgeous brand new accessories at a fraction of your typical retail costs. Checking out the online discount shops for deals on accessories is definitely worth a try, whether or not you decide to purchase your gown from one.

Shoes

Style and comfort is the key. Get something that will complement your dress and the mood of your wedding, but make sure you'll be comfortable in whatever you buy. You're not going to be sitting a whole lot, but you'll be standing and dancing quite a bit...so make sure you'll still be dancing at the end of the night. Keep heels to two inches or less, and go easy on any sparkly accessories. Focus on keeping it simple, elegant, and in tune with your formality.

The most popular color is still white, though accents of silver or gold are often used, and if your dress is another color your shoes should obviously complement it. Most white shoes can be dyed to match a different dress color, too, so keep this in mind when looking at styles.

And don't forget to break your shoes in before the wedding. Wear them around the house a bit to get used to them and scuff the heels to keep from slipping and sliding on smooth surfaces.

Stockings and Lingerie

When it comes to the comfort and shape of your bridal attire, your undergarments are just as important as the dress itself. Talk to your shop's bridal consultant about tips on the right type of bra for the dress you order, and try to purchase everything in time to bring along to your fitting.

Bras

You'll need the right support to be comfortable under that heavy gown and provide the gown with the proper shape. Your bridal shop consultant can give you some pointers on what type of bra goes best with the gown you select. Some details—such as the need for a strapless bra with sleeveless or spa-ghetti strap styles—should be obvious enough. As a general rule, you'll want to use a smooth style bra, as patterns, lace, and other embellishments might show through.

Slips

While most dresses today have slips built into them, you may need to wear another one to improve the way your dress falls.

Slimmers

These elastic undergarments can hide a variety of soggy spots, and lend sleeker lines to the shape of your dress.

Hosiery

Not all brides go for hosiery. Those with a fair amount of natural color to their legs, especially if open-toed shoes are to be used, may choose to forego it. If you'll be using hosiery, select an ultrasheer or shimmery hose in a color that will be compatible with your dress; most commonly white, ivory, or a blush. Do you plan on hitting the dance floor without your shoes? Sheer hose might end up with runs or toe-holes, so you may want to consider tights instead, or knee-highs that you can take off along with your shoes.

Headpiece

Headpieces are accessories like tiaras, combs, floral wreaths or headbands, and they can be worn with or without a veil of sheer material such as organza or tulle. Your veil's material should match that of your dress, and your overall headpiece should flatter and complement your face, dress, and hairstyle. Decide how you want to wear your hair before purchasing your headpiece: certain ones work better with different do's.

You'll probably select your headpiece when you go in for your first fitting, if your shop carries them. If you purchase a headpiece from another source (online, for example, or at a bridal boutique), bring it along during your fitting to see if you may want to alter it in order to better suit your dress.

The length of your veil, if you choose to have one, is traditionally determined by the length of your train: the longer the train, the longer the veil. But feel free to vary the proportions. Try on different types to see what veil length seems to flatter you the most. If you're full-figured and shorter, for example, you may want to avoid a long, billowing veil regardless of the type of

<TIP>

Going Bare

Don't want a headpiece? How about a simple, cute barrette? Or you might want to consider a wreath of fresh flowers. And if stuff on your head just isn't you, no problem: go bare! As with your dress, your hair and anything on or in it should be something you love and feel great in.

</TIP>

dress you're wearing. Many headpieces are made (or can be fitted with) Velcro, hooks, or clips so that the veil can be removed after the ceremony.

When trying on headpieces, make sure you walk around in it, turn your head, and bend over. Is it comfortable? Does it feel loose? Don't buy something that's going to be bugging you all day long, no matter how perfect it looks.

Hair and Makeup

While many brides prefer to do their own hair and makeup for a more natural look, others like the idea of a professional to take care of it and style something special. If your maid of honor, a family member, or one of your bridesmaids is especially good with hair and makeup, you might feel comfortable letting one of them do the honors. If you go with professional hair and makeup salons, you can either swing by the salon the morning of your wedding or have the hairstylist and makeup artist come to you and style you at home. If you want to have your mom and/or bridesmaids done up as well, ask about getting a group discount.

When hiring professional hairdressers and makeup artists, keep in mind that the good ones can book up fast, especially during the peak wedding season. Have your hairdresser and makeup artist both do a trial run or two before your wedding so you can be sure you're comfortable with your look. Don't forget to bring in your headpiece when you meet with the hairstylist.

A manicure and pedicure are additional elegant touches you may want to pamper yourself with.

Jewelry

The key to jewelry as a great bridal accent is keeping it simple. Let your dress and your glowing smile take center stage; jewelry should be in the supporting role. Classic examples of wedding jewelry are a simple string of pearls or a pair of diamond earrings (if your hairstyle lets your ears show), but you can wear anything you like that you feel best reflects your personality and the mood of your wedding. If you don't have jewelry that you feel goes with your attire, consider borrowing it from your mother or another relative. It can be the "something borrowed" component of your attire.

Gown Preservation

Your bridal gown is a treasured memento of your wedding, and you need to be careful with how you store it if you plan on keeping it in good condition throughout the years (your daughter or even granddaughter might wear it at her wedding someday!).

Take it to a professional dry cleaner soon after your wedding (any stains or dirt are best attacked right away). Make sure you choose a reputable cleaner, and preferably someone who has experience with bridal attire. Ask them to test your beading and trim; if you have details that are glued on rather than sewn, the cleaning process could damage your dress by deteriorating the glue.

When you get your gown back from the cleaner, remove any shoulder or bra pads, as the synthetic material in the pads can stain your gown over time. Buy acid-free, linen-free tissue paper and an acid-free box from a craft store (the boxes are commonly used to store photographs or other important documents). Hand press the dress and wrap it in the tissue paper, using the tissue to pad the fabric and guard against creases. Stuff the bodice of your dress and the sleeves with more of the tissue paper, then place the garment into the box.

Don't store the dress in plastic, vacuum-sealed containers, or boxes with cellophane windows, as the lack of air circulation can actually cause the fabric to discolor. Also avoid mothballs: the fumes can be damaging, too.

Store the box in a cool room away from direct sunlight, cigarette smoke, dampness, and other common-sense no-no's. And pack the headpiece separately, since many contain glue, metal pieces, or rubber that can cause a browning of your dress.

Following these precautions, your gown should stand the test of time. Check in on it in a year or so and if you notice any stains you missed previously, or if anything else has happened to discolor the dress, take it back to the cleaner and then wrap and package it away again as before.

<NOTE>

"Something Old, Something New, Something Borrowed, and Something Blue"

If you're into old wedding traditions, this one's about as traditional as you can get, and you've probably heard the phrase more than once already. For years, brides have integrated "something old, something new, something borrowed, and something blue" into their wedding getup. A bit of blue lace in their garter, for example, or blue toenail polish. Perhaps a string of borrowed pearls around their neck and an old penny in their brand new shoe.

Where does this stuff come from?

Symbolically, the "Old" represents the bride's past, and reaffirms her link to her family. The "New" represents success, prosperity, and happiness in her new life to come. "Borrowing" something—traditionally from another happy bride—means good luck, and the "Blue" dates back to biblical times, representing fidelity and purity.

If you like, have some fun echoing what thousands of brides before you have done, and add a little tradition to your ensemble!

</NOTE>

Considerations Worksheet: Bridal Gown

Bridal Gown Budget: $ _____

Silhouette

□ A-line (princess)
□ Ball Gown
□ Sheath
□ Mermaid
□ Basque Waist
□ Empire Waist

Neckline

□ Strapless
□ Off-the-Shoulder
□ Spaghetti Strap
□ Jewel
□ Bateau (sabrina)
□ Halter
□ Scoop
□ Square
□ Sweetheart

Sleeves

□ Cap (short)
□ Puff (short)
□ Three-quarter
□ Fitted (long)
□ Juliet (long)
□ Poet (long)
□ Fingertip (long)
□ Bell (long)

Trains

□ Sweep
□ Chapel
□ Semicathedral
□ Cathedral
□ Extended Cathedral

Bridal Gown Fabric Color

□ Stark White
□ Natural White
□ Ivory
□ _____

Bridal Gown Fabrics

□ Brocade
□ Charmeuse
□ Chiffon
□ Crepe
□ Damask
□ Duchess Satin
□ Dupioni
□ Eyelet
□ Gazar
□ Illusion
□ Linen
□ Mikado

□ Moiré
□ Organdy
□ Organza
□ Polyester
□ Rayon
□ Shantung
□ Silk-Faced Satin
□ Taffeta
□ Tulle
□ Voile
□ Velvet
□ _____

Lace

□ Alencon
□ Belgian
□ Battenburg
□ Chantill
□ Dotted Swiss
□ French
□ Guipure
□ Schiffli
□ Spanish
□ Venise
□ _____

Notes: _____

_____

_____

_____

_____

_____

_____

_____

_____

_____

Checklist: The Bridal Look

Item	Description	Source	Item Cost
☐ Gown			$
☐ Wrap / Shawl			$
☐ Veil			$
☐ Headpiece			$
☐ Petticoat / Slip			$
☐ Bra / Corset / Slimmer			$
☐ Hosiery			$
☐ Garter			$
☐ Shoes			$
☐ Handbag			$
☐ Hankie			$
☐ Gloves			$
☐ Jewelry			$
☐ Makeup			$
☐ Makeup Artist			$
☐ Hair Accessories			$
☐ Hair Stylist			$
☐ Something Old			$
☐ Something New			$
☐ Something Borrowed			$
☐ Something Blue			$
☐			$
☐			$

Total Bridal Look Cost: $

Comparison Forms: Bridal Gowns 1

Appointment Date: _____   Time: _____

Bridal Salon: _____   Years in Business: _____

Address: _____

_____

Sales Contact: _____   Assistant: _____

Email: _____   Phone: _____   Fax: _____

Website: _____   Recommended by: _____

Gown 1

Designer: _____   Size: _____   Price: $ _____

Style: _____

Alterations Required: _____   Cost: $ _____

Gown 2

Designer: _____   Size: _____   Price: $ _____

Style: _____

Alterations Required: _____   Cost: $ _____

Gown 3

Designer: _____   Size: _____   Price: $ _____

Style: _____

Alterations Required: _____   Cost: $ _____

Shoes: _____   Size: _____   Price: $ _____

Style: _____

Headpiece: _____   Price: $ _____

Style: _____

Other: _____   Price: $ _____

Style: _____

Payment Policy: _____

Cancellation Policy: _____

Ordering Deposit: $ _____   Required by: _____

Additional Fees: $ _____

Total Estimated Cost: $ _____

Comparison Forms: Bridal Gowns 2

Appointment Date: _____ Time: _____

Bridal Salon: _____ Years in Business: _____

Address: _____

_____

Sales Contact: _____ Assistant: _____

Email: _____ Phone: _____ Fax: _____

Website: _____ Recommended by: _____

Gown 1

Designer: _____ Size: _____ Price: $ _____

Style: _____

Alterations Required: _____ Cost: $ _____

Gown 2

Designer: _____ Size: _____ Price: $ _____

Style: _____

Alterations Required: _____ Cost: $ _____

Gown 3

Designer: _____ Size: _____ Price: $ _____

Style: _____

Alterations Required: _____ Cost: $ _____

Shoes: _____ Size: _____ Price: $ _____

Style: _____

Headpiece: _____ Price: $ _____

Style: _____

Other: _____ Price: $ _____

Style: _____

Payment Policy: _____

Cancellation Policy: _____

Ordering Deposit: $ _____ Required by: _____

Additional Fees: $ _____

Total Estimated Cost: $ _____

Contact Sheet: Bridal Gown

Date Ordered:

Bridal Salon:

Address:

Sales Contact:

Email:

Phone:

Fax:

Website:

Store Hours:

Gown Designer:

Staple Business Card

Style #:   Size:

Style Description:

Delivery Date: ☐ Home   ☐ Pick-Up

Gown Price: $

Shipping Cost: $

Other Costs: $

Total Cost: $

Deposit: $ Date Paid:

Balance: $ Date Due:

Notes:

Contact Sheet: Gown Alterations

Staple Business Card

Alterations Location: _____

Address: _____

_____

Taylor/Seamstress: _____

Email: _____

Phone: _____

Website: _____

Hours: _____

Special Alteration Instructions: _____

_____

_____

Pressing Instructions: _____

_____

_____

1st Fitting Date: _____ Time: _____

2nd Fitting Date: _____ Time: _____

3rd Fitting Date: _____ Time: _____

Delivery Date: _____ ☐ Home ☐ Pick-Up

Alterations Cost: $ _____

Press Cost: $ _____

Shipping Cost: $ _____

Other Costs: $ _____

Total Cost: $ _____

Deposit: $ _____ Date Paid: _____

Balance: $ _____ Date Due: _____

Notes: _____

_____

_____

Notes:

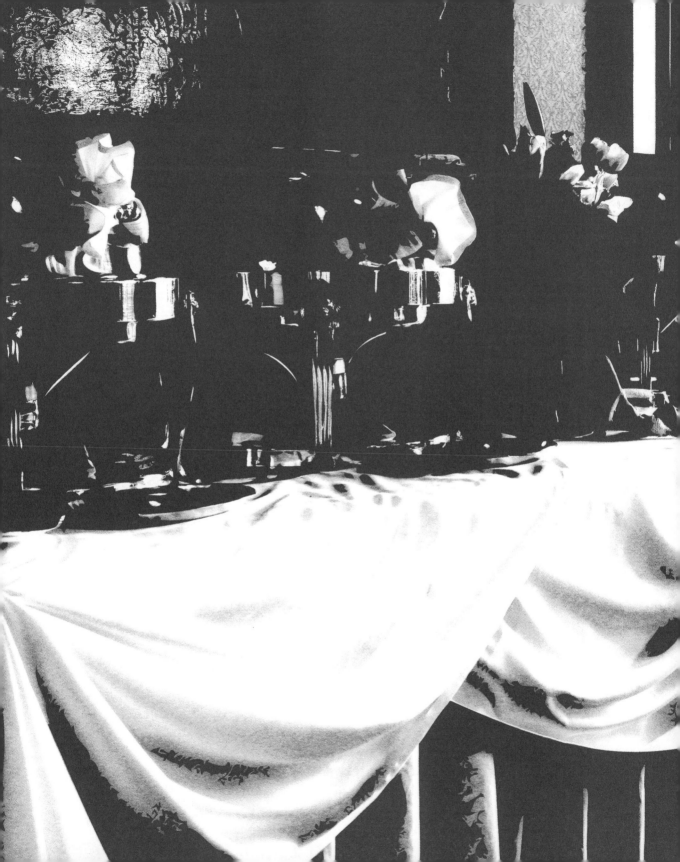

Chapter 11

Choose Your Caterer, Menu and Beverages

- Choosing the Right Caterer

- Creating a Memorable Menu

- Serving Beverages

- Share It! Starting Your Website's Vendor List

- Get It in Writing: Your Catering Contract

- e-Plan It! Use Your e-Resources:

  Online Caterer Hunting
  Your Vendors List

- Worksheets:

  Considerations Worksheet: Caterer, Menu and Beverages
  Comparison Forms: Caterer
  Contact Sheet: Caterer

F ood and beverages are obviously one of the largest and most important components of your reception. Who you choose to handle your wedding day feast and
how you have them do it will significantly impact the overall experience you and
your guests will have.

Choosing the Right Caterer

Your catering service will be handling some of the most important aspects of your wedding reception: food, beverages, decorations and possibly coordination of the event. Whether your caterer is provided by your venue or you hire your own, careful consideration needs to go into accepting the right one. Start early so you can have them booked around eight months before your wedding.

Determine Your Needs

Where do you start when it comes to looking for a caterer and choosing a menu? You'll first need to make a decision on the type of service you want: will it be a sit-down meal or buffet? Family style? Will your hors d'oeuvres be passed by waitstaff, or set out at stations? What kind of meal do you envision? To answer these questions you need to consider the time of your wedding, your style and formality, and how much budget you have to work with.

Time of Day Plays a Role

As we mentioned in Chapter 9, "Find a Reception Location and Lay Out the Details", you have a number of reception time options. You might be going for an early brunch, midday tea affair, four-course dinner, or cake-and-champagne party. Your reception time will dictate the type of menu you and your caterer will be putting together, as well as the drinks you'll be serving.

Style and Formality

How formal is your wedding? Your catering details should be just as formal or informal as the rest if the reception, which only makes sense. The formality of your wedding will affect the way your food is served (see "How to Serve It" in the upcoming discussion on Creating a Memorable Menu) and will influence the actual menu itself. When you discuss your menu and service options with caterers, be sure they're fully aware of your preferred formality level.

Consider Your Budget

Your budget was a major consideration back in Chapter 9 when you decided what day and time to hold your reception. Breakfasts and lunches will typically be less expensive than dinners, and a Friday or Sunday reception can often be planned for less than a Saturday event. Your budget will also play a significant role in deciding the ingredients of your meal (chicken breast versus filet mignon, for example) and how much meal you'll actually serve (elaborate five-course dinner or just a combined meat-and-fish plate preceded by a salad).

> <CROSS-REFERENCE>
> We discussed factors that affect the cost of your wedding in Chapter 5, "Create a Smart Budget and Payment System".
> </CROSS-REFERENCE>

Caterers usually charge by the plate and simply multiply this by your guest count to arrive at a final food cost. To get an idea of what your per-plate cost should be, take the food portion of your budget (it should be set aside as a separate category as we advised in Chapter 5), and divide this amount by the expected guest count. This is an estimate of the upper limit you can spend per person. A good caterer will take your budget into consideration and work with you, showing you different possible menu combinations in a range of prices and ingredients that best fit your means and wedding vision.

> <CROSS-REFERENCE>
> Reception venues and their various policies were discussed back in Chapter 9.
> </CROSS-REFERENCE>

Kinds of Caterers

Depending on the location of reception, you may have one or more choices on the type of catering company you work with: your venue may have an on-site chef or food service company you're obligated to use, while others might have a list of preferred companies that you can choose from. Still other locations will leave it open for you to select anyone you wish.

Food-Only vs. Full Service Catering

Preparing and serving your food are a given, but some catering professionals will do more than that, if needed. Some may assist in coordinating the reception by working with all your vendors to keep things moving according to your timeline. They may provide additional services like your cake, flowers, decorations (votive candles, vases, and other rentals, for example, which we'll discuss next). When interviewing caterers, ask what services they can offer, and what the extra charges are to use them. If you want to bring in your own resources (baker, florist, alcohol, and so forth) are there additional fees to do so? Many catering companies will charge you a corkage or cake-cutting fee as a way of persuading you to use their services over somebody else's.

How About the Rentals?

Linens, dishware, glasses, flatware, tables, chairs, and even outdoor tents are some of the items you might need. What your venue doesn't offer, your caterer just might. Some caterers have their own supply of rental items while others use a rental company and charge you a markup on their own cost. If you'll be obtaining rental items from your caterer, ask if the items are owned by the catering company or if they'll be obtained from a third party. If your caterer is renting the items from someone else, you may find it cheaper going through a rental company yourself and cutting out the middle man.

Handling rentals yourself keeps you in control and is often less costly, but it's one more vendor to deal with, and more work than if you were to just have your caterer take care of it. You'll need to work with the rental company to arrange for delivery and pickup of the items, and if anything breaks you'll usually be held responsible. If your caterer handles the rentals, it's common for them to assume liability for anything that gets damaged. Check your contract to be sure; we'll cover contract points at the end of the chapter.

Thoroughly discuss responsibilities with your venue contact and with your caterer: what will they be taking care of, and what will you need to arrange on your own? Think of everything: lighting, electrical, tables, dance floor, extra chairs, extension cords, and anything else. Don't assume it will be handled unless it's inked specifically into one of your contracts.

Where to Find Them

If your venue comes with its own chef or banquet manager, you're likely limited to using their catering services. Before you settle on one of these venues, make sure you interview the food service personnel and taste their wares. A bit later on, we'll discuss things to consider during your caterer interviews and questions they should be prepared to answer for you.

For those of you who have more freedom in choosing your food service provider, it's time to do some research. The best way to find great caterers is by word of mouth from others who have had positive experiences, so start off by gathering references from those you know and trust. Recently married friends, family members, your wedding coordinator, other vendors, and your chosen venue are all great sources. You'll also find caterers at wedding tradeshows, often cooking up samples for you to taste. Start making a list of caterers to contact based on all your referrals and on/off-line research. If your reception location requires you to use one of their preferred vendors, take their entire caterer list and use that as your list of contacts. Next, you'll narrow the list down further and set up interviews as well as getting started with the real fun of caterer hunting: the tastings!

e-Resource

Online Caterer Hunting

The web has some great resources to help you dig up local vendors, and fast. Get started caterer-hunting in your pajamas over that morning cup of coffee. Check local vendor directories on your favorite wedding portal, search engines, and event websites. Browse caterers' websites for more information, menu samples, and photos of other weddings that they've done. If you find any potentials that pique your interest, add them to your list of contacts.

LocalCatering.com

A service that aims to connect vendor-hunting couples to local caterers. You can either enter in your reception information (location, budget, preferred service type, and so forth) so that the website can send you a list of referrals, or you can just plug in your zip code in the local vendor directory search and see a list of members in your area. We advise that you do the latter; there's really no reason to have referrals sent to you as opposed to checking the list yourself. The local directory search box is a bit hidden; look for it on the right-hand side of the home page midway down, and select "Caterers" as the merchant type.

The Wedding Portal Sites

The portals are always a great way to start off looking for local vendors, though far from an exhaustive list. If nothing else, check out the websites of those caterers you do find and start getting a peek at menus, prices, policies, and photos of food preparation and settings. Also, check out the helpful online articles and read up on posted experiences of other brides regarding caterers you might want to use (and avoid) in the regional message boards.

The results page that LocalCatering.com presents includes links to an informative page for each caterer as well as customers' reviews.

The Search Engines

Don't forget the tried-and-true method of plugging "wedding caterer <city> <state>" into your favorite search engine and seeing what it spits out. Local search engines like CitySearch.com and Google Local (local.google.com) are also great ways of finding caterers in your area. Check out each caterer's website and add any that show potential to your contact list.

Line Up Your Interviews and Tastings

Once you've got a solid list of contacts, start making phone calls. Narrow your list down to those caterers that are: available on your date, friendly and helpful over the phone, and seem receptive and open to your ideas and the type of meal you have in mind. While you're at it, check their websites for photos of other weddings they've done. For those companies that make the cut, arrange an interview to meet them in person.

Come Prepared

Arrive at each interview with menu ideas, clippings from food magazines, even other caterers' menus and ideas (it's okay; they all know you're shopping around). Describe your wedding vision with each caterer, and the type of meal you're thinking of. See what suggestions they provide, and how open they are to your ideas. Do they seem enthusiastic about your wedding? Ask to see sample menus and photos of other weddings the caterer has done that are similar to yours in venue, guest count, and meal type. If you'll need rentals, can the caterer provide them? Ask who would be running the show at your reception, and if it's not the person you're talking to, request that you meet them. It's important that you like and get along with your service professionals, so if you don't feel the vibe, just move on.

Find out about the payment policies and any extra fees that they might charge, such as cake-cutting or corkage fees, gratuities, and so forth. We've put together a good list of questions you'll want to ask towards the end of this section.

Always Ask for a Proposal

If you feel the caterer is still a potential at the end of your interview, make sure you ask for a proposal based on your guest count, the meal types you're considering, and your budget. Request that the caterer come up with a rough estimate on two or more suggested options. Ask that they include an itemized cost list of everything that you'll be charged for: food, rentals, labor, alcohol, any extra fees, and gratuity. The options they give should range in cost and style so that you can get an idea for what this caterer would charge depending on how your meal is served (buffet versus seated) and the type of ingredients used (chicken breast versus filet mignon). Your caterer will prepare the proposal and get back to you within a week or so with an e-mailed or faxed copy of what they come up with.

Enjoy the Tastings

Along with a request for the proposal, set up an appointment for a tasting before you leave the interview. It doesn't matter if you go with this company or not; it's standard practice for catering companies to set up a tasting session for just the two of you or for a small group (bring your most critical family member or friend in this case!). After all, the taste and presentation of the food are the critical factors, and you need to ensure that this caterer will get it right if you're going to be hiring them for your wedding. Another advantage you'll get by attending several tastings (besides a belly full of yummy free food) is ideas. Even though you'll choose one caterer over several others, you can bring the notes of those things you liked about the other tastings to the caterer you choose and have them incorporate it into what they put together for you. Never turn down a tasting, and if a caterer doesn't offer it then thank them politely for their time and scratch them off your list.

When attending tastings, bring along a notepad and jot down what you like and don't like. Don't be shy: let the caterer know about things that don't work for you, and ask if they can change it to better suit your tastes. Make sure you try most or all of the items that will be on your menu, including hors d'oeuvres. How is the food presentation? Does everything work together? Inspect the dishware and make sure it doesn't appear cracked or worn. If you're asking to make significant changes to the menu, request a second tasting.

Your Caterer in Action

Preparing food for a small group is one thing, but preparing the same food for hundreds of guests and getting everything served fresh and hot is quite another. If you're leaning towards a particular caterer, make sure to request that you visit them during another wedding or an event of comparable size as yours so that you can see them in action. How's their performance? Is their process efficient, and does the food go out fresh and hot to every guest? Are there enough waitstaff to handle everyone? How attractive is their setup?

Questions to Ask Caterers

Here's a few things to run by your potentials. Talk to them about your wedding vision and ideas as well; make sure they're enthusiastic and open to what you want.

General

• Are you licensed and insured?

• Will you be able to set out our place cards, favors, and disposable cameras? How about the center-pieces from our florist?

• Do you have experience at our reception location?

• When will we need to provide the final headcount? (Usually you'll need to get the exact number of your guests to your caterer a couple weeks before the wedding)

• Do we have to guarantee a certain number of guests? How many?

• Do you provide any wedding coordination? (like making sure other vendors are sticking to the time-line and adjusting times if need be, cueing the band leader or DJ, letting you know when to cut the cake, and so forth)

Food

• Will we be able to have a tasting to sample our menu items? (This should be a must)

• Would you be doing our cake, or would we need to hire a separate baker? Do you charge a cake-cutting fee? If you're doing the cake, what choices do we have and can we do a tasting? How is the cake delivered?

• Do you use all-fresh food or do you use frozen ingredients?

• Can we add dishes that are not on your menus? (You may want to add a family or ethnic dish)

Beverages

- Can you provide alcoholic beverages? Will we be able to purchase our own?

- Do you charge a corkage fee? If so, how much?

- What type of non-alcoholic beverages can you provide? (Juices, sodas, water, lemonade, tea, coffee)

Service

- What will your staff-to-guest ration be? (For a sit-down meal, there should be one waitperson for every eight to ten guests)

- Who will be the person to oversee our wedding day? Can we meet them?

- What are the average cost differences between having buffet tables, having food stations, and having a sit-down meal?

Pricing

- Can you provide an itemized proposal with a few different menu and service type options and estimates for each?

- Beyond food, service, beverages, and rentals, what other fees and charges would be involved?

- Do you include service gratuity (sometimes called a "service charge") in your base price? How much of this, if any, goes to the waitstaff?

- What is your payment policy and how much of a deposit will be needed to secure our date? What is your cancellation policy?

Rentals

- Are you food-service only, or will you be providing items like dishware, flatware, linens, glasses, salt-and-pepper shakers, and so forth? What would we have to obtain ourselves, and what are your rental fees?

- Can we see the linens, dishware, and flatware that you'll be using for our wedding?

Get It in Writing: Your Catering Contract

Your catering is an expensive purchase with a lot of details involved. Go over it carefully, and make sure all the following is included before signing. Be sure your caterer signs the same copy you do, and that you get your own copy to file away for your records. If your venue is providing your catering services, the same information should be included with their contract.

General

Your written catering contract should list the date, time, and location of your wedding reception as well as the precise room or area if you're holding your affair in a hotel or other place where multiple weddings may be going on.

Food

It should specify the type of service for your meal and hors d'oeuvres and describe the menu in detail. Any ingredient quality assurances should be noted (fresh versus frozen or pre-packaged, for example). You should check to make sure that any details for vendor meals (those of your photographer, band, and so forth) as well as children's meals are specified in addition to the number of such meals you're expecting to serve.

Beverages

Check that your contract includes the brands, number of bottles, price for each, and return policy (you're often able to return unopened cases for a refund). Also check for specifications on non-alcoholic beverages (what kind, how you're being charged, and so forth). The number of bar staff should be noted (shoot for one bartender for every 50 guests), their hourly rate, total hours expected, and any gratuity you're being charged.

Staff

The number of staff, their attire, and what the staff-to-guest ratio will be should be in your contract. You should also see the amount you're being charged per hour, as well as the total number of labor hours. The name of the person in charge who will be present at your reception is helpful to have written down as well. If your cost includes gratuity, it should be noted.

Prices and Policies

The pricing should be clearly stated, along with any gratuity, sales tax, and added fees (corkage fees, cake cutting fees, and the like). Make sure the details of things like payment policy–including the deposit, refund policies, cancellation or overtime fees, and insurance coverage are specified.

<NOTE>

Your Final Headcount

You'll need to get your caterer a final headcount of all your guests two weeks before the wedding. Remember to include any vendors you'll be feeding; if your reception is longer than three hours, you'll need to fuel your photographer, band or DJ, videographer, and so forth.

</NOTE>

Creating a Memorable Menu

You like this, your sweetheart likes that, and you know a lot of your guest like such-and-such...but some members of your family hate it. How do you please the most number of people while being adventurous and different? Can you do it without turning conservative palates off, yet still avoid being too predictably traditional? We've got some tips and advice that should help, as will the creative suggestions you'll get from a good, experienced caterer. Keep in mind that your final selections on food and drinks should be solidified no later than six months before the big day.

What to Serve

Your guests may not remember the color of your bridesmaids' dresses or the particular design of your centerpieces, but they're sure going to remember the food! Aside from the two of you, what they're filling their bellies with is the highlight of your wedding for them, so make it special and memorable. Remember that the reception is your way of thanking everyone–friends and family–for celebrating your marriage with you and being a part of your special day. Make it a meal to remember!

Starting with Your Caterer

Many caterers have house specialties or signature dishes that you can select from. Consider your favorite foods, things about other tastings that you especially liked, and your own ethnic background when personalizing these menus. What can you add or change that would make the meal more personal or give it that touch you're looking for? If you're on the creative side, make sure that you select a caterer who is too, and that they're willing to work with you.

A good caterer will consider your style and budget when suggesting menu options for your wedding. They should give you several options and suggestions, based on their expertise in the business. Even if your budget is tight, they should show you ways to stretch your dollars to get the meal and style you're looking for. Remember that in the hands of a good and experienced chef, even the most simple, inexpensive ingredients can be prepared and presented with flair, and will be more memorable than an expensive variety of foods hurried out by one who is careless or inexperienced. Sometimes less is more, which is good news for your budget but should emphasize the importance of finding the right caterer.

Special Diets

Don't forget to accommodate those guests with special dietary needs or allergies. Kosher and vegetarian options, for example, should be provided; you can get your caterer a more solid number on how many of these dishes you'll need when you hand over your final guest count. A convenient way to handle this is to ask guests to report any special dietary needs via your online RSVP (see Chapter 20 for more about this cool, time- and worry-saving e-resource).

Ethnic Flavor and Regional Specialties

Another budget booster, and a nice touch, is the use of ethnic or cultural dishes. They're a hit with guests, add a personalized touch, and are usually quite economical relative to traditional fare.

Are you marrying in a region well known for a particular food or style? Say clam chowder in New England, Cajun spices in Louisiana? Or perhaps Tex-Mex or southern dishes? Personalize your reception meal even more by finding a way to include regional specialties in your menu. Highlighting your location this way can be a great touch, especially if you have several guests from out of town.

Trends and Special Touches

What's hot these days? Being different! Caterers are having more fun now than ever creating truly dazzling and inventive new ways to prepare and present wedding meals. This doesn't mean you need to go out and spend big bucks on exotic ingredients, either. You (and your caterer) just need to spend some time thinking outside the box. You'd be amazed, for example, how many delicious and ingenious things can be done with boneless breast of chicken.

Another great idea for keeping things interesting while satisfying everyone's diverse palates is to consider having two different proteins share the spotlight in your main course: a beef and fish portion, for example, perfectly balanced and interwoven in their presentation, will give your guests more variety to enjoy while keeping costs low for you (no need to have separate courses for the two).

How to Serve It

How you'll serve your guests will depend on your budget and the formality of your wedding. The main options are sit-down or buffet,

<TIP>

Different Tastes

Your guest list has potentially hundreds of different palates, so how can you be more adventurous in including regional and ethnic additions while still pleasing them all?

The answer: your hors d'oeuvres. You'll have more options to play with, and those guests with shyer, more conservative tastes can bypass anything too over-the-top.

</TIP>

<TIP>

Keep It In-Season

When deciding on your menu, work with foods that will be in season at the time of your wedding. It will be less expensive, and the quality will be better. For example, a dish with fresh tomatoes would work in the summer, but in the winter you'd be better off with a tomato-based sauce over pasta.

</TIP>

<TIP>

Hot Trend: Wine Them and Dine Them

Pair each course of your meal with a different recommended, complimentary wine. Include menus at your table that describe the wines, their places of origin, taste highlights, and why they best compliment their respective courses. Such entertaining, and educational pairings are a big hit with guests and will impress them, both casual wine enthusiast and sophisticated foodie alike. Complete the experience by setting your location at a beautiful winery, and you've got a recipe for a memorable reception.

</TIP>

<CROSS-REFERENCE>

We discussed the style of your meal service in light of the style of your reception back in Chapter 9, "Find a Reception Location and Lay Out the Details".

</CROSS-REFERENCE>

although you can try some popular variations of either style. Regardless of your choice, your goal is to feed your guests a memorable meal with elegance and style.

Sit-Down (Table Service)

The most formal–and expensive–option. This makes things easiest for guests (no standing in buffet lines or walking back from the food table while balancing loaded plates), and they feel pampered. With table service, your guests take assigned seats at their table and are served by waitstaff. The meals are either prepared in the kitchen (American style), on platters beside the tables (French style) and then hand-delivered to each guest. Another option, "service a la Russe" (Russian style), is done by white-gloved waitstaff each carrying a course out on a large tray from which they serve your guests. For a less formal–and less expensive–twist, consider serving your meals family style. In this case, food is brought to the table on large platters and guests help themselves in loading their plates.

<TIP>

Food Station Ideas

- Dim-sum
- Crepes
- Sushi
- Roast beef or other meat carving
- Oyster bar
- Cheese board with warm baguettes and fruit-and-nut garnishes
- Kebobs
- Veggies and dips
- Pasta
- Seafood and shellfish
- Quesadillas
- Chocolate fountain with strawberries, fruit slices, crackers, and marshmallows for dipping

</TIP>

Buffet (Self-Service)

During buffet receptions, one or more buffet tables are kept stocked by your catering staff, or they could be manned to assist your guests, who walk over from their tables to fill their plates. Buffets are less expensive than table service, and guests often have more of a variety to choose from. Avoid making your guests stand in long lines by having your caterer set up more than one buffet table located at opposite sides of the room. Or, set up manned food stations throughout the room. Each food station can have its own theme, type of food, and decoration (a meat carving station, sushi station with chef, pasta

<NOTE>

The Price of Labor

The main reason sit-down meals are often more expensive than buffet-style is the cost of the additional staff involved: you'll need a server for every eight to ten guests, and that doesn't include floor supervisors (captains). The average cost of waitstaff–including bartenders and cooks–is $100 per hour. The hourly cost for the service of captains, who oversee and coordinate the service, is typically $125 to $150.

</NOTE>

station, and so on). It's a great way to add variety, liven up the room, and offer a fun browsing-and-eating experience for your guests.

Cost-Saving Tips

While your food and drinks will typically run you 50% of your entire wedding budget, there's no need to break your budget to make a memorable meal for your guests. Be creative, and make smart choices in your menu and the caterer you choose. Shop around, get detailed proposals, and taste, taste, taste! It's the only way you'll be able to thoroughly compare each of your catering options.

Smart Appetizers

Serve inexpensive hors d'oeuvres, and keep it to no more than four selections (there's no need to serve eight or nine different options, as some caterers will suggest). Or, have your caterer create bread and cheese, fresh fruit, or vegetable displays and just serve a couple varieties of hors d'oeuvres. Instead of having them passed, provide them to your guests at unmanned stations if this will help cut staff. Finally, if you decide to have a lot of appetizers, consider eliminating the first course of your meal.

Have a Buffet

Buffet receptions will usually be less expensive than sit-down meals, and can be just as elegant while providing your guests with more variety. Consider having food stations to avoid making your guests stand in long lines.

Choose the Right Caterer and Menu

Foods that are in season at the time of your wedding will be of better quality and typically less expensive. Serve ethnic dishes, which are more unique, personal, and often more economical. Select a creative caterer that can add flair to inexpensive ingredients like chicken, potatoes, pasta, and broccoli and transform them into elegant, savory dishes.

Serving Beverages

For many people, a wedding reception just isn't a proper celebration without a glass of champagne or other festive beverage with which to toast the bride and groom. Most will also be looking forward to sipping celebratory drinks over hors d'oeuvres and along with their meal.

The bar staff and alcohol might be provided for you by your venue, or your caterer may be the one to stock up and serve your drinks. A popular way to save bucks on booze is to buy your own in bulk at wholesale prices, though you may wind up being charged a stiff corkage fee–which may or may not negate the savings you get. Check with your caterer or venue to find out how you're being charged (by the person or by the bottle), and whether or not you'll need to pay an extra fee if you were to supply your own drinks.

Your Beverage Options

This will depend chiefly on budget constraints and the time of day your wedding reception is held. The cost of alcohol, when its consumption is unchecked, can add up fast, and people drink less earlier in the day and on Sundays. In addition to the quintessential wedding bubbly, you have a lot of options on what to serve and how to serve it.

The Open Bar

This is the most expensive and lavish option, though not necessarily the best. With an open bar, you'll be offering any drink under the sun to your guests and as much as they want of each. You or the individual hosting your reception will then pick up the pricey tab at the end. This is the most generous option for your guests, and they'll no doubt love it... perhaps too much, in fact. Offering an open bar not only drives up your cost more than any other option, but you may wind up with a lot more tipsy and potentially obnoxious, out-of-control guests with such unchecked freedom. This will also increase the number of drinks that are ordered but not finished (although still paid for by you, of course) as people either abandon, misplace, or forget about them.

<TIP>

Hot Trend: Microbrews

If you're limiting your options to beer and wine, why not treat your guests to a variety of microbrews rather than just offering one or two of the same tired labels seen at most events? It's a small touch but will pleasantly surprise your guests, and will really impress the true beer enthusiasts. Leave the usual standbys in your selection as well so that those set in their conventional ways won't be disappointed either.

</TIP>

If you like the generosity statement an open bar makes but are worried about the potential abuse, consider having an open bar just during the cocktail hour, and closing it during the rest of the reception, where you can then limit alcohol to beer and wine at stations or passed by waitstaff. When considering your alcohol options, by all means don't feel obligated to provide an open bar throughout your reception! It's not a requirement, and there are other options (as we mention below) that are just as tasteful and acceptable.

The Limited Bar

You might consider limiting your bar to just serving beer and wine, along with champagne during the cocktail hour and/or the toasts. You may also want to offer an inexpensive traditional mixed drink such as champagne punch, offered and displayed as a fountain. If you're on an especially tight budget, you can save a lot of money by offering such mixed drinks as your sole choice of complimentary alcohol.

While an all-cash bar is usually considered tacky (guests shouldn't have to pay for anything at your reception–including alcohol), serving complimentary beer and wine while also offering mixed drinks at a cash bar can be an acceptable compromise.

Specialty Drinks

Limit your alcohol to champagne and one or two mixed drinks that go well with your reception theme, season, and time of day. Bloody marys or mimosas (champagne and O.J.) work well for early receptions, for example, while margaritas and pina coladas are popular during summer affairs. The amount of alcohol you'll need is far less, and you can use inexpensive alcohol in your mixes to cut your costs even more.

<TIP>

Coffee Bar

During dessert, a great touch is to open a coffee bar that offers cordials like Kahlua, Baily's Irish Cream and Grand Marnier for guests to enjoy with their coffee.

</TIP>

Cost-Saving Tips

To get a rough estimate on how many drinks you'll be serving for cost-calculation purposes, figure on one drink per hour for every guest. So for a 150-guest reception that lasts four hours, your total drink count will probably be something like 600. Keep the following cost-saving tips in mind to help keep these drinks within your budget.

BYOA

Buy your own alcohol wholesale. Just beware of steep corkage fees.

Truncate the Cocktail Hour

A 45-minute cocktail "hour" will cut down on drinks before your meal.

Serve Specialty Drinks

Champagne punch, margaritas, mimosas, pina coladas, and the like can be offered as your sole alcoholic beverage. You can use less expensive alcohol for these mixes, and your booze bill will be significantly lower than if you were serving top shelf alcohol or expensive wine.

Reception Time Matters

People drink more during evening receptions, and in the summer months. Go for a lunch reception or set your date on an off-month. And if your wedding is on a Sunday, many guests will usually cut back on the drinks they have since most will be getting up for work the following morning.

Use Less Expensive Liquor

Consider premium rather than deluxe or top-shelf alcohol. If you're serving wine, you may want to use house wines purchased in bulk. You can serve wine in carafes placed on the tables, which can be filled with inexpensive selections or from magnum containers, which will cost less. Remember that inexpensive wines don't have to mean poor quality wines: do your research and find tasty, low cost options that you might even be able to buy yourself in bulk.

Share It! Starting Your Website's Vendor List

<CROSS-REFERENCE>

Learn more about the advantages of a wedding website in Chapter 4.

</CROSS-REFERENCE>

Besides being very convenient for you, having all your vendor information (name, contact person, phone number, and so forth) in one centralized location that you can access from virtually anywhere is also a great way to share with your guest. And it's great for referrals; any visitor who may be planning his or her own wedding will find this page as useful as you do! Also, it provides your vendors with a central place to check if they ever need to contact any of your other service providers (say your baker needs to call the florist for the cake flowers, or your caterer has to get ahold of your rental company). Centralizing your contacts and information is just plain smart all-around.

e-Resource

This couple's online wedding vendor list includes all the useful information for each of their vendors, including contact numbers, website links, and even referral information for other vendor-hunting couples.

Your Vendors List

It's like an online version of a business card collection for all your vendors and important wedding contacts. The fact that it's online makes it accessible anywhere you might be with Internet access, and it's easy for your vendors to find in case they need to get in touch or coordinate details with another professional you're working with.

If your website service doesn't have a means to create a vendors page, try to at least fit in a list of contact names and numbers for each professional you're hiring–as well as your venues–on another page such as your thank-you's. If your service allows you to create general, or all-purpose web pages, you can also post the information on one of these.

Considerations Worksheet: Caterer, Menu and Beverages

Catering Budget: $ _____

Meal Type

- ☐ Breakfast or Brunch
- ☐ Luncheon
- ☐ Tea
- ☐ Dinner
- ☐ Cocktail and Dessert

Cuisine

- ☐ Thematic:
- ☐ Ethnic:
- ☐ Regional:
- ☐ Seasonal:
- ☐ Continental

Special Meal Requirements

- ☐ Kosher
- ☐ Vegetarian/Vegan
- ☐ _____

Courses

- ☐ Hors d'oeuvres
- ☐ Fruit and Cheese
- ☐ Appetizer
- ☐ Soup
- ☐ Salad
- ☐ Pasta
- ☐ Entrée
- ☐ Dessert

Entrées

- ☐ Eggs
- ☐ Beef
- ☐ Chicken
- ☐ Pork
- ☐ Lamb
- ☐ Seafood
- ☐ Vegetarian
- ☐ Pasta

Beverages

- ☐ Open Bar
- ☐ Limited Bar
- ☐ Beer and/or Wine Only
- ☐ Champagne Toast
- ☐ Specialty Drinks
- ☐ Non-Alcoholic Drinks
- ☐ Provide Own Liquor
- ☐ Liquor Provided By Caterer

Dessert

- ☐ Wedding Cake
- ☐ Groom's Cake
- ☐ Pastries / Tarts
- ☐ Fruit
- ☐ _____

Service Style

- ☐ Cocktails
- ☐ Passed Hors d'oeuvres
- ☐ Hors d'oeuvres Stations
- ☐ Food Stations
- ☐ Sit-Down (table service)
- ☐ Family-Style
- ☐ American
- ☐ French
- ☐ Russian
- ☐ Buffet (self-service)
- ☐ Formal (staff-served)
- ☐ Casual (self-service)

Notes: _____

_____

_____

_____

_____

_____

_____

_____

_____

_____

Comparison Forms: Caterer 1

Tasting Appointment Date: _____   Time: _____

Caterer: _____   Years of Experience: _____

Address: _____

Banquet Manager / Coordinator: _____   Assistant: _____

Email: _____   Phone: _____   Fax: _____

Website: _____   Recommended by: _____

Menu Suggested

Hors d'oeuvres: _____

Appetizers: _____

Entrée(s): _____

Dessert(s): _____

Beverages: _____

Services Available (setup, cake cutting, etc.): _____

Rental Items Available (china, linens, etc.): _____

License and Liability Insurance: _____

Payment Policy: _____

Cancellation Policy: _____

Estimate:

Food Cost: $ _____   Beverage Cost: $ _____   Rental Costs: $ _____

Staff Cost: $ _____   Staff-to-Guest Ratio: _____   No. of Hours Included: _____

Overtime Rate: $ _____

Additional Fees: $ _____

Gratuity: $ _____   Taxes: $ _____

Booking Deposit: $ _____   Required by: _____

Total Estimated Cost: $ _____

Comments:

_____

_____

_____

_____

Comparison Forms: Caterer 2

Tasting Appointment Date: _____   Time: _____

Caterer: _____   Years of Experience: _____

Address: _____

_____

Banquet Manager / Coordinator: _____   Assistant: _____

Email: _____   Phone: _____   Fax: _____

Website: _____   Recommended by: _____

_____

Menu Suggested

Hors d'oeuvres: _____

Appetizers: _____

Entrée(s): _____

Dessert(s): _____

Beverages: _____

Services Available (setup, cake cutting, etc.): _____

Rental Items Available (china, linens, etc.): _____

License and Liability Insurance: _____

Payment Policy: _____

Cancellation Policy: _____

Estimate:

Food Cost: $ _____   Beverage Cost: $ _____   Rental Costs: $ _____

Staff Cost: $ _____   Staff-to-Guest Ratio: _____   No. of Hours Included: _____

Overtime Rate: $ _____

Additional Fees: $ _____

Gratuity: $ _____   Taxes: $ _____

Booking Deposit: $ _____   Required by: _____

Total Estimated Cost: $ _____

Comments:

_____

_____

_____

_____

Contact Sheet: Caterer

Staple Business Card

Date Booked: _____

Caterer: _____

Address: _____

_____

Banquet Manager / Coordinator: _____

_____

Email: _____

Phone: _____

Fax: _____

Website: _____

Menu Tasting Appointment Date: _____

Time: _____

No. of Waitstaff: _____ Staff-to-Guest Ratio: _____

Staff Attire: _____

Package Description: _____

_____

_____

_____

Special Instructions: _____

_____

_____

_____

Final Menu Decisions

Hors d'oeuvres: _____

Appetizers: _____

Soup or Salad: _____

Entrée(s): _____

Dessert(s): _____

Beverages: _____

Rental Items Needed	**Included in Cost**	**Additional Fee**

Contact Sheet: Caterer (continued)

License and Liability Insurance:

Payment Policy:

Cancellation Policy:

Food Cost: $ Beverage Cost: $ Rental Costs: $

Staff Cost: $ No. of Hours:

Overtime Rate: $ Additional Fees: $

Gratuity: $ Taxes: $

Cost per Guest: $ No. of Guests:

Total Cost: $

Deposit: $ Date Paid:

Balance: $ Date Due:

Notes:

Chapter 12

Find a Photographer to Match Your Style

- Photographic Styles

- How to Find the Right Photographer

- Considerations and Tips

- Smart Ways to Cut Cost Without Compromising Your Photography

- e-Plan It! Use Your e-Resources:

  Do Your Photography Hunting on the Web
  Photography Association and Network Websites
  Photographers' Websites and Online Portfolios

- Worksheets:

  Checklist: "Must-Have" Shots
  Considerations Worksheet: Photographer
  Comparison Forms: Photographer
  Contact Sheet: Photographer

Photography is one of the most important elements you'll be planning for the big day. Your flowers will be beautiful, your food and cake scrumptious, and your music will rock. But when all is said and done, your photography will be what preserves the memories of your wedding day for years to come, from the excitement of you getting your hair and makeup ready to the tenderness of your last dance. So if there's one thing you splurge on, splurge here! Don't skimp or try to get your pictures taken care of on the cheap. A good photographer—the right photographer—can bring your memories to life and preserve them for you and your family forever. We'll cover some good ideas on how to save while not compromising quality; but otherwise, go ahead and spend a little extra in this category if you can. You'll be glad you did!

Photographic Styles

Before you start looking to find a photographer for your wedding, spend some time thinking about what style would best suit your taste and preferences. There's really two main schools of thought when it comes to shooting wedding photos: photojournalistic (more spontaneous) and formal (posed portraits), which we'll go over below. While pretty much all photographers will claim the ability to ambidextrously do both, in reality they'll almost always lean more to one style or the other. Familiarizing yourself with these basic styles will allow you to better gauge what you see when you do meet with photographers and start examining their portfolios.

Photojournalistic

News and documentary photographers have a specific style and technique that they use to capture important moments and tell a detailed story about the event they're covering. Well, your wedding is big news to you and yours; why not cover it as such? The photojournalistic style of wedding photography is our personal favorite, capturing all the drama and emotion of your big day with a more candid and documentary-like approach. Photographers favoring this style become a "fly on the wall", keeping a low profile and unobtrusively documenting the highlights of your big day as a visual story.

Does this mean that formal, portrait-style shots are out? Of course not…you'll arrange to have your portraits and posed shots taken at the desired times and with specific people, just as with any formal photographer. A journalistic photographer, however, will otherwise be a shadow in the background, inconspicuous, out of the way, but at the same time everywhere you (and the action) happen to be!

The true-to-life, emotionally charged images you'll get can be some of the most beautiful and power-ful memories of your special day; far more so than portrait shots. You'll get those priceless images of your little niece slyly stealing a slice of cake, or of your mom dabbing a tear from her eye during your first dance.

On the flip side, this spontaneity will mean that you won't always be looking your best in every shot; your hair might be out of place, or you might be caught mouth open in mid-laugh. And since the pho-tographer involves you less in the shots she decides to take, someone important to you might not be featured as much as you'd like if they don't catch your photographer's attention.

Formal

Portrait-style wedding photography seeks perfection. A good portrait photographer will employ soft focus techniques and ideal lighting to ensure that you look flawless. She'll direct groups of family, at-tendants, and guests to assemble and pose in locations she's chosen to make the most dramatic back-drops. While your photographer will normally add candid and spontaneous photos to the mix (more if you direct her to), the bulk of your album will be posed group portraits.

Such formal wedding photos make great gifts to family and friends, and are the kind of traditional heir-looms that will be placed over your mantle and handed down though the generations.

However, some couples feel that posed photographs can appear contrived, especially when com-pared to the more authentic live action of photojournalistic images. Your photographer might also miss capturing a priceless moment or two while she's organizing the groups for their portrait shots.

Color vs. Black-and-White or Sepia Tone

Color shows you everything as it truly was on your wedding day and captures all the details you worked so hard to bring to life, including flowers, favors, and the shade of your bridesmaids' dresses. Black-and-white is classic and timeless; it has a way of bringing out the essence of the emotion in each im-age, focusing on the people and action involved without the cluttered distraction of color. While color is great for capturing the mood of the sky, the flush of your cheeks, and the accents in your bouquet, it leaves less to the imagination. Color also tends to make flaws and blemishes as plain as day, while black-and-white often hides or softens them. Due to the more involved processing procedures of black-and-white, it is usually more expensive than color photography.

Sepia tone is an effect added to black-and-white photographs that alters them from the normal shades of grey to shades of brown. Historically, this effect was produced by adding a pigment from the Sepia cuttlefish to the positive print of a photograph, which prolonged the life of the picture. For this reason you'll often find old or historical photos in a sepia tone. If you like the effect, ask your photographer to add it to your black-and-white wedding photographs in order to capture that elegant and classical "old time" feel.

Although it ultimately comes down to your preference, both color and black-and-white wedding pho-tography have their own distinct charm. So why pick one over the other? Instead, mix your album up with some of both. For example, you might opt to have the majority of your shots taken in black-and-white with a smaller number in color. Or, you could shoot your ceremony in black-and-white and switch over to color or a combination of the two for the reception. If such a mix is what you're after, look for a photographer who can deliver it.

Digital photography makes mixing color and black-and-white photographs even easier. In fact, digital color images can be quickly transferred to black-and-white or even to a sepia tone with professional photo editing software like Adobe Photoshop. If you're interested in this and other kinds of digital editing, make sure to find out how much of it your photographer is willing to do for you.

How to Find the Right Photographer

Determining the wedding photographer that will be right for you will take some time and research. You want someone with a personality that will mesh with yours, someone who is passionate about their work and enthusiastic about your wedding vision. You want to make sure they have the necessary skill, experience, and gear to be worthy of the responsibility of immortalizing one of the biggest moments in your life.

Once the two of you decide what kind of photographer you're looking for, you need to build a list of contacts (from personal references, online resources, bridal shows, and so forth). Check out their websites and online portfolios, if they're available. Narrow down your search as much as possible before making the phone calls and interview appointments. Take the time to visit at least three photographers: the ones you feel are at the top of your list. When you make your decision to go with one, arrange a follow-up meeting to hammer out the specifics, negotiate the final pricing, and sign a contract.

Know What to Look For

When you meet up with photographers, you need to have an idea of what you're looking for. Their personality, skill, style, and equipment quality is of major importance here, and you'll need to know how to compare. Cost is obviously a factor as well, but heed our warning: don't budget shop. Not with photographers. While photographers that are way over your budget are obviously not an option for you, just remember that you want to select one based on their talent and style, not by who's the cheapest.

The Personality

Perhaps more so than any other wedding professional you work with, you want a photographer with a personality that you really like; the chemistry here is vital. Is she overbearing, interrupting you when you talk? Is she too shy and quiet? You want someone who is socially adept and will have a comfortable rapport with you and your guests, but at the same time forward enough to jump in and capture those important moments. Your photographer has to be someone you're totally comfortable with. No matter how skilled and talented they are, if it doesn't click between you, that tension will affect your pictures. Keep in mind that you'll likely want this person shadowing you everywhere, from the bride's bedroom as she's getting ready to the times the two of you step away from the action for a private word and a kiss.

When you meet photographers, explain your vision and your style. How enthusiastic are they about it? You want someone who will be excited about your day…that energy will come through in the pictures, too.

The Portfolio

For every photographer you meet, you'll want to check out their portfolio. Whether you're meeting a photographer at a tradeshow, checking out their online website (most photographers' sites have at least a partial online portfolio), or visiting their studio, you'll want to take a good look at their "book". This is them putting their best foot forward; it's the collection of what they consider to be their best work. If their portfolio doesn't do it for you, move on.

Make sure each photographer shows a strong balance of formal portraits as well as true-to-life spontaneous snaps and fun photojournalistic sequences. If the portfolio is overloaded in one style, you can bet that the photographer would rely heavily on that style for your own wedding.

Does the photographer utilize both color and black-and-white well? Unless you're only going with one color style, make sure that you see good quality shots of each, and in a good balance. Any artistic special effects? Look for examples of the kind of techniques you have in mind.

In general, does this person's work grab you? Is the quality there: vividness of colors, clarity of forms, creativity and attention to the small—but important—details? Is there a good use of lighting? For the formal pictures, how are the poses? Do they look contrived, or do they feel natural? Overall, is the emotion of the day captured throughout?

If you can, look at a finished album. Does it tell a clear story, from beginning to end, of this couple's wedding, complete with all the excitement, emotions, and main players? How's the ratio of formal and spontaneous shots? Ask the photographer how she feels about balancing the formal portraits and photojournalistic story-telling. Make sure her philosophy jives with your own. Ask to see a proof sheet of the album you're looking at; this is the collection of small thumbnails that the couple chose their photos from. A proof sheet tells a lot about a photographer, since this is their work in its raw, unedited form.

<NOTE>

What Happened to My Photographer?

Make sure that the photographer you're talking to is the same one that will be shooting your wedding. Some companies have several photographers that they work with, and the one you're chatting it up with might not necessarily be the one with you on your big day. Likewise, when you're looking at portfolios and proof sheets, make sure they weren't shot by someone else in the studio.

</NOTE>

The Gear

Knowing some fundamentals about film and digital cameras will help you determine whether or not the photographers you talk to are up to par equipment-wise.

First of all, any professional photographer should carry an extra camera or two as a backup: if one camera malfunctions or if it needs to be reloaded with film, the photographer should have a stand-by so as not to miss any potential action.

\<TIP\>

Making Inexpensive Digital Prints and Enlargements

Purchasing your raw digital images is just as significant as purchasing negatives from film-based photos. Rather than narrowing your reprint and enlargement options, digital photographs open some doors for you. Personal photo printers are becoming more and more economical, giving you the power to produce your own prints and enlargements from your computer.

Another useful tip: Costco. Their photo lab is very digital-friendly and allows you great control over selecting prints and enlargements—including quite large enlargements—at a low price.

\</TIP\>

If the photographer is shooting with film, the possible camera types that will be used are known as small format and medium format. Small format cameras use 35mm film, with negatives that are 1" x 1.5" large. Medium format cameras are larger, and use larger film, 2.25" x 2.25". This means that the images can easily be enlarged to a size of 16" x 20" or more and still be crisp and clear. Opt for a photographer who uses a medium format camera for the portrait shots at least; you'll be enlarging a lot of these pictures, and you want the highest possible quality you can get. Don't believe anyone who tries to convince you that 35mm cameras and medium format cameras are of comparable quality. They're not.

For digital cameras, the camera resolution is the quality factor you need to check for. The higher the resolution, the more crisp and clear the images and their enlargements will be. Resolution is measured in "megapixels", and the more megapixels the better. Cameras with a resolution capability of 10 megapixels or more produce photos that can be enlarged up to 20" x 30" and still be of pristine quality.

Should you go digital or film? The look, feel, and quality of the actual photographs will be the same. There will be no difference to your album in the end. Some photographers prefer one medium over the other, but it's just their own individual preference. Some photographers feel that digital gives them an edge: they can switch from shooting color to black-and-white a lot easier and with the same camera. They will usually shoot more pictures than if they were using film, which gives you more photos to choose from. Another great advantage to digital is that all the proofs can easily be posted online for you to browse and choose from, whereas film prints would need to be scanned into a computer to get the same result. Digital cameras don't produce negatives; the raw photos are image files that reside on a computer. This means that they can easily be reworked and touched up to remove minor imperfections using imaging software, which allows the photographer even more control over the finished product. Digital photographs are usually stored by the photographer on CDs, DVDs or similar data media, which are far more durable than chemical-based negatives. Most photo labs can make prints from digital media as well as film negatives.

Any disadvantages to digital? Only to those die-hard traditional film photographers whose opinion (perhaps rightfully so) is that digital takes the true art out of the concept of photography and puts it into the technical world of computers. But for your purposes, you won't see a difference whether your shooter is doing it traditional or tech style.

The Cost

You typically won't be able to get a finalized price until you know precisely what you want, and you should generally save the exact dollar amount talk and negotiations for the second meeting with the photographer you choose to go with. However, there are some cost factors that you can measure to get an idea of how expensive each photographer is relative to one another as you shop around. And do shop around! Keep in mind that photographers who are in high demand will charge a lot more than newbies, and the extra dollars may be very well worth it. Think about how each photographer's portfolio stacks up against the others. Remember, too, that you're paying for their travel time, their shooting time, their development time, the time spent designing your album(s), and the album and prints themselves.

During the comparison stage, you just want to get a feel for: (1) how much each photographer's time will cost, and (2) how much your prints and albums will cost. To determine an estimate for each photographer's time, find out how they charge. Is it by the hour or as a flat fee for the entire event? If it's by the hour, multiply the hourly cost by how many hours you'll want her with you, and find out about any overcharge fees for extra hours. Be sure not to forget your getting ready time: you'll get some great shots here! Ask also if you'll need to pay any travel expenses or other extra fees. Will she charge extra for a bridal portrait or engagement shoot?

Determine about how much this photographer charges for prints and albums. Ask how many pictures she generally takes, and if she can give you a cost-per-print estimate. Since you'll likely want at least a hundred prints, this gives you a starting number for your print cost and a metric to measure against other photographers. Find out what the styles of her albums are and how much the albums generally

---

\<NOTE\>

Let the Negotiations Begin

Once you've shopped around by meeting several photographers, and have narrowed down your search to a photographer whose personality, style, and cost are a winning combo, arrange for a follow-up meeting. Tell them you're interested in using them for your wedding but would like to negotiate a bit on the costs. Using the cost information you collected during your first meeting, and using your comparisons from other photographers you've met, see if you can whittle down the price. Try to negotiate a free engagement shoot, for example, or additional albums for your parents at a lower cost. See if the photographer would consider lowering the cost-per-print if you're willing to purchase the negatives. Just remember that you don't want to skimp on your wedding photography...far more durable than fondant frosting or a gorgeous floral centerpiece, these keepsakes will be with you as captured memories of your special day for years to come.

Do what you can in terms of price negotiation, and then book your chosen photographer for you date...if she's good, she'll be in high demand, especially during the peak months. You don't want to let someone else steal your star shooter away.

\</NOTE\>

run. If she's putting a lot of graphics design or layout work into an album, will she be charging extra for this time? How much will enlargements cost?

Ask the photographer if she offers package deals. Packages are usually a set number of prints and enlargements, along with one or more albums. Prints and enlargements are usually less expensive when ordered as a package.

Know Where to Look

As with all wedding professionals, check for references from those you trust. Look at the wedding albums of friends and family; do any stand out? Were the bride and groom happy with their photographer? Get contact information and add it to your list. Also, attend a wedding tradeshow or two. Bridal shows are a great way to chat with photographers, view their work, and get a feel for their style, personality, and price range. Get business cards from those you're interested in. Add them to your list!

You want to have, at a minimum, three photographers that you actually visit and spend time with to get a handle on their style and tastes. More is better, but it will depend on your available time and how many good prospects you're able to dig up. You should be able to do most of the digging on the web, and even start comparing some portfolios and package prices.

e-Resource

Do Your Photographer Hunting on the Web

You'll save time and get a wider array of choices to look at by hunting for local professionals online. There are vendor directories at the big wedding portal sites, and search engines like Citysearch (www.citysearch.com) and Google Local (local.google.com) can provide leads without the portals' advertising bias. You can check out professional photography associations and link up to photographers' websites, too...most have online portfolios and some include wedding package pricing. Some highly talented and sought-after photographers might even be too long distance for you to visit in person, but you'll still be able to check out their portfolio online and get a feel for their style, then follow up with a phone call or two to ask your questions and gauge your chemistry with them.

When you find photographers online whose style and portfolio stand out for you, add them to your list. You'll hopefully build up a large number of options that you can then take to phase two: the in-person meeting (or phone meeting, if they're long distance and you're especially interested in their work).

Photography Association and Network Websites

The Wedding Photojournalist Association (www.wpja.org) is an association of photographers specializing in a more candid, artistic style and documentary approach. If you're into the photojournalistic look, check these guys out. You can search for photographers in your area and even for those willing to travel to destination locations.

Another great photographer network we found is Event Photography Online (www.ep-o.com). From their home page, make sure you select the second option (Browse Portfolios of Photographers in Your Area). The first option requests a lot of personal information—including your budget—that will let vendors choose for themselves which brides they want to contact, which may be more of an advantage to them than to you.

The Wedding Photojournalist Association can help put you in touch with photographers specializing in a more candid, documentary approach.

But EPO' s local portfolio lookup is a great resource. Just plug in your zip code and set the event type to "wedding". Leave the budget option set to "All Budgets" and style set to "All Styles", then click the Search button. You can expand the search radius if you don't mind traveling a bit for vendor interviews or paying their travel expenses if you happen to select a distant photographer.

The results page lets you choose a photographer and browse a few shots of their work. These are just a couple samples—by no means an actual portfolio—but it lets you rule out those you absolutely aren't interested in, and click over to the websites of those you are.

The Professional Photographer Association (www.ppa.com) provides a link to search for photographers on their website. Click the "Locate a Photographer" link from the rather long navigation menu to be taken to a search page. For the most thorough search, just enter your zip code and click the "Search range of zip codes" checkbox. The results you get back will have a link for each photographer with more information on their work and a little icon next to the names of those who have received a PPA certification. The association claims that certified photographers have passed a written exam and had their work reviewed by a panel of judges (click the certification icon to for more info).

Event Photography Online is a photography network that will let you look up local photographers who are members. Select the second option to browse portfolios of photographers in your area.

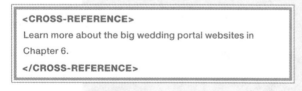

Local search results for photographers using the Professional Photographer Association's Website.

Wedding Channel's results page for a search of local photographers provides thumbnail images of each studio and a link to their website.

<CROSS-REFERENCE>

Learn more about the big wedding portal websites in Chapter 6.

</CROSS-REFERENCE>

Clicking on the "More Information" link of a photographer will provide address and website information (if a website is available). Checking their website or giving them a quick call should verify whether or not they are a wedding photographer; you want to narrow your considerations down to those that specialize in weddings.

Photographers' Websites and Online Portfolios

Whether you find a photographer online, through a friend, or from a business card you obtained at a bridal show, you can get a lot of information before even meeting them if they happen to have a website. And nowadays, most do...complete with a portfolio and sometimes even package prices.

Visiting photographers' websites can greatly cut down your research time by helping you to quickly trim down your contact list as you eliminate photographers whose style and portfolio are obviously not aligned with your tastes. This means you'll be spending less time on the phone and in studios dealing with photographers that aren't right for you.

Search Engines

Another good way to find photographers in your area is to use the local search engines. CitySearch.com provides an interface to enter your keywords ("wedding photography") and a city or zip code. The results that come up contain website links, addresses, and links to maps for directions.

Our favorite, Google Local (local.google.com), provides a similar service and integrates the results with a slick overall map containing markers for all your result locations.

The Wedding Portal Sites: Vendor Directories

The Knot, The Wedding Channel, Modern Bride and others all allow you to search for local photographers. As we mentioned before, photographers in their vendor databases pay top dollar to be on the top of the list while some of the best photographers might be in such demand that they only need to advertise via word-of-mouth, so finding vendors here may be a good start but not necessarily the local cream of the crop.

The Knot (www.theknot.com) also provides a photography-specific page available by pointing your browser to www.theknot.com/wpn; it's full of informative articles on wedding photography and contains an interface to their local database search.

The Knot has a photography-specific section of their website that you can access at www.theknot.com/wpn.

Know What You Want

As you're narrowing down your choices, you'll need to know what to ask your potential photographers to best determine whether or not they'll be right for you. You also want to start preparing a list of those must-have wedding shots: whether you're going for a formal or more photojournalistic style, you want to be able to let your photographer know which shots you are specifically looking for.

Questions to Ask Photographers

Are you comfortable with a photographer's style, skill, and personality? Are they enthusiastic about your wedding vision? Here's some questions to ask the ones with the most potential:

- Will you be personally shooting our wedding? (Some larger studios reserve the right to send any photographer to your wedding, not necessarily the one you're interviewing and getting to know)

<TIP>

Share Them! Posting Your Pics Online

Posting your planning pictures are a great way to share them with your family and friends, and what better spot than your wedding website? Most services provide some number of online photo albums so that you can group your pics together in different categories. If you're planning on posting anything taken by your photographer (samples of your engagement shoot, for example), make sure you get your photographer's permission.

If your wedding website doesn't offer photo albums (most free services don't), check out other online photo sharing services like shutterfly.com, ofoto.com, photos.yahoo.com, or snapfish.com. These sites let you post images up free of charge, as long as you don't mind the advertising banners.

</TIP>

- How do you charge for your time? For prints and albums? (Find out if the photographer charges a flat fee for the whole day, or hourly. If hourly, ask what additional fee will be charged for any extra hours)

- Do you have package deals available? (Often a less expensive way to go)

- Will you charge your travel costs or any other extra fees?

- What type of cameras do you use? If film, will you be using a medium format camera at least for the portrait shots? If digital, what's your maximum resolution? (For film, the photographer should use a medium format camera when taking portrait shots to ensure that they'll retain their quality when enlarged. For digital cameras, make sure the resolution is above 8 megapixels)

- Will you have backup cameras on hand?

- Will you be shooting another wedding or event on our wedding day? (You don't want a photographer who is going to have to run at a specific time, and who can't devote all her attention and energy to your wedding)

- Do you specialize in weddings?

- Can we give you a list of must-take shots?

- Do you develop your own film? (For film photographers, those that develop their own film may turn out better prints than those who ship them off to be developed by outside labs)

<NOTE>

When Should You Take Your Formal Pictures?

This is most often done right after the ceremony, as soon as you become husband and wife, right there at the very spot where you said your I do's. The photographer will arrange groups of family, attendants, and anyone else you may have provided in your must-take shot list to pose with you for your portraits. Meanwhile, the rest of your guests will be waiting for you outside the ceremony location, or will be traveling to the reception spot to kick of the cocktail hour.

If you're worried about the time involved to take your formal photographs, consider having your photographer shoot just the basic formals and leave the rest of your wedding to spontaneous and candid shots. Or have the photographer pull you and others aside during the reception for fifteen minutes or so to get the formal portraits done when you're all at the peak of excitement. Your photographer in this case can select a dramatic backdrop within your reception location to shoot against.

Although traditionally considered bad luck to see the bride before her walk down the aisle, some couples opt to take their formal shots just before the ceremony commences. Whatever time you decide to do your posing, make sure your photographer knows the schedule ahead of time.

</NOTE>

- Will we be able to see our proofs on the web?

- What's your policy for negatives (film) or original image files (digital)? Can we buy them from you? How long do you keep them?

Determine Those "Must-Have" Shots

You should have enough trust in your photographer and her expertise to be confident that she'll be taking the shots that best represent your day. However, you will likely have a good idea of portrait poses, individuals, and details that you want to make sure the photographer doesn't miss. Make a list of these shots and people, and pass them along to the photographer sometime before the big day. Review them with her for her feedback. She'll probably have additional ideas that you might not have even considered.

If your photographer favors more of a spontaneous, photojournalistic approach, you'll definitely want to make sure she has a list of the portraits that you're expecting. The most common include you both together, basking in your post-wedded glow (or pre-wedded, if you opt to shoot your formals before the ceremony...see the discussion on this below) as well as the two of you with each of your families and your bridal attendants. You might also want ones with just your maid of honor and best man, or your grandparents, or out-of-town guests. Make sure your photographer is prepared for the portrait shots you definitely must have, and let her organize the rest.

If you have any photos you'd like to see taken—portrait shots or otherwise—but are afraid your photographer might miss them, add these to the must-take list as well. Remember that these shots aren't guaranteed, but your photographer will do her best to get them in based on how the day unfolds.

Considerations and Tips

The Engagement Shoot

A fun option and a twist on the traditional bridal portrait (discussed below) is the engagement shoot, a photo session with you and your sweetie sometime before the wedding day in the studio or at an outdoor location of your choosing. It could be the two of you taking a romantic stroll down a beach, romping playfully across an open field in a park, holding hands at the location where he proposed, or you might opt for portrait-style elegance in a studio.

These pictures make a great addition to your personal planning album (we'll touch more on this in a bit) and choice shots can be enlarged, framed and placed on your guestbook table at your reception, or just outside the door of your ceremony.

Photographers normally will charge a separate fee for an engagement shoot, but it might be included in the package you select.

The Bridal Portrait

This is a formal session the bride has with the photographer two months or so before the wedding, typically in the studio with the bride donned in her bridal gown and hair styled the same way she'll have it on the big day. Like the engagement shoot, the bridal portrait is optional. The photos you get can be used in your wedding announcement and are often placed, framed, at your reception. If you're interested in having a formal bridal portrait done, ask your photographer if the cost of the session is included in your package.

Your "Planning Album"

Planning your wedding is an adventure! Why not organize a keepsake album to remember all the fun (and crazy) times you're having now? Keep a camera with you always, and have others snap pictures of you trying on your gown, of the bridesmaids trying on their dresses, of the two of you buying your wedding rings, even you at your county clerk's office getting your marriage license! Get pictures of the two of you addressing your invitations, designing your ceremony programs, and anything else you can think of. Add your engagement photo shoot to the mix, and put everything into an album. You can also put the pictures into an online album on your wedding website as you go, so that everyone can share the adventure!

The Getting Ready Shots

With a trusted photographer, the behind-the-scenes moments before the wedding can be captured as part of the story of your day and can be some of the most priceless shots you'll have in your album. Getting ready photos can include shots of the wedding gown hanging in waiting, the bride's hair and makeup getting done, and you each interacting with parents, siblings, and best friends before the main event.

Some photographers' packages don't include the extra hours necessary to cover the getting ready shots (you'd have to pay more), and some couples would rather have their privacy at this time. It's up to you and your photographer whether you'd like to add this prelude to your overall story. If you're game, these photos can be an emotional, anticipation-charged and very charming addition to your album.

Disposable Cameras

Capture your reception from every angle and perspective! Buy disposable cameras in bulk from somewhere like Costco or Wal-Mart, and place them on each individual reception table, or have them passed out by your attendants. Let your guests snap their own shots and highlights. It's generally understood that these are meant to be left behind for the bride and groom, although some misinformed guests might take them home: you may want someone to help you spread the word. After your honeymoon, it will be a lot of fun to take the whole stack of disposable cameras to a good economy photo processor and see what you get!

Ordering Your Photos and Albums

The wait time to start viewing your photos will vary between photographers. Some digital shooters might have the proofs online for you in a few days, while others might spend longer processing and touching them up, and could have them for you in a month or two. Some will hold onto them even longer!

Depending on your arrangement, you might need to set up an appointment to go in and choose your photos, or your photographer might have the proofs online for you to simply select and order prints and enlargements. If you're having an album made, you'll need to interact with your photographer a bit more, especially if the album is a custom made book with a lot of graphics design and layout work done (more common with digital photos).

Consider whether or not you'll be purchasing photos or albums for your parents; this may or may not be in your package deal, if you have one. Talk to your photographer about discounts for parents' albums before you book him to shoot your wedding. As with all albums, make sure the ones you purchase are acid-free. Cheaper albums that are not acid-free will damage your pictures over time.

If your photographer places your photos online to order prints and enlargements, it's a great way to share the pictures with family and friends. Just point them to the ordering website and put the burden of selecting and ordering into their own hands.

Other items you may be interested in ordering from your photographer are CD's or DVD's of your photos, perhaps with a slideshow gallery included. If you have the right equipment, you can even make copies for family and friends. Keep in mind that the resolution quality will be lower, to keep it manageable for regular on-screen viewing. The large resolution original files can usually be purchased separately, as can negatives of film-shot photography. Large resolution is meant for developing prints and enlargements and may be slow to view on the screen, depending on the power of the computer used.

Photographers typically hold onto negatives or large-resolution original images for one to three years after shooting. Check with yours to see how long she'll hold onto them, and when would be the latest you could purchase them.

<TIP>

Preserving Your Negatives

If you're purchasing negatives from film-shot photos, take care to handle and store them properly (digital photos are stored on CD's or DVD's, and don't produce negatives).

Negatives should be kept stored in archival sleeves that the lab or your photographer will typically place them in. If they're not in archival sleeves (for example, if they're just stuffed into a paper sleeve or envelope), stop by an office supply store like Staples or Office Depot and pick up the proper archival sleeves. Chemicals used in paper and plastic will damage negatives (and photos) over time. Negatives should never need to be removed from the archival sleeves; holding the negative against a light while still inside its sleeve will allow you to view the contents just fine. Remember that fingerprint oils and dust can deteriorate the negatives, and once bent or creased, they are damaged permanently. Keep the negatives stored out of the light, in a cool low-humidity room.

</TIP>

Get It in Writing: Your Photography Contract

Your written contract should include your wedding date, the time and location your photographer should arrive (for example, at your house to capture you getting ready), the photographer's name, and whether she'll be using any assistants. All shooting locations should be covered (ceremony, reception, getting ready) with precise addresses and starting times. Make sure your wedding package is laid out in detail as far as cost, number of prints and sizes included, as well as the cost for additional prints should you want them. If your package includes completed albums, check to see that the details of each album are in writing (size, binding, and so forth). Does your photographer charge by the hour? If so, ensure that the overtime fee is specified. A solid contract will also contain a written cancellation and refund policy.

Make sure both you and the photographer sign the contract and that you receive a copy for you records. Place the copy into your "Photos" folder.

Smart Ways to Cut Cost Without Compromising Your Photography

We've been repeating the "don't cut corners on your photography" mantra, and for good reason. The most durable and memorable keepsake you'll have of your wedding will be your photography, so if there's one spending category you want to keep from cutting (and may even want to splurge a little on), it's here. With that said, here's a few smart ideas that will help you manage your budget and at the same time won't compromise the quality of your photography.

<NOTE>

A Word on the "Photographer Friend"

A tempting option for a lot of couples is to allow a friend or family member who's a known shutterbug to handle their wedding photography and eliminate that 10% or so of their overall budget cost.

Our advice: don't do it. We've heard too many stories from brides and grooms who were very disappointed with the results. Must-have shots were missed, entire blocks of pictures came out blurry, dark, or otherwise substandard. One bride complained that her entire ceremony came out underexposed and was basically worthless.

Even if you're confident in your pal's photographic skills, they likely won't give you the results a professional could, with all their knowledge and experience. For this reason, we don't recommend using a student photographer to save cash either; your results just won't be the same. As we mentioned before, you're entrusting someone to capture one of the most significant points in your life, and you have just this one chance to get it done right. While it may be just one concern among many right now, in the future your photographs will be the most lasting keepsake of your special day. You don't want to regret not having done a better job capturing it.

</NOTE>

Build Your Own Album

Placing photos into an album is time-consuming, and many photographers will cut you a break if you relieve them of this burden and take it on yourself. Have your photographer give you the prints and enlargements you order, and create your own album; organize the layout as you see fit. Check online stores like eBay (www.ebay.com) for good quality photo albums at a low cost (make sure they're acid-free!) to save even more. The end result will be a beautiful album made even more personal because you've styled it yourself.

For the best cost-savings, don't order any prints from your photographer. Just buy the negatives or large resolution original digital files and have the prints and enlargements done yourself through an economy lab like the one offered at Costco (order photos online at www.costco.com). Creating your own album this way also keeps you more in control, and you can create as many albums as you like (as gifts for parents and other close relatives, for example).

Wait to Buy Your Negatives

If you are able to wait, buy few or no extra prints (those in addition to your albums or package contents) after your wedding. Wait a couple years or so and then contact your photographer and ask how much she's willing to sell you the negatives or high resolution digital files. Negotiate here for a lower price. Most photographers will be happy to sell them at a discount after some time has passed.

Have Your Bridal Portrait Taken at Your Wedding

If you'd like to have a bridal portrait done but funds are tight, consider having it taken the day of your wedding. If you'd like to use the picture in a published announcement and don't mind waiting until some weeks after the wedding to send the announcement off, this is an option that might work for you. It will save you the cost of an extra session, and since you're already done up in your gown, fab hair and makeup, bouquet, and are complete with that authentic wedding-day glow, the portrait itself will be that much more beautiful and true-to-life.

Checklist: "Must-Have" Shots

Choose those must-have shots you want your photographer to capture.

Before the Ceremony

- ☐ Bride at breakfast
- ☐ Wedding dress displayed
- ☐ Zipping up or buttoning the wedding gown
- ☐ Bride putting on her shoes
- ☐ Bride getting ready (makeup, hair)
- ☐ Bride looking into a mirror
- ☐ Bride looking out a window
- ☐ Bride adjusting garter
- ☐ Bride's mother adjusting her veil or necklace
- ☐ Bride alone
- ☐ Bride with her mother/stepmother
- ☐ Bride with her father/stepfather
- ☐ Bride with both parents and/or stepparents
- ☐ Bride with her maid of honor
- ☐ Bride with her bridesmaids
- ☐ Bride leaving the house
- ☐ Bride with her parents getting into the car
- ☐ Groom alone
- ☐ Groom with his mother/stepmother
- ☐ Groom with his father/stepfather
- ☐ Groom with both parents/ stepparents
- ☐ Groom with his best man
- ☐ Groom with his groomsmen
- ☐ Groom with the bride's father
- ☐ Groom and groomsmen getting boutonnieres
- ☐ Groom before the ceremony
- ☐ Bride arriving at the ceremony location
- ☐ Bride in bridal chamber before the ceremony
- ☐ _____
- ☐ _____

At the Ceremony

- ☐ Ceremony site inside and out, with guests arriving
- ☐ Ushers escorting special guests to their seats
- ☐ Ushers passing out the ceremony program
- ☐ Entire wedding party before the procession
- ☐ Bride holding father's arm before the procession
- ☐ Ceremony musicians
- ☐ Officiant
- ☐ Groom and best man waiting in the altar
- ☐ Bride's mother/stepmother walking down the aisle
- ☐ Groom's parents/stepparents walking down the aisle
- ☐ Wedding party walking down the aisle in the procession
- ☐ Maid of honor walking down the aisle in the procession
- ☐ Flower girl(s) and ring bearer walking down the aisle
- ☐ Bride and her father/stepfather walking down the aisle
- ☐ Father/stepfather giving bride away
- ☐ Groom meeting and seeing the bride for the first time
- ☐ Bride and groom in the altar during the ceremony
- ☐ Readers at the ceremony
- ☐ Guests watching the ceremony
- ☐ Flowers and other decorations
- ☐ Bride and groom exchanging vows, close up and wide shots
- ☐ Ring exchange
- ☐ Other traditional cultural rituals
- ☐ The kiss
- ☐ Bride and groom leading the recessional
- ☐ Bride and groom outside the ceremony location
- ☐ Signing of the marriage license
- ☐ Bride and groom alone
- ☐ Bride and groom with ceremony officiant
- ☐ Bride and groom with parents/stepparents
- ☐ Bride and groom with families
- ☐ Bride and groom with the wedding party
- ☐ Bride and groom with special guests
- ☐ Bride's and groom's hands displaying rings
- ☐ Guests blowing bubbles or throwing flower petals
- ☐ Bride and groom getting into the car
- ☐ Bride and groom in the backseat of their car
- ☐ _____
- ☐ _____

Checklist: "Must-Have" Shots (continued)

At the Reception

☐ Bride and groom arriving
☐ Bride and groom getting out of car
☐ Bride and groom greeting their guests
☐ Big group picture, all guests with bride and groom
☐ Outside and inside of the reception site
☐ Entire tent (if applicable)
☐ Signing of the guestbook
☐ Place card table
☐ Gift table
☐ Table centerpieces
☐ Place settings and wedding favors
☐ Site decoration details
☐ Guests at cocktail hour
☐ The receiving line (if applicable)
☐ Entrance of the wedding party
☐ Entrance of the bride and groom
☐ Bride and groom's table (head table)
☐ Individuals giving toasts
☐ Close-up of a dinner serving or the buffet setup
☐ Bride and groom at parents' tables
☐ Group pictures of guests at each table
☐ Bride and groom's first dance
☐ Bride and father/stepfather dance
☐ Groom and mother/stepmother dance
☐ Guests dancing
☐ Reception musicians
☐ Bride and groom dancing
☐ Bride and groom talking to guests
☐ Guests' candid shots
☐ Wedding cake and table decorations
☐ Groom's cake (if applicable)
☐ Bride and groom cutting the cake
☐ Bride and groom feeding each other cake
☐ Bride and groom toasting
☐ Throwing / catching of the bouquet
☐ Groom taking off the bride's garter
☐ Throwing / catching of the garter
☐ Bride and groom with the catchers of the bouquet and garter
☐ The getaway car
☐ Bride and groom leaving
☐ Guests blowing bubbles or flower petals
☐ Bride and groom driving away
☐ _____
☐ _____

Guests shots that shouldn't be missed: (Provide a seating chart to your photographer so guests can be easily located)

_____
_____
_____
_____
_____
_____
_____
_____
_____
_____
_____
_____

Considerations Worksheet: Photographer

Photography Budget: $

Photography Style

☐ Photojournalism (candid photos, some portraits)
☐ Formal (posed portrait-style photos, some candids)

Photography Type

☐ Digital
☐ Film

Events to be Covered

☐ Engagement Session / Bridal Portrait
☐ Getting Ready
☐ Ceremony
☐ Reception
☐ Going Away

Film Color

☐ Color
☐ Black-and-White
☐ Sepia
☐ Mixture

Package Contents Required

☐ Coffee Table Book Album(s)
☐ Wedding Album(s)
☐ Insert-style Album(s)
☐ Prints Only
☐ Enlargements
☐ Negatives / Digital Source Files
☐ Presentation Box

Notes:

Comparison Forms: Photographer 1

Appointment Date: _____   Time: _____

Photographer: _____   Years of Experience: _____

Address: _____

_____

Contact: _____   Assistant: _____

Email: _____   Phone: _____   Fax: _____

Website: _____   Recommended by: _____

Style (Journalistic, Formal): _____   Type: ☐ Digital   ☐ Film   ☐ Both

Film Color: _____   Backup Equipment: _____

Package Description: _____

_____

_____

Full Day Rate: $ _____   Cost per Hour: $ _____   Cost per Extra Hour(s): $ _____

Insurance Coverage: _____

Payment Policy: _____

Cancellation Policy: _____

Booking Deposit: $ _____   Required by: _____

Additional Fees: $ _____

Total Estimated Cost: $ _____

Comments: _____

_____

_____

_____

_____

_____

_____

_____

_____

_____

_____

_____

Comparison Forms: Photographer 2

Appointment Date: _____ Time: _____

Photographer: _____ Years of Experience: _____

Address: _____

Contact: _____ Assistant: _____

Email: _____ Phone: _____ Fax: _____

Website: _____ Recommended by: _____

Style (Journalistic, Formal): _____ Type: ☐ Digital ☐ Film ☐ Both

Film Color: _____ Backup Equipment: _____

Package Description: _____

_____

Full Day Rate: $ _____ Cost per Hour: $ _____ Cost per Extra Hour(s): $ _____

Insurance Coverage: _____

Payment Policy: _____

Cancellation Policy: _____

Booking Deposit: $ _____ Required by: _____

Additional Fees: $ _____

Total Estimated Cost: $ _____

Comments: _____

_____

_____

_____

_____

_____

_____

_____

_____

_____

_____

_____

_____

Contact Sheet: Photographer

Date Booked:

Photographer:

Address:

Contact:

Email:

Phone:

Fax:

Website:

Package Description:

Staple Business Card

Special Instructions:

Photo Session Location 1:   Time:

Photo Session Location 2:   Time:

Photo Session Location 3:   Time:

Photo Session Location 4:   Time:

Exclusive reservation time from   to

Will engagement session / bridal portraits be taken?   ☐ Yes   ☐ No

If yes, cost for session: $ Session Date: No. of Pictures:

Wedding Album Cost: $ Pickup Date: No. of Pictures:

Negatives/Source Files Cost: $ Release Date:

Total Cost: $

Deposit: $ Date Paid:

Balance: $ Date Due:

Notes:

Chapter 13
Make a Scene with the Right Videographer

- Do I Need a Videographer?

- Videography Styles

- How to Find the Right Videographer

- Ideas to Cut Cost

- e-Plan It! Use Your e-Resources:

    Do Your Videography Hunting on the Web
    Videography Association Websites
    Videographers' Websites and Online Demos

- Worksheets:

    Considerations Worksheet: Videographer
    Comparison Forms: Videographer
    Contact Sheet: Videographer

V ideography allows you to immortalize your wedding beyond photography, to preserve the action and sounds of your special day in ways never before possible. How do you find the right one, and what are the things to look for?

Do I Need a Videographer?

Some couples just don't like the idea of a wedding video and want nothing more than a good photography package to preserve their memories. But before skipping over this chapter altogether, take a few moments to consider what you'll be getting with a good videographer, and how the possibilities offered by the latest technical gear and editing equipment stack up to your friend's camcorder or to photography alone.

What Videography Will Give You

Couples often feel as though their wedding day went by in a blur. After months of planning and effort, the big day comes in a rush, and everything happens so fast and with such emotion that before they know it, the day is over. A good wedding video is like a time machine that can take you back to your wedding day any time you like. You can experience all the sounds, action, subtle details and endearing moments all over again, including those you might have missed or might otherwise forget. It's a living documentary that will be available to your children, their children, and so on. Imagine being able to watch your grandparents' wedding, or their grandparents'!

Do the words "wedding video" invoke thoughts of a cheesy soundtrack, amateurish screen wipes and complete, unbroken coverage of the chicken dance? Today, digital video and editing technology make it easier and more affordable than ever to create wedding videos as engaging and sophisticated as quality television documentaries, complete with voice-over interviews, flashbacks, professional scene cuts, special effects and more. The style you choose is up to you, but you have more choices for capturing the sights, sounds, and action of your special day now than ever before.

Professional or Amateur?

Common question: "I have a friend or family member with a camcorder. Can't he take my wedding video?"

Our view on going the amateur route with photography and videography is that you should resist the temptation. These are real mementos of your day, and you don't want just anybody with the responsibility of capturing such a special time in your life. We've heard countless stories about individuals missing important events, running out of batteries, and in general just producing shaky or dizzying footage. You'll inevitably have those guests who bring their own cameras and camcorders, and the highlights they capture will be great, but certainly not a complete story of your day. And you have to ask yourself:

even if a friend or family member was charged with the responsibility of documenting all the special moments and details of your wedding, will they be able to enjoy themselves as much?

A professional videographer will use his experience, artistic sense and eye for detail to capture the details and moments as completely as possible. Modern editing techniques, soundtrack mixers, and special effects can produce a video you'll love to watch again and again and will be proud to show to others.

Ultimately, the choice is yours, of course. If you're on a mega-demanding budget, can barely afford a good photography package, and are having a small, intimate affair—perhaps with just immediate family and the closest of friends—go ahead and ask one of those attending (or accept their offer) to handle the role of videographer. You can even have the raw footage professionally edited at a later date when you can better afford it, producing a more compact, sophisticated overall production. A professionally edited video is one you'll be more apt to watch often and show others. Just keep in mind that the quality of video produced by consumer cameras are almost never up to par with the kind of equipment that a good pro would use (see the section on Gear later in this chapter).

Videography vs. Photography

Ask a photographer and he'll probably tell you that photography is more important. Ask a videographer and he'll stress the equal importance of both. The real question is, how important is videography to you? Remember that while you can't put your wedding video in a frame above the mantle or pull it out of your wallet to show a friend, a photograph can't capture the sound of your voices exchanging vows or the sounds and activity of your reception party.

When it comes to wedding videos, there's something about the live-action capture of such a special moment that can take you back like nothing else. Consider how popular movies are today as a way of telling a story. Videography is quickly becoming less of an optional side-kick to photography and more of an equal partner in preserving the memory of your day.

Videography Styles

Individual videographers will bring a style all their own when putting together a production that captures your day, whether it's more formal and traditional or hip and humorous. When selecting videographers, spend the same time talking with them and feeling out their style as you did when selecting your photographer. Check out their demos and decide if their tone follows with your own vision. Remember that a lot of the magic of molding a wedding video, at least for the cinematic styles, happens during the editing, so ask how much interaction and input you'll have during their editing process.

Depending on the mood you're trying to capture, additions to your wedding video such as a photo montage, the inclusion of childhood photos and video clips, or out-takes and bloopers can make a wedding video more nostalgic, romantic or even humorous. The possibilities are pretty broad, and a lot of fun. We'll go over some such additions later, but in general your video will fall somewhere in between the two basic videography styles:

The Cinematic Documentary

This style involves extensive editing to highlight the important events, moments, and details that result in an engaging, fast-moving story. Transitions and back-and-forth scene cutting are worked in along with voice-over dialogue by you or those close to you. The soundtrack is mixed in to highlight the mood and atmosphere of each scene, and the entire production has a coherent documentary-like feel to it.

Most good cinematic style wedding videos are shot with two cameras: this allows multiple perspectives of the most important events that can then be mixed in the finished video. It also allows one camera to focus on the main action while another can scope for charming little details and additions to be worked in later as enhancements. This style requires a lot more attention to detail and a considerable amount of post-shooting work. Editing can often take up to 30 or 40 hours on a computer after the footage is collected.

A "highlights" reel is sometimes included, which we highly recommend. This is your entire day boiled down to a 15 minute or so fast-moving collection of all the main scenes, endearing moments, and hilarious bloopers, set to an appropriate soundtrack. The editing is key here. It takes a lot of work to produce, but the result is a truly entertaining snapshot of your day that you will want to watch again and again. You can proudly show it friends, family, coworkers—you name it! Highlights like this are incredibly entertaining and if done properly can captivate even the most attention-deficient audience, giving them a solid feel for the emotion, atmosphere, and beauty of your wedding day in a short amount of time.

The Straight Shot

From beginning to end, this is a single-camera take of your wedding without edits or anything especially fancy. It's what you'll get if you have a friend or relative shoot your day with a camcorder. If you do hire a videographer, this is going to be your most basic and inexpensive option, because no extensive editing will be done to the raw footage, except maybe a title page and some background music. Some companies might add screen wipes and similar effects to make the scene cuts and transitions smoother. Expect to have this style of video delivered shortly after your wedding, since little post-shooting work will be done on it.

Watching a straight-shot wedding video is going to be like watching any other home movie: kinda lengthy, with a lot of manual jumping ahead to the good parts. At least you'll have the sights and sounds of your wedding preserved to revisit when you wish, and you can always send the raw footage in to be professionally edited at a later date.

Consider the Extras

As you go over the packages offered by videographers, check to see if they include the following fun extras that might interest you. If they don't, discuss the options with the videographer and see if they're willing to add anything into the deal.

Childhood Photos and Video Clips

You might want to supply the videographer with photos of each of you growing up, as well as some old video footage that you might have collecting dust in your parents' garage. If you're into this kind of "memory montage", it might be a nice way to start off the wedding story.

Getting Ready Sequence

This is always a winner, as long as you don't mind the camera there with you while you're fixing yourself up (you might have your photographer there as well!). If you each have a cameraperson with you (one with the groom and his entourage and one with the bride and hers), this makes for a great behind-the-scenes documentary that can be edited to go back and forth between both perspectives. A lot of fun, and a great way to remember all that pre-wedding excitement.

Highlights Reel

We mentioned this when discussing the cinematic format above. It's a great way to condense all the emotion, excitement, and visual impact of your wedding in a fast-paced whirlwind look at the big day from getting ready to reception. This is great for showing pals all the glory of your wedding in a time-frame that can fit anywhere and without boring them to death with the flowery minutia.

Out-takes and Bloopers

This is a fun option to separate those especially hilarious or outrageous moments from the rest of the video. Extra cool is when they're added to the end of the video, movie-style, during the scrolling of the "credits".

DVD Menus and Chapters

If your videographer is providing your video on DVD (we highly suggest this...see our DVD section in "The Gear"), ask if you'll have a complete intro sequence, menu, and chapters like a real DVD movie. This technique, called "DVD authoring", adds a great finishing touch and a cool convenience to your wedding video, enabling you to jump immediately to specific sections. Go straight to your "Getting Ready" chapter, then jump over to your "Highlights", and after that to "Best Wishes", for example. If your videographer simply transfers the footage to a DVD, you may not be provided with this feature.

Specially Designed Cases

Some videographers provide your wedding videos in custom cases designed like those of real movies. You may have a creative title, movie blurbs, PG rating, and the works. Whether you add input or let your videographer come up with the content themselves is up to you. A fun touch that might be included in your package.

How to Find the Right Videographer

So how are you going to find the right video wiz for you? Start off by knowing where to look: get references from family, friends, bridal fairs, online (see the following e-Resource), and more. We'd suggest getting contacts for at least six local videographers with whom you see some potential. Use the information and demo clips on their websites to help eliminate the ones whose styles are definitely not aligned with your own tastes. Don't scratch anyone off your list initially because they're too expensive, and don't settle on the first company whose online demo clips you're enamored with.

Once you've settled on six top picks, give them each a phone call or send an e-mail to request a demo tape or DVD. When you have time to watch the full demos, consider the quality, technique, and style. We'll go over what to watch for in a bit. Based on the strength of the demos, trim your list further to no more than three solid candidates. Call each and set up an appointment.

Spend some face time, ask questions, and negotiate the costs. We'll advise you next on what to ask and what to look for in terms of personality, gear, and skills. When you pick your winner, go over the fine print before signing a contract. The objective throughout is to shop smart and keep your options as open as possible in order to hire the videographer best suited to your taste and budget.

Know Where to Look

Check first for those trusty referrals. Do any friends or family members have great stories about a videographer that really worked for them? Ask to see their video, and if it moves you, add the videographer to your list. You can also check with your photographer to see if they've worked with any videographers in the past that they would recommend.

Bridal fairs are a great place to meet and chat with videographers, and many have demos playing of weddings that they've shot. But, even if you think you might be interested in them, don't sign up on the spot! If they're pushing you to do so, you don't want to work with them anyway. By shopping around and going through the entire selection process we outline here, you'll give yourself the best advantage in finding the right videographer.

e-Resource

Do Your Videography Hunting on the Web

Now it's time to make use of some available e-Resources to help in finding great local videographers. Even those who you found through other avenues will most likely have a website, and you'll be able to get a lot of useful information there: package details, policies, prices, and even demo clips. If you discover that one of the videographers on your list is too expensive, don't scratch them off the list yet. Seeing their demo and the quality of their work will be great comparative help later on. Plus, if you find that nobody compares with them, you can always negotiate and try to massage your budget categories.

Videography Association Websites

The Wedding and Event Videographers Association (WEVA) is a good spot to check for potentials. Visit them at www.weva.com and click on the "Bride's Guide" link in the left-hand menu.

You have two choices to search for videographers here: you can enter your wedding information using an online form (click on the "Find A Videographer" link) so that videographers contact you, or you can search by state for videographers' websites. We recommend you stay in control of your own research and review the videographers they list by state. While these lists don't cover all their members, it lets you start looking at videographers'

The Bride's Guide section of WEVA, the Wedding and Event Videographers Association.

websites immediately. We're also skeptical of any service that asks for too much personal information; it gives the advantage to their members and not to you. Click the "Member Links By State" link from the Bride's Guide menu, and select your state. You'll get a list of cities sorted alphabetically, and each city on the list will contain one or more videography entries, with website links. Check the websites and add any that interest you to your list of potentials

You'll notice that WEVA's lists contain videography professionals that may not necessarily specialize in weddings. A quick phone call or visit to their website should clarify this. Make sure you only spend time investigating those with weddings as their specialty.

Videographers' Websites and Online Demos

Like photographers' websites, those of videographers usually list package details, policies, and samples of their work.

In addition to giving you basic pricing and package details, the websites will allow you to get a feel for the videographers' styles even before you receive a complete demo. Scratch a videographer off your list when it's apparent that their quality and style do not agree with your tastes.

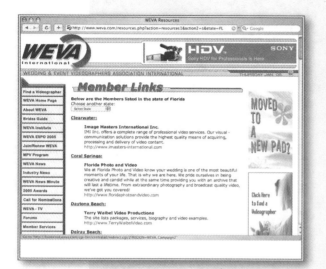

State-specific videography entries are listed by city in WEVA's videography directory.

Search Engines

See what contacts you can drum up using the search engines. Google (www.google.com), Citysearch (www.citysearch.com), and Google Local (local.google.com) have been the ones we've used so far in this book. Just make sure that the companies you find specialize in weddings; the search engines might give results that are a little too general at times. A quick phone call or perusal of the company's website should make it clear enough. If any videographers show potential, add them to your list.

The Wedding Portal Sites: Vendor Directories

A great resource for checking out a lot of videographers at once is to do a local vendor search on your favorite portal site. You'll get a list of vendors in your area, complete with a little thumbnail for each and a link to their website. This should give you a wide variety of wedding videography websites to browse so you can get a feel for how the various packages and online demo clips compare.

The Knot's videographer search provides a list of videographers in your area with basic information, a contact form, and website link for each.

Know What to Look For

Once you've built up a list of five or six contacts (if you have more on your list, narrow them down to six favorites, or you won't have time to view all the demos), send a request to each videographer for their demo tape, as well as any pricing and package information if they don't have it posted on their website. You'll be using this information to narrow your list down to three potential videographers to actually interview. You'll want to make sure their personality and gear is up to the task of capturing the memories and emotions of such an important day so that you and your family can relive them forever!

The Demo

Position, perspective angles, lighting, and sound all come from experience, and the best way to gauge the experience of each videographer—as well as to see if their personal style fits with what you want—is to look at their demo tapes. Go over each videographer's demo carefully. Can you see the difference in their styles? Compare each demo and see which aspects of each you like and dislike.

While reviewing demos, watch the entire wedding videos, not just highlight reels. Yes, this may take some time, but it's the only way to really see the quality of the work. During the ceremony scenes, how are the classic shots? Look

<CROSS-REFERENCE>

Learn more about the big wedding portal websites in Chapter 6, "The Online Wedding Portals: Ideas and More Galore".

</CROSS-REFERENCE>

for things like a view down the aisle to the altar, as well as from the opposite direction as the bride makes her way arm-in-arm with Dad towards the altar (and the camera). How are the close-ups during the vows? Do you see both the bride's and the groom's faces? Notice how the perspectives cut back and forth (if they do at all; this kind of complete coverage is difficult to get without two cameras). An important thing to take note of during the ceremony is the sound: are the vows clear? Do the readers, musicians, and singers come out loud or are they distant and muffled?

When viewing the reception scenes, pay attention to the coverage and editing. Is it smooth, and are the transitions between scenes done professionally? Is the sound clear and balanced? Is it choppy, distorted, or too loud? How is the positioning of the cameras: are the scenes composed together well?

The video should tell the story of the wedding and capture the mood, the excitement, and emotions of the day. Details and close-ups should be included that add to the story and drama. The bride and groom shouldn't be the only focus; the wedding party and individual guests should be given attention as well. If the style is more cinematic, how is the overall pace of the video? It should move at the right speed, without skipping over so much that you feel lost and without languishing in the same spot so much that you find yourself getting bored. The entire result should be engaging and entertaining. Take note of any special effects. Do they actually add to the video, or are they just plain cheesy? How about the music; does it go with the scenes? For each demo you review, think about how it makes you feel. Which ones capture you the most and tell the story the best way, conveying all the emotion and energy of the day? These are the ones you want to focus on.

In general, the sound and lighting throughout the video should be clean and consistent. If you see a trend in washed-out faces, dark shadows that hide the details, and jumpy editing containing gaps or awkward transitions, it's a bad sign. Remember that these demos should be their best work.

The Cost

Your actual price will depend on the package you select, the options you prefer, the experience of the videographer and how much time is involved. The typical wedding requires the continuous work of two camerapersons over five hours or more, followed by up to 40 or 50 hours of post-shooting editing work to get all that raw footage worked into a smooth, professional production.

For each demo, take note of the basic package cost of the company who sent it (you should be able to swipe this info from their website). This will give you a good idea of the quality of work that can be delivered for each price range. The least expensive price you'll find will probably be around $800 and the more expensive companies will charge anywhere from $2,000 to $5,000 and up. Select three videographers that you like who fit more or less in your budget (you can negotiate with them when you meet) and make an appointment with each one.

The Personality

Upon narrowing your selection down to three companies whose quality of samples you find to your liking, it's time to spend some actual face time with the videographer or videographers who will be shooting and editing your wedding production. We list some questions you want to pose each videographer a bit later.

When meeting a videographer, try to get a feel for their personality. You will probably have already seen (and approved of) their demo, but an in-person meeting is essential for gauging the chemistry you have with them. Like your photographer, you'll want to be comfortable with this person who will be shadowing you on your special day. When you describe your wedding vision, are they enthusiastic? Notice how well they listen to you. If they interrupt, change the subject, or seem otherwise uninterested in what you have to say, they'll probably be just as likely to exclude your input when it comes to editing your video.

Look for someone with good people skills; you don't want an obnoxious or obtrusive person shoving a video camera in your guests' faces. A good videographer knows how to be transparent and out of the way, but always there at the right time and place to catch the important shots.

The Gear

As you're interviewing each videographer, take note of the equipment they use. Some videographers will flaunt their gear, but just remember that experience is more important than how flashy their stuff is. A $1,000 dollar video camera in the hands of an experienced videographer and editing wizard will give you a priceless wedding production, while a $15,000 camera in the hands of an amateur will always be amateurish.

<NOTE>

Are You My Videographer?

Like photographers, large companies often employ several videographers, and the one(s) they send to your wedding might not even be the individual you're talking to during the interview. Some companies will send you a demo containing the work of their best videographers and send less experienced ones to your wedding. As you gauge personality, make sure the individual or individuals you talk to will actually be at your event, and verify that the demo you reviewed contains their work.

Another thing to keep in mind is that the editing is a large component of the finished video, and this is independent of who shoots the actual footage. You can ask who will be editing the video—it may or may not be the person who shoots the video—and meet them as well. Ask if the person editing your wedding was involved with editing the demo you viewed.

</NOTE>

Digital or analog?

What's the difference between digital cameras and analog (tape)? It really comes down to the quality of the picture: Super VHS and Hi-8 cameras produce output with a quality of 400 lines of resolution while digital produces 530 lines of resolution, a substantially superior quality (VHS has a paltry 230 lines of resolution, in case you were interested). In this day and age, you really want to go digital. The latest digital cameras are smaller, offer exceptional color quality and low-light capabilities, and produce output that can be fed directly into a computer for editing.

Should you have one or two cameras?

Two cameras will cost more, but the cost will be worth it, especially if you're shooting for a cinematic style (see our earlier discussion on styles). Unless your budget just won't allow it or you're planning to have a straight-shot video taken, ask for two cameras. It will bring greater depth to your video: you'll get extra points of view that will allow for more professional and polished editing. Make sure you clarify with each videographer whether or not your second camera is truly a second cameraperson, and not just a camera on a tripod.

What kind of audio equipment?

You want to make sure that you're going to be given a wireless microphone for your vows, otherwise this priceless moment might not be properly captured. Good videographers will have invested well into their audio. Some might actually use devices called sound recorders, which are small enough to be placed inside a pocket and can also be left at the podium or in the location of your singers. Sound recorders record their audio onto a digital disk or flash memory, and must be synchronized with the video later during editing. The advantage is that there will be no danger of interference or loss as there is with some wireless microphones, and the quality of the sound captured is very high.

What format will you receive your video on?

Trust us: you want your video on DVD. Don't settle for VHS. There's no need for that kind of substandard technology in this day and age with something so important as your wedding video. There is no loss of quality when going from a digital master to DVD like there is with VHS. A DVD is forever, and will last for generations while a VHS tape will eventually deteriorate (it wears out a little each time it's watched, in fact). If you can, get your videographer to include a full intro sequence and an interactive menu with chapters, which will let you jump to certain sections (getting ready, ceremony, reception, highlights, and so on) just like a real movie. This is not just a great finishing touch, but an incredible convenience and you'll enjoy your little production a whole lot more with the added control in navigating it.

Questions to Ask Videographers

Here's some questions you'll want to pose to the three or so videographers you interview. Think of any more that apply to your situation and preferences and make absolutely sure you're comfortable with them before you sign any contract.

- Will you be the one shooting my wedding? Was your work on the demo you sent me? (You want to be talking to the one who will actually be there and whose work you reviewed)

- How long have you been in business? (Experience is key with videographers)

- What format do you shoot on? (Digital is the superior choice, and what you should be looking for)

- What kind of audio equipment do you use? How will the vows be recorded? (Make sure you'll at least be wirelessly mic'd up for the vows)

- Will you have emergency equipment on hand in case something goes wrong?

- Can I get my wedding video on DVD or is this an extra charge? Will the DVD have an introductory sequence and a chapter menu?

- How long will the finished video be? (Most people agree that 30 minutes is too superficial and longer than 2 hours is too boring. Look for a videographer that will keep it between the two extremes, and divide it into chapters, such as "getting ready", "ceremony", "reception", and so forth. See if the videographer will include a 15-minute or so "highlights" chapter for a quick snapshot of your overall day.)

- How many cameras will I have at my wedding? (This should be detailed in your package and contract as well. If you have a second camera, make sure it's a live cameraperson and not a stationary tripod)

- How long will you be covering the wedding? What's your fee for extra hours?

- Will you cover our getting ready period or rehearsal? Is this included, or will it be an extra cost? How much?

- Do you interview guests during the reception? How do you do it? (This makes a nice addition to the wedding video, often as a separate chapter of "best wishes". How they obtain these gems depends on their style: will they be approaching your guests themselves, or will they have a camera off to the side and allow guests to come to them?)

- Can you explain exactly what kind of editing, music, and effects are included in the package(s) I'm interested in?

- Will I be able to buy the unedited master footage? How much will this cost?

- How much do you charge for extra copies?

<NOTE>

If you're interested in learning more about DVD technology, check out www.dvddemystified.com/dvdfaq.html

</NOTE>

- How long will it take to get my finished video?

- Will I see a preview or "rough cut" of my video to offer feedback before the final editing?

- Will you be charging for transportation or any other additional fees?

- How familiar are you with my ceremony and reception locations?

- Have you worked with our photographer before?

Get It in Writing: Your Videography Contract

Your videography contract should clearly state your wedding date, your videographer's name, the exact time and address of each location your videographer will be arriving at (if both of you will be filmed during your getting ready period, make sure both addresses are included). Your package should be laid out in detail, including cost, number of cameras, hours included, any editing points you've agreed on, and how many copies you will be receiving. There should be a total cost in the contract, any extra fees (overtime rates, travel charges, and so forth), and estimated dates you'll receive the "rough cut" preview and final video.

Ideas to Cut Cost

As with photography, your wedding video is a durable, lasting keepsake of your big day. It will capture the memories and emotions of your wedding in vivid live action and sound, and you don't want to regret not having this record later. Be careful on cutting too many costs here. However, managing a wedding budget is always a challenge, and you'll need to compromise as much as possible to fit it all in. Here are some ideas for making videography work on tight funds.

Avoid Getting Charged for Extra Hours

Unless your videographer is charging you a flat fee for the day, you'll be billed extra for hours above and beyond what you contract for. Avoid this by knowing up front how much time you'll need the camera and negotiate to get this time into your contract. Never underestimate the power of negotiation! If your package doesn't quite cover the hours you think you'll need, try to get the videographer to squeeze the extra time into your contract. Once you sign that contract, any extra time you realize later on that you need will come at an extra cost.

Use a Single Camera

We discussed the benefits of having an extra camera in this chapter, but if you're strapped, a single camera will do in the hands of an experienced videographer who knows how to get the best angles and shots. Strong editing skills and an overall knack for storytelling, which you should be looking for anyway, should compensate for some of the missed perspectives and details.

Cost-Effective Duality

If you can find a company offering both photography and videography, you'll probably save by having them do both. Just be careful that their quality and experience in both areas is acceptable to you. Examine their photography portfolio and video demos thoroughly.

Make Your Own Copies

If you're getting your wedding video on DVD (you should be!), the quality of any copies you make with a DVD recorder will be just as high as the original, unlike videotape, which degrades when it's copied. Just make sure you have your videographer's permission to do this; you don't want to step on any copyright toes, and your contract might make copying the video illegal. See if your videographer will sell you the rights and provide a master copy; it will probably be cheaper to buy this and make as many copies as you like than buying individual copies from the videographer.

Go for a Straight Shot Capture and Edit Later

Can't afford those fancy edited packages? Don't drop your entire videography; prepare for the future. Go ahead and purchase the most basic service you can, which is usually one or two cameras that film your big day straight through and provide you with a lengthy video that has been only minimally edited. Some companies will let you purchase the raw footage without any editing at all (see the sidebar), which is even better. In either case, the low editing demand will result in a very low price for you. The finished video won't be the slick, professional production you'd get with all that editing, but if you hired a good videographer, it will be detailed, thorough coverage of your day. And with the complete footage in hand, you can always send it off to be professionally edited later when you can better afford it. If you were to scratch videography off altogether, such an opportunity will be irretrievably lost.

<NOTE>

A Word on Master Copies and Raw Footage

A master copy is a high grade version of your wedding video. When the videographer creates your wedding DVDs and sends them to you, they may be in a compressed format, which allows more video to fit onto a single disc. Ask your videographer if this is the case and if so, request a master copy; the master is what you'll want to use to make copies, as it's the highest quality version of your wedding video possible. If your videographer does not provide the master (typically to keep you from making your own copies and ensure that you buy from them), try and negotiate a length of time where the master will eventually revert to you, usually after a year or so of your wedding.

Raw footage is the raw, uncut and unedited recording of your wedding: every second of it! Raw footage will likely span multiple DVDs, as they are uncompressed and can contain several hours of recorded footage, especially if multiple cameras are used. Videography companies will usually be happy to sell you the raw copies for a reasonable fee.

</NOTE>

Considerations Worksheet: Videographer

Videography Budget: $ _____

Videography Style

☐ Cinematic Documentary (extensive editing)
☐ Straight Shot (less or no editing)

Video Type

☐ Digital
☐ Analog

Events to be Covered

☐ Rehearsal
☐ Getting Ready
☐ Ceremony
☐ Reception
☐ Going Away

Package Contents Required

☐ One Camera
☐ Two Cameras
☐ DVD Video
☐ VHS Video
☐ Complete Raw Footage Included
☐ Extra copies: _____

Video Extras

☐ DVD Menus and Chapters
☐ Special Effects
☐ Childhood Photos and Video Clip Additions
☐ Getting Ready Sequence
☐ Highlights Reel
☐ Out-takes and Bloopers
☐ Best Wishes from Guests
☐ Specially Designed Cases
☐ _____

Notes: _____
_____
_____
_____
_____
_____
_____
_____
_____
_____
_____
_____
_____
_____
_____
_____
_____
_____

Comparison Forms: Videographer 1

Appointment Date: _____ Time: _____

Videographer: _____ Years of Experience: _____

Address: _____

_____

Contact: _____ Assistant: _____

Email: _____ Phone: _____ Fax: _____

Website: _____ Recommended by: _____

Style (Documentary, Straight Shot): _____ Type: ☐ Digital   ☐ Analog

Backup Equipment: _____

Package Description: _____

_____

_____

_____

Video Extras: _____

_____

Full Day Rate: $ _____ Cost per Hour: $ _____ Cost per Extra Hour(s): $ _____

Insurance Coverage: _____

Payment Policy: _____

Cancellation Policy: _____

Booking Deposit: $ _____ Required by: _____

Additional Fees: $ _____

Total Estimated Cost: $ _____

Comments: _____

_____

_____

_____

_____

_____

_____

_____

_____

_____

Comparison Forms: Videographer 2

Appointment Date: _____ Time: _____

Videographer: _____ Years of Experience: _____

Address: _____

Contact: _____ Assistant: _____

Email: _____ Phone: _____ Fax: _____

Website: _____ Recommended by: _____

Style (Documentary, Straight Shot): _____ Type: ☐ Digital ☐ Analog

Backup Equipment: _____

Package Description: _____

_____

_____

Video Extras: _____

Full Day Rate: $ _____ Cost per Hour: $ _____ Cost per Extra Hour(s): $ _____

Insurance Coverage: _____

Payment Policy: _____

Cancellation Policy: _____

Booking Deposit: $ _____ Required by: _____

Additional Fees: $ _____

Total Estimated Cost: $ _____

Comments: _____

_____

_____

_____

_____

_____

_____

_____

_____

Contact Sheet: Videographer

Staple Business Card

Date Booked: _____

Videographer: _____

Address: _____

_____

Contact: _____

Email: _____

Phone: _____

Fax: _____

Website: _____

Package Description: _____

_____

_____

Video Package Extras: _____

Special Instructions: _____

_____

Video Shooting Location 1: _____ Time: _____

Video Shooting Location 2: _____ Time: _____

Video Shooting Location 3: _____ Time: _____

Video Shooting Location 4: _____ Time: _____

Exclusive reservation time from _____ to _____

Will there be one or two cameras available?   ☐ One   ☐ Two

If two, name of assistant: _____

Wedding Video Cost: $ _____ Pickup Date: _____ No. of Copies: _____

Raw Footage Cost: $ _____ Release Date: _____

Total Cost: $ _____

Deposit: $ _____ Date Paid: _____

Balance: $ _____ Date Due: _____

Notes: _____

_____

_____

Notes:

Chapter 14
Book Your Music and Entertainment

- Ceremony Music

- Reception Music

- e-Plan It! Use Your e-Resources:

  Online Music Sampling
  Adding Your Song to Your Wedding Website
  Start Your Entertainment Hunting Online

- Worksheets:

  Considerations Worksheet: Wedding Music
  Comparison Forms: Ceremony Music
  Comparison Forms: Reception Music
  Contact Sheet: Ceremony Music
  Contact Sheet: Reception Music

Without a doubt, music is a vital and important facet of your overall wedding. Just think of how important a soundtrack is to a movie. Music sets the mood and atmosphere of your day, adds to the romance, and—of course—is the lifeblood that fuels your party. It accompanies and highlights all those special, emotional moments from the ceremony's prelude to your last dance. In this chapter we'll help you plan your tunes and set the stage for a perfect soundtrack to a perfect day.

Ceremony Music

Your music sets the mood and atmosphere for your wedding, and the first impression your guests will have is at the ceremony. Whether it's building up a breathless anticipation during the prelude, providing the guiding flow for the processional, or creating an emotional highlight during special reflective moments, ceremony music does more than just build the ambiance for this all-important event. It's an integral part of the ceremony itself.

Considerations and Options

When deciding what to play at your ceremony and who will play it, you'll need to think about the formality of your wedding and the the unique characteristics and restrictions of your location. Make careful, effective selections but avoid extravagance; it's generally a good idea to keep the ceremony music simple to avoid overshadowing the vows themselves.

Music to Match Your Mood

Keep your wedding vision in sight throughout your decisions. Is the mood you'd like to capture solemn and formal or more fun-filled? Traditional or contemporary? Consider your location as well; a formal ceremony held in a breathtaking cathedral will call for different

---

<TIP>

Music Timetable

Keep up with your checklist in Chapter 2 and use the following guide to make sure you're on track:

10 months before: Start contacting prospective entertainers. Make arrangements to see them in action, or at least review their demo CDs.

8 months before: Hire your musicians.

5 months before: Get special requests (ethnic music, for example) to your band or DJ so they have enough time to prepare.

1 month before: Finalize your music preferences, such as a must-play song list, a banned song list, and other notes.

1 week before: Touch bases and confirm starting time, date, and location, and review your wedding day schedule.

Rehearsal day: Your ceremony musicians should be present to practice at your ceremony rehearsal.

</TIP>

instrumentation and style of music than an informal back-yard affair.

Perhaps you'd like to add selections that have special significance to the two of you, like the first song you slow-danced to. There will be specific key moments during your ceremony when such music would be an effective addition (we'll cover the various music-worthy moments in a bit). Think of anything you can incorporate into your choice of music and style to personalize it: ethnicity, religion, the season, even your wedding's theme.

Instrumentation plays a major role in setting the mood (think of the mood difference between a violin, classical guitar, and a fiddle). Organ music is the traditional choice of instrumentation, but your mood and preferences might dictate any number of alternatives: a harp, group of violins, trio, or string quartet for example. You might even go with something that has ethnic or cultural flair, like Scottish bagpipes or a Greek mandolin. Remember that certain instruments can get swallowed up by very large sites. A harp, for instance, will get lost in a big cathedral.

<CROSS-REFERENCE>

We went over comparing and settling on ceremony spots in Chapter 8, "Determine Your Ceremony Details and Location".

</CROSS-REFERENCE>

<TIP>

Name That Tune!

Want to search through a list of popular ceremony music and hear sample clips from each? Check out the "Online Music Samples" e-Resource we cover in the upcoming section on reception music.

</TIP>

Site Restrictions

Check with your ceremony location for any restrictions on the type of music or instruments you can include. Many places of worship have strict policies on this. Catholic churches, for example, often will not allow certain secular (non-religious) music, while Orthodox Jewish ceremonies prohibit any music at all.

If you're marrying in a public location such as a park or beach, there may be noise policies and time restrictions to deal with. Ask the powers that be (county, state or city officials) what compliances you need to keep in mind.

Find out if your location includes an organist or other musician and if you're obligated to use their services or can bring in someone else of your own choosing. You might be required to pay fees to the provided musicians even if you bring in your own.

Musical Ceremony Components

Let's go over the basic music-worthy components of most western-style weddings. Your location's music director or coordinator should be able to work with you in deciding which songs would work best at which times, and when you may prefer the solemnity of silence. Here are the basics:

Prelude

This is the anticipation-filled beginning of your wedding day. The location's doors open, guests take their seats, and the anticipation begins! Aside from the beauty of the location itself, this is your guests' first sensory impression. Soft instrumental tunes or a vocal solo should be played no later than 30 minutes before the time indicated on your invitations. Even if you've decided not to include music in the rest of your ceremony, consider at least playing something subtle during the prelude. Good prelude music will set the mood and entertain guests as they wait for the ceremony to begin, without distracting from the energy and anticipation in the air.

You may want to give your musician(s) a heads-up as to the basic genre that you want to be played during the prelude and leave the choice of individual songs up to them. Popular genre choices include love songs, jazz, broadway or romantic classical. Pick a genre that complements the rest of your ceremony's musical selection.

<TIP>

Commission a Unique Processional

A bride is hard pressed to think of a moment more emotional and special than her walk down the aisle. Yet most opt for familiar and traditional when it comes to the music that will highlight their processional. Even those who try to think beyond Wagner will find music that was once unique a decade or so ago, such as Pachelbel's "Canon in D", is now common. Choosing contemporary tunes is one alternative, but it might end up really dating your wedding.

We have another option for the bride wanting to keep her distance from the rest of the flock: consider having original ceremony music commissioned just for you. Few of us are lucky enough to have friends or family members that are talented musical composers, but there are professional wedding composers available. Do a Google search (www.google.com) for the keywords "Wedding Compositions" or "Original Wedding Music", or check the big portals. A wedding composer will consult with you to get a feel for the emotions and mood you're going for—you can even specify the instruments to be used—and they'll produce an original piece tailored just for you. After the wedding, frame your original score and display it alongside your wedding pictures. How's that for unique?

</TIP>

Processional

As the bridal party and the bride make their way down the aisle, a bold majestic piece is typically played to mark the dramatic moment and also to keep pace as everyone proceeds in order to their places. Often, a separate piece is played for the bride; the most traditional by far is Wagner's "Bridal Chorus", popularly known as "Here Comes the Bride". As with the rest of your ceremony music selections, your own choices can be as personal or traditional as you like.

Interlude (Key Moments)

You can choose to add music to highlight special moments during the ceremony such as between readings, the lighting of the unity candle, the exchange of rings, or anywhere else you deem appropriate. Classical tunes, contemporary songs of special importance to you, and even traditional cultural or folk songs are all fair game. Know a talented friend or family member? Have them lend their pipes and personalize your ceremony with a song, or hire a trio or singer to do the honors. These are emotional moments, so back them up well.

Recessional and Postlude

You are now husband and wife! The music that plays as you walk up the aisle hand-in-hand should be giddy, excited, and triumphant—to match the mood of the moment and to honor the importance of the change that's just taken place. Even if you're actually returning to take photos, your recessional should highlight you going out with a bang. The postlude that is played afterwards as guests file out should continue the excitement and upbeat mood and get everyone ready for the coming party. Since the postlude can last anywhere from ten minutes to half an hour, consider giving the musicians a genre and letting them select the songs themselves, as you may have done for the prelude.

Booking Your Ceremony Tunes

If your site doesn't come with its preferred musicians or if you'd just like to hunt for your own options, gather referrals from friends or family as always. Ask your site coordinator, officiant and other wedding vendors as well. You might also want to check with local colleges, symphonies and music schools to get contacts for local trios, quartets and singers.

If you can, try and see a live performance by the musicians you're considering, or at least listen to a demo CD. Hearing is believing, and you don't want to leave it to your special day to find out that these guys are really not the style you were looking for.

Also, it's best for all or most of the musicians to attend your wedding rehearsal, so let them know the date and time far enough in advance for them to fit it into their schedules.

Questions to Ask Ceremony Musicians

- Are you experienced with weddings?

- Can we see you perform, or can you provide us with a demo CD?

- Are you familiar with our music choices? Will you need us to provide sheet music for you?

- What kind of equipment, if any, does the ceremony location need to supply for you?

- What is your dress code?

- How much setup time do you need?

- What is your fee? Do we need to pay any travel fees or any other additional expenses?

Get It in Writing: Your Ceremony Music Contract

The musicians you choose should provide a detailed contract that specifies your wedding date, ceremony location, and the time they will arrive (accounting for setup time). Any necessary equipment they'll supply or will need from the location should be inked out as well. What will they play, and when? Ask that this be included and that any flexibility (possibly playing longer during prelude and postlude, for example) is indicated. Look for a clear specification of the fees and any extra charges. A solid contract will also state the names of the musicians and any backup substitutes in case an emergency arises.

Reception Music

A party without music is like a car without gas: it's not going to go too far. Your reception music will set the stage, create the mood, and keep the party moving. It should capture your own unique compilation of favorite and meaningful picks while also appealing to all your guests, as diverse in age and taste as they may be.

Considerations and Options

Bring out your wedding vision again and think about your ideal image of a wedding reception. Does it feature a live band or is it spun by a DJ? Are there separate musicians for the cocktail hour? What type of music? Is there dancing?

Band or DJ?

Some are of the opinion that a live band is more traditional than a DJ, and certainly a big orchestra in a grand ballroom will create an atmosphere for a very formal wedding that can't quite be matched. Something about the energy of a live band is dramatic and just party-moving infectious. But a good DJ brings a flexibility to the music you're able to play that no band can offer, no matter how open-minded and resourceful their repertoire. And with a DJ, the songs you're grooving to are the original versions you and your guests know and love, rather than someone else's cover. DJ's also usually cost less than a band and play nonstop, while a band will need to take breaks. Both DJ and bandleader can act as your master of ceremonies (or emcee), announcing events as they occur and keeping your reception schedule rolling. Your selection for either type of entertainment will be key; both a DJ and a band can be fantastic, weak, or just plain cheesy.

Whether you hire a DJ or musicians for the bulk your reception entertainment, you may also want to consider separate musicians for your cocktail hour. You can always have your DJ play soft background instrumentals during the pre-dinner mingling, for example, or you could add the drama and elegance of a string quartet or jazz ensemble. How you mix and match your entertainment will depend on the vision you have of your reception as well as budget constraints.

Choosing Your Music

Your choice of music will take into account your own favorites and preferred styles to be sure, but you also want to move your guests, especially if you're featuring after-dinner dancing. How do you make everyone happy when your guest list spans a vast array of generations and tastes?

While this may at first seem an impossible task, keep in mind that DJ's and musicians experienced in weddings satisfy such a need at nearly every wedding they perform. The art of genre-blending and feeling the crowd is one they should have a solid mastery of. From 30's-era big-band hits to Disco to 80's to today's faves, every genre is unique and has its own distinct way to get people moving.

If you know that your group's tastes are aligned predominately with your own, give your performer(s) the heads-up. Often, though, you'll want to go for variety, relying on their experience and crowd-reading talent. Specify lists of songs you absolutely must hear, genres you'd like featured more than others, and songs you want banned (you may be dead set against YMCA, the Hokey-Pokey and the Electric Slide, perhaps)...but otherwise leave the general selections up to them.

e-Resource

Online Music Sampling

Sometimes, while you're considering your ceremony and reception tunes, it helps to browse a list of popular choices to jump-start your ideas. Even more helpful is the ability to hear sample clips from the listed songs; after all, you may not know what Mozart's Adagio Violin Concerto #4 means, but if you heard a sample of the piece you just might recognize it. You could then request it by name from your musicians or add it to your playlist.

Such playable lists can be found on the Internet for free. Try searching for "wedding music" on Google (www.google.com) and see what the latest available are. A great resource we found was available at WedAlert.com (www.wedalert.com/songs/). It divides its playable music library into categories for ceremony, reception, cocktail hour, first dance, parents' dance, last dance, group event, and even ethnic and religious. The reception selections are divided even further into subcategories like 50's, 70's, Hip Hop, Waltzes, and so forth. It can be a big help when building your music lists and making song selections.

WedAlert.com provides lists of popular music choices in a number of categories. You can even listen to sample clips to help identify those songs whose names you're not sure of.

Adding Your Song to Your Wedding Website

Give your guests a taste of your wedding atmosphere before the big day by posting your first dance, processional, or just something special to the two of you as background music on your wedding website. For those friends and family who aren't able to attend your wedding it may be their only exposure to it.

WedShare.com allows you to choose background music from their pre-loaded royalty-free selections or upload your own songs in MP3 format.

Check with your wedding website service to see what your musical options are. Most allow you to choose from a number of preloaded selections or upload your own tunes. Make sure that your visitors are able to turn music on and off as they please. Forcing them to listen to your special song, as beautiful as it is, will keep them from staying very long.

Musical Reception Components

The Big Three musical moments in your reception are commonly specified as cocktail hour, special and ethnic dances, and general after-dinner dancing. Your band or DJ will probably break it down even more, though, so here's a list of moments you may want to consider:

Cocktail Hour

As guests are sipping, munching and mingling, create a relaxed and romantic atmosphere that's as formal or informal as the rest of your wedding's style. Music should be background ambiance, allowing people to easily chat. A string quartet, jazz combo or the like make excellent choices. If your budget won't allow the additional splurge on extra performers, have your DJ play some mellow background instrumentals or club-like lounge tunes, depending on your style.

The Entrance

Enter the stars of the wedding! As your entourage and finally the two of you are introduced by your DJ or bandleader and make your way into the main reception area, you may want to highlight the entrance with music. You could go for a grand piece, something funky, or music that highlights your culture and heritage.

The Meal

Why not add ambiance to the meal? Depending on the time of day, you may be serving a dinner, lunch, or even breakfast. Like the cocktail hour, it's nice to provide a bit of relaxing background ambiance from either musicians or some appropriate selections from your DJ.

Special Dances

You'll be providing your tunesmiths with specific selections for your first dance, the bride's father/daughter dance, and the groom's mother/son dance. Are there any ethnic dances or group activities you want to include? Let your entertainers know!

Bouquet and Garter Toss

Whether it's a drum-roll, countdown, or fun contemporary choice, music often accompanies the traditional bouquet toss. Ditto for the garter removal and toss...it's up to you how low-key or wild you want to go.

Cake Cutting

Most of the romantic rituals of wedding receptions benefit from a soundtrack, and the cake cutting is no exception.

General Dancing

Select music with your guests in mind, as we discussed earlier. Most good DJ's and bands know how to provide entertainment that successfully spans genres, generations, and tastes to make the party a blast for everyone: from your picky high school nephew to your waltz-loving grandfather. Let your music makers know if there's specific styles, eras, or genres that you want highlighted or avoided. You should also provide a list of any songs you absolutely must have played...and those you won't touch with a ten-foot pole even if they're requested.

Finding and Booking Musicians or a DJ

As you'd expect, the best way to find good entertainers will be through referrals from those you trust. Have you been to a wedding recently where the DJ or band was fantastic? Talk to the bride and groom to get the contact. Your other vendors may also know of some good musicians, trios, singers, and DJ's. For everyone you're considering, make sure that you either see them perform live or watch a tape or DVD of them at another event (sometimes called an "audition tape").

When consulting with the band or DJ you select, go over your musical tastes and preferences. Give them instructions as to how you want your wedding party to be introduced, and make sure they have a detailed schedule of your reception with times for the various events (introduction, dinner, cake cutting, and so forth) so that they can efficiently emcee.

e-Resource

Start Your Entertainment Hunting Online

Most DJ's, DJ companies, and musicians have informative websites that include fees, policies, equipment, song lists, photos of the entertainers and sample clips. Do a local search for the area of your wedding location using your favorite search engine with keywords like "Wedding Music", "Wedding DJs", or the type of music or group you're looking for: jazz, swing, salsa, brass ensemble, string quartet, orchestra, and so forth.

Association Websites

Check out the websites of professional associations. The American Disc Jockey Association, for example (www.adja.org), can point you to local DJ's and provides informative articles and tips. Search for DJ's in your area, and link directly to their websites for more information.

The Big Portals

Check out portals like The Knot (www.theknot.com/music/) and WeddingChannel.com (click local vendors > musicians and DJ's) for articles, song lists, and portfolios of local entertainers. Visit their websites and add any potentials to your list.

Booking Musicians

Finding a talented, professional, and quality performer or group of performers with the right style requires some time and effort. There are a lot of options out there, and some will be better suited to your tastes and style than others. Here's some advice to guide your way.

Booking Agencies - First, let's take a look at what it means for a performer or group to be represented by a booking agency as opposed to being self-managed. You'll find both during your searches, so what's the difference? Agencies that represent musicians are businesses, and they charge the artists a fee for the service of promoting them to you the customer. The agency takes their cut of the fee you're charged, so prices for agency-represented musicians can be higher than self-managed groups unless the musicians are working for rates below industry standard. Another thing to consider is that while self-managed groups are experienced in playing together, some agency-represented musicians are independent and the agency is the one that organizes them to play together at a wedding. Make sure you always ask if the group you're hiring has experience playing together; if not, the potential lack of chemistry between the individual musicians could detract from the quality of your music.

Self-Managed Groups - They'll be experienced playing together and, without the added agency fee, are often available at more reasonable prices. This isn't to say that agency-represented groups should be avoided. Just make sure you ask plenty of questions and shop around to compare your options.

Professional or Amateur - This is going to come down to how you feel about the individual performer(s). Students and part-time musicians may be incredibly talented and play beautifully, but they'll lack the experience of full-time professionals. Professionals who live and breathe music may be more expensive but better able to grasp the vision of what you want your music to be. They'll be able to select the perfect music for you and pull it off just right.

Five Steps to Booking Your Musicians - First, make initial contact with the musicians you're considering and check their availability. Popular ones can book up a year or more in advance.

Second, get to know their sound. Check out their website, listen to sample clips, and request a demo CD. Performers are notoriously busy, so it may not always be possible to meet with them before signing the contract to secure your date. Review their promotional material carefully. If you can see them perform live, so much the better; you'll be able to evaluate their stage presence, demeanor, and the style with which the bandleader introduces songs and activities.

Third, request a quote personalized for your event. Give them all the specifics as to date, location, duration, and so forth. Make sure that the quote is provided in writing (e-mail counts).

Fourth, review and sign the contract, securing your date (we'll cover contract points in a bit).

Fifth, the group or a representative of the group will set up a consultation to go over your style, vision, list of songs to be played (and banned) and generally get a feel for what you want your music to accomplish. For cocktail hour or dinner performers whose roles are solely background ambiance, the consultation will be simple, possibly even over the phone. Make sure that you finalize things like breaks, start and end times, and any details you feel are unique to your situation.

Questions to Ask Musicians

- Have you performed at many weddings? Do you have references we can contact?

- Are you experienced as an emcee? Are our preferences compatible with your style? (More low key, more interactive, or however vocal you'd like them)

- If you were to describe your music style, what would it be?

- What's your standard attire for a wedding reception? Can you accommodate our preference?

- Do you use a standard playlist? Can you play special songs that are important to us, including ethnic selections?

- Can you take requests?

- How many breaks do you take, and for how long? Do you have recorded backup music or another musician to take over during the breaks?

- Do you provide your own sound system? What are your technical requirements? (Check with your reception location to make sure they can be accommodated)

- How much setup time do you need?

- What are your rates and overtime fees? If we need you to play overtime, will you be able to?

Get It in Writing: Your Musician Contract

When booking musicians, you'll need to provide a 20% to 50% deposit, but don't pay any more than this until their performance is over. The only leverage you'll have against singers or musicians being no-shows or otherwise not living up to the contract is the 50% balance due that you can potentially decrease.

Make sure your contract includes date, time, location, and the total estimated hours that the group will play. The contract should note how many breaks will be taken and whether or not they'll provide recorded music during those times. Names of the band members and substitutes (in case of emergency) should be listed, along with the instruments they'll bring. Also, look for a break-down of the equipment they'll use and anything that you or the location will need to provide. Solid contracts will include any emcee duties as agreed, dress code, the rate you've settled on, and a cancellation and refund policy. See that you and a representative of the musicians each sign the same copy of the contract, and file a copy away in your "Music" folder.

Booking a DJ

There are a lot of DJ's out there, easily found using online searches, the big wedding portals, or through referrals from family and friends. Don't shop based on price alone: most of the very inexpensive ones are either part-time or newer DJ's looking for more exposure. The consequence of hiring either is a lack of experience. Established pros might charge a bit more, but the extra experience, crowd-reading knowledge and professionalism you'll be getting is probably well worth it.

As with musicians, hearing is believing, and you should catch the DJ you're considering in action at an event that's comparable in location and spirit to your reception. At the very least, watch a video of an event that he's worked. Does he read the crowd and mix the music well? Does he take requests professionally? Does he keep the crowd moving? And—very important—how's the cheese factor? Steer clear of DJ's who chatter endlessly, crack goofy jokes and are just plain obnoxious.

Arrange a consultation with each potential DJ to get some one-on-one time, ask questions and discuss your wedding vision. They should be excited about being a part of your day and on the same level with your tastes and preferences. Bring up genres you're into and ask the DJ to pull out a few examples from his library. Go over the must-play and banned-music lists; how does he react? Make sure the personality of the DJ is one that you are compatible with and can see directing your reception.

Questions to Ask DJ's

- Have you performed at many weddings? Do you have references we can contact?

- Are you experienced as an emcee? Are our preferences compatible with your style? (More low key, more interactive, or however vocal you'd like)

- What's your standard attire for a wedding reception? Can you accommodate our preference?

- Can you play special songs that are important to us, including ethnic selections? (You may need to provide your own CD's in some cases)

- What are your technical requirements? (Check with your reception location to make sure they can be accommodated)

- If we need you to play overtime, can you? What is your overtime fee?

- Will you play continuous music? (With a DJ, the music should never stop)

- How extensive is your musical library? (Should be at least 5,000 songs)

- What kind of equipment do you use?

- If we want theatrical lighting, can you provide it? Is there an extra fee for this?

- How much setup time do you need?

- What is your rate?

Get It in Writing: Your DJ Contract

You'll most likely put down a 50% deposit up front to book your date with a DJ, with the remaining balance due on the day of your wedding. Don't forget to factor in a 10% to 15% tip if you feel the DJ does a good job for you.

Make sure your contract includes date, time, location, and the total estimated hours that the DJ will work; setup times should be outlined as well. The DJ's name and a substitute (in case of emergency) should be noted. Also, look for a break-down of anything that you or the location will need to provide. Solid contracts will include any emcee duties as agreed, dress code, the rate you've settled on, and a cancellation and refund policy. See that you and the DJ sign the same copy of the contract, and file a copy away in your "Music" folder.

Considerations Worksheet: Wedding Music

Music Budget: $

Ceremony Musician(s)

- ☐ Organist
- ☐ Soloist
- ☐ Choir / Ensemble
- ☐ Instrumental
- ☐ Live
- ☐ Recorded

Ceremony Music Components

- ☐ Prelude
- ☐ Processional
- ☐ Interlude (key ceremony moments)
- ☐ Recessional
- ☐ Postlude

Reception Band, DJ or Musician(s)

- ☐ Band
- ☐ DJ
- ☐ Vocals
- ☐ Instrumental

Reception Music Components

- ☐ Cocktail Hour / Receiving Line
- ☐ Introductions
- ☐ Dinner
- ☐ Couple's First Dance
- ☐ Father - Daughter Dance
- ☐ Mother - Son Dance
- ☐ Group / Ethnic Dances
- ☐ Open Dance
- ☐ Cake Cutting
- ☐ Bouquet Toss
- ☐ Garter Toss
- ☐ Last Dance

Reception Dance Music Preferences

- ☐ 1940's / Big Bands
- ☐ 50's
- ☐ 60's
- ☐ 70's Rock / 70's Disco
- ☐ 80's / 80's Modern Rock
- ☐ 90's / 90's Rock
- ☐ Ballroom
- ☐ Cha Cha
- ☐ Classical
- ☐ Country
- ☐ Ethnic
- ☐ Foxtrot
- ☐ Group Participation Dances
- ☐ Hip Hop
- ☐ House
- ☐ Jazz
- ☐ Karaoke Sing-Along
- ☐ Latin
- ☐ Motown
- ☐ Old School / Funk
- ☐ Polka
- ☐ Rap
- ☐ R&B
- ☐ Reggae
- ☐ Rock / Pop
- ☐ Rhumba
- ☐ Salsa / Merengue
- ☐ Samba
- ☐ SoulSwing
- ☐ Tango
- ☐ Techno / European Techno
- ☐ Top 40
- ☐ Waltz
- ☐ _____

Notes:

_____
_____
_____
_____
_____
_____
_____
_____

Comparison Forms: Ceremony Music 1

Appointment Date: _____ Time: _____

Musician(s): _____ Years of Experience: _____

Address: _____

_____

Contact: _____ Agent: _____

Email: _____ Phone: _____ Fax: _____

Website: _____ Recommended by: _____

Demo available?   ☐ Yes   ☐ No   _____

Your Reviews: _____

_____

_____

Audition Location: _____ Date and Time: _____

Type of Music: _____

Equipment: _____

Payment Policy: _____

Cancellation Policy: _____

Number of Hours Required: _____

Cost per Hour: $ _____ Cost per Extra Hour(s): $ _____

Booking Deposit: $ _____ Required by: _____

Additional Fees: $ _____

Total Estimated Cost: $ _____

Comments: _____

_____

_____

_____

_____

_____

_____

_____

_____

Comparison Forms: Ceremony Music 2

Appointment Date: _____   Time: _____

Musician(s): _____   Years of Experience: _____

Address: _____

Contact: _____   Agent: _____

Email: _____   Phone: _____   Fax: _____

Website: _____   Recommended by: _____

Demo available?   ☐ Yes   ☐ No

Your Reviews: _____

Audition Location: _____   Date and Time: _____

Type of Music: _____

Equipment: _____

Payment Policy: _____

Cancellation Policy: _____

Number of Hours Required: _____

Cost per Hour: $ _____   Cost per Extra Hour(s): $ _____

Booking Deposit: $ _____   Required by: _____

Additional Fees: $ _____

Total Estimated Cost: $ _____

Comments: _____

Comparison Forms: Reception Music 1

Appointment Date: _____ Time: _____

Band, DJ or Musician(s): _____ Years of Experience: _____

Address: _____

_____

Contact: _____ Agent: _____

Email: _____ Phone: _____ Fax: _____

Website: _____ Recommended by: _____

Demo available?   □ Yes   □ No

Your Reviews: _____

_____

_____

Audition Location: _____ Date and Time: _____

Type of Music: _____

Equipment: _____

Number of Breaks: _____ Length of Breaks: _____

Payment Policy: _____

Cancellation Policy: _____

Number of Hours Required: _____

Cost per Hour: $ _____ Cost per Extra Hour(s): $ _____

Booking Deposit: $ _____ Required by: _____

Additional Fees: $ _____

Total Estimated Cost: $ _____

Comments: _____

_____

_____

_____

_____

_____

_____

_____

_____

_____

Comparison Forms: Reception Music 2

Appointment Date: _____ Time: _____

Band, DJ or Musician(s): _____ Years of Experience: _____

Address: _____

Contact: _____ Agent: _____

Email: _____ Phone: _____ Fax: _____

Website: _____ Recommended by: _____

Demo available?   ☐ Yes   ☐ No

Your Reviews: _____

_____

Audition Location: _____ Date and Time: _____

Type of Music: _____

Equipment: _____

Number of Breaks: _____ Length of Breaks: _____

Payment Policy: _____

Cancellation Policy: _____

Number of Hours Required: _____

Cost per Hour: $ _____ Cost per Extra Hour(s): $ _____

Booking Deposit: $ _____ Required by: _____

Additional Fees: $ _____

Total Estimated Cost: $ _____

Comments: _____

_____

_____

_____

_____

_____

_____

_____

_____

Contact Sheet: Ceremony Music

Date Booked: _____

Ceremony Musician(s): _____

_____

Address: _____

_____

Contact: _____

Email: _____

Phone: _____

Fax: _____

Website: _____

Type of Music: _____

Attire: _____

Package Description: _____

_____

Special Instructions: _____

_____

Music Selection Requests (if any)

Prelude: _____

Bridal Party's Processional: _____

Bride's Processional: _____

Interlude: _____

Recessional: _____

Postlude: _____

Exclusive reservation time from _____ to _____

Gratuity (if any): $ _____

Total Cost: _____

Deposit: $ _____   Date Paid: _____

Balance: $ _____   Date Due: _____

Notes: _____

_____

_____

Staple Business Card

Contact Sheet: Reception Music

Staple Business Card

Date Booked:

Band, DJ or Musician(s):

Address:

Contact:

Email:

Phone:

Fax:

Website:

Type of Music:

Attire:

Package Description:

Special Instructions:

Music Selection Requests (if any)

Cocktail Hour / Receiving Line:

Bridal Party Introduction:

Bride and Groom Introduction:

Dinner's Background Music:

Couple's First Dance:

Father – Daughter Dance:

Mother – Son Dance:

Group / Ethnic Dances:

Cake Cutting:

Bouquet Toss:

Garter Toss:

Last Dance:

Other:

Exclusive reservation time from   to

Gratuity (if any):

Total Cost: $

Deposit: $ Date Paid:

Balance: $ Date Due:

Notes:

_____

_____

_____

_____

_____

_____

_____

_____

_____

_____

_____

_____

_____

_____

_____

_____

_____

_____

_____

_____

_____

_____

_____

_____

_____

_____

_____

_____

_____

_____

_____

_____

Chapter 15

To Give and to Receive: Buy Gifts and Set Up an Accessible Gift Registry

- Registering for Gifts

- Giving

- Receiving

- e-Plan It! Use Your e-Resources:

  Online Registries for Stores and Other Services
  Your Website's Gift Registry Page
  Online Wedding Favor Ideas
  Recording Gift Information in Your Guest Database

- Worksheets:

  Checklist: Registry Basics
  Contact Sheet: Gift Registries

W hether you feel 'tis better to give than to receive or vice versa, weddings include a lot of both. This chapter will cover some of the joyous giving and getting you'll be experiencing before and after you say your I do's. A lot of info management will come into play, but—lucky for you as an e-planner—you've got some nifty resources to help out.

Registering for Gifts

Today, setting up a gift registry that's convenient for both you and your guests is easier than ever. Registries are pretty much all computerized now. You can start, edit and update your list online and give guests the opportunity to shop and ship from the web. And gone are the worries of how to get the registry info out to your guests; your wedding website will let them find it easily.

Considerations and Timetable

If you want your gift registry available for your bridal shower and other pre-wedding parties, get started on it six to eight months before the wedding. When setting out to build your registry, take into account your needs and lifestyle. What things do you need when starting your new life together? Which would be the biggest help? You may well be living on your own or together already, and perhaps the last thing you want is another toaster or serving platter. Besides traditional kitchenware and household goods, registries and online services exist that allow guests to shower you with gifts towards your honeymoon, the down payment of a house, that flashy new game console your sweetheart's been eyeing, or even a new car. Think outside the gift box! And even if you're sure you have everything you need now, is a bigger house in your future? You may need some of the household essentials found in a traditional registry more than you think.

<CROSS-REFERENCE>
For more on bridal showers and other fun pre-wedding parties, check out Chapter 22.
</CROSS-REFERENCE>

Why Have a Gift Registry?

A gift registry is an incredible convenience, not just for you but also for your guests. It lets them know just what you want and provides a list of items to choose from, which makes it easy for them. Because most stores automatically update your registry as gifts are purchased, a gift registry decreases the number of duplicate items you'll receive.

Even if you feel that the tradition of gifts is tacky and you don't want any, guests will bring them. And without a registry, they're forced to guess what to buy for you, which can result in mismatched kitchen sets, linens that clash with your style, or a dozen toasters. You might add a line like "No gifts, please" or "Your presence is your present" to your invitations. But while it's a nice way to let guests know that a gift isn't mandatory, some will want to give you something anyway. Friends and loved ones will find it enjoyable to give you something to celebrate your day with, and being told they can't will make some feel awkward. As we mentioned, a registry doesn't have to cover traditional items at all, so think about what your needs are and consider some of the alternatives: sports, travel, electronic goods, and so forth. If you absolutely don't want gifts, consider letting your guests donate to your favorite charity in your name.

Go for Elegance

Even if you've already got plenty of dishes, silverware, and kitchen appliances, your wedding is the chance to upgrade to a newer, elegant collection. Why? Because even if you've been on your own or living together for a while, your wedding day is the start of a new life, so why not start off fresh? And if you and your sweetie love to entertain, a gorgeous set of china with matching serving platters and accessories is perfect for inviting family and friends to dinner parties. And don't underestimate the simple luxury of trading in your old kitchen appliances for new, state-of-the-art models with all the extras. Or those worn bath towel sets and bedroom linens for name brand designs you both will love. Such classy and elegant collections can be pricey, so why not let someone else pick up the tab?

Being Charitable

If you don't want to receive wedding gifts, one way to let friends and loved ones contribute to your happiness is to ask that donations be made in your name to your favorite charity. An ideal place to pass along this request is on your wedding website's registry page (we'll cover this more in a bit). Another option is to have your website link directly to online charity registries like GlobalGiving (www.globalgiving.com/registry) or JustGive.org (www.justgive.org/weddings/index.jsp). Using these or similar services, you can set up an online registry and select a charity or nonprofit organization to which your guests' donations will go. Guests can be linked there from your wedding website just like any other online gift registry. As always, be sure to also let your family and attendants know to pass along the info to those guests that shun technology and don't have Internet access.

Registry Timetable

- Start thinking about your registry once you get your initial wedding plans in place and have a solid date. Talk about what you'll need, what your style will be, and where you'd like to register. Do some preliminary shopping together. For traditional items, use the checklist at the end of this chapter to determine which items you'll need and which you already have or otherwise don't want.

- Check out the online registry services. Shopping and building a registry online is the ultimate convenience, whether it's traditional gifts you're after or something more unique: a car, computer, honeymoon funds...you name it. Even if you have a comfortably traditional registry, your second (or third) choice could be something a bit different. Check out the e-Resource a bit later on for exclusively online registries that allow you to point, click, and add everything from a waffle iron to a computer or even a BMW to your wish list. Keep in mind, though, that for those items you gotta see and feel, you can't beat going into the store and choosing them in person.

- About six to eight months before your big day (or whenever will be early enough for your pre-wedding parties and showers) open a registry at the store or stores you select. When you go into the store you may need to set an appointment. Start your registry even if you only have a few months left or less, since most gifts won't be purchased until right before the wedding. And don't register more than a year in advance; you don't want your selected items to be discontinued or to go out of stock. During the initial meeting, your registry consultant will show you how to use the store's portable registry scanner, a handheld device that you use to scan the barcodes for items you'd like to include in your registry. Make sure you ask your registry consultant about seasonal items (that may be discontinued) and other things to watch out for.

- Shop away! Do an initial run through your list and browse the store's appropriate departments, selecting the items you like with the scanner as you go. You can always return to the store to continue shopping and to update new items. Check your registry online and make any changes or additions there, as well.

Getting the Word Out

Traditionally, guests had to find out about your wedding registry by word of mouth. While you can go ahead and include the info on your shower invitations, it's always been considered bad form to mention your registries on the invitations for your wedding. Enclosing a registry card is a gray area generally agreed to be best avoided. Lucky for you, you have an advantage as an e-planner, which is your wedding website! Put your website address on everything, from your invitations and other stationery to your e-mail signatures. Guests will find your registry information there while they're browsing the rest of your wedding info. It's a fool-proof, etiquette-safe and hassle-free solution. Have your parents, attendants, and close friends spread the word about your registry as well. In fact, they should be spreading the word about your wedding website already.

One modern-day etiquette blunder you'll want to avoid is the guest e-mail notification feature that many online gift registries offer, which sends out your registry info to your guests' e-mail addresses on your behalf. They tout it as a convenient way to get the information out to your guests, but it's tacky and demanding. It serves the online services well in getting their advertisements out to a targeted audience, but that's about it. If any online registries you use offer this option, make sure you decline it.

Traditional and Unique Ideas

The "Registry Basics" checklist at the end of this chapter will give you a guide to most traditional items that you'll find in department stores and "lifestyle" shops like Crate & Barrel or Williams-Sonoma. Tableware, flatware, and glassware (both everyday and formal) as well as cookware, kitchen appliances and bedroom linens are the main categories you'll be working with.

But your options are as open as you want them to be. Some nontraditional items that are quickly becoming registry favorites are honeymoon and travel costs, personal electronics, financial gifts (stocks, home down-payment contributions and so forth), sports equipment, wine, art, and home-improvement goods.

Selecting and Visiting the Stores

With your needs and preferences in mind, think about the kind of stores you want to register with. It can be pretty much any store you want, although those with computerized registry systems will be most convenient. If a store you love doesn't have a gift registry, talk to the manager. Most will be more than happy to work something out.

Keep your guests' convenience in mind. Does the store have a number of locations to make it easy for everyone to visit? You may love that little one-shop import store downtown, but for any guests that live out of town, you're limiting their options. Stores with online gift registries are a great way to ensure a broader access, allowing guests to shop and ship from the web or go in to visit, whichever they prefer. Keep in mind that not all of your guests may have Internet access or feel comfortable buying on-line. Your goal should be to make gift buying as convenient and hassle-free as possible for your family and friends.

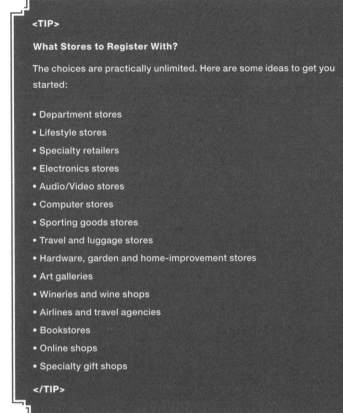

<TIP>

What Stores to Register With?

The choices are practically unlimited. Here are some ideas to get you started:

• Department stores

• Lifestyle stores

• Specialty retailers

• Electronics stores

• Audio/Video stores

• Computer stores

• Sporting goods stores

• Travel and luggage stores

• Hardware, garden and home-improvement stores

• Art galleries

• Wineries and wine shops

• Airlines and travel agencies

• Bookstores

• Online shops

• Specialty gift shops

</TIP>

Don't feel the need to limit yourself to one store, either. You may want to stick to a traditional registry for your first choice and try something more unique for your second (or third). Perhaps an electronics store, honeymoon registry, or one of the all-inclusive online registries we'll introduce a bit later.

What to Ask Registry Consultants

Many department stores and upscale shops that offer gift registries will have a registry consultant to assist you. This person will meet with you upon starting your registry, discuss your options, demonstrate how the store's system works, and be on hand to help you with any questions or issues you may have. Stop into the store you're considering, pick up any information they have and see if you need to set an appointment. They're usually less busy on weekdays and off hours. The registry consultant will be able to get you started and should be able to answer the following questions:

• Does the store have an on-line gift registry? Is it updated automatically when guests purchase gifts, and can I log in to update it myself over the web?

- Will the store mail or fax my registry to out-of-town guests that don't have Internet access, so they can place orders by phone?

- Can the store ship gifts ordered online or by phone to my address?

- Will the store's return policy allow me to exchange duplicate gifts or any other items I decide I don't want or need? Do I have a deadline that items need to be returned by?

- Does the store have a completion program allowing me to purchase items you didn't receive after my wedding for a discount? How long after my wedding is this program active?

- How long after my wedding will my registry be kept active? (Your list should remain active for a year or more, so that friends and family can continue to order from it for the holidays or other events if they wish)

e-Resource

Online Registries for Stores and Other Services

Online registries give your guests more options. If they're comfortable online, they can point and click their way through your wish list and even ship items to your door right from the web, in minutes. Or, they can always take the traditional route and go into the store to buy; but at least they can preview their selection first and even print it out to take with them.

For you, the advantages are even greater. Gone are the days when you had to run all changes, additions, or removals by your store's registry consultant. Just log in at home and make all the changes you like there. You can even see which items have been purchased and which haven't, making it easy for you to stay on top of your registry selection as time goes on. And if you're pressed for time or just not in the mood for driving, shop for items online and add them to your registry without setting foot in the store. You might opt to do some quick shopping for certain items online, and leave others—those you definitely want to see and feel in person—for a later store visit.

Online Store Registries

When you meet with your store's registry consultant, she should be able to provide you with the online information you need (website address, name, password, and so forth). Some retail locations—Macy's is an example—allow you to create a registry online without even going into the store. Check online shops and the websites of your favorite stores for links to their gift registry page.

Online gift registries will all have a login page that allows you to sign in to view or edit your registry. Most stores' registries will also give you the opportunity to see which items have been purchased already.

If you want to allow your guests to view your registry online, you'll need to give them the web address of the login page for each of your registries. By entering all or part of your names, the registry locator will allow guests to quickly find and view your gift registry. The best alternative to this, as we'll see later, is to link guests directly to your registry from your wedding website.

Other Gift Registry Services

Aside from stores' registries, other services exist online that let you register for anything from honeymoon expenses to college tuition to a downpayment on your dream home. Just checking the big portals or doing an online search for "wedding registries" gives you a good sample of everything that's out there. Unlike stores' registries—which are free—some services pocket a percentage of the overall gift amount, which may be a dealbreaker for you. Some of what these services provide can be more or less handled by your wedding website anyway, with a flexible enough registry feature and some creativity on your part. We'll get to your wedding website's registry page in a bit, but first let's discuss how these other registry services work, and what you can expect from them.

Honeymoon Registry Services let you create a dream honeymoon itinerary, and then set up a registry so that your guests can buy portions of your trip. They might buy you a romantic dinner, for example, or your rental car costs for a day. It's set up like a regular registry with a quantity needed, quantity received, and amount, but in the end you get a single check from the service—minus their fee, of course. Fees can range anywhere from 6% to 9% of the overall amount you receive from your guests.

Some honeymoon registry services will coordinate your travel arrangements as well, although this may come at an additional fee. Make sure you read the FAQ section of any service you're considering to find out what percentage of your guests' gifts they keep.

HoneyLuna.com and The Big Day Travel (www.thebigday.com) both retained 9% of your overall wedding gift as their service fee at the time of this writing. The Honeymoon (www.thehoneymoon.com) was a service we found that charged a variable fee, which starts at 8.85% and decreases the more your guests give. These amounts may have changed, so be sure to check their fees.

Cash Contribution Registry Services let you set up a registry for things like home down-payments, school tuition, and anything else you need hard cash for. (Essentially, the honeymoon registries we just discussed are really specialized cash contribution services). Remember that many guests will bring cash gifts to your reception anyway, but a cash contribution registry enables you to let guests specify where they want their monetary gift to go, rather than just slipping you a check. It will help with your thank-you card writing, too, as you can specify how you enjoyed—or plan to enjoy—the "gift" they funded for you.

Some cash registries, like Greenwish.com, wire your guests' gifts directly to your bank account. Others, including aperfectweddinggift.com, use the popular online merchant service PayPal (www.paypal.com) to get you your funds. Both services take a cut of the guests' gifts for themselves as a service fee, similar to the honeymoon registries.

Add a new gift registry to your website by posting links to the store's registry login page and perhaps a store locator. Some services even let you group your registries into separate categories.

Customized Registry Services let you create a wish list from more than one store as a single registry. FindGift.com is a free service that includes a gift search engine to search for gifts to put in your registry. The registry lets guests know what you want and where to find them, although it doesn't actually integrate with the stores. It therefore relies on your guests' cooperation to return to the registry and check the gifts off once they've purchased them. Essentially, it functions like a wish list, which should be included in the gift registry feature of most good wedding website services. If your own wedding website doesn't offer this option, you may want to consider a service like FindGift.com for your wish list. See if you can link to it from your website.

Felicite.com is another customized registry service that allows you to build a single registry list from several different stores, but it is actually integrated with the stores themselves and handles your purchasing and registry updates for you. Felicite.com, however, charges your guests a percentage of the gift cost as a service fee.

Online Shops exist that sell just about anything you could imagine. Art, wine, travel tickets, computers, books…you name it. See if your favorite online shop has a registry program and link to it from your wedding website. 67 Wine & Spirits (www.67wine.com), for example, has a wedding registry program that makes a personal and unique gift option for those couples partial to wine.

Your Website's Gift Registry Page

What really drives all this online registry convenience is your wedding website. Your guests will browse your website and find your registry page along with all the photos, stories, directions, and other essential info. The registry page of a good wedding website should provide a list of stores and other registries you're set up with, and ideally have a link for each so that your guests can go straight to any one of them from this central starting point. A wish list is another feature your service may provide for you to include on your registry page. Items in a wish list can be located at any store or may be monetary contributions (a $90 romantic candlelight dinner on your honeymoon, for example). Having your registries accessible from your wedding website is an easy, sure-fire way for guests to find them with minimum etiquette hassle and fuss.

Linking to Your Stores' Registries

Add a link from your website's gift registry page to every online registry you have, whether they are store registries, honeymoon registries or any other specialty gift services. Your objective is to have a single list of registries so that your guests can find them all from one location and jump easily to the website of each. As an added convenience, you may want to add a link to each of your registries' store locator pages. Most stores have a page on their website where visitors can enter an address and locate a nearby store, which your guests will appreciate. Some wedding website services are more helpful than others, and may even provide the registry website addresses and store locator links for all the most popular stores automatically.

> **<TIP>**
>
> **Consolidating Your Registries**
>
> While it's great to have more than one type of registry (sports, electronics, traditional, and so forth) keeping track of all of them can become an unruly burden if you go overboard. Having them all centralized and accessible from your wedding website will help you as much as it will your guests, but resist the urge to register with every store under the sun. If you're considering two or more stores with a similar theme or type of wares, decide which has the most of what you want and settle on that one exclusively. Too many registries to juggle will be difficult to maintain later on, and you'll be increasingly likely to have duplicate or similar items sneak into more than one of your lists.
>
> **</TIP>**

Adding a Wish List

In addition to linking with other registries, your wedding website may be able to host its own. If your wedding website provides a "wish list" feature, you should be able to upload your own photo thumbnails, descriptions, prices, and store locations for any items you've got your eye on. You might even want to emulate your own honeymoon itinerary like the honeymoon registry services we mentioned previously. For guests wanting to provide you with the monetary gifts described in your wish list, you can either have them provide a check at your wedding or use an online credit card merchant like PayPal (www.paypal.com). With some tasteful creativity and a good, flexible wedding website service, your registry page can cover the full gamut of gift styles and types. Provide your guests with as broad a range of options as possible, and let them choose what they would feel most comfortable and enjoyable to give.

Building and Managing Your Registry

Ready to shop? There's a lot of ways to tackle it, especially with the extra option of online browsing. You can start online or in the store, with the main objective at first being simply to feel out your options. Study the registry checklist that the store gives you and the one at the end of this chapter. These are traditional essentials—by their nature very general—so scratch off what you're not interested in and make notes on those extra goods you are. You can either decide to tackle the whole list at once or divide-and-conquer (kitchen gizmos and tableware today, bed linens this weekend). To maximize your online advantage, you might want to hang around the stores just long enough to check out those things you need to see and feel in person, and then leave the rest to shop for online.

Store Shopping

In the stores you'll be given a hand-held scanner that you tote around and use to zap the barcodes of those items you want added to your list. Scratch off items from your checklist as you go. It's obviously best to do this registry-building together, but if one of you is extremely adverse to long shopping excursions either break it up into smaller trips or have one person scout it out and narrow options before you make the final decisions together in the store or even online. Don't ever feel you need to rush a decision; anything you add (or don't add) to your registry can be removed or re-added later.

The Cost Ratio

Make sure you consider the budgets of your guests. You want a broad range of gift prices for them to be able to select from. Aim for the majority of your items in the $50 to $100 range. Some expensive items are fine to add for those guests with the desire and means to purchase, as well as for those who may pool together for a group gift. Don't forget to add plenty of less expensive choices as well. These will be appreciated by guests on a budget, and can be purchased for showers and other pre-wedding parties.

As for overall number, a good rule of thumb to shoot for is two or three items for every expected guest you plan to have. Many friends and family members will dip into your registry for easy gift choices during holidays and other special occasions, so make sure you're stocked up. Does it sound like too much to shop for? You don't have to finalize everything now. Get a good mixture of gifts up on your registry and add to it later as items are purchased and time goes by (see the registry maintenance discussion below). At least you'll have a selection up for your showers, and most guests will buy gifts for your wedding closer to the big day anyway.

Easy Registry Maintenance

You can quickly see if your available gift registry items are running low by logging onto your registry online. Most online registries will show you in real-time which items have been purchased, so you can tell at a glance if you need to stock up on more goods. Always check that you have a good cost ratio available and that any items you receive early are getting checked off the list.

Review your registry printouts and online reports frequently during the time you're busy shopping and building your lists. Eliminate any duplicate items you have or items you might have added in more than one registry. No need to get more than one brand of toaster oven, and if you're using an online-only registry, the shipping for returns can get expensive.

Giving

Give a token of appreciation to those who have been there for you during the wedding planning journey. Big or small, it's your choice. If you're hard pressed and on a tight budget, don't underestimate the power of a thoughtful card or handmade gift. It's traditional to give something to thank your bridesmaids, groomsmen, ring-bearer and flower girl, but some couples also provide gifts to their parents, ceremony readers, or anyone else who helps make their wedding day happen. And don't forget something special for each other!

Gifts for Your Attendants

They've stood by your side, given you support, run errands and organized your prewedding parties. Show them each some love—and thanks—with a gift, whether it's along the traditional lines of something they'll wear on your wedding day (jewelry, cufflinks, and so forth) or something unique and different. Pass out gifts at the rehearsal dinner, bridesmaids' luncheon, or any other attendant get-together.

To Personalize or Not to Personalize

When considering what to get your troops, you need to decide if you'll be giving the same gift for everyone or personalizing it further by matching each attendant with something that's especially up their alley. While personalizing your gifts can add an extra thoughtful touch, it's usually easiest with a smaller wedding party. Instead of identical cufflinks for the guys you might give suitcase cufflinks for that friend who loves to travel, for example, dollar signs to the accountant, and scuba masks for the diving buff. Or go totally different: an MP3 player for the music-loving technophile, restaurant gift certificate for the foodie, and stylish photo frames for the shutterbug. Often, bride and grooms spend a little more on the best man and maid of honor.

If your time is short or you're hesitant about one person's gift being perceived as "better" than another's, it's perfectly acceptable to go the identical route. And with very large wedding parties, this is often the most practical way to go. Choose something you know everyone will love—one for the guys and one for the girls—and buy the gifts in bulk. You can still get something a bit different for the honor attendants to let them know that the extra help they're putting in is appreciated.

Junior Attendants

Junior bridesmaids or groomsmen, the flower girl, ringbearer, and any other bridal party tot in your entourage will be thrilled to get even a simple gift that shows them the importance of their part in your big day. Whether it's their first nice jewelry or real cufflinks, a set of bride-and-groom teddy bears, or photo of you with them in an heirloom frame, it will make them feel special.

<TIP>

Who to Thank?

Think about all those who helped pull off your day. Did someone host a pre-wedding luncheon? Perhaps a relative has agreed to house out-of-town guests. Did you get a friend or sister to help with those time-consuming invitations or ceremony programs? Chances are your loved ones have done a lot to make your day a success, and all of them are great candidates for a thank-you gift.

Depending on your budget, that gift may be a wrapped item, a centerpiece from your reception, (you can even have the DJ pause the music for you to present them with a message of thanks), a card, or even dinner at your place after the wedding to check out your pictures and video. A great use for your new dinnerware! The important thing is to let them know how much their help and support means to you.

</TIP>

Some Ideas

Stumped for bridal party gift ideas? Here are some options to get your creative juices flowing:

Traditional

- Wedding day jewelry

- Engraved jewelry boxes, toasting glasses, flasks, lighters, or cigar holders

- Wallets

- Money clips

- Silver-plated business card cases

- Cufflinks

- Beer steins

Budget

- "Memory Basket": handmade photo collage of you with each of your bridesmaids and a CD of special music, placed in a cute gift bag

- Goodie bag with scented candles, bubble bath, and other relaxing bath treats

- Magazine subscription, each catering to the recipient's interests

- Group nosebleed tickets to a baseball or basketball game

- Box of chocolates

- Each of their favorite movies on DVD

Hobby

- Symphony tickets

- Photo frames or leather album

- Hobby or craft store gift certificate

- Cooking lesson with a master chef

- Subscription to a related magazine

Luxurious

- Day spa treatment

- Elegant throw

- Cashmere sweater

- Night at a luxury hotel

- Gourmet restaurant dinner for two

- Silk pajamas or nightgown

Beauty and Health

- Gift certificate for yoga sessions

- Health magazine subscription

Artsy

- Pottery or jewelry-making session at an art studio

- Art supplies

- Craft book or magazine subscription

Active

- Sporting good store gift certificate

- Day of horseback riding

- Rock climbing, scuba diving, or other activity session

Electronics

- Software

- MP3 Player

- PDA

Other

- Concert or sports tickets

- Gourmet coffee or tea

- Wine

- Membership to a beer- or cigar-of-the-month club

- Offer to pay some or all of their attire expenses

Gifts for Each Other

Giving each other something special the day of or before your wedding is a nice way to celebrate all the work and successes of your relationship and wedding planning journey. What you get your sweetie doesn't have to be expensive, either. How about a DVD of the movie you saw on your first date, or a CD of songs that are most special to you? A card with a heartfelt message is another way to share how happy you are about this special day; for an added personal touch, handcraft it yourself.

Some traditional gifts are pearl or diamond earrings for her and an engraved watch for him, though this could very well be above and over your budget's capacity. If you like, talk about it ahead of time and set a price limit so you'll each have an idea of how much to spend.

<CROSS-REFERENCE>

Refer to the discussion on online jewelers in Chapter 3, "The Journey Begins"; most of the same tips for engagement rings apply to wedding sets as well.

</CROSS-REFERENCE>

Your Wedding Rings

Although they're sometimes not thought of as such, your wedding rings are also gifts to each other, and very special ones, too. Some couples decide to purchase each other's rings as their sole wedding gifts to each other, along with a card or other sentimental keepsake.

Start shopping for your wedding ring set four to six months before the big day. You can see if the shop where you purchased the engagement ring will give you a deal for returning, but you should still check out a few other stores to get a feel for the variety in styles and prices. Make a decision in time to pick up your rings about a month or so before the wedding day. Getting the rings fitted and having any inscriptions made on the inside (most jewelers should do this for free) will take a bit of time, and if the rings come back too loose or too tight you'll need extra time for the resizing. Make sure you leave yourself plenty of room for last minute modifications.

Wedding Favors

An often-overlooked detail of your wedding reception is the favors you give out to your guests. Favors have a triple purpose, really: they serve as thank-you gifts for your guests' attendance and support, memoirs of your special day, and also as decoration accents for your tables. Simple or extravagant, the style of your favors will be a reflection of the rest of your wedding's formality and theme as well as your own very unique personalities. Don't hesitate to think outside the box here. While many couples like the tradition of mints or jordan almonds in tulle, others strive for creativity and uniqueness, and your guests will love a break from the expected norm in the goodies they get.

Things to Consider

We'll start with cost, although this should by no means be the sole guide to your choice of favors. Take the total amount you've budgeted for your favors and divide by the number of expected guests to get your target cost-per-favor. You'll want to have about 25 extra favors too, just to be safe.

How personalized do you want the favors? Will you be able to include your names, wedding date, and any special message? Ribbons, inscriptions, and calligraphy are all possibilities for personalization.

Think about assembly. How demanding and time-consuming will it be to create or bundle together the favor you have in mind? Can you enlist any help from friends or family?

How's the decorative potential? Will the favors boost the atmosphere of your reception? Does the favor's style match your wedding formality and theme?

Is the favor practical? In other words, does it have a potential use for your guests (eating is an excellent use, by the way!)...or will it be something they'll toss or put away to collect dust? Some favors look gorgeous and cute when they're arranged together on a table, but quickly lose their appeal when brought home separately by each guest.

Will you have a place to store the favors after they're assembled or purchased? How will you transport them to the reception location, and how will they be distributed? You might choose to have favors preset at the tables; they could even take on yet another role as placeholders (lavender soaps wrapped in decorative paper with guests' names, for example). You could also lay favors out on a separate table or have them handed out personally.

e-Resource

Online Wedding Favor Ideas

Online shops like www.beau-coup.com and hansonellis.com are full of ideas, catalogs, and articles for all kinds of fun favor possibilities. Get your inspiration and how-to's as well as search for online discounts. These online shops cover the latest trends and recommended picks. Even if you're thinking of handcrafting your own gifts, you'll find such websites to be a useful source of ideas.

For ecological favor ideas, such as tree saplings or forget-me-not seed packages, check out Evergreen Memories (www.evergreenmemories.ca).

Ideas

Above all, let the theme and style of your wedding guide your choice of favors. Here's a few ideas:

Edible

- Chocolates or truffles. Buy or handcraft decorative boxes to enclose them

- Frosted cookies

- Little jars of honey or jam

- Fortune cookies with a special message inside

- Sparkling cider mini-bottles

- Custom-labeled bottles of wine

Handcrafted

- Decoupage flowerpots

- Miniature wreaths made of herbs with a symbolic representation, like rosemary for remembrance

- Potpourri- or rose petal-filled lace sachets

- Handcrafted or hand-decorated boxes filled with candies or other goodies

- Homemade candles or soaps

- Custom-created CD with your favorite music, labeled with your names and wedding date

Practical

- Bookmarks

- Key rings

- Letter openers

- Lottery tickets

Ecological

- Packets of seeds or little saplings to be planted

- Natural objects native to the area or relative to your theme: seashells, miniature pine cones, etc. Affix ribbons with your names and wedding date.

- Break-away centerpieces like several small pots of miniature rosebushes that can be distributed among the guests at each table

- Miniature lucky bamboo plants

- Donation to your favorite charity in the name of each guest. Distribute cards on ornate paper describing the charity and the donation

Traditional

- Jordan almonds or mints wrapped in tulle and white ribbon

- Votives with scented candles

- Hershey's kisses

- Slice of the groom's cake in a decorated box

- Wedding bubbles or bells

- Placecard frames

Gift Baskets for Out-of-Town Guests

Welcome baskets are an optional touch of thoughtfulness that will be well appreciated by those guests who travel a distance to be with you on your special day. Have it waiting for them as they arrive at their lodging, whether it is at a hotel or the home of a relative. You can arrange for this ahead of time with the management of the hotel where your guests will be staying. Ask about it early on so that they'll be prepared to distribute your baskets to the appropriate rooms.

The welcome basket can contain anything you like: wine and truffles, gourmet cheeses, crackers and fruit, a city guide and disposable camera, or a certificate for a massage or other amenity at the hotel.

Receiving

While plenty of guests will bring gifts to your wedding reception, many will find it convenient to ship items directly to you. The incoming goods may start with one here and there at first, but the closer to your big day, the more they'll come. Getting all those goodies is great, but you can bet there's plenty of etiquette and expectations surrounding gift-getting. Keep on top of your records, pace your thank-you notes, and deal quickly and efficiently with duplicate orders, broken items, and other situations requiring your attention. Avoid the procrastination pitfall and make receiving your wedding gifts the pleasure it should be.

Gift Record-Keeping

To keep everything going smooth and organized, make sure you have a record-keeping system in place before you even set up your gift registry. If your wedding website has a guest database with gift information capability, yours may already be in place already (we'll cover your website's gift tracking in the next e-Resource).

As the gifts come in, save the enclosed card, mailing label and invoice; you'll need these for exchanges or returns. Note the following information for each gift:

- The sender's name

- The sender's mailing address

- A description of the gift

- Date the gift arrived

- The store the gift was shipped from

- Comments (write down anything that comes to mind. It will help you when filling out your thank-you cards)

- The date you sent out your thank-you card

This information can be tracked on paper, on a spreadsheet or—the most timesaving and efficient way—in your wedding website's guest database.

e-Resource

Recording Gift Information in Your Guest Database

The online guest database that was introduced in Chapter 7, "Manage Your Guests and Attendants" is one of the most practical and time-saving tools, in part because it's so versatile. You used it to manage your guest list, your RSVP's, your contact information, and now you can use it to track your gifts and thank-you cards. Since you already have all the information (name, address, and so forth) together, it saves time by avoiding any re-entry of information and keeps everything conveniently organized in one place.

Most of your guest information should already be entered in your online database. When a sender's gift arrives, do a quick search on their name, add the information into the gift field (date, description, store, and so forth) and save. When it comes time to write thank you notes, you can easily do a search on those guests whose gifts you have received. Write your cards as you step through each resulting guest entry, and check the "Thank-You Card Sent" box for each so you'll know later which guests you've already thanked.

Using a centralized database like this makes it easy for you to keep up with your received gifts and track your correspondence, all in one easily accessible place.

Gift Etiquette: Accepting, Returning and Exchanging

Most of this gift etiquette stuff is just common sense and being considerate, but it doesn't hurt to take a look at some of the following reminders. In all the excitement and fuss, you don't want to drop the ball anywhere.

To Bring or to Ship

Many guess will find it convenient to ship your gifts directly, but some will bring them to the reception. Make sure you have a table set up for this purpose in a safe yet out of the way area. Assign someone to accept gifts from guests as they arrive and make sure this helping soul has a roll of scotch tape to secure the accompanying card to each gift right away. One of the biggest gift problems newlyweds face is trying to match gifts up with a jumble of loose, non-attached cards and wind up with potentially many gifts whose senders are unknown. You'll also need to arrange someone to help transport your gifts home after the reception.

Money Gifts

If you'd like gifts of monetary joy, spread the word through friends, family, and possibly an online cash contribution registry option (described earlier in the chapter). Definitely do not put your request for green on your invitation, as it looks almost like you're charging admission for attending your wedding. Not cool. Guests will either send your cash in the mail or bring it to your reception, along with a card. You could have a a card box to receive such gifts at the reception. Record monetary gifts in your records just as you would any other.

Broken or Damaged Gifts

It's bound to happen: a gift arrives, you open the package, and..oops! It's damaged. Luckily, items from your registry should be no problem to replace. Notify the store's customer service right away, and you'll be able to swap your damaged goods with a pristine item.

If the gift is not from your registry, check to see if there's a postal insurance stamp on the package. If so, you're in luck: return the gift to the sender with a thank-you card and explanation so they can get reimbursed by the post office and send you a new gift. If the package was not insured, it's best to bite the bullet and chalk the gift up as a casualty of shipping. Send a normal, gracious thank-you card to the sender and don't mention the damage, or they'll probably feel obligated to purchase another gift for you.

Duplicates

Some gifts are good to have duplicates of: sheets, place settings, towels, breakable items, and anything else that can wear out easily. Stash them away to replace used items later. For those gifts you definitely don't want more than one of, though, you'll want to exchange. Three toasters or two identical blenders are probably not going to be needed.

Most registries will be very open about exchanges, but do it soon after you receive the gift. Send your thank-you card to each sender of the duplicate item as if you were keeping theirs. No need to mention the exchange. And don't ever ask a guest where they bought your gift so you can exchange it.

Unwanted Gifts

Sometimes you receive something that's just not your style. You should feel free to return it to the store it was purchased from and trade it for something you do want, if the store information is provided. It's your call whether or not to keep the original gift instead, to avoid potential hurt feelings if the sender comes by for a visit. Either way, send a gushing thank-you letter just as you would if the item was more up your alley, and don't mention the exchange if you do choose to make one.

Absent Gifts

Perhaps you haven't received a gift from a close friend or family member and fear it may have been lost in the mail. Resist the urge to ask about it. If the guest did send a gift and hasn't heard from you about it or received a thank-you card, they'll eventually bring it up.

Unnamed Gifts

At best you may have one or two gifts that either don't have cards or have cards that are loose and unattached. At worst, you may wind up with many such anonymous packages. Try contacting the store and see if you can glean any information that way. Purchase date, store location, and anything else they can tell you may help narrow down the puzzle. Beyond that, it's just good old process of elimination. Find out who you have on your guest list that you're missing a gift from and see if you can enlist friends or family to help find out discreetly who sent what. Don't ask guests yourself.

Gifts for a Postponed/Cancelled Wedding

If your wedding is put on hold, you'll obviously be sending out announcements to your guests, and you can go ahead and hang on to the gift. If your wedding is cancelled, though, all gifts—shower, engagement, and wedding—need to be returned to the sender.

Showing Your Thanks: How to Manage and Write the Thank-You Cards

The most important thing to remember in all this gift-getting frenzy is to send a prompt note of thanks for everything you receive. A handwritten note is absolutely imperative. Since gifts will start coming in as soon as you announce your wedding plans, stock up on stationery early. There's a lot of white, ivory, and colored stationery out there for the purpose. Alternatively, you might want something that matches your invitations.

Some Words of Advice

So how prompt is prompt? You should send out your message of thanks no later than a month after the gift is received, and for gifts received before your wedding, etiquette rules suggest even earlier: two weeks. For gifts received after your wedding, it's okay to take a little more time. You get up to three months for those. But any later than that can be taken as rude or unappreciative. People will be waiting to hear what you thought about their contribution to your new life.

<TIP>

Preventing Anonymous Gifts

As we mentioned before, it's a good idea to assign a gift attendant and make sure they're equipped with scotch tape. Ask them to securely affix all accompanying cards to the gifts as they're received. It could save you a lot of time and identity sleuthing later on.

</TIP>

Handwriting is a must; never type or print your thank-you cards. Having bad writing isn't an excuse, either: your chicken scratch will make the message that much more personal.

The important thing to remember when sending out notes of thanks is to keep up with it! You're going to be getting gifts nonstop for months, and if you let those pile up...well, heaven help you. Keep records and descriptions of all gifts received, as we mentioned earlier, and send thank-you notes out a group at a time. Writing five a day for twenty days is something anyone can manage, and it will result in good, sincere notes. Imagine the alternative: a hundred cards at a time! That's enough to give anyone writer's cramp.

Also: split up the task between you and your sweetie. Who says the bride has to write them all? Or the groom? The groom's friends and family will no doubt prefer a message from him, and the bride's will be thrilled to get a message from her.

<CROSS-REFERENCE>
We'll cover stationery in more detail in Chapter 20, "Send Invitations and Manage Your Responses".
</CROSS-REFERENCE>

How to Write a Good Thank-You Note: Our Three-Step Guide

The task might seem daunting. How will you come up with personal, unique ways to thank potentially hundreds of guests? The answer: use a formula. These three straightforward steps are a derivation of what most wedding pros will advise.

Step 1: Identify the Goods. Name or describe the gift you received.

Thank you so much for the china place setting.

Step 2: Mention how you and your sweetie (mention his or her name) will use it.

Peter and I love having company over and these will get a lot of use!

Step 3: Add a personal comment in a sentence or two. It's up to you and your relationship with the particular guest. If they came from out of town, this is a perfect spot to thank them for the travel.

We were so happy you were able to make it to our wedding. Thank you for coming so far to make our day that much more special!

Wrap up your note by signing it (it's not required that both of you sign). That's it! As long as you give yourself fifteen or twenty minutes a day, you should easily be able to stay on top of them all. If you do find yourself in a dire situation and it looks like you won't be able to get the thanks out in time, go ahead and send general printed cards first, but make sure you follow up soon with a written note as soon as you're able.

Checklist: Registry Basics

Choose those items essential to you.

Bakeware

☐ Ovenware Set
☐ Silicone Baking Mats
☐ Bundt Pan
☐ Cake Pans
☐ Cookie Sheets
☐ Muffin Pans
☐ Mixing Bowls
☐ Measuring Cups and Spoons
☐ Cooling Rack
☐ Rolling Pin
☐ Ramekins and Soufflé Dishes
☐ Pie / Tart / Quiche Pans
☐ Bread / Loaf Pans
☐ Pizza Stone and Peel
☐ Spatulas / Mixing Spoons
☐ _____

Cookware

☐ Cookware Set
☐ Fry Pan / Skillet
☐ Grill Pan / Griddle
☐ Pot Rack
☐ Roasting Pan and Rack
☐ Sauce Pan
☐ Sauté Pan
☐ Steamer Insert
☐ Stockpot
☐ Tea Kettle
☐ _____

Cutlery

☐ Knife Block Set
☐ Boning Knife
☐ Bread Knife
☐ Carving Knife
☐ Chef's Knife
☐ Cleaver
☐ Kitchen Shears
☐ Paring Knife
☐ Slicing Knife
☐ Stake Knifes
☐ Utility Knife
☐ Sharpening Steel
☐ _____

Flatware

☐ Dinner Knifes
☐ Dinner Forks
☐ Soupspoons
☐ Salad / Dessert Forks
☐ Teaspoon / Dessert Spoons
☐ Salad Serving Set
☐ Butter Knifes and Spreader
☐ Hostess Set
☐ Cake / Pie Server
☐ Formal Set Pattern
☐ Casual Set Pattern
☐ _____

Glassware

☐ Goblets
☐ Iced-Beverages Glasses
☐ Red / White Wine Glasses
☐ Champagne Flutes
☐ Old-Fashioned Glasses
☐ Cocktail Glasses
☐ Beer Mugs
☐ _____

Bar and Wine

☐ Champagne Cooler
☐ Ice Bucket and Tongs
☐ Wine Rack
☐ Wine Opener
☐ Punch Bowl Set
☐ Cocktail Shaker / Tools Set
☐ _____

Tableware / Dinnerware

☐ Dinner Plates
☐ Salad / Dessert Plates
☐ Bread / Butter Plates
☐ Cups and Saucers
☐ Cream Soup Bowls
☐ Soup / Cereal Bowls
☐ Rim Soup Bowls
☐ Vegetable / Fruit Bowls
☐ Serving Platters / Trays
☐ Serving Bowls
☐ Coffee / Tea Service
☐ Water Pitcher

Checklist: Registry Basics (continued)

☐ Mugs
☐ Gravy Boat
☐ Sugar and Creamer Set
☐ Salt and Pepper Set
☐ Condiment Dishes
☐ Formal Set Pattern
☐ Casual Set Pattern
☐ _____

Small Appliances

☐ Blender
☐ Coffeemaker
☐ Coffee Grinder
☐ Espresso Machine
☐ Food Processor
☐ Hand / Stand Mixer
☐ Toaster / Toaster Oven
☐ Microwave
☐ Waffle Iron
☐ Popcorn Popper
☐ _____

Other Favorite Kitchen Items

☐ Cutting Boards / Mats
☐ Cheese Grater
☐ Colander
☐ Electric Can Opener
☐ Electric Knife / Sharpener
☐ Fondue Set
☐ Juicer
☐ Multi-Cooker / Pasta Cooker
☐ Rice Cooker / Steamer
☐ Roasting Pan
☐ Salad Spinner
☐ Spice Rack
☐ Storage Containers
☐ Thermal Carafe
☐ Turkey Fryer / Fish Cooker
☐ Vacuum Food Sealer
☐ Wok / Stir Fry Pan
☐ _____

_____

Linen (Bed, Bath, Kitchen)

☐ Comforter / Duvet
☐ Blankets
☐ Fitted / Flat Sheet Sets
☐ Pillows and Shams
☐ Mattress Pad
☐ Bed Skirt
☐ Shower Curtain / Liner / Rings
☐ Bath Mats
☐ Bath / Guest Towels
☐ Bath Robes
☐ Kitchen Towels / Dishcloths
☐ Pot Holders / Oven Mitts
☐ Place Mats / Napkins / Rings
☐ _____

General Accessories

☐ Luggage
☐ Picture Frames
☐ Framed Art
☐ Wall Frames / Mirrors
☐ Photo Albums and Boxes
☐ Wall / Alarm Clocks
☐ Lamps
☐ Vases
☐ DVD / CD Racks
☐ _____

Contact Sheet: Gift Registries

Registry: _____

Address: _____

_____

Registry Consultant: _____

Email: _____

Phone: _____

Fax: _____

Website: _____

Login Email Used: _____

Password: _____

Account Number: _____

Staple Business Card

Setup Date: _____

Completion Program Description (if any): _____

Registry Categories: _____

Return / Exchange Policy: _____

Registry Expiration Date: _____

Registry: _____

Address: _____

_____

Registry Consultant: _____

Email: _____

Phone: _____

Fax: _____

Website: _____

Login Email Used: _____

Password: _____

Account Number: _____

Staple Business Card

Setup Date: _____

Completion Program Description (if any): _____

Registry Categories: _____

Return / Exchange Policy: _____

Registry Expiration Date: _____

Chapter 16

Settle on Your Attendants' Dresses and Formalwear

- Styling Your Bridesmaids

- Fashion for the Guys

- Dressing Your Child Attendants

- Moms and Dads

- e-Plan It! Use Your e-Resources:

  Idea Shopping for Bridesmaid Dresses
  Dress Designers' Websites
  Online Bridesmaid Dress Bargains
  Formalwear Websites

- Worksheets:

  Considerations Worksheet: Bridesmaids' Look
  Considerations Worksheet: Groomsmen's Look
  Contact Sheet: Groom's Formalwear

Time to style your entourage! How you want your group to look will depend on the formality of your wedding to a great extent, as well as your overall theme and colors. Just remember that as long as everyone feels great, they'll look great…and that will make you look all the better on the big day and in your pictures. So suit them up in style, and get their feedback as to what's comfortable for them, too.

Styling Your Bridesmaids

It's up to you to decide how you want your gals to look while backing you up on your wedding day. In general, you'll want their style to complement that of your dress and overall theme, but you've got a lot of options. These days, the emphasis is less on everyone looking identical and more on how they work together as a group.

Color and Style

Once the big order for the all-important wedding gown is placed, you're ready to start thinking about how to dress your entourage. When thinking about dress styles, consider a look that will coordinate well with your gown and echo the formality of your wedding. Color will be a matter of preference, and should be chosen to match your theme. Most bridesmaid dresses are simple in design and often in a solid color, but there's a wide selection of looks to choose from.

Should your bridesmaids wear the same style and color dress? This is often the case, but you don't have to make them completely identical. You may want to give your girls a bit more freedom in customizing their look—especially if age, body type, and skin tone vary widely in your group. We'll go over some tips on balancing the variation if you decide to allow it. Most brides also set their maid of honor apart in some way, whether it's a slight difference in the dress (modified style or color shade) or a different bouquet that signifies their special status.

Length

Bridesmaids' dresses come in a variety of lengths, and it's your choice as to how much skin you want your girls to show. As a general rule, the length of their dresses should match well with your gown. If you're wearing a floor-length gown, for instance, your girls shouldn't be wearing something short. For formal weddings, their dresses shouldn't be any shorter than tea length.

Floor -The hem completely skims the floor.

Ballerina - This dress style is extra full, with the hem falling to just above the ankle.

Tea - The hem falls to mid-calf.

Intermission or Hi/Low - The hem falls diagonally: high on one side, low on another. Or, it falls just below the knees in the front and to the ankles in the back.

Knee - The hem just reaches the knees.

Street - The hem just covers the knees.

Mini - The hem falls above the knee.

Different Styles?

Keep in mind that some dress styles are better designed for a specific body type than others. The A-line style, for example, flatters a taller, more slender build. A shorter bridesmaid might find that she needs to do a lot of alteration in order to be comfortable, while a sheath silhouette would likely flatter her form a lot more. You may want to consider choosing dresses that are the same color and of the same fabric, but in different styles to best compliment each of your bridesmaids' figures. You can select two or three style options, for example, and let each of your bridesmaids choose the one she feels most comfortable with.

Different Colors?

Just as certain dress styles compliment specific body types, certain color shades compliment specific skin tones and may not flatter others as well. Think about selecting a dress available in a few varying shades of your wedding color (like purple, lavender, and periwinkle), and then allowing your bridesmaids to choose the shade they feel goes best with their skin.

<CROSS-REFERENCE>

We covered dress silhouettes, necklines, and fabrics in detail in Chapter 10, "Play Dress-Up: Create Your Wedding Day Look".

</CROSS-REFERENCE>

Finding the Right Dress

Six months or so before your wedding is a good time to start thinking about settling on your bridesmaids' look. You should probably plan on at least one group shopping trip if possible, to get your girls involved in the decision and obtain their input on the dresses that you're leaning towards.

Try narrowing down the decision on your own at first, either online or at dress salons (you can bring your maid of honor along to help). While you're considering color, style, designer, and so forth, don't forget to think about cost, too. Bridesmaids are traditionally responsible for purchasing their own attire, so you don't want to put an inconvenient financial burden on them. We'll be giving you some e-secrets to pass along to help ease their costs (check out the Online Dress Bargains later on in this section).

e-Resource

See bridesmaids' dresses matching your search criteria on The Knot, and click on each for detailed information and local stores.

Dress Designer Bill Levkoff's website (www.billlevkoff.com) lets you have the photographed models "try on" different colors of each dress.

Idea Shopping for Bridesmaid Dresses

We talked about this in Chapter 10: you can shell out five bucks or more on a bridal mag, or hit the most comprehensive online dress catalogs for free, and have the power to search them based on color, designer, and price range. Just as you did with your wedding gown, you can look at a wide variety of styles, colors and fabrics, and narrow down your search quickly and easily. If you find a great dress that you like, you can locate stores near you (and your girls) with an easy click and obtain an address and phone number, or hop over to the designer's website and get more info.

The Knot (www.theknot.com), has one of the best online dress and gown catalogs there is. Click on the "Gowns" link at the top of The Knot's home page and navigate to Bridesmaids using the left-hand menu. From here, you can browse dress articles and browse or search the catalog. To search, choose a designer, a price range, and/or color.

For each dress you're interested in, click on the "Save to my notebook" link to bookmark the gown in a kind of idea shopping cart so you can refer to it later. Check out the dress' designer by clicking on their site, or look at the list of stores in your area that carry it. From here it's easy to give them a phone call to see if they have it in stock, and arrange to stop by (possibly with your maid of honor or a bridesmaid as your try-on model) to examine it further.

Check out the other portals as well, including The Wedding Channel's "Fashion and Beauty" section (www.weddingchannel.com/wedding-fashion/wedding-dress/bridesmaid-dress.html) and Brides.com's "Dress Gallery" (www.brides.com/fashion/dresses/gallery ... click "bridesmaid").

Dress Designers' Websites

If you find a dress or style you like, consider checking out the designer's website for other models that might be up your alley. Bill Levkoff's website (www.billlevkoff.com), for example, sports a slick interface that lets you change the dress colors on the pictured models to get an idea of how each style would look in your color.

Most designers' websites will have a store locator so that you can search for stores in your area that carry their products.

Dress Shops

Hit bridal salons (such as the spot you purchased your wedding gown), bridal warehouses, and formal-wear stores to actually see the dresses and feel the fabric. Go armed with information you've gleaned off the web (see the e-Resources above), including styles you like—make a list of style numbers—and designers. Visit the online resources ahead of time to find which shops to go to that carry the designs you're looking for. A good idea is to bring your maid of honor or another bridesmaid along to try on dresses you're considering.

Ordering and Fitting

Your bridesmaids will all need to be fitted for the dress you select, in order to obtain the right size and make any necessary alterations. Consider getting everyone together and going in to your dress shop for a group fitting, at which time you can see how everyone will look in the dress you've selected and place all the orders at once (your bridesmaids traditionally pay for their own attire). If there are a few

<NOTE>

Some Popular Dress Designers' Websites

After Six	aftersix.com
Alyce Designs	alycedesigns.com
Jasmine	belsoie.com
Bill Levkoff	billlevkoff.com
Jim Hjelm	jimhjelm.com
Dessy Creations	dessy.com
Jordan	jordanfashions.com
Jessica McClintock	jessicamcclintock.com
David's Bridal	davidsbridal.com
Watters and Watters	watters.com

</NOTE>

different dresses that you're considering, you can all decide together which one to go with. This will also make them feel like they have more of a say as to what they'll be wearing.

If your girls live in different parts of the country, you'll need to take steps to make sure they can all be properly fitted. One option is to use a dress designer whose line is available from a national chain, so that your bridesmaids can find a shop local to them to get fitted and have any alterations done conveniently on their own. Alternatively, have your remote maids send in their measurements and buy all your dresses from the same shop (this will ensure your dresses are all from the same dye lot). The shop you purchase the dresses from will ship them to your bridesmaids so that they can have their alterations taken care of by a local tailor or seamstress.

e-Resource

Online Bridesmaid Dress Bargains

A dress can be a big expense for your girls, so pass along the same tips we gave you when searching for your wedding gown. Online dress shops sell the same items that your local retail outlets do, but with discounts up to 20%, 30%, or even 50% off what you'll find in the dress shops. If you find a great deal online, you and your bridesmaids may want to consider taking it, but you'll want to actually see the dress and have the girls—or your maid of honor—try it on in a shop first.

How to Find the Best Deal

A good strategy is to start off by browsing ideas online as we mentioned in the previous e-Resource, "Idea Shopping for Bridesmaid Dresses". Narrow down the look you want, perhaps with a few specific designers and style numbers noted down that you'll want to try out. Using the online sources, find local shops that carry the dresses you're interested in, and make appointments to see them. Make your final decision after seeing the dresses, just as you normally would. Bring along your bridesmaids or maid of honor to try them on and provide their feedback. Get quotes for the dresses you like; you'll want to compare the shop's price with what you find online.

> <CROSS-REFERENCE>
>
> We discussed finding great online deals for your wedding gown in Chapter 10, "Play Dress-Up: Create Your Wedding Day Look".
>
> </CROSS-REFERENCE>

Don't commit to anything at the shop just yet. Armed with all the specifics and a price, go back to the web now and check the online dress shops. If you find the same dress for significant savings, you might want to pass the reference on to your bridesmaids to purchase it online—they'll appreciate your saving them the bucks. Just keep in mind that shipping will add to the overall cost (although you'll probably be able to cut out the sales tax), and the dresses will likely need to be pressed since they'll wrinkle during shipping. If your girls don't feel the online savings are worth it for the dress you're looking at, they can always head back to the dress shop and make their purchases there.

The Sites

So where do you find these online discounters? There's plenty of dress sites on the web, but be careful who you're dealing with. Make sure they are authorized dealers of the designs they feature (meaning that they work directly with the manufacturer) and that they accept returns and will refund payments if you and your bridesmaids are not satisfied for any reason. The following are some of the better bargain sites:

BrideSave.com

As seen in our previous discussion on wedding gowns in chapter 10. Click the "Bridesmaids" menu link to get to the bridesmaid dress search page. Enter in your criteria and click the "Find Dress" button to begin browsing their selection. If you have the item numbers of dresses you may have tried on and liked in a bridal shop, enter them each into the keyword search box at top of the page.

Results for your criteria are listed in familiar catalog style, including price. Clicking on a dress for more information allows you to select individual sizes and obtain exact prices for each. See how the prices compare with your local retailers' offerings.

eBay's "Wedding Apparel" Section (www.ebay.com)

As we've shown you before, eBay can be a source of tremendous savings for many items, including brand new wedding attire. It's worth it just to run the dress number by the Wedding Apparel section's search and see if you come up with anything. One or more of your bridesmaids might find your design and style in their size and be able to get their dresses for a real bargain.

Find eBay's wedding apparel section by selecting the "Clothing, Shoes, & Accessories" category from their home page and clicking on "Wedding Apparel > Bridesmaids" from the menu that is presented next. From there you can browse the dresses listed to see the price ranges and designers offered or search for specific dresses you're interested in. To do a search, just enter in a designer name and item number in the search box provided.

NetBride (www.netbride.com)

NetBride offers more designers that BrideSave.com (above), but doesn't list their prices in a catalog; you need to request an e-mail quote. Click on "Bridesmaids Dresses" and then "Price Quote" to submit a request for a price quote on a specific dress (you provide the designer and item number). If you've gone into dress shops already, you can compare the quoted price with what your local retailers are giving you to see how much of a discount you can get. If you can save your girls a lot of bucks, pass the ordering information on to them!

Get It in Writing: Your Dress Contract

Whether the purchase is made on or offline, dress orders should specify the designer, color, specific style number, details, and total cost of the dress being purchased. Make sure a delivery date is given, and that all additional fees are listed, such as pressing, alterations, and so forth (if your bridesmaids are purchasing a dress online, they'll be using a tailor, seamstress or local dress shop for the alterations). Be clear about the refund and cancellation policies of the store or online discounter you're buying from; it should be provided in your contract or listed on their website.

Shoes and Accessories

Pick a shoe style for your bridesmaids that matches your wedding theme and their dresses. All your bridesmaids should wear the same style, color, and heel height. You may want to do the shopping for the right shoe style yourself, or go with all the girls and shoe shop in a group so that they can try on different looks and provide feedback on what feels most comfortable to them.

If you also want your bridesmaids to wear matching accessories (like gloves or a shawl, for instance), make sure you let them know so they have enough time to round it all up.

Fashion for the Guys

The bride may be the star of the wedding (some modern-day groomzillas might object), but all eyes will be on the groom as well. The attire of the groom and groomsmen will depend on tradition, your reception time, and the formality level of your wedding. They'll traditionally wear identical tuxedos or suits, with the groom's attire being slightly different to set him apart: a different color vest or cummerbund perhaps, or a white dinner jacket while the other guys wear black.

Quick Guide to Mens' Formalwear

Not sure what an ascot is, or the difference between a vest and a waistcoat? Here's a quick rundown:

Jackets

Cutaway (morning coat) - A very formal daytime jacket that's short in front with a long tapering tail in back. Most often black or charcoal in color and worn with striped trousers, wing-collared dress shirt, and an ascot.

Dinner Jacket - A white or ivory jacket with peaked lapels or a shawl collar, worn with formal black satin-striped tuxedo trousers.

Double-Breasted Jacket - A jacket with two rows of buttons down the front.

Full Dress (tails) - A very formal evening jacket that is short in front with two long tails in back. It's worn with a white tie and a vest.

Lapel - The extension of a jacket's collar that folds back against the breast.

Notched Lapel - A lapel with an inward-pointing triangular cut at the collar line.

Peaked Lapel - A lapel with an upward-pointing triangular cut that forms a broad V-line look.

Single-Breasted Jacket - A jacket with a single row of buttons down the front.

Shawl - A rounded lapel without cuts.

Stroller (walking coat) - A semiformal jacket with a tuxedo cut. Color is black or gray, and it's often paired with striped trousers and a waistcoat.

Shirts and Vests

Turn-Down (point) Collar - Like that of a business suit, but in a more formal type of fabric.

Lay-Down (spread) Collar - Less pointy than a turn-down collar but otherwise similar.

Wing Collar - The most formal style, it consists of a stand-up band with fold-down tips, and can be used with an ascot or bow tie.

Vest - Worn under a jacket to cover the trouser waistband instead of suspenders or a cummerbund. The groomsmen's vests (and ties) may optionally match the color of the bridesmaids' dresses.

Waistcoat - Similar to a vest, but cut lower in the front. It's a more formal look and works especially well with a morning jacket or full tails.

Ties

Ascot - A broad scarf looped under the chin and secured to the collar with a tie-tack or stickpin. Worn with a formal wing collar shirt and most often with a morning jacket.

Straight (four-in-hand) Tie - Similar to a business tie, but in a more formal type of fabric. Worn with a turn-down or lay-down collar.

Bow Tie - A short tie in a formal fabric and shaped like a bow. It can be worn with any type of collar.

Other Accessories

Boutonniere - A small floral arrangement pinned to the left lapel of the guys' jackets. Typically, the groom's boutonniere matches the bride's bouquet, and the groomsmen's matches the bouquets of the bridesmaids. The fathers' boutonnieres can either be the same as the groom's, the groomsmen's, or you may want to add something different to it to set them apart.

<CROSS-REFERENCE>

For more on florals, refer to Chapter 17, "Paint Your Wedding Colors with Flowers and Décor".

</CROSS-REFERENCE>

Cuff Links and Studs - Decorative metal fasteners used in place of shirt buttons.

Cummerbund - A pleated sash of brocade, satin, or silk worn to cover the trouser waistband instead of suspenders or a vest. The pleats are worn facing up. The groomsmen's cummerbunds (and ties) may optionally match the color of the bridesmaids' dresses.

Suspenders (braces) - Worn instead of a cummerbund or vest and helps to keep the trousers pulled up and in place.

The Traditional Gear (or, What to Wear and When)

Here's a few hints for sticking to tradition in your guys' attire. Remember that ultimately the choice is up to you, so feel free to break the rules if you'd like! As with the bridesmaids' attire, the important thing is that you're all comfortable—you'll look and feel better, and it will show on the wedding day and in your pictures.

Daytime Reception, Semiformal

The groom and groomsmen wear nice suits with dress shirts and straight (four-in-hand) ties.

Evening Reception, Semiformal

You can wear suits as in a semiformal daytime wedding, or black tuxedos if you prefer, along with wing-tipped or turn-down collar shirts that are white or ivory (to match the bride's dress). Optionally, cummerbunds and vests may match the bridesmaids' dresses in color.

Daytime Reception, Formal (100 or more guests, before 5 p.m.)

Wear gray strollers and waistcoat, with striped trousers and striped ties. You can also wear formal suits with vests or cummerbunds, or a black tuxedo anytime after noon.

Evening Reception, Formal (100 or more guests, after 5 p.m.)

Wear black tuxedos, white or ivory dress shirts, and bow or straight ties with vests or cummerbunds.

Daytime Reception, Very Formal (200 or more guests, before 5 p.m.)

The guys might wear cutaway or morning coats, with charcoal gray pinstriped trousers. Shirts will be wing-collared, with striped ties or ascots.

Evening Reception, Very Formal (200 or more guests, after 5 p.m.)

Wear full dress tailcoats, white bow-ties, white wing-collar shirts and waistcoats. Not necessary these days is sporting white gloves and black top hats, unless it fits your theme.

Renting and Fitting

Most grooms rent their formalwear. Shops will often rent the groom his tux for free as long as a minimum number of groomsmen rent theirs at the same shop. Step into a few shops with your sweetheart and check out their selection and prices before settling on one that you'll go with. When you pick a shop, you'll sit down with the store representative and decide on your choices (type of formalwear, jacket, shirt, tie, cufflinks, accessory colors, shoes, and so forth). You'll also be asked about the number of groomsmen, fathers, and anyone else who will be renting. You'll take your measurements, make a deposit to reserve the date, and be on your way. After that, you'll just need to inform the rest of the guys to go in at their convenience and get their measurements taken as well. When the suits come in (typically a few days before the wedding), you'll all need to go in and get fitted to make sure the right attire was ordered and that everything fits.

What to Look for When Fitting a Suit or Tuxedo

In order to make sure that you'll have time to make any emergency changes if the wrong color, size or style is provided to you, go in to try on your attire no later than three days before your wedding. Your salesperson should be able to assist you, but here's a quick guide to making sure you've got the right fit:

Button up your shirt and make sure it's not too tight at the neck. Remember that you'll have a tie on there, too. It should fit comfortably at your shoulder and waist as well. Put your jacket on over it, put your hands at your sides, and make sure that a quarter to a half inch of the shirt's cuff shows below the sleeve of the jacket. With your fingers extended, the bottom hem of your jacket shouldn't be any lower than your middle finger. Check to make sure your jacket is comfortable when you stand and sit up with it buttoned. It shouldn't feel tight at the neck or shoulders, and shouldn't hang too loose.

If you're wearing a vest, check that it's not too tight or loose and that the bottom of the vest falls just over the waistline of your trousers.

Sit and stand with your trousers buttoned up to see if you're comfortable in them. Most have adjustable waists. Put your shoes on and make sure that the trousers' hem just skims your heel in the back.

If Your Groomsmen Aren't Local

If you pick a shop with stores near all your groomsmen, they'll all be able to go in and get fitted at a shop that's close to them. The guys will go to their stores to pay for their tuxes when they pick them up a few days before the wedding.

Alternatively, your chosen formalwear shop can provide you with measurement cards to send or e-mail to the guys so that they can go in and get measured at any clothing store near them (most will do this for free). You'll collect everyone's measurement cards afterwards and provide them to your shop to complete the rental order.

Get It in Writing: Your Formalwear Contract

When signing your formalwear contract, make sure the following points are included and that you each sign one copy. Keep another copy for your records in your "Bridal Party Attire" folder.

Check for the style of the suit or tux you ordered, the accessories you specified (ascot, cuff-links, and so forth) as well as the colors of your vests/cummerbunds and ties. The contract should specify the number of suits rented (be sure to include all groomsmen and the dads) and the dates your attire will be ready for pickup, which should be a few days or so before the wedding. The contract should also specify the total rental cost, how much deposit you're paying, the payment schedule, and any additional charges like cleaning fees or late return fees. As always, go over the refund and cancellation policy and be sure you're comfortable with them before signing.

e-Resource

Formalwear Websites

Idea-browsing online isn't just for the girls. Going into formalwear stores and sifting through their styles, colors, and vest patterns takes time. Why not do it online? Most formalwear stores have websites that allow you to check out the styles they offer and perform searches based on your style preferences.

WeddingChannel.com

The portal sites have resources for the guys, too. You may want to check out the online tuxedo galleries and browse the posted articles to get a feel for the type of look you want before visiting the stores. From the WeddingChannel.com home page, click "Fashion and Beauty" and navigate to "Tuxedo Search" to look at various styles based on your preferences. Most designers allow you to purchase online or provide links to their stores, which may interest you if you're considering purchasing rather than renting. Otherwise, use the galleries solely as an idea-and-comparison tool. WeddingChannel.com also offers several articles covering men's fashion in their "Groom's Corner".

The Knot (www.theknot.com)

Click on "Grooms" from The Knot's home page to access the resource page for the guys: everything from tips for groomsmen to helpful articles and formalwear galleries. There's even a boutonniere gallery to give you ideas for those manly floral accents.

Dressing Your Child Attendants

The parents of children in your wedding party are traditionally responsible for purchasing clothing for the tots, but it's up to you how you want them to look. Check into the same resources you used when hunting for bridesmaids' dresses; most shops and websites have a children's section. Remember that above all you want little boys and girls to be in something that will be comfortable for them. Otherwise, your wedding will be a long one not only for them but also their parents.

Flower Girls

Little girls' dresses should contain elements of the bridesmaids' attire, such as color, style, or even length. While they're often white, you can pick any color or pattern that you (and she) like. Consider a sash whose color matches the bridesmaids' bouquets, or a pattern that echoes some details of the bride's gown. Look into department stores and children's clothing shops for adorable little party dresses that may not necessarily be labeled as "flower girl dresses", which will probably save the purchaser a pretty penny.

Ring Bearers

If it's a little girl, use the flower girl tips above. If it's a little boy, consider a dark blue or black suit in cooler months or a white linen suit in summer months.

Moms and Dads

It's a big day for your parents as well! Make sure you let them know everything they need to get styled right and look (and feel) great on the big day. Pass along the formal wear rental info to Dad, and make sure Mom knows your formality and color. She should also have contact info for your sweetie's mom—and vice versa—in case they want to call and swap attire suggestions.

Moms

First of all, both moms don't need to look alike. You shouldn't have to instruct them on what to wear (or not to wear) beyond advising them of your wedding formality and any colors you think might go well with your color scheme. Given the basics, they should take them into consideration and wear what they each feel comfortable in. The one way they really should match is in formality, just so one mom doesn't feel uncomfortably over- or under-dressed.

Dads

Pops has it easy enough: the same attire the groomsmen are using should be donned by the dads, along with a special boutonniere to set them apart from the rest of the crowd.

Considerations Worksheet: Bridesmaids' Look

List ideas and preferences you have for your girls' look, and give them a copy to get their input. When it's time for try-ons, go in together so you can choose the best options together.

Dress Length

- ☐ Ballerina
- ☐ Floor
- ☐ Intermission or Hi/Low
- ☐ Knee
- ☐ Mini
- ☐ Street
- ☐ Tea

Neckline

- ☐ Strapless
- ☐ Off-the-Shoulder
- ☐ Spaghetti Strap
- ☐ Jewel
- ☐ Bateau (Sabrina)
- ☐ Halter
- ☐ Scoop
- ☐ Square
- ☐ Sweetheart

Sleeves

- ☐ Cap (short)
- ☐ Puff (short)
- ☐ Three-quarter
- ☐ Fitted (long)
- ☐ Juliet (long)
- ☐ Poet (long)
- ☐ Fingertip (long)
- ☐ Bell (long)

Accessories Options

- ☐ Wrap/Shawl
- ☐ Jewelry
- ☐ Hair Accessories
- ☐ Gloves
- ☐ _____

Dress Color Options

_____
_____
_____
_____

Shoe Color Options

_____
_____
_____

Dress and Accessories Options

Description and Style #	Store Information	Cost
		$
		$
		$
		$
		$
		$
		$
		$

Notes:

_____
_____
_____
_____
_____
_____
_____

Considerations Worksheet: Groomsmen's Look

Think about how you'd like the guys to be styled (including the dads).

Coat/Jacket Style

□ Cutaway (morning coat)
□ Dinner Jacket
□ Double-Breasted Jacket
□ Full Dress (tails)
□ Single-Breasted Jacket

Shirts and Vests

□ Turn-Down (point) Collar Shirt
□ Lay-Down (spread) Collar Shirt
□ Wing Collar Shirt
□ Vest
□ Waistcoat

Ties

□ Ascot
□ Straight (four-in-hand)
□ Bow Tie

Accessories Options

□ Cuff Links and Studs
□ Cummerbund
□ Suspenders (braces)
□ Gloves, Top Hat (ultra formal!)
□ _____

Attire Color Options

_____
_____
_____
_____

Shoe Color Options

Rental Attire and Accessories Options

Description and Style #	Store Information	Cost
		$
		$
		$
		$
		$
		$
		$
		$

Notes:

_____
_____
_____
_____
_____
_____
_____
_____
_____
_____
_____
_____

Contact Sheet: Groom's Formalwear

Staple Business Card

Date Ordered: _____

Formalwear Store: _____

Address: _____

Contact: _____

Email: _____

Phone: _____

Fax: _____

Website: _____

Package Description: _____

Special Instructions: _____

Jacket/Coat:	Trousers:	Shirt:
Neck:	Vest:	Shoes:

Accessories: _____

Fitting Date:	Time:
Pickup Date:	Time:
Return Date:	Time:

Returned By Who? _____

Total Cost: $

Deposit: $	Date Paid:
Balance: $	Date Due:

Notes:

Notes:

Chapter 17

Paint Your Wedding Colors with Flowers and Décor

- Your Floral Choices

- Selecting and Working with a Florist

- e-Plan It! Use Your e-Resources:

  Online Bloom Browsing
  Florists on the Web
  Online Floral Discounters

- Worksheets:

  Considerations Worksheet: Flowers and Décor
  Comparison Forms: Florist
  Contact Sheet: Florist

From the mood-setting beauty of your ceremony and reception arrangements to the bouquet you'll carry with you down the aisle, your wedding flowers will make a big statement about your style, formality, color, and theme. They're so integral to your day that they can even be a theme all on their own! In this chapter we'll walk you through the choices you need to make when selecting the right blooms and finding a florist to bring it all together. We'll even look at some online discounts and budget-bending whole-sale bargains.

Your Floral Choices

You may already have a good idea about the type of flowers you're going for. Perhaps you've got a favorite, or maybe your wedding theme is summer daisies. Either way, Mother Nature's got plenty of beautiful possibilities for you to choose from, and some will work better than others with your theme, season, and location.

<NOTE>

Your Floral Timetable

10 months before: Gather ideas and florist referrals. Once you have your ceremony and reception locations nailed down and your dress is ordered, you can start some serious flower-hunting. Your goal is eventually to meet with at least two or three florists.

8 months before: Decide which florist you prefer and book their services for your date.

6 months before: Finalize your flower choices, arrangement details, and color choices with your florist.

1 month before: Have your florist provide you with a sample of your centerpiece and be sure you're happy with the style and colors. Make any changes or adjustments.

1 week before: Confirm details like delivery locations and times, and arrangement count.

</NOTE>

Things to Consider

Here are some key points to keep in mind as you think about the type of flowers you'd like to use on your big day, and how you'd like to use them:

Your Color and Theme

Select varieties in shades that echo your wedding colors. Don't worry about trying to match colors up perfectly (there's over a hundred shades of pink, for example) but instead choose shades that blend together and complement each other well. You may want to use a type of flower as your overall wedding theme, perhaps playing off its special meaning.

Season and Availability

Varieties that are in season will give you the most flower power for your buck. They'll be more affordable as well as fresher and therefore more beautiful. Make these the most abundant flowers in your bouquets and arrangements. And if you're marrying in a hot month (especially if your ceremony or reception will take place outdoors), go for more durable flowers like roses instead of quick-to-wilt options like hydrangeas, tulips or gardenias.

<TIP>

Choose Available Flowers

Spring - Anemone, azalea, camilla, dianthus, garden rose, hyacinth, hydrangea, jasmine, lilac, mimosa, pansy, peony, primrose, ranunculus, sweet pea, tuberose, tulip, viburnum, violet.

Summer - Bachelor's button, bells of Ireland, blue lace, blue salvia, cattleya orchid, clematis, cornflower, delphinium, eremurus, honeysuckle, hydrangea, larkspur, lysimachia, phlox, Queen Anne's lace, rosemary, sedum, sunflower, sweet william, tuberose, zinnia.

Fall - Bouvardia, cockscomb, China aster, dahlia, euphorbia fulgens, grape ivy, hydrangea, statice, viburnum berries, yarrow.

Winter - Amaryllis, cyclamen, eucalyptus berries, heather, Christmas rose, holly, juniper pine gardenia, narcissus (daffodil), pepper berries, poinsettia, santolina.

Year-Round - Alstroemeria, baby's breath, calla lily, chrysanthemum, cymbidium orchid, daisy, dendrobium orchid, freesia, gardenia, gerbera, gladiolus, iris, ivy, lily, lily of the valley, nerine, phalaenopsis orchid, rose, September aster, snapdragon, stephanotis.

</TIP>

Location

The scale of your arrangements will depend on the scale of your site. A grand cathedral will require larger flowers and an overall larger arrangement size than a small chapel or intimate location. And take into consideration the characteristics of the site itself; you may be blessed with a location whose inherent beauty requires little decoration, while a more plain setting might need a bit more help.

Style and Formality

Different flowers, vases and arrangements complement different levels of formality. Think about the different style and message that a woven basket of wildflowers gives as opposed to a tall, square glass vase with a few calla lilies.

<TIP>

The Symbolism of Flowers

Apple blossoms—Good fortune	Anemone—Expectation
Baby's breath—Innocence	Bluebells—Constancy
Blue violets—Faithfulness	Calla lily—Magnificent beauty
Camellia—Perfect loveliness	Carnations—Distinction
Chrysanthemum—Wealth, truth	Daisy—Share your feelings
Forget-me-nots—True love	Freesia—Innocence
Gardenia—Joy, purity	Gerbera—Beauty
Holly—Foresight	Iris—Faith, wisdom
Lilac—First love	Lilies—Purity, innocence
Lily of the Valley—Happiness	Magnolia—Love of nature
Orange blossoms—Purity, fertility	Orchids—Love, beauty
Roses—Love	Stephanotis—Marital happiness
Sunflower—Adoration	Tulip—Passion

</TIP>

Budget

Flowers can be pricey, especially if yours include out-of-season blooms or a time-intensive arrangement style. As you'd expect, the more flowers you need, the higher the price tag. Increasing your guest or attendant count usually directly increases your cost of flowers, since more tables mean more centerpieces, and more attendants mean more bouquets and boutonnieres.

Here are some money-saving tips to keep in mind as you try to find flowers that match your budget: use local in-season varieties and simple yet elegant centerpieces to cut down on labor costs. Even groups of a single in-season flower can work. Pick large flowers, as they fill up space better. And check out the e-Resource later in the chapter on buying flowers online at wholesale prices. If there are any flower wholesalers in your area, give them a visit on a day they're open to the public, or check out a local farmers' market.

Still looking into ceremony and reception locations? Choose an ornate spot that won't need a lot of extra decoration. And have your ceremony arrangements do double duty: assign someone the task of transferring them to your reception location after the ceremony is over.

e-Resource

Online Bloom Browsing

Want to get a head start on flower types, bouquet styles, centerpiece ideas and sample arrangements? Check the web for pictures, articles and ideas. This is another one of those areas the big portals can come in real handy. Mine them for ideas and print out anything that catches your eye; you'll use this information when talking to florists later on.

The Knot's flowers and décor section (www.theknot.com/florists/) is packed with useful info. There are picture galleries for bouquets, centerpieces, and boutonnieres. Also available are glossaries for bouquet types and floral terms, as well as a ton of useful articles.

WeddingChannel.com has a number of flower galleries as well: bouquets, wedding party flowers, boutonnieres, centerpieces, arches and decor, and more. You'll find useful articles and tips here as well. Just click on Planning > Flowers and Decor from the WeddingChannel.com home page.

Find bouquet and centerpiece ideas from BRIDE'S magazine at www.brides.com/flowers/. Check out their photo slideshows, Q&A articles, and guides.

Ceremony Floral Components

Check with your site manager or officiant and find out what your decorating restrictions are. Is there a church florist or decorating manager that you'll need to work with? See if your location has vases, candelabras, and other items that you can use or rent. If other couples will be marrying at your location that day, ask for their contact information and arrange to share the cost of the ceremony flowers. And keep in mind the location itself; if it's already stunning and ornate, consider yourself lucky and cut back on the added décor. See if your florist can meet you at the location—or show her photos at the very least—to generate ideas and ensure that you don't over- or under-decorate.

Ceremony flowers should draw attention to the altar or stage and to you the couple, so at a minimum plan on having two arrangements, one on either side of the altar. As your budget permits, you might include additional touches like pew decorations (every other row or every third row to be cost-effective), a floral arch and arrangements on columns or windowsills.

Bridal Bouquet

The bouquet you carry down the alter will be in the spotlight (on the day of and in your photos). Bouquet styles and possible flowers to include abound, so you'll have a lot of options to cover with your florist. Make sure your choices complement your body type and gown. In general, a petite bride or elaborate gown is best paired with a smaller and simpler bouquet. A more extravagant, irregularly shaped bouquet matches up better with a larger or taller bride, or a less elaborate gown.

Have your florist create a "throwing" bouquet that you can use for the bouquet toss if you'd like to keep and preserve yours.

\<TIP\>

Carrying Your Bridal Blooms

Bouquets can be heavy, especially larger ones. Don't overcompensate by carrying yours too high; your hands should rest just above your hipbones.

If your bouquet includes lilies, make sure your florist removes the stamens (the long stalks in the center) or you'll wind up with bright yellow pollen stains on your gown. Likewise, have the hollow stems of flowers like daffodils wrapped up to prevent sticky drippings.

\</TIP\>

Floral Headpieces

Rather than a tiara or headband, you may want to adorn yourself with a delicate wreath of flowers. These are pinned in place and can have a veil attached if you prefer. Other members of your party that you might want to crown in gorgeous blooms are bridesmaids and flowergirls. Include flowers in a color from the bridesmaids' bouquets. For an added touch of delicate elegance, you could also attach thin satin ribbons.

Flowers for Bridesmaids

The bouquets for the bridesmaids will normally be smaller than the bride's cluster but complement the same style and type of flowers. Add colors that work well with their dresses. You may want your maid of honor's bouquet to be a bit different to emphasize her special status. It could be larger perhaps, or in a slightly different color shade.

```
<TIP>

Ensure a Fresh Delivery

For the freshest floral results, ask that your flowers be well misted and
wrapped in cellophane or waxed paper when they're delivered.

</TIP>
```

Child Attendants

Fowergirls look adorable with a floral headpiece and a little flower basket, pomander (a small flower-covered ball suspended from the wrist with a satin ribbon) or small bouquet. They traditionally spread rose petals, but if your location doesn't allow it, consider having them pass out single long-stem roses as they make their way down the aisle.

If your ring bearer is wearing a suit or little tuxedo, you can have a miniature boutonniere of the style the groomsmen are wearing on his left lapel.

Boutonnieres

These arrangements are small—often a single flower bud or cluster of small ones—and pinned to the left lapels of the groomsmen, dads and possibly grandfathers. The groom's boutonniere can include the dominant flower in the bride's bouquet, and the rest of the guys might echo the bridesmaids' flowers. The dads' can look like that of the groom or the groomsmen...your choice.

Corsages

It's traditional to provide mothers, grandmothers, and other special honor attendants (close relatives, ceremony readers, and so forth) a pin-on or wrist corsage. Another option is to give them each a small bouquet, or "tussie-mussie", to carry.

Reception Floral Components

Your choice of reception flowers will depend largely on your location and budget. Floral touches are appropriate anywhere you'd like to focus your guests' attention: the guestbook, cake table, serving stations or buffet tables, on mantels and staircases, and—of course—on your tables as centerpieces. Depending on your available funds and how ornate the site already may be, work with your florist to come up with a good fit. As you did with the ceremony location, have your florist meet you at the reception site or show her some pictures to get ideas going. Play off your wedding theme and select varieties that match well with your colors. Remember that high ceilings and large rooms benefit most from tall, larger centerpieces and small spaces need something less distracting. If you like the drama that tall centerpieces provide but don't have the budget for them, think about having half of your centerpieces high and half low to cut the cost. Alternate them throughout the room for some aesthetic visual texture.

Centerpieces

Decorate your tables according to the rest of your wedding's theme and formality. The more guests you have, the more tables—and therefore centerpieces—you'll need, so one of the biggest floral cost factors is guest count. But don't let a tight budget deter you! Simple, elegant, and eye-catching centerpieces can be created with votive candles, single large-flower clusters, and unusual vases or urns found at discount stores or online at bargain sites like eBay (www.ebay.com). Candles are an inexpensive yet appealing alternative (or addition) to flowers; set votive candles on pedestals to raise the light and surround them with scattered rose petals. Or have rose petals floating in glass vases filled with water, lit up romantically with floating candles.

Make sure that your beautiful arrangements don't become an obstruction to your guests' views, especially if your centerpiece arrangements are on the large or tall side. Place especially tall centerpieces up on pedestals or on narrow columns so that they're above everyone's heads and out of the way while still looking great.

Other Reception Touches

Along with flowers, you can choose to add other festive décor to your reception. Your florist, site manager, or caterer may be able to help with some of the setup. Candles, for starters, are a great mood-setting, romantic, and inexpensive way to accent your location. Votives, candlesticks in majestic candelabras, and floating candles are all possible choices. Tulle can be draped over table cloths, wrapped around votives and flower vases, or hung in ethereal clusters from the ceiling. Tulle also pairs up great with well-placed strings of white twinkle-lights. Ice sculptures can add a dramatic touch to winter weddings, especially when illuminated with the right lighting. Attractive picture frames with adorable photos of the two of you can be placed in spots like the reception entrance and guestbook table.

Selecting and Working with a Florist

After familiarizing yourself with the various floral components, it's time to find someone to make it happen. When it comes to the look and atmosphere of your wedding day, your florist is a major player in the results. Make sure you choose one with creativity, artistic style, and taste that you trust and respect.

Finding Your Floral Artist

Give yourself enough time to meet with at least two or three florists to get a handle on their different styles, creativity, and what they can offer. You want someone who is open to your ideas and excited about your wedding vision and the potential of your location. Make sure you're prepared by reviewing this chapter's prior discussion on floral choices, and have a folder of ideas ready. Bring along magazine clippings, photos of your site, website printouts, and fabric swatches from the bridal gown and bridesmaid dresses.

Ask around for recommendations from family and friends, other brides, and your other wedding vendors—including your location's site manager.

e-Resource

Florists on the Web

For each of your recommended florists, see if they have a website. Find out by doing a search, checking their business cards or by giving each a quick call. If they do have a website, you can get another step ahead by browsing their catalog of arrangements and bouquets online.

If you're hunting for florist leads, you can find those in your area on the big wedding portals or by using local search engines. See what other brides in your area are recommending on the message boards. Rather than selecting from the big portals' directories, our recommendation is to use the local search engines, or—if you prefer the old-school method—Yellow Pages. Your most cost-effective florists are often the small shops that are probably not paying the bucks to be listed on the big portals, and instead get most of their business via word-of-mouth. Chances are there's a good shop or two near your wedding location, and they probably even have experience with your chosen site.

Set Up Consultations and Compare Proposals

Your first meeting with a florist will gauge her personality and give you a look at her work and style. Look through photos of previous weddings. Do you like what you see? If the formality of her work doesn't fit, or the example arrangements are sparse and you prefer a fuller look, move on. Does the florist seem to understand and appreciate your vision? Look around the shop and take in the arrangements on display. Are they creative and appealing? Are the flowers healthy? Feel out the florist's personality, too. If the chemistry's not there, your floral vision won't be, either.

Have each florist you meet go through all the available wedding options in detail, from ceremony arrangements to your bouquet to centerpieces to reception accents. Get specific flower names and see examples or photos of everything you're not familiar with.

If the florist is still a potential after your initial meeting, ask her to compile a full proposal for you and arrange a follow-up meeting to go over it. When considering proposals, make sure that everything is itemized in detail: type and number of arrangements, the flowers used, material and rental costs, and any setup or delivery fees. See if there's any further adjustments you can make to lower the total price. Using these proposals and your opinion of each florist's style and abilities as guides, make your final decision on which one to go with.

Questions to Ask Florists

- Can you prepare a proposal for me based on my location, budget, preferences and initial decisions?

- What flowers will be in season on my wedding date? Which ones are available in shades that complement my colors?

- Do you have experience working at my ceremony and reception locations?

- Can you provide recommendations on flower types and arrangement styles that work best with my budget?

- Can you deliver flowers to different locations? (Centerpieces and other reception flowers to the reception location, ceremony flowers to the ceremony location, bouquets to the bride's house, and so forth. If flowers can only be delivered to one or two places, you may need to assign someone the task of distribution to your various locations)

- How many weddings do you expect to be handling on my wedding date?

- Who will be in charge of delivering and setting up flowers? With our wedding time in mind, when would you start? How long does the delivery and setup take?

- Are there other decorative items you could provide? (Vases, columns, votives, potted ficus trees, and so forth)

- Would you be able to work with our baker to provide flowers for the cake?

- On delivery, how will you ensure the freshness of the flowers? Will they be well misted and wrapped?

Get It in Writing: Your Florist Contract

When you've selected a florist, make sure the following is inked out in your contract. Keep a copy in your "Flowers" folder:

Delivery details should be spelled out clearly as far as exact times, locations, and date. The name of the person responsible as well as that of an acceptable substitute should be listed.

Look for an itemized list of every bouquet, arrangement, boutonniere, headpiece, and anything else you've agreed upon. For each arrangement, its size and the types and colors of flowers to be used should be indicated. Any rental items and accessories you've requested should be noted as well.

Your contract should include those flowers that are acceptable substitutes in case the ones you've selected are unavailable. You can also request that anything unacceptable as substitutes be listed (no chrysanthemums or nothing pink, for instance).

Finally, make sure the total cost, payment policy, deposit amount, and refund policy are included.

e-Resource

Online Floral Discounters

You might want to buy your own flowers and provide them to your florist to save cost (see if your florist is okay with this). Or perhaps you're a do-it-yourselfer and feel you have enough creativity and people-resources to put arrangements together without professional help. In any case, the web can give you access to bulk blooms at big discounts.

Bargain Sites

Online bargains abound, and flowers are no exception. Many distribution services exist that ship fresh flowers from the U.S. and South America for a fraction of the cost you'd pay a florist or re-tailer. Check out the following online stores we have listed. To scout out others, just do a search on the web for "discount flowers" or "discount wedding flowers". Do some e-shopping and compare the deals you find.

The Grower's Box (www.growersbox.com)

A great spot to pick up bulk flowers fresh from growers in Central and South America and the U.S. They have available blooms divided by flower type in the main menu. Browse the varieties, colors and prices.

Big Rose (www.bigrose.com)

If you've got roses on your to-buy list or if your wedding theme is a rosy one, don't miss checking this site out. They have all kinds of useful tips, care guides, and over 50 varieties of roses available at discount prices. They even have a wedding section with instructions on creating rose bouquets, boutonnieres, and centerpieces.

Flowerbud.com

Another bulk flower source, Flowerbud.com also sells assembled bouquets. See if they have your preferred flower types available.

Wholesalers

Another option is buying in bulk from growers and wholesalers, businesses that supply florists and retailers with a resale permit. The general public can also get big discounts on bulk orders for weddings and other parties. Markets for wholesale flowers are also a great source for vases, ribbons, and other décor-related goods. Interested? Here's the scoop:

At Big Rose (www.bigrose.com), you can buy discount roses in bulk and find step-by-step instructions on how to create your own bouquets, boutonnieres, and centerpieces.

To find wholesale flower markets in your area, check out the Wholesale Florist and Florist Supplier Organization (www.wffsa.org) and click "Find a Wholesaler". You can also check the Yellow Pages under "Florists—Wholesale or use a local search engine to see if you pick up any additional leads. Local farmers' markets are another great source of bargain blooms; see if any are in your area and if they'll be active around the time of your wedding.

If you or someone you know has a resale permit (sometimes called a reseller's badge) see if they can help out by acting as your buyer, or visit the wholesaler during public hours. Without a resale permit, you'll need to pay sales tax.

Check out your nearest wholesale market and get familiar with how it operates and what you can find there. Remember that different flowers will be available at different times of the year. As with the flowers you'll get from the bargain websites we just discussed, blooms sold in wholesale markets will still be in bud form, so make sure you allow a day or two for the flowers to open up. When it comes time to get your flowers, you may want to set an alarm and hit the sack early: markets open as early as 2:00am and the good stuff goes fast.

Vendors closest to the entrance usually charge the highest prices, so make sure you scout the whole place before purchasing. For the flowers you choose, stems should be freshly cut and the buds should be firm; avoid sellers that have withered or browning blooms in their mix.

<TIP>

Preparing Bulk Flowers

After obtaining flowers from an online discounter or wholesaler, remove any wrapping material and stand them in a tub or sink filled with cold water. Before you arrange your flowers, make fresh cuts on the stems. For roses, cut the stems underwater. Always keep the flowers cool, out of direct sunlight and well misted to ensure longer-lasting freshness

</TIP>

Considerations Worksheet: Flowers and Décor

Flowers and Décor Budget: $

Personal Floral Needs

☐ Bridal Bouquet
☐ Toss Bouquet
☐ Bridesmaids Bouquets
☐ Groom's Boutonniere
☐ Groomsmen's Boutonnieres
☐ Fathers' Boutonnieres
☐ Mothers' Tussie-Mussie or Corsages
☐ Flower Girl's Pomander
☐ Flower Girl's Petal Basket / Stem Roses
☐ Floral Headpieces
☐ Grandmothers' Tussi-Mussie or Corsages
☐ Grandathers' Boutonnieres
☐ Other Special Attendants' Flowers
☐ _____

Ceremony Floral Needs

☐ Entryway Arrangements
☐ Altar / Huppah Arrangements
☐ Arch / Canopy Flowers
☐ Pews and Aisle Decorations
☐ Rose Petals for Tossing / Décor
☐ _____

Reception Floral Needs

☐ Entryway Arrangements
☐ Head Table Arrangements
☐ Bride and Groom's Chair Decorations
☐ Centerpieces
☐ Buffet Table Arrangements
☐ Cake and Cake Table
☐ Guestbook Table
☐ Escort Card Table
☐ Powder-room Arrangements
☐ _____

Other Decoration Needs

☐ Candles and Holders
☐ Aisle Runner
☐ Fabric / Tulle
☐ Lighting
☐ Bubble Machine / Bubbles
☐ _____

Seasonal Flower Types Required

☐ Spring
☐ Summer
☐ Fall
☐ Winter
☐ Year-Round

Notes: _____

_____

_____

_____

_____

_____

_____

_____

_____

Comparison Forms: Florist 1

Florist: _____ Years of Experience: _____

Address: _____

Designer: _____ Assistant: _____

Email: _____ Phone: _____ Fax: _____

Website: _____ Recommended by: _____

Flowers and Décor	Description of Flowers and Colors	Cost
Bridal Bouquet		$
Toss Bouquet		$
Bridesmaids' Bouquets		$
Boutonnieres		$
Tussie-Mussie or Corsages		$
Pomanders / Petal Basket		$
Stem Roses / Toss Petals		$
Floral Headpieces		$
Ceremony Arrangements		$
Pew / Aisle Decorations		$
Entryway Arrangements		$
Head Table Arrangements		$
Centerpieces		$
Buffet Table Arrangements		$
Cake and Cake Table		$
Guestbook Table		$
Other Ceremony Decorations		$
Other Reception Decorations		$

Payment Policy: _____

Cancellation Policy: _____

Will florist make sample centerpiece / other arrangements after booking?   ❑ Yes   ❑ No

If yes, extra cost (if any): $ _____

Rental Fees: $ _____

Delivery Fees: $ _____

Booking Deposit: $ _____ Required by: _____

Additonal Fees: $ _____

Total Estimated Cost: $ _____

Comments: _____

Comparison Forms: Florist 2

Florist: _____   Years of Experience: _____

Address: _____

Designer: _____   Assistant: _____

Email: _____   Phone: _____   Fax: _____

Website: _____   Recommended by: _____

Flowers and Décor	Description of Flowers and Colors	Cost
Bridal Bouquet		$
Toss Bouquet		$
Bridesmaids' Bouquets		$
Boutonnieres		$
Tussie-Mussie or Corsages		$
Pomanders / Petal Basket		$
Stem Roses / Toss Petals		$
Floral Headpieces		$
Ceremony Arrangements		$
Pew / Aisle Decorations		$
Entryway Arrangements		$
Head Table Arrangements		$
Centerpieces		$
Buffet Table Arrangements		$
Cake and Cake Table		$
Guestbook Table		$
Other Ceremony Decorations		$
Other Reception Decorations		$

Payment Policy: _____

Cancellation Policy: _____

Will florist make sample centerpiece / other arrangements after booking?   ☐ Yes   ☐ No

If yes, extra cost (if any): $ _____

Rental Fees: $ _____

Delivery Fees: $ _____

Booking Deposit: $ _____   Required by: _____

Additonal Fees: $ _____

Total Estimated Cost: $ _____

Comments: _____

Contact Sheet: Florist

Staple Business Card

Date Booked: _____

Florist: _____

Address: _____

_____

Designer: _____

Email: _____

Phone: _____

Fax: _____

Website: _____

Package Description: _____

_____

Special Instructions: _____

_____

Flower's Delivery Location 1: _____   Time: _____

Flower's Delivery Location 2: _____   Time: _____

Flower's Delivery Location 3: _____   Time: _____

Flowers and Décor	Description of Flowers and Colors	Quantity	Cost
Bridal Bouquet			$
Toss Bouquet			$
Bridesmaids' Bouquets			$
Groom's Boutonniere			$
Groomsmen's Boutonnieres			$
Father's Boutonniere			$
Mother's Tussie-Mussie/Corsages			$
Flower Girl's Pomanders			$
Petal Baskets / Stem Roses			$
Toss Petals / Décor Petals			$
Floral Headpieces			$
Ceremony Arrangements			$
Pews / Aisle Decorations			$
Entryway Arrangements			$
Head Table Arrangements			$
Centerpieces			$
Buffet Table Arrangements			$
Cake and Cake Table			$

Contact Sheet: Florist (continued)

Guestbook Table $

Other Ceremony Decorations $

Other Reception Decorations $

$

$

Will florist make sample arrangements?   ☐ Yes   ☐ No

If yes, extra cost (if any): $ View Date: Time:

Rental Fees (if any): $

Delivery Fees: $

Total Cost: $

Deposit: $ Date Paid:

Balance: $ Date Due:

Notes:

Chapter 18
Design a Cake to Remember

- All About Wedding Cakes

- Selecting and Working with a Bakery

- e-Plan It! Use Your e-Resources:

  Online Bakery Searches and Idea Gathering

- Worksheets:

  Considerations Worksheet: Wedding Cake
  Comparison Forms: Bakery / Cake Designer
  Contact Sheet: Bakery / Cake Designer

Time to skip to dessert! The celebrated wedding cake takes many forms these days, with styles and colors ranging from traditional looks to unique spectacles that sweetly reflect wedding theme and season. And for the latest trends, don't pay for those bridal mags: you can find all the best ideas right on the web. This chapter will guide you through the process of selecting a baker, choosing the right cake, and saving a buck or two while presenting your guests with a memorable treat for their eyes as well as their mouths.

All About Wedding Cakes

Wedding cakes have a rich tradition and history, descending directly from ancient fertility rituals of flinging wheat and rice at the newlyweds, or breaking whole loaves of bread over the bride's head. Sound unappetizing? Maybe, but no more so than some wedding cakes, built more for looks and style than for flavor. Break away from the dry, tasteless, cardboard-cake stereotype! Nowadays, the yummy factor is making a comeback, and your goal should be a dessert that's not only beautiful—indeed, a work of art in many cases—but truly delicious as well.

What You Need to Know

Your reception site or caterer may offer to provide your wedding cake, and it may be included in your contract and pricing scheme. While this sounds like an easy out (killing two planning birds with one stone), you really want to consider your alternatives unless you're totally pressed for time. Independent bakers that specialize in wedding or special event cakes will almost always be able to offer more options and, since cakes are their specialty, a better quality cake. Unfortunately, your reception site or caterer will probably impose a cake-cutting fee for bringing in an outside cake, and the fee could very well be substantial (up to $2 per person or more!)…it's a call you'll have to make based on your situation and preferences. If your caterer is including the cost of a cake in your contract, see if they'll let you bring in an outside cake and waive the cutting fee for the same contract price.

Whether you plan on obtaining the cake from your caterer or from a specialty bakery, don't settle on anything without first having a tasting session; all bakeries, caterers, and reception sites should offer one. Oftentimes they will have a special day per week set up just for tasting. Bakeries vary wildly in their pricing, taste quality, skill and overall product. Know what you're buying before you buy it, or be prepared for a dry, flavorless cake that won't impress you or anyone else. Set up several tasting appointments with different bakeries (including your caterer, if they offer wedding cakes). Take notes and compare, using the worksheets at the end of this chapter for guidance.

Your Options

Bakeries are going to throw all kinds of things to consider your way. Arm yourself by already having an idea of what you want before going in. Magazine clippings or photos printed from web sites that show examples of what you're interested in are great, so start collecting now. Review the discussion points below and then check out the e-Resources at the end of the chapter for a good starting point.

Size

The size of your cake and the number of tiers (layers) will depend on your guest count and whether or not you're having an additional dessert served. Today's cakes should be yummy enough that they can easily be the sole dessert, so providing an additional choice of sweets is not necessary nor will it be expected.

<TIP>

What to Bring to the Bakeries

• Your "Cakes" folder, preferably filled with all your photos, magazine clippings, and printouts of online examples showing what you're interested in and where your preferences lean.

• A general idea of your guest count.

• Your wedding day vision details (season, outdoor/indoor reception, formal/informal, and so forth).

• Swatches of your wedding colors.

• Information regarding your florist and wedding flowers, especially if you're considering fresh flowers on your cake.

• A solid idea of your cake budget.

</TIP>

Another consideration when figuring overall cake size is whether or not you'd like to save the top layer to be frozen and later thawed at your first wedding anniversary. This very traditional practice sounds romantic in theory, though the quality of once-frozen wedding cake is not quite going to be on par with fresh. Instead, or in addition, you may want to buy a small cake of the same flavor and recipe from the same bakery for your anniversary.

Shape

What shape cake would you like? Round is traditional, but how about square, heart shaped, or hexagonal layers? Contemporary cakes are shaped in several styles, even multiple ones (alternating circular and hexagonal layers, for example). Consider, too, if you'd like your layers in uneven heights, such as top and bottom layers that are taller than the middle ones. Nowadays, stacked layers—as opposed to columns in between—have the contemporary edge in popularity.

• Round: Traditional and elegant, the round shape is the most familiar and versatile.

• Square: Square tiers, with their hard lines and angles, give a very bold, modern look.

• Off-kilter or Twisted Square: Square tiers where each layer is rotated 45 degrees as though the cake were turning on an axis.

• Hexagonal: Modern like the square, but with an added flair and creativity. The six-sided tiers make a bold statement even without embellishments.

• Petaled or Scalloped: Curvy, flowerlike tiers.

<TIP>

How to Preserve the Top Layer

- Unpack the cake from the box and remove any plate or platter for return to the bakery.
- Freeze the cake for at least three hours, or just leave it in the freezer overnight.
- Remove the cake from the freezer and enclose it in plastic wrap, then put it back into the box.
- Wrap up the box in plastic wrap.
- Using a blow dryer, heat up the plastic until it seals against the box, without any openings.
- Keep the cake in the freezer for a year.
- The day before your anniversary, take the cake out of the freezer to thaw. Remove all the plastic wrap before thawing.

</TIP>

- Tiers: The separate layers of a tiered cake.

- Columns: Variable length pillars used to separate and support the different layers of a tiered cake.

- Scattered: Cake layers that are separated as individual cakes rather than tiers of a single structure. Presented on varying levels (either by pillars or other decorative supports) on the cake table.

- Stacked Tiers: A cake whose tiers are stacked directly on top of each other, without columns or spaces in between. More popular these days than column-separated tiers.

Flavor

Consider your favorite flavors and each baker's available variety. While tasting, make notes as to what cake flavors, fillings, and frostings you particularly like. Use the comparison worksheets at the end of this chapter. Traditional white, yellow, or chocolate flavors are common choices, but how about banana cream or butter pound cake? Mocha fudge? Your taste choice may also be influenced by the season. Some bakers report that many couples opt for tropical combos in the summer, such as key lime and coconut, with richer chocolate or mocha being more popular in the winter. How about asking your baker to customize a flavor for you? Just keep in mind that the farther from the norm you stray, the more likely you will be to wind up with cake flavors that some of your guests will find not to their liking. The two of you may love carrot cake, for example, but you can be sure that someone on your list hates it, or worse, is allergic to carrots.

If you're set on exotic flavors, consider a multi-flavored cake (a different flavor per layer). You'll be able to dabble in the interesting while keeping at least your largest layer more traditional. As always, you can also offer other desserts in addition to your cake, ensuring that you've got something available for everyone.

Icing

What's going to be the icing on your cake? There are two big favorites: the first is buttercream frosting, mainly made of butter and similar to the birthday cake frosting you're used to. Buttercream is tasty and can be used to create very beautiful and elegant designs and patterns. The second finishing favorite is fondant, made with gelatin and corn syrup. Fondant is very smooth and stiff, and can be shaped and styled into a variety of fabric-like effects that are not possible with buttercream frosting. Fondant is also very durable, does not require refrigeration, and stands up well against the heat, where buttercream frosting is far more perishable.

If fondant is so durable and elegant, what's the catch? Price and taste. Fondant designs tend to be pricier due to the increased time and labor involved, and while it looks cool, most fondants are usually kind of chewy and tasteless. Ask the bakeries you visit to let you taste samples of their fondant and buttercream. Bakeries will often create cakes with a layer of buttercream frosting underneath a styled, protective layer of fondant. This keeps the cake moist and allows your guests to peel off the fondant layer from their slice and still enjoy the tastier buttercream frosting beneath.

- Buttercream: Made mostly of butter, it's the traditional rich and creamy icing used on most birthday cakes. It's easy to color, flavor, and shape into various decorations and styles, but doesn't stand up well in high temperatures.

- Fondant: Composed of gelatin and corn syrup, this icing gives cakes a smooth, shell-like appearance. It can also be folded and twisted into a variety of cool fabric-like styles.

- Ganache: This combination of cream and chocolate can be used as an icing or cake filling. Be careful with humidity or heat; both can cause it to soften and melt.

- Marzipan: A mixture of almonds, egg whites, and sugar that results in a paste to mold flowers, fruits and other decorations. It can also be rolled and shaped into sheets and used as an icing similar to fondant.

- Whipped Cream: Tasty and beautiful, it can't usually be used as a wedding cake topping simply because it needs to be refrigerated until the last possible moment.

Decoration

Cakes can be decorated with all sorts of things: flowers (fresh or sugar-based), stripes, polka dots, brushes of silver or gold edible paint, and even fresh or sugar-based fruit. Bakers and professional cake designers can do amazing things with pulled sugar and gum paste (a mixture of gelatin, starch, and sugar)…from sculpting fruits and flowers that look dead-on realistic to satiny shapes and woven basket designs that you have to taste to believe they're actually edible! A popular idea is to bring a photo of your wedding dress pattern and have your baker match it for the cake detail. All these decorations run up a bill of course, so work within your budget, browse online photo galleries and magazine photos, then decide if any of these special effects are worth spending the bucks on.

A word on fresh flowers: remember that you'll need to coordinate with your florist and baker in order to get the blooms on your cake at the right time. You'll also want to verify that your flowers are pesticide-free; etiquette rules tend to frown on poisoning your beloved guests.

- Basketweave: Piped decoration that is interwoven with vertical and horizontal bands like a basket.

- Cornelli: Piped decoration in with a lacy finish.

- Dragees: Tiny, hard decorative balls of sugar that are coated in a silver or gold edible paint.

- Gum paste: A sugar, cornstarch, and gelatin paste used to mold long-lasting, extremely lifelike fruits and flowers. Not as tasty as marzipan, but so durable that the flowers and shapes it creates can be kept as keepsakes for years.

- Piping: Decorative paste squeezed out of a pastry bag and formed into different shapes and designs with interchangeable metal tips.

- Pulled Sugar: Sugar and corn syrup that's boiled in water to form a malleable, glassine paste used to shape all sorts of beautiful decorations from flowers to satiny bows.

- Royal Icing: Milk, egg whites, and confectioner's sugar combine to form a paste used to create decorative dots and latticework. It's hard and brittle when dried.

Color

In the past, all-white cakes were all the rage, but these days bright colors are in, from hot pink to moss green. Let the season of your wedding guide your color choice. If you're going traditional, consider an ivory-colored cake with white detail. You might also want to accent it with pulled-sugar flowers that look satiny and real, in the shade of your wedding colors.

Theme

If you have a wedding theme, you may want to consider adding details from the theme to your cake. A wedding at a winery with a harvest theme might include fresh grapes on the cake (as well as on the centerpieces), or you could add a subtle design pattern of butterflies to the cake if your wedding has a butterfly theme. And, of course, here's no need to stick to the traditional look at all; if you're both wanderers and your theme is travel, why not have a cake designed to look like a stack of suitcases?

Final Touches

Today's trendy wedding cakes are topped with heirloom porcelain figures, sugar-based monograms or flowers, and even jewelry. The old plastic bride-and-groom cake toppers are yesterday's style, seldom used unless you're resurrecting your parent's or grandparents' historical pieces.

The Groom's Cake

Something you may hear mentioned is the groom's cake, an old southern tradition where a smaller, richer cake was displayed alongside the lighter wedding cake. The groom's cake, traditionally a dark fruitcake, was cut up and boxed for each guest to take home after the wedding. Supposedly, a single girl who slept with a boxed slice of the groom's cake under her pillow would dream of her future husband.

Due to the added overhead of cutting and serving an extra dessert, this tradition is not a common practice these days. If you decide to revive it, have fun and be creative. Couples often design the groom's cake after a particular interest or hobby of the groom's, so it might be shaped like a football or something even wilder. Go all out on flavor, too, as the groom's cake is usually a richer confectionary than the wedding cake (can you say mocha fudge with extra-rich chocolate mousse filling?) You can box slices of the cake up for guests as it was traditionally done, or just serve it as an alternative to the wedding cake.

Delivery

You'll want to ask each baker you consult with if they can deliver to your reception location and what their delivery fee is. To save money, you can pick it up yourself (or have a designated person pick it up for you), but if your cake is even slightly elaborate you'd be best leaving this task to a professional. The last thing you want on the morning of your wedding day is four or five expensive layers of collapsed, disassembled wedding cake.

<CROSS-REFERENCE>

Slices of the groom's cake in boxes personalized with your names and wedding date can serve as your wedding favors. Check out Chapter 15 for more on favors and other gift ideas.

</CROSS-REFERENCE>

Selecting and Working with a Bakery

Make appointments to visit several bakeries and cake designers in order to compare taste quality, styles, and workmanship. Make sure you do your homework ahead of time and have compared web resources (we'll get to these next), magazine clippings, and details like those outlined in the previous section. Compare your favorites and note things that are common to all: are they a specific shape, color, or style? What is essential to your wedding cake?

e-Resource

Online Bakery Searches and Idea Gathering

Start your idea hunting with the big wedding portals by browsing cake styles and reading about the latest trends. Print out photos of cakes and even close-up shots of details that you find interesting. Use these along with magazine clippings to boil down your preferences in look and style. Of course, you'll have to visit the bakeries themselves to settle on taste!

The Knot (www.theknot.com) and WeddingChannel.com allow you to browse photo galleries and look up articles on wedding cake styles, trends, and options. There's galleries for traditional, floral, and unique cakes as well as cake accessories. Check out the online articles, tips, and local bakery directories, too. Click the "Planning" link from WeddingChannel.com's home page and then select "Cakes" to access their wedding cake info zone.

WeddingChannel.com

Browse cake ideas and find informative articles on portal websites like WeddingChannel.com

The cake corner of Brides.com can be found at www.brides.com/weddingstyle/cakes

Brides.com is brought to you by the editors of BRIDES Magazine, one of the Fairchild mags (like Modern Bride). Go to www.brides.com/weddingstyle/cakes to view photo slideshows of different cake styles. They also have some wedding cake guides and how-to's for your reading pleasure.

Local Bakery Hunting with Search Engines

As always, you'll find the local search engines to be especially helpful in locating local bakeries and cake designers. Use the keywords "Wedding Cakes" in the search bar at Google Local (local.google.com) to see a map with vendors in your area, directions, website links, and reviews by other brides. Try Citysearch (www.citysearch.com) and Yahoo Local (local.yahoo.com), too.

Where Else to Look

As always, solicit referrals from those you trust. Recently wed friends and family members are the best source of tips on good bakeries (and ones to steer clear of). Ask your caterer or other wedding vendors, such as your photographer or florist, for recommendations or connections.

Browse the web sites and wedding portals we list in the e-Resources section for ideas and pictures of styles that appeal to you; print everything out and keep it in a "Cakes" folder to bring to the bakeries you will be visiting. Make a note of local bakeries listed in the online vendor directories, and get even more information about them up front by browsing their website if they have one.

Look up bakeries in your yellow pages and seek out those that are dedicated to weddings or special occasions.

Bridal fairs are a great place to chat with bakers and taste their wares, as they usually provide samples at such events.

Do you know someone who is a whiz with baked goods? You might be able to save money and personalize your cake even more by having a skilled friend or family member reprise their famous recipe. Keep in mind that baking for a family get-together is one thing, but baking for hundreds of wedding guests is quite another. Such home-grown options are best done for smaller, more intimate affairs.

Questions to Ask Bakeries

- Can we see photos of your previous work?

- Can we schedule a tasting? (this is mandatory! If a bakery doesn't offer tastings, move on)

- Would you provide references that we can contact?

- Will you be able to do a custom designed cake for us? (bring along photos or printouts of designs and styles you have in mind)

- What kind of ingredients do you use? (Better ingredients will mean a better cake: fresh fruits, farm-fresh dairy products like butter and cream, and so forth)

- How long before our wedding will the cake be prepared? (The closer to the wedding that your cake is prepared, the fresher it will be and the better it will taste. Most cakes typically take 3 to 5 days to prepare)

- How many wedding cakes do you do per week? (Try to get an idea of how much time the bakery will be devoting towards each cake)

- If I want fresh flowers on my cake, will you take care of them or will you need to coordinate with my florist? Will I need to get the flowers to you from the florist myself?

- How are your cakes priced: by the cake or by the slice? Do special fillings or designs cost more? Will my custom design cost more? (Get a price list and a list of fillings and flavors).

- How flexible can you be in adapting your designs to my budget? (Their designs and pricing may too rigid for what you have in mind)

- Do you rent accessories such as cake toppers, cutting knives, stands, fountains, and so forth? Are they included, or is it an additional fee?

- Is the top layer included in the price?

- Are you licensed by the state health department?

- Do you do deliveries? Will you deliver to my reception site? How much do you charge for this service?

Money-Saving Ideas

Buy a Sheet Cake

Order a smaller showcase cake for everyone to admire, and have a sheet cake of the same flavor, icing, and so forth prepared to be cut behind the scenes. The sheet cake will cost a fraction of the price of a large, fancy wedding cake.

Decorate the Cake Yourself

If you have a creative eye, buy your cake with simple icing and no design or decoration, then adorn it yourself with flowers or rose petals. You can even find marzipan, cake ribbons, sugar-based flowers and other decorations at your local pastry shop.

Don't Use Fondant

Use buttercream instead of fondant. Some more complicated designs can only be done in fondant, but it's labor-intensive and expensive. Buttercream can still do very beautiful and intricate designs, and often this is all you'll want or need.

Don't Have the Cake Delivered

Pick it up yourself or have a designated person take care of it. Some designs, especially the more complicated ones, are best handled by a professional and need intensive setup, so talk with your baker about it ahead of time if you're planning on picking up your own cake; you'll want to choose a design that will be easily transported and set up.

Order Less Cake

Especially in the case of buffet weddings, not every guest will want cake, and cakes are typically priced per-slice. If you have a guest count of 175, you're not likely to need more than a 150-slice cake, especially if you're offering other desserts.

Don't Order a Custom Design

Pick from your bakery's book of styles rather than personalizing a design.

Cut the Frills

Multiple flavors and lots of details can dramatically increase the cost of a cake. Go for simple but good; one great-tasting flavor, one yummy filling, and a minimum of decorative detail.

Hire a Home-Based Baker

Home-based bakers are often less expensive due to their reduced overhead, and can design some really beautiful cakes. Just make sure they're legit and licensed by the state health department (see the What to Ask Bakeries section).

Get Your Cake Topper on eBay

There's a great assortment of contemporary and stylish wedding cake accessories on eBay (www.ebay.com) for a fraction of the normal retail price.

<CROSS-REFERENCE>
In Chapter 21, "Countdown Considerations", we'll get into finding online bargains for all your wedding accessories at sites like eBay.
</CROSS-REFERENCE>

Use Other Goodies

Smaller baked items like cupcakes, arranged on tiers and decorated, can be very beautiful and elegant, and a lot cheaper than a wedding cake.

Fool Them with Foam

If you like the look of more layers but aren't feeding enough guests, have your bakery ice a bogus styrofoam center layer or two.

Considerations Worksheet: Wedding Cake

Wedding Cake Budget: $

Wedding Cake Style

□ Traditional
□ Modern
□ Simple
□ Ornate
□ Unique

Wedding Cake Shape

□ Round
□ Square
□ Off-Kilter

□ Hexagon
□ Octagon
□ Petaled / Scalloped

Wedding Cake Structure

□ Tiered, Stacked
□ Tiered, with Columns
□ Number of Tiers

□ Sheet Cake
□ Individual Cakes Scattered, Not Stacked
□ Croquembouche / Cupcakes / Desserts

Wedding Cake Decorations

□ Fresh Flowers
□ Sugar Flowers
□ Fruit

□ Cake Topper
□ Icing Decorations
□ _____

Wedding Cake Icing

□ Buttercream
□ Fondant
□ Ganache

□ Whipped Cream
□ Marzipan
□ Royal Icing

Wedding Cake

Theme Ideas

Groom's Cake   □ Yes   □ No

Theme Ideas

_____

_____

_____

Flavor(s)
Choose different for each layer if desired.

Flavor(s)

_____

_____

_____

Colors

Colors

_____

_____

Notes:

_____

_____

Comparison Forms: Bakery/Cake Designer 1

Appointment Date: _____ Time: _____

Bakery/Cake Designer: _____ Years of Experience: _____

Address: _____

_____

Contact: _____ Assistant: _____

Email: _____ Phone: _____ Fax: _____

Website: _____ Recommended by: _____

Bakery Specialties: _____

_____

Favorite Flavors from Tasting: _____

_____

Favorite Fillings from Tasting: _____

Favorite Icings from Tasting: _____

_____

Styles, Shapes and Structures Available: _____

_____

Decorations Available: _____

_____

Rental Items Needed: _____

_____

Payment Policy: _____

Cancellation Policy: _____

Cost per Slice: $ _____ Cost per Layer: $ _____ Number of Layers: _____

Wedding Cake Cost: $ _____

Groom's Cake Cost: $ _____ Description: _____

Delivery Cost: $ _____

Rental Fees: $ _____

Additional Fees: $ _____

Booking Deposit: $ _____ Required by: _____

Total Estimated Cost: $ _____

Comments: _____

_____

_____

_____

Comparison Forms: Bakery/Cake Designer 2

Appointment Date: _____   Time: _____

Bakery/Cake Designer: _____   Years of Experience: _____

Address: _____

_____

Contact: _____   Assistant: _____

Email: _____   Phone: _____   Fax: _____

Website: _____   Recommended by: _____

Bakery Specialties: _____

_____

Favorite Flavors from Tasting: _____

_____

Favorite Fillings from Tasting: _____

Favorite Icings from Tasting: _____

_____

Styles, Shapes and Structures Available: _____

_____

Decorations Available: _____

_____

Rental Items Needed: _____

_____

Payment Policy: _____

Cancellation Policy: _____

Cost per Slice: $ _____   Cost per Layer: $ _____   Number of Layers: _____

Wedding Cake Cost: $ _____

Groom's Cake Cost: $ _____   Description: _____

Delivery Cost: $ _____

Rental Fees: $ _____

Additional Fees: $ _____

Booking Deposit: $ _____   Required by: _____

_____

Total Estimated Cost: $ _____

_____

Comments: _____

_____

_____

_____

Contact Sheet: Bakery/Cake Designer

Date Booked: _____

Bakery / Cake Designer: _____

Address: _____

_____

Contact: _____

Email: _____

Phone: _____

Fax: _____

Website: _____

Staple Business Card

Wedding Cake Description: _____

_____

Special Instructions: _____

Style and Shape: _____   Structure: _____

Decorations: _____

No. of Layers: _____   Icing(s): _____   Color(s): _____

Layer   Flavor   Filling   Size

_____

_____

_____

Cost per Serving: $ _____   No. of Servings: _____   **Wedding Cake Cost: $** _____

Groom's Cake Description: _____

Special Instructions: _____

Style and Shape: _____   Structure: _____   Decorations: _____

No. of Layers: _____   Icing(s): _____   Color(s): _____

Flavor: _____   Filling: _____   Size: _____

Cost per Serving: $ _____   No. of Servings: _____   **Groom's Cake Cost: $** _____

Security Deposit on Rentals: $ _____   Date Returned: _____

Security deposit refundable after items returned?   ❏ Yes   ❏ No

Delivery Cost: $ _____   Delivery Time & Location: _____

Total Cost: $ _____

Deposit: $ _____   Date Paid: _____

Balance: $ _____   Date Due: _____

Chapter 19
Arrange Transportation

- Transportation to Fit Your Style and Budget

- Selecting a Vehicle Company

- Other Transportation Considerations for the Big Day

- e-Plan It! Use Your e-Resources:

  Car e-Shopping
  Online Limousine Directory

- Worksheets:

  Considerations Worksheet: Wedding Day Transportation Service
  Comparison Forms: Wedding Day Transportation Service
  Contact Sheet: Wedding Day Transportation

When deciding on your wedding day transportation, you'll need to consider your own wheels, those of your bridal party and parents, as well as basic parking accommodations and shuttling of your out-of-town guests. In this chapter, we'll help you look at all your vehicle options and draw up a timeline for everyone, ensuring that nobody is left stranded without a ride. Shopping and researching for your transportation can easily be done online, complete with virtual tours of the cars' interiors. Lastly, we'll consider other transportation issues that may come up, like valet parking or guest shuttles for hotel and airport.

Transportation to Fit Your Style and Budget

When it comes to your wedding transportation, not just any wheels will do. Whether you want to make a big entrance, pamper yourself and your entourage in luxury, or go for accommodation and efficiency, there's a car (or truck...or sleigh...or balloon!) for you.

What You Need to Know About Limo and Car Rentals

A typical wedding package for a limo includes three hours or more of service and costs anywhere from $200 to $500. Choosing more exotic vehicles like vintage antique cars or a stretch Hummer can more than double the price, so the choice is yours based on your budget for wedding day wheels (more on vehicle options later).

As suggested by your planning calendar in Chapter 2, you should begin shopping for your wedding day transportation six to eight months before the wedding, and should definitely have made a choice and reserved your date six months prior. If you wait too long, you might not be able to get a vehicle you like.

If your wedding is during the spring prom season, act even sooner! Those prom attendees book up the limo services and leave procrastinating couples with few, if any, real options. Prices are often higher during these times, and some car companies may impose a larger hourly minimum than the typical three hours. Shop early and keep your options open.

While you're shopping for cars, make sure you specify the number of passengers you expect. If you want your attendants to ride with you but your party is a large one, you may not be able to accommodate everyone together without shelling out more dough. Most limousines can usually only carry up to ten passengers, and for a wedding this may be even less; you'll need extra space considering the wedding dress and everyone's formal wear. Some larger specialty vehicles can accommodate more, but these are a bit tougher to find and, of course, are more expensive.

When booking your date, you'll usually be required to provide a credit card number or deposit. The balance is typically due on your wedding day. Make sure to call your car company the day before your wedding and confirm your pickup times.

Create Your Transportation Schedule and Timeline

Start off by making some important initial decisions on which to base the rest of your transportation plans. To do so, you'll need to keep your wedding vision and style preferences in mind, as well as your budget.

Decide Who's Riding

Before you start looking at cars, decide for whom you want to provide transportation. Consider that the bride, groom, your parents and bridal party all need to get from your getting-ready locations to the ceremony site. After the ceremony, you all need to be moved to the reception location, unless the reception is taking place in the same general area. When the party is over, you and your new spouse will need a ride to your first night accommodations and everyone else will need transportation home or to their hotel.

It's up to you to decide how everyone gets around and whether you want to provide transportation or have most people drive themselves. Consider the following scenario:

The bride, together with her parents and/or bridesmaids ride together in a limo from the bride's house to the church. The best man drives the groom, and the groomsmen drive each other, as do the groom's parents. After the ceremony, the limo takes bride and groom to the reception location, while the bridesmaids ride with friends, family, or their significant others. The bride's parents also ride with family. After the reception, the bride and groom drive off in a getaway car that has been brought by a family member or friend to the reception (and decorated by the best man, groomsmen, and anyone else who wants to pitch in). The parents and bridal party all generally have their own cars to get home afterwards.

Only one rented car is needed in this case, the girls can prepare and relax together, and there's enough cars at the end for everyone to get rides home without any hassle. Consider a second car (it doesn't have to be rented or fancy) to take the bridesmaids to the ceremony site if the bride prefers some private time in the limo with her parents. Adjust the schedule as you see fit, and as your budget allows. Just make sure nobody is left stranded!

If you have a little more budget to spend on transportation, you may want to substitute a second or even third rented car for anybody in the above scenario. A nice touch is to offer transportation for the groom's parents if they are from out of town. Keep in mind that some vehicles, like a vintage Rolls or a horse-drawn buggy, will only be able to carry two or three passengers.

Write It All Down

For each person or group, make a timeline specifying how they're getting from place to place. The timeline might go something like this for the groom and for the bride's parents:

Groom

2:00pm - Best man gives ride to church
3:00pm - Ride together in limo to reception
10:00pm - Ride together with bride in getaway car to hotel

Mom and Dad

2:00pm - Ride together with bride in limo to church
3:00pm - Ride with Uncle Mark and Aunt Jen to reception
10:00pm - Come home with Stacy

Do this for everyone you expect to provide transportation for. When this is solidified and makes sense to you, type it up on the computer for your own reference; file a printout away in your "Transportation" folder. For each person you're transporting, make a printout of their individual schedule and include directions to each location (you can even include maps from MapQuest or Google). Add emergency contact numbers—you, your maid of honor, or a designated person who's good with directions—and distribute the schedules sometime just before the wedding; the rehearsal dinner is a good time to do it. This will save a lot of confusion and potential problems on the big day.

Vehicle Options

Limousines, combining style and function, are the most popular choice for wedding day wheels. They're elegant, roomy, and available in most cities. But there's a wide array of choices for you to consider, from vintage classics such as an Excalibur Rolls Royce to the modern luxury of a Bentley or Lincoln. Do you really want to make an entrance? How about a fire engine or horse-drawn carriage? Here's some unique ideas to consider:

Antique cars can be rented or borrowed from a friend. Some styles resemble carriages, and add the Cinderella touch without the horses.

A flashy sports car like a Ferrari could add the perfect touch to the right kind of wedding.

Nothing quite beats a getaway in a hot-air balloon!

Ride together from ceremony to reception on board a fire engine. Ask about it at a local fire station.

If your wedding is set for the winter or at a ski resort, a horse-drawn sleigh is a romantic touch.

Check out some of the more exotic limos, like stretch SUV's, Hummers, and Ford Explorers. They're pricier, but they have more room and can comfortably hold more passengers than a traditional limo.

Selecting a Vehicle Company

Before shopping for cars, you should know how many people you're transporting and how many cars you want to rent, as discussed in the previous section. You might even have an idea on the type of car you're looking for. Your next step is to start shopping!

Review the list of questions that follow and keep them in mind while you're searching online directories or thumbing through the phone book. The web resources (see the following e-Resources) are truly a godsend here, letting you browse photos of the companies' cars, review their policies, and check prices when available. You can even view virtual tours of the cars' interiors. Compare styles and vehicle types to narrow down your selection based on your preferences. Contact the companies to discuss your options and inquire if the type of car you like is available on your date. Make an appointment to visit the company or companies you're leaning towards to get a first-hand look at their cars. This is especially advisable if you're looking to rent a vintage or antique ride.

When you're ready to book your date, make sure you get a signed contract with the vehicle of your choice. Have the company put everything they offer in writing.

Questions to Ask Vehicle Companies

- How old are your cars? (Unless you're going for antique or vintage, the newer the better)

- How many years have you been in business?

- What is your hourly minimum?

- What are the available sizes of your cars, and how many people can fit comfortably in each?

- What is your cancellation policy?

- Do you offer a wedding package?

- What extras does the price / package include? (Champagne, television, sunroof, and so forth)

- Does the price include gratuity?

- How will the driver be dressed? Can we see photos of your drivers?

- Are you a member of the National Limousine Association? (Or another industry association if the vehicle is not a limo. Companies that belong to industry associations usually must adhere to service standards and insurance regulations)

- If we rent more than one car, is there a discount offered?

- Does gas and mileage cost extra or is it included with the price?

- If there's an emergency can you provide a back-up vehicle?

Car e-Shopping

Most limo companies have a web site enabling you to view photos of their vehicles inside and out. Web sites also list their policies, any associations the company is a member of, and often rates as well. If the company offers wedding packages, the price and package inclusions will usually be listed for comparison.

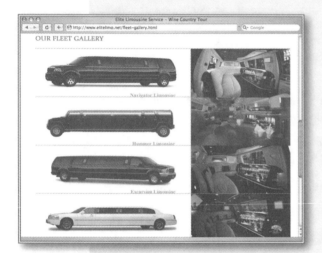

Check out available vehicles, including interiors, at car companies' websites.

When shopping for transportation, don't just go by price alone. Take care to note the company's reputation (outside referrals or recommendations), policies, and association memberships, if any. Make sure you're dealing with a reputable company that will provide quality service.

For companies in your area, you can look in the phone book (web pages are often listed along with phone numbers) or use a search engine like Google Local (local.google.com) and search using the keywords "wedding transportation <your city> <your state>".

Fleet Comparisons

Websites for car companies enable you to quickly and easily compare styles, colors, and capacities. Based on your budget and preferences, you can eliminate those vehicles that don't work for you and quickly narrow down your choices.

Virtual In-Car Tours

Some websites offer virtual tours of the cars' interiors. By clicking left, right, up, and down arrows, you can move the tour's "camera" any direction you like and get a pretty good feel for the car's interior atmosphere.

Online Limousine Directory

www.limos.com

This company's website allows you to "virtually" explore their vintage cars' interiors.

Limos.com, an online limousine directory, is a great resource not only for locating car companies but also for obtaining tips and advice. Plug in your wedding date, location, and the number of passengers, and then select either "Wedding Transfer" or "Wedding Package" (for complete packages) to search for reputable companies with cars available on your date. Wedding packages often include extras like champagne or roses. The limos.com search result provides a list of companies and available vehicle types, as well as links to the companies' websites.

Other Transportation Considerations for the Big Day

Aside from your own cool wheels, think about guest parking issues and transportation between hotels, the airport and your wedding site.

To and from the Airport (and Surroundings)

You'll need to arrange to pick up friends and relatives that arrive from out-of-town and aren't planning on renting a car. Since you're going to have enough on your plate in the days leading up the main event, you may very well want to get some assistance here. You can also check the hotels your guests are staying at to see if they offer shuttle service to and from the airport.

In addition to airport shuttles, some hotels offer shuttle service to and from other locations as well, as long as the distance is reasonable. When deciding where to reserve accommodation blocks for your out-of-town guests, make sure you check out nearby hotels and ask if they provide this type of service. Some might offer it for free, others at an additional cost. For guests without a car, a service like this is a nice, added convenience and saves on taxi fares.

Guest Valet Service

Some wedding and reception sites have limited parking, or parking that isn't directly adjacent to the site. If your heart is set on a location, you don't have to let parking issues become a deal-breaker; you just may have to spend a bit more time and effort (and funds) to accommodate.

What you'll need to decide is whether you want to help your guests get to and from their cars, or help their cars get to and from your guests. A shuttle service can be arranged for the former, or valet service for the latter. Valet service is usually preferred, as it is more of a luxurious touch and eliminates the need for guests to wait at remote locations for a shuttle. Some sites will offer valet service in their wedding packages, and some may require you to obtain it separately on your own.

If the valet service is included in your site package, be sure to ask for the information of the company being used, as well as their insurance policy. If you're shopping for parking service on your own, make sure they can provide you with the same insurance information and that they agree to assume all liability in the case of any accident. Any contract between you and a parking service should clearly state that they have full responsibility for any incidents and claims that may arise. The company should also disclose the dollar amount of their liability per accident.

Considerations Worksheet: Wedding Day Transportation Service

Transportation Budget: $ _____

Transportation Needs

☐ Bride and Groom	☐ Family and Attendants	☐ Out-of-Town Guests
☐ To Ceremony	☐ To Ceremony	☐ To Ceremony
☐ To Reception	☐ To Reception	☐ To Reception
☐ To Wedding Night Hotel	☐ To Hotel or Home	☐ To Hotel
☐ To Airport	☐ To Airport	☐ To Airport
☐ _____	☐ _____	☐ _____

Type of Transportation Needed

Bride and Groom

☐ Limousine	☐ Own Car	☐ Hot-air Balloon
☐ Classic / Vintage Car	☐ Rental Car	☐ Plane / Helicopter
☐ Luxury Car	☐ Horse-drawn Carriage / Sleigh	☐ Fire Engine
☐ Town Car	☐ Boat / Gondola	☐ _____

Family and Attendants	**Passenger(s)**	**Destination(s)**
☐ Stretch Limos (10-12)		
☐ Limos (6)		
☐ Town Cars (4-6)		
☐ Vans (7)		
☐ Own Cars		
☐ Other:		

Out-of-Town Guests	**Passenger(s)**	**Destination(s)**
☐ Shuttle		
☐ Rental Cars		
☐ Vans (7)		
☐ Bus (52)		
☐ Other:		

Parking Attendants needed?	☐ Yes	☐ No
Valet Parking Service needed?	☐ Yes	☐ No

Total Number of Cars Needed:

To Ceremony: _____

To Reception: _____

Post-Reception: _____

Other: _____

Comparison Forms: Wedding Day Transportation Service 1

Appointment Date: _____   Time: _____

Transportation Service: _____   Years in Business: _____

Address: _____

Contact: _____   Driver: _____

Email: _____   Phone: _____   Fax: _____

Website: _____   Recommended by: _____

Vehicle Model / Type: _____   Color: _____   Capacity: _____

Package Description: _____

_____

_____

Vehicle Amenities: _____

_____

Complementary Items: _____

_____

_____

Full Day Rate: $ _____   Cost per Hour: $ _____   Cost per Extra Hour(s): $ _____

Emergency back-up vehicle and driver available?   ☐ Yes   ☐ No

Insurance Coverage: _____

Payment Policy: _____

Cancellation Policy: _____

Booking Deposit: $ _____   Required by: _____

Additional Fees: $ _____

Total Estimated Cost: $ _____

Comments: _____

_____

_____

_____

_____

_____

_____

_____

Comparison Forms: Wedding Day Transportation Service 2

Appointment Date: _____   Time: _____

Transportation Service: _____   Years in Business: _____

Address: _____

_____

Contact: _____   Driver: _____

Email: _____   Phone: _____   Fax: _____

Website: _____   Recommended by: _____

Vehicle Model / Type: _____   Color: _____   Capacity: _____

Package Description: _____

_____

_____

Vehicle Amenities: _____

_____

Complementary Items: _____

_____

_____

Full Day Rate: $ _____   Cost per Hour: $ _____   Cost per Extra Hour(s): $ _____

Emergency back-up vehicle and driver available?   ☐ Yes   ☐ No

Insurance Coverage: _____

Payment Policy: _____

Cancellation Policy: _____

Booking Deposit: $ _____   Required by: _____

Additional Fees: $ _____

Total Estimated Cost: $ _____

Comments: _____

_____

_____

_____

_____

_____

_____

_____

Contact Sheet: Wedding Day Transportation

Date Booked: _____

Transportation: _____

Address: _____

_____

Contact: _____

Email: _____

Phone : _____

Fax: _____

Website: _____

Package Description: _____

_____

Staple Business Card

Special Instructions: _____

_____

Qty.	Vehicle Model, Color, Capacity	# of Hours	Cost per Hour	Total Cost
			$	$
			$	$
			$	$

Pick-up Location: _____ Time: _____

Drop-off Location: _____ Time: _____

Pick-up Location: _____ Time: _____

Drop-off Location: _____ Time: _____

Exclusive reservation time from _____ to _____

Are gratuities included in fee?   ❑ Yes   ❑ No

If no, gratuity amount: $ _____

Additional Fees: $ _____

Total Cost: $ _____

Deposit: $ _____ Date Paid: _____

Balance: $ _____ Date Due: _____

Notes: _____

_____

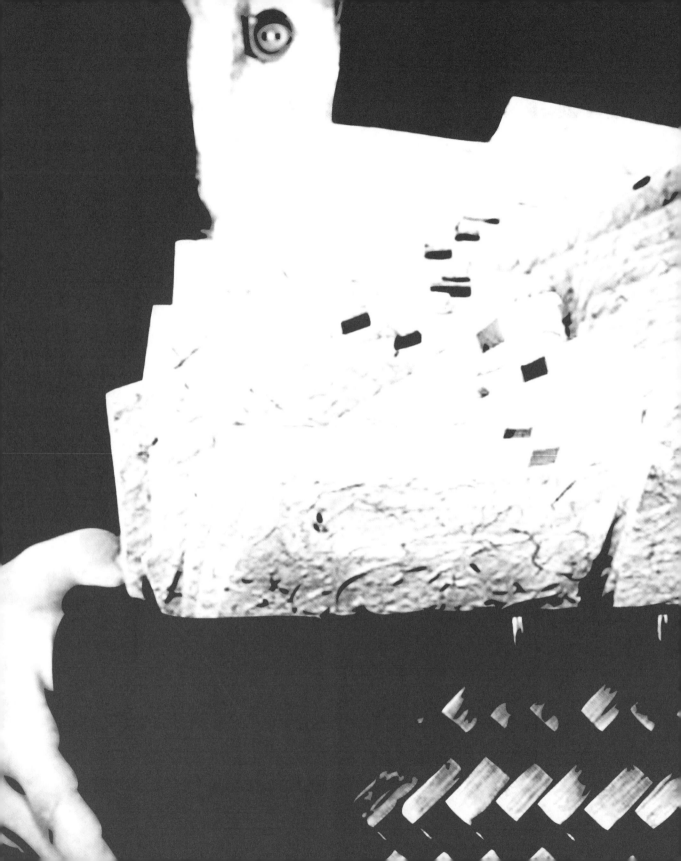

Chapter 20

Send Invitations and Manage Your Responses

- All About Printers and Wedding Stationery

- Finding a Stationer

- Addressing and Sending Invitations

- Handling Your Responses

- e-Plan It! Use Your e-Resources:

  Invitation Wording Ideas
  Online Stationers
  Free Calligraphic Fonts
  Online RSVP

- Worksheets:

  Considerations Worksheet: Stationery
  Comparison Forms: Stationers
  Contact Sheet: Stationer

D ealing with wedding invitations requires attention to lots of details: printing techniques, paper, wording and addressing etiquette, managing your responses and headcount, and more. This chapter takes it a step at a time and covers everything you need to know without overwhelming you with all the hoity-toity minutia you're not likely to need or care about. And we've got some great e-Resources to help out, like an online RSVP feature to take care of the response management for you while you sleep off your invitation assembly all-nighter.

All About Printers and Wedding Stationery

You'll want to order invitations around four to six months before the wedding. Give yourself plenty of time to assemble and address them so you can mail them out no later than six weeks before the big day. Before you shop, let's go over the need-to-know stationery facts and lingo.

The Anatomy of a Wedding Invitation

If you're newbies to the world of the wedding invite, it helps to get a handle on all the components involved. Many are optional, and many more can change based on the formality of your wedding. If you're having an informal affair, you might even forego the traditional invitation completely and use simple cards, notes or save a tree and do the whole thing online.

For our purposes, let's take a traditional wedding invitation, all sealed and stamped and ready to go. We'll peel into this thing like an onion.

Outer Envelope - This contains and protects everything else. The recipient's name and address is handwritten on the outside according to traditional outer envelope etiquette (we'll cover this later), and a postage stamp is applied; the postal service's "love" stamps are a nice touch. A return address (yours) is often printed on the flap of the outer envelope to ensure that any undeliverable invitations are returned to you.

Inner Envelope - As the flap of the outer envelope is opened, the inner envelope is revealed, printed side up and flap down so that the recipient's name is immediately visible. It is ungummed and unsealed, with the recipient's name handwritten according to traditional inner envelope etiquette (and yes, we'll cover that, too). While the outer envelope may arrive scuffed and abused from its journey, the inner envelope should be pristine.

Invitation - Inside the inner envelope is the invitation itself. It's traditionally printed or engraved with black, brown or gray ink on rich white or ivory paper. The wording is up to you, but many follow a traditional format.

Enclosures - These are extras like maps, reception cards, response cards and so forth that are stacked on top of or between the invitation itself...we'll get to the specifics next. There may also be a slip of tissue between the invitation wording and enclosures, historically used to protect the ink from blotting. The order of enclosures, from bottom to top, goes like this (not all of these may be present): tissue paper, reception card, map card, then response envelope with response card tucked under the flap. The response envelope is usually pre-printed with your address and has a stamp applied so invitees need only ink their response, seal it, and drop it in the mail.

All Kinds of Enclosures

As we mentioned, these are optional extras that might be added in with the invitation itself. Keep in mind that more enclosures mean more stationery cost, more postage, and more invitation assembly time. A better bet? Post all this stuff on your wedding website, and inform everyone more conveniently for free.

Response (or RSVP) Card

The response card is the note that guests send back to you to let you know if they're attending or not. They're also known as RSVP cards (from the French *répondez s'il vous plaît*, meaning "please reply"). You'll normally tuck them inside the flap of a pre-stamped and pre-addressed return envelope for quick and easy mailing back to you. If you're accepting responses by phone or e-mail only, let guests know on the card, and omit the return envelope. Remember that for your (and your guests') convenience, you should also offer online RSVPs at your wedding website—a feature we'll discuss towards the end of the chapter when "Handling Responses". If online RSVP is your sole response method, notify your guests on the response card. Keep a contingency plan in mind for those tech-phobic guests that shun the Internet.

Response cards should set a deadline for guests to respond. The printed wording may go something like:

The favour of a reply is requested
by the sixteenth of May

After this, you have a number of options. You might leave the rest of the card blank, letting guests enter in their own message; the cards could then become keepsakes for you. Or you might write the exact names of the individuals invited and have a column for "Accepts" and one for "Regrets" so that they each can simply check off their response. This has the added benefit of restricting guests to those you invite, rather than leaving it open for them to bring any number of people they wish. You might also want to have checkboxes for meal choices in order to collect the number of each preference for your caterer.

All of this functionality and more is offered to you automatically on your website's online RSVP page. The good thing about such e-RSVPs, as we'll see later, is that all the headcount, meal count, adult count and kid count stats are tracked and updated for you automatically.

Reception Cards

Provide the time and location of the reception if it's in a different location than the ceremony. An example:

Reception
immediately following the ceremony
The Bay Lodge
332 Pacific Coast Drive
San Francisco

Accommodations and Map/Directions Cards

Let everyone know where your guest accommodations are located and how to get to your ceremony and locations spots. You can also print maps and directions to the reception area on the back of your ceremony programs.

Special Transportation Cards

Inform your guests if you've arranged for a shuttle or other vehicle service to transport them to a remote or out of the way site.

Rain Cards

If you're having an outdoor wedding, a rain card could notify guests of an alternate location in case the weather sours.

Within-the-Ribbon or Pew Cards

For especially large weddings, these can designate special seating arrangements for family members and close friends—typically close to the alter, or "within the ribbon". They should instruct your ushers where to seat the individual(s). Pew cards can also be sent out separately to the guests once they've accepted the invitation.

Choosing Your Style

Your invitation is the first tangible component of your wedding that guests will experience. It should introduce your style and formality, letting guests know what to expect (including dress code). Invitations can even give a hint of your theme and a first glimpse of your overall wedding vision. To that end, here are some of the decisions you'll make:

Printing Technique

Engraving - This is the most formal, traditional, and—yes—expensive option. It also takes the most time. A custom metal plate is used to press the text into the paper from behind, resulting in a raised top surface and indented back.

Thermography - The most popular method. A resinous powder is applied to the ink and it is heated, resulting in raised lettering very similar to engraving at a much lower cost.

Lithography or Offset Printing - Standard printed stationery without any kind of texture to the lettering. This method is the most cost-effective and is often used for informal invitations. It's also the only choice for very textured paper that won't support raised lettering.

Alternatives - If your guest list is a small one and you have beautiful penmanship, you may want to draw up your own invitations for that extra touch of personalization. Or you may want to hire a calligrapher to do it. There are also nice, printable do-it-yourself packages out there and some truly gorgeous calligraphic computer fonts as a cost-effective alternative to pricey and time-consuming calligraphy. Check online or at your local craft shop.

Paper Stock and Ink

Traditional invitation stock is white, cream or ivory, though newer contemporary designs are often rich with color. Cotton/linen blends are elegant and more expensive options. Keep in mind that heavier paper or larger dimensions will cost more and will increase your postage expenses.

For ink, black or dark gray is traditional, but most printers can lay your text out in one of a variety of colors.

Invitation Wording

The purpose of your invitations is to inform your guests as to the time and place of the wedding, the names of the couple getting married and the names of the wedding's sponsors. How you word yours will also reflect the style and mood you envision. Feel free to add your personality to the prose, but otherwise keep it simple and straightforward. Have the following etiquette pointers in mind for formal wedding invitations:

No Abbreviations - With the exception of Mr., Mrs., Dr. and Jr. you should spell everything out: street names, states, titles, numbers, dates and so forth.

No Nicknames - Proper, full names only. And be consistent; if you use the groom's middle name, use the bride's middle name as well. Traditionally, the bride's surname is not included unless it is different from her parents'.

Name the Sponsors - The wording should reflect the individuals hosting the wedding.

Religious or Civil? - Traditionally, the wording "request the honour of your presence" hints that the ceremony will be religious while "request the pleasure of your company" implies a civil ceremony.

Wording Examples

The Bride and Groom Hosting:

> Ms. Christina Anne Morgan
> and
> Mr. Steven Lee Smith
> request the honour of your presence
> at their marriage
> Saturday the sixteenth of June
> at one o'clock
> Grace Cathedral
> San Francisco, California

Bride's Parent's Hosting:

> Mr. and Mrs. Randall Morgan
> (or Randall and Lisa Morgan) – less formal
> request the honour of your presence
> at the marriage of their daughter
> Christina Anne
> to
> Steven Lee Smith
> Saturday the sixteenth of June
> at one o'clock
> Grace Cathedral
> San Francisco, California

Both Parents Hosting:

Mr. and Mrs. Randall Morgan
(or Randall and Lisa Morgan) – less formal
request the honour of your presence
at the marriage of their daughter
Christina Anne
to
Steven Lee Smith
son of
Mr. and Mrs. Scott Smith
(or Scott and Amanda Smith)
Saturday the sixteenth of June
at one o'clock
Grace Cathedral
San Francisco, California

e-Resource

Invitation Wording Ideas

To see all sorts of wording variations and styles, and to get those creative juices flowing, hit the web. Go to Google (www.google.com) and do a search for "wedding invitation wording". Sites like VerseIt.com have plenty of ideas to browse through, along with etiquette guidelines and tips.

At the VerseIt.com home page, click on "Verse It" and select "Weddings" from the event menu. You'll be able to select wording based on theme and hosts: bride's parents hosting, both parents hosting, bride and groom hosting, and so forth. It's a great source of ideas on invitation wording that you might otherwise have never even considered.

Got writer's block? VerseIt.com has the cure with a huge online collection of invitation wording ideas to browse through.

<TIP>

As with all other information, everything in your ceremony program can also be posted on your wedding website. Give guests the scoop on your site's Ceremony page.

</TIP>

<TIP>

Check local stores for program or brochure kits that you can print on your computer and assemble yourself to save money. Or ask that a creative friend or relative give you a hand making them from scratch.

</TIP>

Additional Stationery Items

Order other paper goods that you may need together with your invitations and enclosures—especially if you want them to match in style. The more things you buy at once, the more of a discount you're likely to get. When it comes to printing, bulk orders are the way to go.

Ceremony Programs

This is a great way to make your guests feel more a part of the ceremony, and is especially useful if you're including ethnic or cultural rituals, or special readings. Why have your guests whispering to each other trying to figure out what's going on? Inform them with an attractive program that reflects your wedding's style and can become a keepsake as well.

What kind of information is typically included in programs? The names of your wedding party, for starters, along with their relationship to you. Include an itinerary so your guests will know what's coming up next, and add any readings that will be given so they can follow along. Explain cultural customs or special rituals if it's an interfaith or intercultural wedding. Couples also often include an acknowledgment or thank-you passage dedicated to parents, friends, and other loved ones (swipe the text from your website's Thank You page!) as well as directions from the ceremony spot to the reception. If you've moved or will be moving after the wedding, you can put your new address here, too.

<CROSS-REFERENCE>

We cover gifts and writing thank-you notes in Chapter 15, "To Give and to Receive".

</CROSS-REFERENCE>

Informal or Thank-you Cards

Get plenty of these! You want to start sending out the thank-you's as soon as your gifts begin arriving.

Gift-received Cards

If you've got a long honeymoon lined up, a big guest list or otherwise anticipate that you won't be able to get your thank-you's out in time, consider these pre-printed notes. They'll inform guests that you've received their gift and that a written message from you will soon follow.

Name Cards

These can be sent separately, with your invitation or with a wedding announcement. They let friends, relatives and business associates know that you'll be changing your name.

Wedding Announcements

After your ceremony, you may want to send a formal announcement to those individuals you were unable to invite to the wedding in order to spread the news.

Save-the-Date Cards

If your wedding date falls on a holiday weekend or you are otherwise worried that your guests may make alternate plans, these notices can be sent out before the invitations—right away, in fact. They simply inform the recipient of your wedding date and can be sent as soon as you settle on the date itself to avoid potential conflicts in plans. A great alternative idea is to send a Save-the-Date e-card and cut the extra stationery cost. If your guests' e-mail addresses are all stored in your online guest database, sending such a broadcast is easily done.

Finding a Stationer

Now that you know your stationery possibilities, it's time to decide what you want and find out where you can get it. Choices abound from online bargain shops to pricey upscale boutiques. You can even do some or all of it yourselves.

Selecting and Purchasing Your Stationery

Before scoping out stationers, make sure you're rock solid on your wedding date, the times for your ceremony and reception, the correct names and addresses of your locations, your guest count, and a set stationery budget. When you purchase, order at least fifty extras; you're going to be doing a lot of handwriting, which means a lot of mistakes, and you'll probably want to keep some as keepsakes.

Shopping Around

Hit up local stationery stores and upscale wedding boutiques to see samples, ask questions, and get written price estimates. Know an artistic friend or graphic designer? See if they'll put together a one-of-a-kind design tailored just for you. If your guest count is small and fairly manageable you may want to check into printable do-it-yourself kits and calligraphic printer fonts to make your own.

Details for an invitation at InvitationConsultants. com. Get an instant quote and explore all your customization options with a few easy clicks.

Online Stationers

Don't feel like driving to the local shops? Start checking out invitation possibilities immediately at online stationers and one-stop invitation websites. Most will save you a pretty penny over a local stationer or boutique, and you can often find the same or similar designs. Get cool tips and etiquette advice online too, even if you plan on purchasing from a local stationer after idea-browsing. Always order a sample of the design you're interested in before placing an order from an online stationer; samples are usually a few bucks apiece, but you want to see and feel what you'll be buying. Check with your favorite search engine to see what's available in addition to the following:

InvitationConsultants.com

With thousands of invitations, announcements, and greeting cards, this online store has a lot of options to browse through. Go through their collection by color, theme or season.

FineStationery.com

This is another stationer with thousands of products available, including name-brand invitations with thermography and engraving options. It's easy to build your stationery package, customize it, and obtain immediate quotes.

Mygatsby.com

Offers quality invitations as well as a helpful "word wizard" to build your invitation wording, an etiquette guide, glossary, and more.

Renaissance Writings (www.renaissancewritings.com)

Some very interesting and unique handcrafted invitations for that extraordinary touch.

Questions to Ask Stationers

- What type of printing styles and paper stock do you have available?

- Do you have one or more catalogs of samples that we can browse through?

- Can you offer samples and advice on invitation wording?

- For our guest count, what will the cost be for the invitations we're interested in? How much additional for each enclosure? (Make sure that you're quoted the complete cost including paper and printing, with no hidden extras)

- Can you print our map cards and directions? How much will this cost?

- Will we be given proofs of everything (invitation, enclosures, envelopes) to preview and check for errors before the order goes to the printer?

- How long will the order take to be completed?

- Would you be able to recommend a calligrapher to address our envelopes?

- Is it possible to receive our envelopes in advance so that we can start addressing them?

Addressing and Sending Invitations

Address and assemble your invitations in time to send them out six to eight weeks before the big day. This will give everyone a few weeks to respond (set a deadline on your response card) and, if you get several regrets, will allow you to invite people on your "wish list" a few weeks before the wedding.

Create an Invitation "Assembly Line"

There's a lot of detail involved in a finished wedding invitation, and you've got potentially hundreds to prepare. Use our tried-and-true method for eliminating as much error and oversight as possible!

Get It Weighed

First thing's first: when your stationery comes in, check through the separate boxes of invitations, envelopes and enclosures. Make sure the design, wording, stock and ink color are as they should be. Then assemble a single invitation completely (including any maps, tissue paper, and even the stamp on the return envelope) and take it down to the post office to get it weighed and measured. Heavy invitations and nonstandard dimensions will push up your postal cost. Purchase enough stamps to send out all your invites and to put on all the response envelopes. The post office sells special floral and "love" designs that you might want to choose from. If you've got international guests, get enough postage to cover the cost of their invitations while you're at it.

Know Your Recipients

You should have this taken care of before your stationery comes in. Put together a complete list of all your guests' full names, mailing addresses, and the names of their accompanying children, spouses, or dates. If you're using your wedding website's online guest database, you can easily export all this to a printed list.

Assemble the Invitations

Clear a table and set everything up like an assembly line, from envelopes to invitations to enclosures. Build stacks of all your invitation components and make sure they're of equal number (50 envelopes, 50 invitations, 50 response cards, and so forth).

Assemble invitations one at a time, and don't have more than two people working on them at once; there's too much potential for confusion. Stamp all the return envelopes before you get started. For each invitation:

- Address the outer and inner envelopes (see below for envelope etiquette) and prepare the response card. Tuck the response card under the flap of the response envelope, with the text showing.

- Stack the enclosures, face up. On the bottom of the stack should be the tissue paper (if any), then the reception card, then the map cards and any other enclosures. On the very top of the stack place the response envelope and card.

- For a single fold invitation with text on the outside only, place this stack of enclosures on top of the invitation. For multi-fold invitations or those with text inside the fold, put the stack of enclosures inside the first fold. Insert the whole thing into the inner envelope.

- Leave the inner envelope unsealed and place it into the outer envelope flap down, so that the hand-written names on the inner envelope are visible. Leave the outer envelope unsealed for now, and move on to the next invitation.

When you're done with this batch, all your stacks should be empty since you started with equal numbers. If you have any extras, you missed something (this is why we didn't seal the outer envelopes yet). Check your invitations and see where the problem is. Otherwise, seal the outer envelopes, stamp them, put them aside and create stacks for the next batch.

Pace yourself, work together, and the mountain will eventually move for you. When mailing your invitations, take them into the post office and ask that they be hand-cancelled. Not all postal employees will do it, but it looks nicer than the messy machine-cancellation and can prevent invitations from getting damaged in the machines. Check off the guests' "invitation sent" flag in your guest database to keep track of those you've sent invites to. Another good idea is to mail yourself an invitation with the others; this way you'll know when local invitations have been delivered.

Envelope Address Etiquette

As was the case with your invitation wording, envelope addresses should not contain abbreviations. They should also be handwritten (don't use stick-on printer labels). You can hire a calligrapher if you've got the coin to spare, or bribe a friend or relative that has exquisite penmanship (tell them it's their wedding gift to you).

---

e-Resource

Free Calligraphic Fonts

Another option, although most etiquette experts would rise up in opposition to this, is to run the entire envelopes through your printer and use a high quality calligraphic font, which can be almost indistinguishable from handwritten calligraphy. Ultimately, it's your call; some feel this works great for them while others insist on their actual handwriting's personal touch. Handwriting fonts can be purchased or downloaded for free from websites like 1001freefonts.com, highfonts.com, search-freefonts.com, and simplythebest.net/fonts.

When addressing outer envelopes, write the full name of the recipient and, of course, include their address. Remember not to abbreviate! On the inner envelope, write just the surname of the recipients. Write their accompanying guest's name here too, if you're not sending a separate invitation to them. If this recipient has children under the age of 18 that are invited, include their first names on the inner envelope as a list—oldest to youngest. Children 18 and up (or 16 and up, it's your call) should be sent their own invitation, even if they're living with their parents. Here are a couple examples:

Addressing Envelopes for an Unmarried Recipient

Outer Envelope: Ms. Rebecca Walker
              332 Oak Drive
              Chicago, Illinois 60617

Inner Envelope, if No Guest: Miss (or Ms.) Walker

Inner Envelope, if with Guest: Miss (or Ms.) Walker and Mr. Davidson

Addressing Envelopes for a Married Couple

Outer Envelope:	Mr. and Mrs. Lawrence Morgan 83 Chestnut Circle Houston, Texas 77381
Inner Envelope, if No Kids:	Mr. and Mrs. Morgan
Inner Envelope, if with Kids:	Mr. and Mrs. Morgan John, Rachael, and Daniel

Handling Your Responses

As the response cards come in, make a note of each guest's response on your guest list and update your total current headcount. If you're using your website's guest database and are allowing online RSVP, many guests may have already done it for you.

Call any guests who haven't sent a response by your deadline. You need to get a final headcount to give to vendors like your caterer, and also to know if you'll be able to invite anyone on your "wish list".

e-Resource

Online RSVP

Activate your wedding website's RSVP page and let guests know that they can send their response instantly, even if they're also submitting the paper response card. Online RSVP will take even more hassle out of your schedule by tracking responses, the number of adults/children attending, their meal options, and updating your overall headcount right in your online guest database.

For smaller, informal affairs or for other events like the bridal luncheon you can even send e-invitations and use your online RSVP as your sole means of accepting responses. It makes it a lot easier having your website automatically manage your list for you.

Getting It Started

Go to your wedding website's RSVP manager. If you're using the WedShare.com service, get there by clicking on "Available Features" in the SiteBuilder pane of your Control Panel. Select "Online RSVP" to bring up the event manager.

Select to edit the default wedding event, or create a new one if it doesn't already exist. With WedShare.com's service, you'll notice that you can specify all sorts of things about your event in addition to adding the same informative notes that are on your invitation:

WedShare.com's online RSVP manager lets you create events, view the results, and export responses. Wedding event responses update the included guest database as well.

Photo - You may or may not want to add a photo. It could be the two of you, your ceremony location, or anything you like.

RSVP Wording - Specify exactly what is asked and how the options available should read. ("Will you be attending?"..."We accept"..."We regret we will be unable to attend", and so forth. Choose anything you like).

Guest Selection - Specify which guests are invited to this event, or simply select to include everyone in your guest database. Individual selections are useful for inviting only specific guests to small events like the rehearsal dinner. If a guest is not invited to an event, he will not see it as an option when he visits your website's RSVP page. If a guest is invited to more than one event, he will be presented with a menu to select from.

Reserve Seats - In your guest database, you can reserve a specific number of seats for each guest. Your RSVP page won't allow them to respond with a greater headcount than you've reserved. You can also specify whether or not your RSVP page should display the number of seats reserved for their party.

Meal Selections - Optionally, you may set up any number of meal selections for your guests to choose from. Be as specific as you like: you can simply specify "beef", for example, or be as thorough as "herb crusted filet mignon, grilled asparagus, baby carrots wrapped in scallions and basil red potatoes".

Additional Questions - Specify other questions, such as asking guests if they have special requirements or allergies.

Save your RSVP event, activate it, and you're good to go! All guests in your guest database can now go to your wedding website's RSVP page and submit their responses. You can view the results from your RSVP manager or see the updates in your guest database. Watch your headcount adjust and update on its own. View, export and print all the response statistics, meal information, special requirements and other notes—most of which you'd never be able to capture with standard conventional response cards.

Considerations Worksheet: Stationery

Stationery Budget: $ _____

Invitation and Enclosure Options

☐ Ceremony Invitations
☐ Reception Cards
☐ Response or RSVP Cards
☐ Accommodations Cards
☐ Maps and Directions Cards
☐ Special Transportation Cards
☐ Rain Cards
☐ Within-the-Ribbon or Pew Cards
☐ _____

Additional Stationery Items

☐ Ceremony Programs
☐ Favor Tags
☐ Gift-Received Cards
☐ Informal or Thank-you Cards
☐ Name Cards
☐ Place Cards
☐ Save-the-Date Cards
☐ Table Cards
☐ Wedding Announcements
☐ _____

Invitation Style

☐ Formal
☐ Casual
☐ Contemporary
☐ Unique
☐ Handmade
☐ _____

Printing Style

☐ Engraving
☐ Thermography
☐ Lithography
☐ Calligraphy
☐ Computer Calligraphy (Print Yourself)
☐ _____

Invitation Wording

☐ The Bride and Groom Hosting
☐ Bride's Parent's Hosting
☐ Groom's Parent's Hosting
☐ Both Sets of Parents Hosting
☐ _____

Personalization Choices

☐ Font Type: _____

☐ Envelope Liners: _____

☐ Ink Color: _____

☐ Monograms: _____

☐ Motifs: _____

☐ Stock Color: _____

Notes: _____
_____
_____
_____
_____
_____
_____
_____
_____

Comparison Forms: Stationers 1

Appointment Date: _____   Time: _____

Stationer: _____   Years in Business: _____

Address: _____

Contact: _____   Assistant: _____

Email: _____   Phone: _____   Fax: _____

Website: _____   Recommended by: _____

Samples available?   ☐ Yes   ☐ No

Your Thoughts: _____

Design Styles: _____

Personalization Options: _____

Enclosures Available: _____

Payment Policy: _____

Cancellation Policy: _____

Invitation Cost: $ _____   Quantity: _____

Envelope Liner Cost: $ _____   Quantity: _____

Reception Card Cost:$ _____   Quantity: _____

Response Card Cost: $ _____   Quantity: _____

Thank-you Card Cost: $ _____   Quantity: _____

Other Enclosures Cost: $ _____   Quantity: _____

Delivery Cost: $ _____

Turnaround Time (printing and shipping): _____

Additional Fees: $ _____

Total Estimated Cost:$ _____

Comments: _____

_____

_____

_____

_____

_____

_____

_____

Comparison Forms: Stationers 2

Appointment Date: _____ Time: _____

Stationer: _____ Years in Business: _____

Address: _____

Contact: _____ Assistant: _____

Email: _____ Phone: _____ Fax: _____

Website: _____ Recommended by: _____

Samples available?   ☐ Yes   ☐ No

Your Thoughts: _____

Design Styles: _____

Personalization Options: _____

Enclosures Available: _____

Payment Policy: _____

Cancellation Policy: _____

Invitation Cost: $ _____ Quantity: _____

Envelope Liner Cost: $ _____ Quantity: _____

Reception Card Cost:$ _____ Quantity: _____

Response Card Cost: $ _____ Quantity: _____

Thank-you Card Cost: $ _____ Quantity: _____

Other Enclosures Cost: $ _____ Quantity: _____

Delivery Cost: $ _____

Turnaround Time (printing and shipping): _____

Additional Fees: $ _____

Total Estimated Cost:$ _____

Comments: _____
_____
_____
_____
_____
_____
_____
_____
_____
_____

Contact Sheet: Stationer

Date Ordered: _____

Stationer: _____

Address: _____

_____

Contact: _____

Email: _____

Phone: _____

Fax: _____

Website: _____

Stationery Design: _____

Printing Style: _____

Package Description: _____

Special Instructions: _____

Invitations: _____

Envelope Lining: _____

Reception Cards: _____

Response Cards: _____

Informal / Thank-you Cards: _____

Other Enclosures: _____

Delivery Cost: $ _____   Delivery Date: _____

Total Cost:$

Deposit: $ _____   Date Paid: _____

Balance: $ _____   Date Due: _____

Calligrapher Cost: $ _____   Delivery Date: _____

Notes: _____

_____

_____

_____

_____

Staple Business Card

Chapter 21
Countdown Considerations

- Managing All the Details

- Covering Your Last-Minute Bases

- e-Plan It! Use Your e-Resources:

  Your Planning Calendar
  Online Accessory Bargains

- Worksheets:

  Checklist: Wedding Day Emergency Kit
  Worksheet: Reception Seating Chart
  Contact Sheet: Wedding Day Vendors

The big day is finally approaching! A lot happens between "Will You?" and "I Do", and much of the final two weeks will be devoted to tying up all the loose ends and making sure the details are taken care of so that everything comes together right and your big day goes off without a hitch. This chapter will give you a heads-up on everything you'll need to prepare for to make this potentially hectic and stressful period go as smoothly as possible.

Managing All the Details

With all the little things and not-so-little things to manage as the wedding day gets closer, it's easy to let something slip through the cracks. Touching bases with vendors, managing guests, packing for your honeymoon and fitting time in for prewedding get-togethers are just the tip of the iceberg. Even though you've been carefully planning for months, the last weeks can be the busiest, and it's times like these when Murphy's Law reigns supreme. Good time and detail management will keep the hectic, stressful stuff to a minimum and make the anticipatory buildup more enjoyable.

e-Resource

Your Planning Calendar

A tool you won't be able to do without—from the beginning of your planning journey to any last-minute craziness—is a good calendar. But traditional paper-and-ink ones will only go so far. They've got limited space (you can only hold so much information in a two-inch by two-inch square), they can only be in once place at one time (usually home, especially if they're large), and if you're looking for something specific you need to leaf through it page by page. Plus, if you need to make a lot of changes it's going to get messy.

An e-Calendar just makes sense. And if it's available as part of your wedding website, it's accessible anywhere you can get on the web: home, his work, her work, or halfway across the world where your sweetheart is on a business trip. At the same time! You can load it with info—forget about space limitations—categorize your events, search through them instantly, and even designate which events should be publicly viewable. This lets guests know when they can and can't reach you, and what the scheduled time and place are for the rehearsal dinner or dress-shopping trips. View it in different modes: month, week, day, or year, depending on your needs.

Your planning calendar is a powerful tool, so use it! Any meeting, reminder, deadline, or even just notes-to-self should be posted. It's a central place to track details and keep everything organized and under control. Remind and inform yourselves, your vendors, attendants, and anyone else. And if you need to take your info to go, just print it out or export it to iCal format or to a handheld PDA.

Covering Your Last-Minute Bases

As the clock winds down, make sure you've taken care of the essentials. Set deadlines and mark your planning calendar for all your countdown considerations, including the following:

Finalize Your Guest List and Seating Plan

In Chapter 7, "Manage Your Guest List and Attendants", we discussed setting a deadline for your guests to respond (usually three or four weeks before the wedding). We also suggested inviting those on your "wish list" depending on how many decline your invitation.

Well, the two-week mark is the point of no return. If guests haven't responded by now, you need to call them and get a solid yes or no. At this point it's necessary to give the final headcount to your caterer. So divide the list of procrastinators up between you, your sweetheart and perhaps your family, and start making the calls.

A Reception Floor Plan

Draw out a quick sketch of your reception facility and make photocopies to act as templates for you to doodle on (some locations will have a template that they can give you). Note where everything will go: your guestbook table, gifts, DJ booth or band stage, dance floor, head table, guests' tables, and so forth.

Your online planning calendar as seen by your guests. Only events, notes, and information designated as public are displayed.

It's easy to add, edit, search and categorize your notes and deadlines with a good online planning calendar.

<CROSS-REFERENCE>

We covered reception and ceremony accessories in Chapter 17, "Paint Your Wedding Colors with Flowers and Décor". In Chapter 11, "Choose Your Caterer, Menu and Beverages", we went over items your caterer might provide, and Chapter 10, "Play Dress-Up", touched on accessories for your bridal look.

</CROSS-REFERENCE>

Add a Seating Chart

If you have more than fifty guests, you probably want to do them and yourselves a favor and draw up a seating chart. We discussed this and other reception details in Chapter 9, "Plan the Party".

Talk to your reception coordinator about how many guests will fit comfortably per table, and based on your final headcount decide how many tables you'll be needing. Draw each table in on a copy of your reception floor plan, including the head table, and number them. On a separate chart (spreadsheets work great for this), designate a column for each table and decide who goes where. You and your sweetheart may want to split this job (you can each do your own guests).

Share the Plan with Your Vendors

Go over your final floor plan with your reception coordinator, caterer, florist, and other applicable vendors to verify that everyone's on the same page. You can also add copies to your vendors' information packages (see the upcoming discussion on "Touching Bases with Your Vendors").

Gather Your Accessories

Getting a hold of all the little things is something that will be ongoing throughout your planning. But as the countdown proceeds and you find yourself in last minute land, you'll want to check that you haven't missed anything, which can be easy to do. Lay claim now on anything you haven't already rounded up.

Make sure you've got keepsake items like your toasting glasses and cake cutting set for starters. If you want them engraved—say, with your monogram and wedding date—many gift shops will do it either on the spot or within a day or so. Don't forget ceremony items like your ring pillow, flower basket, candles, and so forth. For the reception, check off items like your guestbook, signing pen, a cute box or birdcage for any gift cards your guests will bring, disposable cameras, wedding favors, and decorative items like candles, votives, silk flowers, vases, and potted plants. You may be able to rent a lot of this, so check with your florist and caterer to see what they can provide. And how about your wearable accessories? Your garter set, wedding jewelry, shoes, lingerie, headpiece and veil are all things you should be able to include in the "got it" column by now.

e-Resource

Online Accessory Bargains

Save a bundle by e-shopping for your accessories. Everything we mention above, from toasting glasses to potted palms, can be found online. Many couples just head straight to boutique shops and gift stores for their accessories and pay some dramatically marked up retail prices.

Online stores like RedEnvelope (www.redenvelope.com), Beaucoup Wedding Favors (www.beau-coup.com) and Exclusively Weddings (www.exclusivelyweddings.com) are great places to shop for deals and ideas. And for some of the best money-savers you'll find, check out eBay (www.ebay.com). Couples on a tight budget (and who isn't?) would be truly remiss not to browse this gold mine of bargains. The auction site has thousands of wedding-related deals on everything from apparel to décor.

Go to eBay and do a search on any accessory or item you're looking for: "disposable cameras", "wedding toasting glasses", "wedding garter", etc. Or, just put the word "wedding" into the search field for a list of all the wedding categories available.

Plug the word "wedding" into eBay's search field to get a listing of all the categories with wedding-related items.

Finalize the Wedding Day Timeline

A detailed timeline of everything that has to happen on your wedding day isn't just a smart preparation step. It's an essential component of your countdown planning and one that you, your attendants, and vendors will be relying on.

Make a master timeline for yourself, and smaller vendor-specific timelines for your wedding professionals. The limo driver's timeline, for example, should include the pickup time at your getting-ready location, the drop-off time at the ceremony spot, and so on. Your photographer's timeline should include the time she's scheduled to arrive for your getting-ready shots, portraits, and all the major points in your day to give her a good idea of when to expect everything occurring (like cocktail hour, dinner, special dances, cake cutting). Do the same for your videographer, DJ, caterer, reception coordinator, and everyone else. It takes some time, but getting this nailed down now will save you a lot of potential headaches and mistakes on the big day.

Do your master timeline on the computer so you can cut-and-paste when building your vendor time-lines. Just set up two columns, one for the time and one for the event that has to occur. Here are a few sample excerpts:

10:00am	Bouquets and boutonnieres arrive at bride's house
10:30	Hairdresser arrives at bride's house
	Photographer arrives at bride's house
	Videographer arrives at bride's house
11:00	Second videographer arrives at groom's house
11:30	Maid of honor arrives at bride's house
•	
•	
•	
2:45pm	Limo leaves ceremony location with bride and groom
3:00	Cocktail hour begins
	Take portrait shots at reception site
4:00	Guests invited into dining room
4:15	Bridal party Introduction
4:20	Toasts
•	
•	
•	
5:30	First dance
	Father/daughter dance
	Mother/son dance
5:45	Open dancing
•	
•	
•	

Not everything will happen as planned, of course, but having a solid idea of when things should happen—for yourselves and others—will help coordinate the flow of events and keep everyone on the same page.

Touch Bases with Your Vendors

A week or two before the wedding, pay a phone call or visit to all your wedding day players to recon-firm times, locations, and other points of importance. Make an information package for each vendor with applicable excerpts of your timeline, addresses, directions, and contact phone numbers (you, the groom and the maid of honor or other reliable individual). Include a copy of your floor plan for those that need it (like your caterer). Get the information packages to each vendor—by hand, e-mail, or fax—during the final week.

Once your big day launches, remind yourself to relax and trust your professionals to do their jobs. You did your part researching, interviewing and selecting the best, so let them take it from there.

Prep Your Look

Don't forget those trial-runs with your hair stylist and makeup artist. A week before the wedding, double check that they've got you in their appointment books for the day of.

Pick up your dress and make sure it fits; get any emergency last-minute modifications taken care of right away. Have your mom, maid of honor or other trusted individual help you put everything on beforehand, including your headpiece and other accessories. Don't wait until the wedding day to decide that changes need to be made or to discover that something's missing from your ensemble.

The groom should go in a couple days before the wedding to pick up rented formal wear. Any later than this and there might not be enough time to accommodate potential problems like attire that doesn't fit or jackets or shirts ordered in the wrong style.

The bride should leave time for a manicure and pedicure, too. And if at all possible, spend the evening before the wedding relaxing! Schedule your rehearsal early enough that you can get to bed on time and have a good night's sleep.

Pack for the Honeymoon

Don't leave this to the last minute. Pack as much as possible a week before the wedding so it's out of the way, and shop for all those little items you're missing: insect repellant, sunscreen, swimming gear and so forth. Confirm your flight plans and hotel reservations, and have your itinerary printed out and ready to go along with your passport.

Watch the Weather

Keep an eye on the weather report. If you're planning an outdoor event and the skies are looking threatening, make preparations. Ask your attendants and relatives to bring as many umbrellas as they can get, and check with your location coordinator to make sure that your backup location is good to go. See if you can round up plenty of space heaters and other warming (and drying) comforts. You might also want to have family and attendants help you phone all your guests with the potential change in location. Post it on your wedding website, too.

<NOTE>

Wedding-Day Emergency Kit

Gather some essentials and put them in a small bag to have on hand during the big day. Use the emergency kit checklist at the end of this chapter for an idea of things you may want to have with you.

</NOTE>

Checklist: Wedding Day Emergency Kit

Bride's Ceremony/Reception Items

☐ Groom's Wedding Ring
☐ Ceremony Programs
☐ Written Vows or Poem
☐ Bridal Bouquet/Other Arrangements Delivered
☐ _____

Bride's Emergency Kit

☐ Fully Charged Cell Phone
☐ List of Contact Numbers (vendors, bridal party)
☐ Makeup and Small Mirror
☐ Perfume
☐ Deodorant
☐ Lotion
☐ Small Hair Brush or Comb
☐ Hairpins/Ponytail Holder
☐ Breath Mints/Dental Floss
☐ Small Brush-and-Toothpaste Kit
☐ Eye Drops/Lens Solution
☐ Extra Contact Lenses
☐ Sewing Kit/Safety Pins/Scissors
☐ Clear Nail Polish/ Super Glue/Nail File
☐ White Chalk (for gown spots or smudges)
☐ White Masking Tape (for quick hem adjustments)
☐ Tissue/Wipes
☐ Antacid/Allergy Medication/Pain Reliever
☐ Bottled Water
☐ Energy Bar/Other Snacks
☐ Clear Band Aids
☐ Tampons/Pads (if needed)
☐ Spare Change/Bills/Credit Card
☐ Wedding Night Bag (placed in get-away car)
☐ Honeymoon Itinerary, Tickets, Passport, etc.
☐ Honeymoon Suitcases (placed in get-away car)
☐ _____

Groom's Ceremony/Reception Items

☐ Bride's Wedding Ring
☐ Marriage License
☐ Written Vows or Poem
☐ Payment Envelopes (Officiant, Musicians, etc.)
☐ _____

Groom's Emergency Kit

☐ Fully Charged Cell Phone
☐ List of Contact Numbers (vendors, bridal party)
☐ Cologne
☐ Deodorant
☐ Small Brush or Comb (if needed)
☐ Breath Mints/Dental Floss
☐ Small Brush-and-Toothpaste Kit
☐ Eye Drops/Lens Solution
☐ Extra Contact Lenses
☐ Antacid/Allergy Medication/Pain Reliever
☐ Bottled Water
☐ Energy Bar/Other Snacks
☐ Spare Change/Bills/Credit Card
☐ Wedding Night Bag (placed in get-away car)
☐ Honeymoon Itinerary, Tickets, Passport, etc.
☐ Honeymoon Suitcases (placed in get-away car)
☐ _____

Notes: _____
_____
_____
_____
_____
_____
_____
_____
_____
_____
_____
_____

Worksheet: Reception Seating Chart

Name or number each table and group your guests according to the number that each table will comfortably seat. Photocopy this page or go online to www.eplanyourwedding.com to download and print out copies of this worksheet.

Total Number of Guests: _____

Table: _____   **Table:** _____

_____   _____

_____   _____

_____   _____

_____   _____

_____   _____

_____   _____

_____   _____

_____   _____

_____   _____

No. of Guests: _____   **No. of Guests:** _____

Table: _____   **Table:** _____

_____   _____

_____   _____

_____   _____

_____   _____

_____   _____

_____   _____

_____   _____

_____   _____

_____   _____

No. of Guests: _____   **No. of Guests:** _____

Worksheet: Reception Seating Chart (continued)

Table: _____

_____
_____
_____
_____
_____
_____
_____
_____
_____

No. of Guests: _____

Table: _____

_____
_____
_____
_____
_____
_____
_____
_____
_____

No. of Guests: _____

Table: _____

_____
_____
_____
_____
_____
_____
_____
_____
_____

No. of Guests: _____

Table: _____

_____
_____
_____
_____
_____
_____
_____
_____
_____

No. of Guests: _____

Contact Sheet: Wedding Day Vendors

Wedding Coordinator:

Phone: _____ Cell: _____

Balance Due: _____ Tip: _____

Hairstylist:

Phone: _____ Cell: _____

Balance Due: _____ Tip: _____

Makeup Artist:

Phone: _____ Cell: _____

Balance Due: _____ Tip: _____

Photographer:

Phone: _____ Cell: _____

Balance Due: _____ Tip: _____

Videographer:

Phone: _____ Cell: _____

Balance Due: _____ Tip: _____

Florist:

Phone: _____ Cell: _____

Balance Due: _____ Tip: _____

Officiant:

Phone: _____ Cell: _____

Balance Due: _____ Tip: _____

Ceremony Musicians:

Phone: _____ Cell: _____

Balance Due: _____ Tip: _____

Reception Site Manager:

Phone: _____ Cell: _____

Balance Due: _____ Tip: _____

Contact Sheet: Wedding Day Vendors (continued)

Catering:
_____

Phone: _____ Cell: _____

Balance Due: _____ Tip: _____

Bakery:
_____

Phone: _____ Cell: _____

Balance Due: _____ Tip: _____

Band/DJ:
_____

Phone: _____ Cell: _____

Balance Due: _____ Tip: _____

Transportation Service:
_____

Phone: _____ Cell: _____

Balance Due: _____ Tip: _____

Notes:
_____
_____
_____
_____
_____
_____
_____
_____
_____
_____
_____
_____
_____
_____
_____
_____
_____
_____
_____

Notes:

Chapter 22

Enjoy Those Pre-Wedding Parties

- Showers

- Bridesmaids' Luncheon

- Bachelor/ette Bashes

- The Wedding Rehearsal and Rehearsal Dinner

- Online Invitations and Event RSVPs

- e-Plan it! Use Your e-Resources:

  Your Website's RSVP Page and Event Center
  Online Event Managers

- Worksheets:

  Guest List: Bridal Shower/Bachelorette Party
  Guest List: Bachelor Party
  Guest List: Bridal Luncheon
  Guest List: Rehearsal and Dinner
  Comparison Forms: Rehearsal Dinner Location
  Contact Sheet: Rehearsal and Dinner Locations

You have your hands full planning your wedding, and probably don't relish the thought of organizing even more events. But don't worry: pre-wedding parties boast you as the guest of honor, and many are handled by someone else. So sit back, enjoy, and bask in the attention. And when you do need to organize a rehearsal or some socializing time, you'll have online event managers and automated RSVP features to offload some of the time and hassle.

Showers

Aside from the engagement party (covered in Chapter 3), your bridal shower will probably be the first pre-wedding bash you have. It's a chance for your relatives and best friends to come together, get to know each other, and—of course—"shower" you with gifts and attention!

When?

Bridal showers are typically held one to two months before the wedding. As with most pre-wedding parties and get-togethers (with the exception of the rehearsal), you don't want it to be any closer than that to the big day; too many activities too close to the wedding will swamp an already hectic schedule. Just revisit Chapter 21, "Countdown Considerations", to see what we mean.

Who Plans and Organizes It?

Not you. The bride is the guest of honor here, so let others handle the details and just enjoy it!

Traditionally, this party is arranged and organized by the maid of honor, the bridal party as a group, a close friend, or (less common) a relative. While it's often considered inappropriate for parents, sisters, and grandparents of the bride to throw the shower (to some this is perceived as the family "asking" for gifts), they may want to help with the cost by picking up part of the catering tab or offering their home as the shower's location.

> **<CROSS-REFERENCE>**
> We went over your online guest database and how to easily export lists of names in Chapter 7, "Manage Your Guests and Attendants".
> **</CROSS-REFERENCE>**

You'll want to get together with the person hosting your shower to make sure they have the right guests on the list (see below). If you think they might be planning a surprise shower, make sure they have access to guests' names and contact info. Your fiancé might be able to assist them in this area, but if you want to be sure, write up a list of names or print out the appropriate contacts from your online guest database.

Who's Invited?

The bridal shower is traditionally an intimate affair that includes just the bride's attendants, her family, relatives of the groom (mother, sisters, and so forth), and close friends. The average guest count is between 20 to 40, and any more than that is probably too many. Obviously, anyone invited to a wedding shower should be invited to the wedding as well, unless it's an "office shower" thrown by your coworkers or your wedding will take place out of town. If you're going to be having multiple showers, you should probably avoid duplicating the guest lists; inviting the same guests to too many gift-giving events can make the whole thing an unwelcome financial burden.

The person or persons planning and hosting your shower will be responsible for sending out the invitations. They should include the name of the planner, the bride's name, date and location, as well as a notice if it's to be a surprise. An RSVP e-mail or phone number is usually provided as well. Check out the e-Resource later in this chapter if you want your guests to be able to send an RSVP for the shower from your wedding website; you can give the access information to your planner to set it up.

What Happens and Where?

The shower is usually held at the home of the person planning it, or at a relative's house (a sister, aunt, or the mother of the bride, for example). Commonly, a luncheon or tea party is held, but it can be as creative and unique as the planner wishes: a pool party, picnic, or barbeque are all possibilities. The bride will open her gifts, and the planner might even have games on the agenda. Make sure that all your gifts are recorded (have someone create a list with the name of each guest and their gift) so you can send thank-you notes soon after the shower.

One popular option that works especially well if you're having multiple showers is the "theme" shower. For example, you might have a linen shower, a kitchen shower, lingerie shower, and/or a Tupperware shower. It helps prevent duplicate gifts and gives you a chance to receive items you may need more than others.

Bridesmaids' Luncheon

Your attendants will be running errands, backing you up, providing emotional support, and...well, attending to you...throughout the planning and on the big day. The bridesmaids' luncheon is a fun, traditional way to get your girls together and show them your appreciation.

When?

This get-together is usually held a few weeks before the wedding. Yes, this is one of the busiest times of your planning, but the time demand is pretty low, as you'll see.

Who Plans and Organizes It?

This one's in the bride's court. Along with your bridesmaids' gifts, it's your way of saying thanks to those who will be serving as your attendants.

Who's Invited?

You'll invite your maid of honor and all your bridesmaids.

What Happens and Where?

While traditionally a luncheon, this get-together can be an actual restaurant outing, lunch at a friend's, or even a round of cocktails after a day of dress shopping. It's just a way of getting the girls together and thanking them, so you can do it your style and any way that fits your busy schedule. You can give your girls their gifts at this get-together, or wait until the rehearsal dinner.

You might also want to have a traditional bridesmaids' cake baked for the event. Such cakes contain a token inside (a ring, charm, or thimble) and—as bridal lore goes—whoever gets the slice with the token will be the next to wed.

Bachelor/ette Bashes

Whether it's a foray into Vegas, a night on the town, or some drinks and poker (for him) and a pajama party with the girls (for her!), bachelor/ette parties are an optional but time-honored tradition for you both to get together with your closest friends and party before the big day. You'll often hear that the sake of the party is your last big night as a single guy/gal, but we know it's really your upcoming marriage you're celebrating. In fact, a traditional custom for the groom-to-be (just slightly less known than the stripper-jumping-out-of-the-cake routine) has long been to fill his and his groomsmen's glasses and toast his new bride. The glasses were then shattered so that they could never be used for a less worthy purpose.

When?

These parties are usually held during the last couple weeks before the wedding, preferably three days or more before the wedding day itself.

Who Plans and Organizes It?

Not you! The best man and maid of honor traditionally get the fun of planning and organizing each of your big night out.

Who's Invited?

It's your call. Who do you feel most comfortable to get together and hang out with in such an intimate setting? Your attendants are a given. Your best man will get the guys together for the bachelor party, and your maid of honor will do the same with the girls for the bachelorette bash. Feel free to enforce any invitation list wishes you may have.

What Happens and Where?

Anything. Anywhere! This is a chance to get out with your buds and celebrate your upcoming marriage (and last night of singlehood), so do it your way and have fun! Even if your hosts insist on surprising you with their party agenda, slip them a hint or two on your preferences (if you'd like to keep it low key, for example, but you know your friends want to plan a crazy bar-hopping night out, you'd better let them know!).

The Wedding Rehearsal and Rehearsal Dinner

You'll need to rehearse the details of your ceremony before the big day, so it will be necessary to get everyone together to do the run-throughs and distribute important information. As a show of appreciation to those taking time out of their days to rehearse, you'll be arranging a dinner afterwards for everyone to socialize, exchange gifts, and just enjoy the evening. It's also a great opportunity to invite all your guests from out of town to get together with you and meet everyone, too.

When?

You'll typically rehearse your wedding ceremony the day before the wedding. Your church or site coordinator will be able to fill you in on the details and schedule.

Who Plans and Organizes It?

Traditionally, the groom's parents have been the ones to host the rehearsal dinner. If they're hosting yours, they may do some of the dinner planning, but you'll likely need to be involved either way, especially with the rehearsal itself. You'll need to make sure that the right people are invited (see below) and also that communication is ongoing with the church or ceremony location regarding scheduling of the rehearsal and music.

Who's Invited?

Typically, the complete bridal party is invited, with or without their spouses or significant others (your call), as well as your parents and immediate families. You may also want to invite the out of town guests so that the get-together serves the dual function of rehearsal dinner and welcome party.

You can invite those who you'd like to attend by email, phone, or with mailed invitations. Provide directions and a contact to RSVP at. If you have a wedding website with an RSVP page that allows for multiple events (see the following e-Resource), it can be very helpful to have the invited guests visit your website to send in their RSVPs as well as obtain map locations, driving directions, and even menu options.

Others who might make an appearance at your rehearsal are your wedding coordinator (if you have one) and your videographer. Check with these individuals to see if they plan on attending.

What Happens and Where?

At the Rehearsal

The rehearsal normally takes place at your ceremony location. Have the parents and bridal party, as well as anyone else who will be taking place in the ceremony (speakers, singers, and so forth) to assemble and rehearse everything, from procession to recession. Your officiant may be present to provide guidance, or you may be assisted by a site coordinator.

```
<CROSS-REFERENCE>
We went over planning your ceremony details in Chapter 8.
</CROSS-REFERENCE>
```

Since you have everyone together, now is a good time to delegate wedding day duties, too. Have a written or typed outline of tasks prepared ahead of time (you should have discussed everything with the individuals already, at least over the phone). Pass out packets with maps for the locations (ceremony, reception, hotel) as well as a timeline and emergency contact phone numbers to your attendants. Make sure everyone's up to speed for the next day!

At the Dinner Party

The rehearsal dinner immediately follows the rehearsal, provding a chance for gifts to be exchanged, toasts to be given, and for everyone to spend some time socializing and generally discussing the stars of the event: you two! The rehearsal dinner is usually an informal get-together and can be held at a catering hall, private room at a restaurant, pizza parlor, home of a friend or relative, or anywhere else that suits you.

This is a good time to give gifts to your attendants and to exchange your own wedding gifts if you like. Some couples also give their parents a gift at this time as a show of appreciation for hosting the wedding or for all their support through the planning.

Wrap up the night early enough to get home and rest up. At the end of the dinner, you and your sweetie traditionally part and won't see each other again until you meet to exchange your I-do's. You've got a big day tomorrow, so get a good night's sleep!

Online Invitations and Event RSVPs

Your time will become more and more a precious commodity the closer your wedding day becomes. As your centralized information source, let your wedding website keep all of your guests informed with maps, directions, times, locations, and even menus for your parties and get-togethers. Your website's RSVP page, if enabled with multiple events, can handle all your pre-wedding parties and more. With your guests checking your website for info, your phone will be quieter, and you'll be able to see who's coming, who can't make it, and who hasn't responded with just a few clicks. And if you'd rather post your event information online but off your wedding website, there's other services that can help, too. The online resources will make your event planning and response management a snap!

e-Resource

Your Website's RSVP Page and Event Center

Most wedding website services include an option for guests to view the date, time, and location details of the ceremony and reception, and send or update RSVP responses online. Some services also allow you to include events other than your wedding. Guests invited to multiple events in this case would be presented with the option of selecting which event they would like to view and respond to. Make sure that your service allows you to tailor your guest list for each event. Your rehearsal dinner, for example, should only be displayed as an option for those guests who are invited to it—namely, your family and attendants. All other guests should not even be able to see it as an option.

> **<CROSS-REFERENCE>**
> We discussed the advantages of a wedding website in Chapter 4, and also covered how to get a free or low-cost website live and on the Internet in minutes.
> **</CROSS-REFERENCE>**

For most services, you are provided an RSVP response page so that you can log in and view the results of your event at any time. The WedShare.com service, for example, allows you to administer and view your event results from your control panel. For your wedding event, it will also update your overall wedding headcount and guest manager details. We'll step through a wedding website event manager using the WedShare.com service as an example. Most good wedding website services will have a similar interface that you can follow along with.

Enabling Your RSVP Page

Chances are, you've already set up your website's RSVP page to enable guests who visit your site to submit their RSVP responses to your wedding online. Chapter 20, "Send Invitations and Manage Your Responses", gives a detailed introduction to activating this incredibly convenient feature. What we'll be discussing here is creating other events in addition to your wedding and enabling specific invited guests to access those events and respond to them.

<CROSS-REFERENCE>
Review Chapter 20 for activating the RSVP feature of your wedding website.
</CROSS-REFERENCE>

To administer your events on a WedShare.com website, click the "Available Features" option in the SiteBuilderTM pane of your Control Panel. Find the "Online RSVP" feature in your list of active features and click its "Edit" link. If your online RSVP page isn't activated yet, just click the "Activate" link to get it started.

Creating a New Event

Creating, editing, and removing events is pretty straightforward. Click the "Create New Event" button to create as many events as you'd like. New events will appear in your event list, and can be independently edited, activated, deactivated, or deleted. You can also review and export your guests' responses. Events won't be visible to your website's visitors until you activate them.

The administrative interface for WedShare.com's Online RSVP Feature has helpful instructions built in. Click the "Create New Event" button to start a new event.

For full details on creating, editing and managing your events, review the e-Resource "Allow Guests to RSVP Online" in Chapter 20. You can set your event up to request just the basics (yes/no, how many), as well as collect any additional information you might need. If your event includes dinner and you have a group menu with specific options, you can add a menu to your event and let guests select menu options online. Telling your restaurant or caterer how many of each menu options you'll need can smooth the dinner out considerably, especially if you've got a large group.

For every event you set up, you can allow all your guests (those in your online guest database) to visit the event, or you can select from a list. You'll find that having your RSVP page and guest manager both integrated with your wedding website is a great time-saving feature for this and other online planning tasks.

Include all the pertinent information for each event. In addition to automating most of the basics, WedShare.com's RSVP manager allows you to add images for your events and as much informative content as you need. Since it's online and at the service of your guests, they'll be able to use it to obtain a map, directions, time, place, and more. A quick phone call telling them to check out the event on your website's RSVP page can make things a lot easier for you than filling out a bunch of invitation cards or repeating it all a couple dozen times over the phone. During the countdown stage before the wedding, you'll need every free minute you can get!

You can start an event, save what you've got, and come back later to touch up the info; events are deactive by default, so your guests won't see them initially. Once you have your event set up the way you want it, just activate it to enable those guests who have been invited to view and respond to it.

Online Event Managers

There are some other great online event managers that you can use to manage your events and responses if you're using a free wedding website service that doesn't do on-line RSVPs, or if your wedding website service doesn't offer a complete event manager. Some you may have even used before: Evite, for example (www.evite.com), lets you do much of the functionality described above for free using e-mailed invitations to your guests and a slick, easy-to-use interface. Evite even has a custom wedding interface, allowing you to create themed invitations and even set up gift registries on your invitation pages.

A wedding RSVP page from a couple's wedding website using WedShare.com.

Register

Go to www.evite.com and click on the "Plan an Event" link. Register with Evite before setting up your events, otherwise you'll be interrupted to do so during the sending process. Remember to use your wedding-specific email address when registering. Evite will send you a confirmation email with a link you'll need to click on in order to complete the registration process. The whole process takes just a few minutes.

Creating a New Event

Evite calls their events "Invitations", since all your guests will receive an invitation e-mail linking them to the page you create. Use the "Create Your Invitation" form to build your online invitation. Select "Wedding Themes" as your event type in order to give your invitation the appropriate design. A small thumbnail of what your invitation will look like is given at the top left of the page.

It's easy to send an invitation to your pre-wedding parties using Evite's online invitation builder.

A wedding rehearsal invitation set up with Evite.

Fill out your guests' email addresses, the wording you'd like to use, and preview it to make sure you've got everything down right. The preview will show you how your invitation will look to your guests (you can preview the e-mail that will be sent out, as well). When you've got everything set the way you like, click "Send" to fire it off. If you haven't registered yet, Evite will request you to do so when you send the invitation.

Editing Your Event and Viewing Your Results

Log in to Evite with your e-mail and password in order to view the results, make changes, and do other host-related stuff. You'll be provided with a list of your events and options to edit or review the results of each.

Guest List: Bridal Shower/Bachelorette Party

Bride: fill out the names and contact information for the guests you would like invited to your bridal shower and/ or bachelorette party. Give the information in advance to your maid of honor or the individual organizing the bash, to help send and track the invites.

Photocopy this page or go online to www.eplanyourwedding.com to download and print out copies of this work-sheet.

Name:

Address:

Email: Phone:

□ Date Invitation Sent

□ Date RSVP Received   Attending: □ Yes   □ No   □ Maybe   Number of Guests:

□ Date Sent Thank-You Note

Gift Received:

Name:

Address:

Email: Phone:

□ Date Invitation Sent

□ Date RSVP Received   Attending: □ Yes   □ No   □ Maybe   Number of Guests:

□ Date Sent Thank-You Note

Gift Received:

Name:

Address:

Email: Phone:

□ Date Invitation Sent

□ Date RSVP Received   Attending: □ Yes   □ No   □ Maybe   Number of Guests:

□ Date Sent Thank-You Note

Gift Received:

Guest List: Bridal Shower/Bachelorette Party (continued)

Name: _____

Address: _____

_____

Email: _____ Phone: _____

☐ Date Invitation Sent _____

☐ Date RSVP Received   Attending: ☐ Yes   ☐ No   ☐ Maybe   Number of Guests: _____

☐ Date Sent Thank-You Note _____

Gift Received: _____

Name: _____

Address: _____

_____

Email: _____ Phone: _____

☐ Date Invitation Sent _____

☐ Date RSVP Received   Attending: ☐ Yes   ☐ No   ☐ Maybe   Number of Guests: _____

☐ Date Sent Thank-You Note _____

Gift Received: _____

Name: _____

Address: _____

_____

Email: _____ Phone: _____

☐ Date Invitation Sent _____

☐ Date RSVP Received   Attending: ☐ Yes   ☐ No   ☐ Maybe   Number of Guests: _____

☐ Date Sent Thank-You Note _____

Gift Received: _____

Name: _____

Address: _____

_____

Email: _____ Phone: _____

☐ Date Invitation Sent _____

☐ Date RSVP Received   Attending: ☐ Yes   ☐ No   ☐ Maybe   Number of Guests: _____

☐ Date Sent Thank-You Note _____

Gift Received: _____

Guest List: Bachelor Party

Groom: fill out the name and contact information for the guests you would like invited to your bachelor party and give the information in advance to your best man or to the individual organizing the bash, to help send and track the invites.

Photocopy this page or go online to www.eplanyourwedding.com to download and print out copies of this worksheet.

Name:

Address:

Email: Phone:

☐ Date Invitation Sent

☐ Date RSVP Received   Attending: ☐ Yes   ☐ No   ☐ Maybe   Number of Guests:

☐ Date Sent Thank-You Note

Name:

Address:

Email: Phone:

☐ Date Invitation Sent

☐ Date RSVP Received   Attending: ☐ Yes   ☐ No   ☐ Maybe   Number of Guests:

☐ Date Sent Thank-You Note

Name:

Address:

Email: Phone:

☐ Date Invitation Sent

☐ Date RSVP Received   Attending: ☐ Yes   ☐ No   ☐ Maybe   Number of Guests:

☐ Date Sent Thank-You Note

Name:

Address:

Email: Phone:

☐ Date Invitation Sent

☐ Date RSVP Received   Attending: ☐ Yes.   ☐ No   ☐ Maybe   Number of Guests:

☐ Date Sent Thank-You Note

Guest List: Bachelor Party (continued)

Name:

Address:

Email: _____ Phone:

☐ Date Invitation Sent

☐ Date RSVP Received   Attending: ☐ Yes   ☐ No   ☐ Maybe   Number of Guests:

☐ Date Sent Thank-You Note

Name:

Address:

Email: _____ Phone:

☐ Date Invitation Sent

☐ Date RSVP Received   Attending: ☐ Yes   ☐ No   ☐ Maybe   Number of Guests:

☐ Date Sent Thank-You Note

Name:

Address:

Email: _____ Phone:

☐ Date Invitation Sent

☐ Date RSVP Received   Attending: ☐ Yes   ☐ No   ☐ Maybe   Number of Guests:

☐ Date Sent Thank-You Note

Name:

Address:

Email: _____ Phone:

☐ Date Invitation Sent

☐ Date RSVP Received   Attending: ☐ Yes   ☐ No   ☐ Maybe   Number of Guests:

☐ Date Sent Thank-You Note

Guest List: Bridal Luncheon

Bride: fill out the names and contact information for your bridesmaids and maid of honor to organize the attendance of your bridal luncheon.

Photocopy this page or go online to www.eplanyourwedding.com to download and print out copies of this worksheet.

Name:

Address:

Email: Phone:

☐ Date Invitation Sent

☐ Date RSVP Received   Attending: ☐ Yes   ☐ No   ☐ Maybe

Gift:

Name:

Address:

Email: Phone:

☐ Date Invitation Sent

☐ Date RSVP Received   Attending: ☐ Yes   ☐ No   ☐ Maybe

Gift:

Name:

Address:

Email: Phone:

☐ Date Invitation Sent

☐ Date RSVP Received   Attending: ☐ Yes   ☐ No   ☐ Maybe

Gift:

Name:

Address:

Email: Phone:

☐ Date Invitation Sent

☐ Date RSVP Received   Attending: ☐ Yes   ☐ No   ☐ Maybe

Gift:

Guest List: Rehearsal and Dinner

Typically includes family members, bridal party, officiant, wedding coordinator, flower girl and ring bearer with their parents, closest friends and out-of-town guests. If necessary, include any other special guests and ceremony musicians. Photocopy this page or go online to www.eplanyourwedding.com to download and print out copies of this worksheet.

Name: _____

Address: _____

_____

Phone: _____   Cell: _____

Email: _____   Website: _____

☐ Date Invitation Sent _____

☐ Date RSVP Received _____   Attending: ☐ Yes   ☐ No   ☐ Maybe   Number of Guests: _____

Name: _____

Address: _____

_____

Phone: _____   Cell: _____

Email: _____   Website: _____

☐ Date Invitation Sent _____

☐ Date RSVP Received _____   Attending: ☐ Yes   ☐ No   ☐ Maybe   Number of Guests: _____

Name: _____

Address: _____

_____

Phone: _____   Cell: _____

Email: _____   Website: _____

☐ Date Invitation Sent _____

☐ Date RSVP Received _____   Attending: ☐ Yes   ☐ No   ☐ Maybe   Number of Guests: _____

Name: _____

Address: _____

_____

Phone: _____   Cell: _____

Email: _____   Website: _____

☐ Date Invitation Sent _____

☐ Date RSVP Received _____   Attending: ☐ Yes   ☐ No   ☐ Maybe   Number of Guests: _____

Guest List: Rehearsal and Dinner (continued)

Name: _____

Address: _____

_____

Phone: _____ Cell: _____

Email: _____ Website: _____

☐ Date Invitation Sent _____

☐ Date RSVP Received   Attending: ☐ Yes   ☐ No   ☐ Maybe   Number of Guests: _____

Name: _____

Address: _____

_____

Phone: _____ Cell: _____

Email: _____ Website: _____

☐ Date Invitation Sent _____

☐ Date RSVP Received   Attending: ☐ Yes   ☐ No   ☐ Maybe   Number of Guests: _____

Name: _____

Address: _____

_____

Phone: _____ Cell: _____

Email: _____ Website: _____

☐ Date Invitation Sent _____

☐ Date RSVP Received   Attending: ☐ Yes   ☐ No   ☐ Maybe   Number of Guests: _____

Name: _____

Address: _____

_____

Phone: _____ Cell: _____

Email: _____ Website: _____

☐ Date Invitation Sent _____

☐ Date RSVP Received   Attending: ☐ Yes   ☐ No   ☐ Maybe   Number of Guests: _____

Comparison Forms: Rehearsal Dinner Location 1

Rehearsal Dinner Date: _____ Time: _____ Rehearsal Dinner Budget:$ _____

Rehearsal Dinner Location: _____

Address: _____

Contact: _____

Email: _____ Phone: _____ Fax: _____

Website: _____ Recommended by: _____

Location Amenities   **Parking   Information**

☐ Private Room   ☐ Outdoor Area   ☐ Free Ample Parking   ☐ Paid Parking Lot /Garage

☐ Bar Area   ☐ Game Room   ☐ Limited Free Parking   ☐ Street Parking

☐ Mingling Area   ☐ Other   ☐ Valet Parking   ☐ Other

Cuisine Type and Description   **Special Meals Required and Quantity**

☐ Regional   ☐ Thematic   ☐ Vegetarian   ☐ Kosher

☐ Ethnic   ☐ Other   ☐ Vegan   ☐ Other

Courses Available for Guests   **Beverages Available for Guests**

☐ Hors d'oeuvres   ☐ Salad   ☐ Open Bar   ☐ Specialty Drinks

☐ Appetizer   ☐ Pasta   ☐ Limited Bar   ☐ Own Liquor Provided

☐ Fruit / Cheese   ☐ Entrée   ☐ Non-Alcoholic Beverages ☐ Other

☐ Soup   ☐ Dessert

Other Special Requests: _____

Can rehearsal dinner site provide a special limited menu option for guests? ☐ Yes   ☐ No

(If yes, have them email or fax to you the menu options and descriptions to choose from, including price ranges.)

Type of Payment Accepted: _____

Cancellation Policy: _____

Reservation Required by: _____

Additional Fees: $ _____

Total Estimated Cost: $ _____

Comments: _____

Comparison Forms: Rehearsal Dinner Location 2

Rehearsal Dinner Date: _____   Time: _____   Rehearsal Dinner Budget:$ _____

Rehearsal Dinner Location: _____

Address: _____

_____

Contact: _____

Email: _____   Phone: _____   Fax: _____

Website: _____   Recommended by: _____

Location Amenities

☐ Private Room   ☐ Outdoor Area

☐ Bar Area   ☐ Game Room

☐ Mingling Area   ☐ Other

Parking Information

☐ Free Ample Parking   ☐ Paid Parking Lot /Garage

☐ Limited Free Parking ☐ Street Parking

☐ Valet Parking   ☐ Other

Cuisine Type and Description

☐ Regional   ☐ Thematic

☐ Ethnic   ☐ Other

Special Meals Required and Quantity

☐ Vegetarian   ☐ Kosher

☐ Vegan   ☐ Other

Courses Available for Guests

☐ Hors d'oeuvres   ☐ Salad

☐ Appetizer   ☐ Pasta

☐ Fruit / Cheese   ☐ Entrée

☐ Soup   ☐ Dessert

Beverages Available for Guests

☐ Open Bar   ☐ Specialty Drinks

☐ Limited Bar   ☐ Own Liquor Provided

☐ Non-Alcoholic Beverages ☐ Other

Other Special Requests: _____

_____

Can rehearsal dinner site provide a special limited menu option for guests? ☐ Ye   ☐ No

(If yes, have them email or fax to you the menu options and descriptions to choose from, including price ranges.)

Type of Payment Accepted: _____

Cancellation Policy: _____

Reservation Required by: _____

Additional Fees: $ _____

_____

Total Estimated Cost: $ _____

_____

Comments: _____

_____

_____

_____

Contact Sheet: Rehearsal and Dinner Locations

Rehearsal Date:

Time:

Date Reserved:

Ceremony / Rehearsal Location:

Address:

Site / Event Coordinator:

Officiant:

Email:

Phone:

Website:

Staple Business Card

Dinner Reservation Date:

Time:

Date Reserved:

Confirmed Reservation Time,
Date and Location on:

Rehearsal Dinner Location:

Address:

Contact:

Email:

Phone:

Fax:

Website:

Total Number of Guests Attending:

Location Amenities:

Parking Information:

Cuisine Type and Description:

Special Meals Required and Quantity:

Courses Available for Guests:

Beverages Available for Guests:

Contact Sheet: Rehearsal and Dinner Locations (continued)

If rehearsal dinner site provides a special limited menu option for your guests, include the menu options below and get a head count on the preferences in advance.

Menu Options	Quantities Needed and Cost per Plate
1.	
2.	
3.	
4.	
5.	
6.	
7.	
8.	
9.	
10.	

Payment Policy:

Cancellation Policy:

Rentals Required:

Rentals Cost: $

Additional Fees: $ (corkage, setup, cleanup, etc.)

Gratuity: $ (if not included in total)

Total Cost: $

Notes:

Chapter 23

Don't Forget the Legal Considerations

- Marriage License

- Name and Address Changes

- Prenuptial Agreements

- e-Plan it! Use Your e-Resources:

    Your County Clerk's Website
    Online "Name Change Kits"

- Worksheets:

    Considerations Worksheet: Legalities
    Considerations Worksheet: Name and Address Changes

From marriage licenses to name-changes to prenups, make sure you're up to speed with the many legal requirements and options that a new wedding brings. By accounting for these details in advance, you'll be set for smooth legal sailing to the big day ahead.

Marriage License

Before you get married, the state wants to make sure that all legal requirements have been met for your happy union. They'll need to verify that you're both of legal age, and if previously married, that you're legally divorced or widowed as well. Some states also require a medical exam (blood test). There's usually a specific window of time that your marriage license will be valid, so you don't want to neglect this important detail. The three-month mark before your wedding is normally a good time to take care of it; your checklist (Chapter 2) will give you a reminder.

Who to Contact

Each state has slightly different requirements and procedures regarding marriage certificates, so you'll need to contact the appropriate agency in the county where your marriage ceremony is to take place. The agency responsible for issuing marriage licenses is the county clerk (sometimes known as the county clerk-recorder or county recorder). Look up the phone number or website for the appropriate county clerk and find out what you'll need to obtain the marriage license, where to go to file the paperwork, and what your time window is.

e-Resource

Your County Clerk's Website

If you're lucky, your county clerk may have an informative website to answer all your questions and even let you download forms to print out and sign before coming in. You can probably find it doing a search on your county with the keywords "county clerk <county name>" using a search engine like Google (www.google.com). For example, the county clerk-recorder for Santa Clara County in California has a website at www.clerkrecorder.org.

Requirements

You'll both need to visit the county clerk together, so make sure you've completed any prerequisites (the blood test, for instance) and bring along all the necessary paperwork. Also, keep in mind that if you're getting married out of state, you'll need to take care of this when you both arrive, so plan on allowing enough time.

Call the appropriate county clerk or visit their website to make sure you're bringing along everything you need. Usually, you'll need your birth certificate, a photo ID, and divorce or death certificates if necessary. The following is some information to ask about:

The Santa Clara County clerk-recorder's website provides all the necessary information regarding marriage license requirements, and even allows couples to download the associated paperwork in .PDF format.

- What is your time window? Is there a waiting period after obtaining the marriage license, and does it expire?

- What are the age requirements? (Your parents may need to sign if one of you is not of "legal" marrying age in your county)

- If you're not a resident of the county you plan to wed in, are there any additional procedures or requirements involved?

- Is a medical exam or blood test required? (If an AIDS test is required, make sure to get this done three months or so ahead of time, as results can take up to eight weeks to get back)

- What fees are involved, if any?

- What type of identification is required?

- If divorced or widowed, are divorce or death certificates required?

Name and Address Changes

If you'll be switching mailing addresses, you can start notifying the post office and all those nice people that send you bills in advance, to minimize any mixup or lost mail. You won't need to take any action regarding name changes until after your wedding, although you may want to give your employer a heads-up. Since the agencies responsible for changing your legal name (the Social Security agency, Passport Agency, and Department of Motor Vehicles) require a marriage certificate, you won't be able to run the name change errands until after your wedding, and most likely after your honeymoon. If you're going to be doing any air travel for your honeymoon, just keep the tickets in your unmarried name, since the name on your tickets need to match your photo ID and passport. Don't worry; you'll have plenty of time to get the name change legalities out of the way when you get back. And that's assuming you're changing your name in the first place...we'll discuss that, too.

Name Change Options

The traditional switch of a bride's last name for that of her husband's is still the most common marriage name-change scenario, although it's not required. Your own choice will depend on personal circumstance and preference. The following are some of the options that couples today have gone with:

Traditional (Bride Takes Her Husband's Name)

Once the only choice a bride had, the traditional taking of her husband's name is just one in a variety of choices today, but is still the most customary. It's usually regarded as a sign of dedication and a symbol of union with her new spouse. Begin the metamorphosis by signing your new married name on your marriage certificate and all further documents, and take care of the paperwork and name-change errands in the next section to make it official.

No Name Change (Bride Keeps Her Maiden Name)

After years of building a name, changing it—especially if it is professionally well-known—can be difficult. You may want to forego the custom and keep your own names, saving you the professional pains as well as long lines at the DMV. Just be ready for miffed in-laws and curious questions as to why you're not "honoring" hubby's family name.

Bride Uses Her Husband's Name Socially and Her Maiden Name Professionally

A compromise chosen by some brides whose maiden names are professionally established is to continue using their maiden name professionally but use their husband's socially. You don't have to take care of any name-change duties in this instance, but just make sure to keep all legal paperwork—including your joint tax return—under your maiden name to avoid any confusion. One side-note is that the IRS may request a notarized copy of your marriage certificate at tax time.

Combine the Names (Hyphenation or Middle Name Change)

A contemporarily popular option is for the bride (and the groom in some cases) to combine both last names using a hyphen, typically hers first and then his. Rebecca Smith becomes Rebecca Smith-Jones, for example. Sometimes, the bride opts to change her middle name instead; Rebecca becomes Rebecca Smith Jones. You'll need to follow the same name-change steps as the traditional method. If the groom doubles up his name as well, you'll both need to run through the name-change errands together.

Groom Takes His Wife's Name

While not customary, this is sometimes done if the bride cannot easily change her name for professional reasons, and they both want the same last name to keep it socially straightforward. His family's feathers could be ruffled, though, so be prepared with a diplomatic explanation if you anticipate a problem.

Who to Notify

If either of you will be changing your names and/or your residence addresses, read up! Whether it's the bride who's switching, the groom, or both, you need to make sure everything's legit and that all personal, professional, and legal contacts are fully aware of your name change and/or move. For the name change(s), some of these entities are going to want to see an official marriage certificate (not a photocopy)...specifically, the Department of Motor Vehicles (DMV) and passport agency. While you'll visit the DMV yourself, you're probably going to mail in the passport request, including marriage certificate, so have your County Clerk issue you an extra certified copy or two for this purpose.

e-Resource

Online "Name Change Kits"

The information given in this chapter is a quick but complete summary of what you'll need to do. By taking care of the following paperwork, notifying the contacts listed, and using a little common sense, your name change duties should be relatively painless. However, if you'd like more information, try doing a Google search on the keywords "marriage name change" and you'll get a ton of informative links, as well as a slew of "Name Change Kits" that range anywhere from $20 to $50 and up for a packet (or CD) of forms, checklists, and letter templates. The choice to purchase is yours, although you should be fine with the information in this book and a few phone calls.

The portal site WeddingChannel.com is one of many online wedding companies to offer a "name change kit".

Step One: Contact the Social Security Administration

The first hoop you'll need to jump through is to get a new social security card. The DMV will require that you already have this taken care of this. After you obtain your marriage certificate (and any certified copies) from your county clerk, Call 800-772-1213 to hear an automated walk-through of the steps, or go to www.socialsecurity.gov for the information and form download. The new card is free, so don't buy into online companies offering to do this for a fee.

Step Two: Amend Your Passport

There's no fee for this service unless you take longer than a year to get the form in. You can get more information and download the necessary name-change form at travel.state.gov (click on the Name Change link). You'll need to mail your current passport, a certified copy of your marriage certificate (not a photocopy), and the application form to your nearest passport agency. They'll send you the same passport back with your updated information printed on the inside cover.

Step Three: Visit the Department of Motor Vehicles

The DMV requires you to stop by in person. Call in and make an appointment ahead of time if you can. Ask what forms and information you'll need to bring in (you'll need the updated social security info and your marriage certificate for sure). If you've changed your middle name, some DMV offices have been reported to ask for your modified passport. Ask your office if they will require this.

Step Four:

Order replacements for documents that contain your previous name, such as checks, credit cards, and business cards.

Step Five:

Have your employer change your name in their records. If you're a student, do the same thing with your school so they update your registration information.

Step Six:

Change the name on your vehicle's registration. Contact your bank, your mortgage and insurance companies to let them know of your name change. Ask what documents or letters you might need to mail or fax in.

Step Seven:

Contact the registrar of voters for your county, the post office, and your utility companies. Basically, anyone you pay a bill to should be notified of your name and/or address change.

Step Eight:

Notify everyone else! Family and friends, associates and acquaintances, you name it. You can send stationery made just for such a purpose, or leave it to the next time you contact them. You'll be putting your new name on the thank-you cards you mail out, holiday cards, your wedding website, and other correspondence as well.

Prenuptial Agreements

There's nothing romantic about the word "prenup", but you'll find that most legal and financial experts give prenuptial agreements the nod as a smart financial planning step before tying the knot, especially in particular circumstances. The fact is that should your marriage end in an unfortunate death or divorce, your finances will be in the hands of the courts unless you have a valid prenuptial agreement that keeps such decisions in your own control.

A prenuptial agreement is a contract made between two people before they get married, specifying what each person is bringing into the marriage and how assets should be divided up in the case of death or a divorce. With more and more couples these days establishing themselves professionally at a younger age, and marrying at an older age, they are bringing more hard-earned assets into marriage than ever before. This, combined with the fact that couples simply don't want the courts to be the one to dictate what happens in the case of an unfortunate end to the marriage, is leading to an increase in the popularity of prenuptial agreements.

Who Are They For?

Legal experts say that prenuptial agreements aren't just for the rich and wealthy. Any of the following is a good reason to consider a prenuptial agreement:

- You have a home, stock, retirement fund, or other assets

- You are the owner or co-owner of a business

- One of you is a good deal wealthier than the other, or will be supporting the other for any reason (such as through school)

- You anticipate receiving an inheritance

- You have kids from a previous marriage

- You'll be supporting dependent loved ones, such as elderly parents

- You foresee a large increase in your future income for any reason

How to Go About It

First of all, you need to be honest with your sweetheart. Sit down and discuss your concerns openly and plainly, and as early as possible. It's not a romantic subject, and many people take it as a lack of commitment towards the future marriage, so it needs to be very clear why you feel a prenup would be in both your best interests.

Write down a list of your assets and what, in general, you'd like the contract to say. It doesn't have to be specific, but having a lot of the initial decisions out of the way will save you money, since fees for prenuptial agreements depend on how long they take to draft. Having information ready and being on the same page before bringing the lawyers into the picture will be to your advantage.

We'd also advise you to obtain separate attorneys to make sure that the agreement is seen as valid by the courts later on; prenups have been thrown out on the basis that both parties didn't have fair representation. Likewise, don't hide anything or try to slant the agreement in a way that is overly beneficial to one party. A judge may throw out a prenup if it appears to be taking advantage of one party, or if it is discovered that certain facts have been withheld. Be fair and honest, as with anything else.

Keeping It Updated

Review your agreement every few years, and revise it if necessary. Prenuptial agreements are not written in stone. After 10 years of marriage you might want to relax some of the terms, for example. Some people even include a "sunset clause" in their agreements that allows their prenup to expire after a certain length of time—say, 10 or 15 years. These and other choices will be up to you to decide, so talk it over and come to the conclusions together.

Considerations Worksheet: Legalities

Marriage License Requirements

Items Required	Have	Bride Needs	Groom Needs
☐ Driver's License (proof of age and identification)	☐	☐	☐
☐ Birth Certificate (proof of citizenship)	☐	☐	☐
☐ Divorce Degree (proof of divorce)	☐	☐	☐
☐ Death Certificate of Previous Spouse (if widowed)	☐	☐	☐
☐ Doctor Certificate	☐	☐	☐
☐ Blood Test Results	☐	☐	☐
☐ Parental Consent	☐	☐	☐

Considerations for Prenuptial Agreement

☐ Real Estate
☐ Retirement Funds
☐ Stocks and Other Assets
☐ Business Ownership
☐ Large Saving Accounts
☐ Will Be Supporting Spouse
☐ Anticipate an Inheritance
☐ Children from Previous Marriage
☐ Have Other Dependent Loved Ones to Support
☐ Foresee Large Increase of Income
☐ _____

Notes:
_____
_____
_____
_____
_____
_____
_____
_____
_____
_____
_____
_____
_____
_____

Considerations Worksheet: Name and Address Changes

Check the name/address boxes for those items you'll need to change. As you take care of the change for each item, check its "changed" box.

	Bride			Groom		
Consideration Items	Name	Address	Changed	Name	Address	Changed
☐ Social Security	☐	☐	☐	☐	☐	☐
☐ Driver's License	☐	☐	☐	☐	☐	☐
☐ Car Registration	☐	☐	☐	☐	☐	☐
☐ Voter's Registration	☐	☐	☐	☐	☐	☐
☐ Passport	☐	☐	☐	☐	☐	☐
☐ Post Office	☐	☐	☐	☐	☐	☐
☐ Employer Records	☐	☐	☐	☐	☐	☐
☐ Stocks / Bonds	☐	☐	☐	☐	☐	☐
☐ 401K Plan	☐	☐	☐	☐	☐	☐
☐ Pension Plans	☐	☐	☐	☐	☐	☐
☐ Health Insurance	☐	☐	☐	☐	☐	☐
☐ Life Insurance	☐	☐	☐	☐	☐	☐
☐ Doctor / Dentist	☐	☐	☐	☐	☐	☐
☐ Bank Accounts and Checks	☐	☐	☐	☐	☐	☐
☐ Credit Card Accounts	☐	☐	☐	☐	☐	☐
☐ Property Insurance	☐	☐	☐	☐	☐	☐
☐ Home Loan	☐	☐	☐	☐	☐	☐
☐ Property Titles	☐	☐	☐	☐	☐	☐
☐ Leases	☐	☐	☐	☐	☐	☐
☐ Utilities	☐	☐	☐	☐	☐	☐
☐ Auto Loans	☐	☐	☐	☐	☐	☐
☐ Auto Insurance	☐	☐	☐	☐	☐	☐
☐ Wills / Trusts	☐	☐	☐	☐	☐	☐
☐ School Records	☐	☐	☐	☐	☐	☐
☐ School Loans	☐	☐	☐	☐	☐	☐
☐ Other Loans	☐	☐	☐	☐	☐	☐
☐ Subscriptions	☐	☐	☐	☐	☐	☐
☐ Memberships	☐	☐	☐	☐	☐	☐
☐ Business Cards	☐	☐	☐	☐	☐	☐
☐ Stationery	☐	☐	☐	☐	☐	☐
☐ Taxes	☐	☐	☐	☐	☐	☐
☐ _____	☐	☐	☐	☐	☐	☐

Notes: _____

_____

_____

_____

_____

_____

_____

Notes:

Chapter 24

Create the Ultimate Honeymoon Getaway

- Pick Your Hot Spot: Choosing a Destination

- Budget Your Trip

- Get It Booked

- Tips and Suggestions for a Great Honeymoon Getaway

- e-Plan It! Use Your e-Resources:

  Travel Guides on the Web
  Destination Finders
  Online Travel, Hotel, and Rental Car Booking
  Your Website's Honeymoon Page

- Worksheets:

  Considerations Worksheet: Honeymoon Budget
  Considerations Worksheet: Honeymoon
  Checklist: Packing Suggestions
  Contact Sheet: Honeymoon Accommodations

When the dust finally settles, it's time for a break! And a good one, too: you've spent months planning, organizing, and coordinating a million and one details. You've entered a new stage in your lives together, and have just spent the weekend hosting family and friends. Happy? Of Course! Drained? Definitely! You deserve a custom-made, romantic getaway just for the two of you to relax, unwind, and reflect on everything that's happened. From picking the right spot to budgeting your fantasy trip to getting it all booked, check out the following guidance and advice to help make your honeymoon everything you deserve it to be.

Pick Your Hot Spot: Choosing a Destination

What's your idea of a dream honeymoon? This may be different for both of you...your sweetheart might be up for an action-filled adventure while the only action you might care for is lifting your margarita glass and soaking up sun on a Caribbean beach. Compromise and combine your pleasures. Select a destination that provides opportunities for both relaxation and action; you can always hit the beach or pool for a nap while your sweetie takes a mini-excursion. You're not obligated to stay at each other's side 100% of the time, and you may very well crave some private time when the hustle and bustle of the wedding planning is finally over. You'll always look forward to your rendezvous afterwards!

When thinking about honeymoon destinations, go over your options together and pick a spot with something in it for both of you. Your goal should be to come up with two or three possible destinations that you can research further before comparing the estimated cost demands of each and making a decision (we'll discuss costs more in the upcoming discussion on Budgeting Your Trip).

<TIP>

What to Do, and When

Follow your checklist in Chapter 2 to plan your honeymoon getaway, and don't let it slip through the cracks until the end! Get better airfare deals and more destination variety by doing things early. Plus, you'll have one less thing to deal with when things start picking up towards the end of your planning. Here's a time guide to this chapter:

12 months before: Think about a destination.

9 months before: Do your research.

6 months before: Set your budget.

5 months before: Book It.

</TIP>

Beaches and Cruises and Resorts, Oh My!

When considering where to go, try to imagine yourself at your dream spot, just like you did when en-visioning your perfect wedding. What's the climate like…is it sunbathing-friendly, hot and tropical? Or is it dusted in powdery snow, with a warm fire to snuggle in front of? Do you imagine yourself being pampered at an all-inclusive resort (massages, martinis, and yummy meals) or touring across Europe? How about privacy…are you two secluded, free to slowly explore (each other!) or bathed in big-city lights? Are you mobile, relaxing on a cruise or riding the rails over beautiful country? Use your imagina-tion, add your own ideas, and research the following e-Resources to find the perfect spot.

Action-Packed or Rest-and-Relaxation?

Your destination choice will be influenced by whether your idea of a romantic honeymoon getaway is more relaxing or adventuresome. You may want to do some of both, so be sure the spots you look into will accommodate that. For example, an oceanside resort that offers nearby jungle or forest excur-sions, kayaking, and snorkeling should satisfy both the beach bum and adventure junkie in you. Or, split your honeymoon up into mini-getaways: spend the first half recuperating from the stresses of wedding planning at an all-inclusive resort, and for the second half grab a guidebook, your backpack, and hit the trails to do some fun exploring.

Helpful Resources

It's a good idea to start doing some serious research into your honeymoon destinations around nine months or so before your wedding. Find information and trip suggestions on the locations you're considering; do it from home in a snap with online travel guides and destination sites like the ones we suggest below. You can also look in maps, brochures, and tour guides for leads. Check out the travel section at a local bookstore. Don't forget to ask friends and coworkers for recommendations on spots they liked, too.

e-Resource

Travel Guides on the Web

Lonely Planet (www.lonelyplanet.com)

An excellent online travel guide and one of the best resources to find destinations and cool spots off the beaten path, Lonely Planet's website will be an immeasurable help in researching more about your potential destinations. Click on the map and zero in on fun-sounding locations to learn more. As an example, the page for Italy is packed with informative articles and allows you to select from a dropdown box to explore individual regions like Venice, Rome, or Naples.

Fodor's (www.fodors.com)

Click on the overview map on fodors.com and browse locations from Acapulco to Zurich. You'll have access to features, visitor-rated sights and attractions, maps, and articles covering all the topics you'd expect from a solid print guidebook. Click on the "Booking" link and you'll be taken to Fodor's partner, Expedia.com. We'll cover Expedia and other forms of online (and offline) travel booking later in the chapter.

Destination Finders

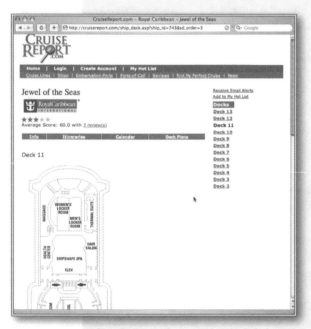

CruiseReport.com lets you explore the deck plan and profile of popular cruise ships.

BedandBreakfast.com

This site is a great resource for finding and researching B and B's. Each spot is presented with extensive information covering the type of establishment, property details, and room rates. You'll also find photos, maps, contact info, and website links.

Cruise Lines International Association (www.cruising.org)

Thinking about a honeymoon cruise? The Cruise Lines International Association (www.cruising.org) allows you to search cruises based on destination, cruise line, and cruise duration.

CruiseReport.com

This comprehensive resource maintains a third-party database of cruise ship information, itineraries, sailing dates, and more. You'll find information on destinations, major cruise lines, consumer reviews, and even the deck plans of popular cruise ships. Check out the reviews to read other visitors' cruise experiences and to post your own.

Budget Your Trip

In order to get everything booked properly and take advantage of the lowest possible travel prices, try to have a honeymoon budget nailed down no later than six months before your wedding. If your engagement length itself is six months or less, get this taken care of while you plan your overall wedding budget. You may be asking how you're going to finance your honeymoon fund with all the other expenses you have to deal with, especially if you're footing the entire wedding bill yourselves. Let's discuss what to expect, how to save, and why you need to get everything planned and booked early.

```
<CROSS-REFERENCE>
We covered building a smart wedding budget in Chapter 5.
</CROSS-REFERENCE>
```

What? More Budgets?

We know you've probably had your fill of budgets by now and may be doing all you can in order to get your wedding pulled off without slipping into the black hole of debt. But look at it this way: you're experts at budget management at this point, as well as masters of the art of financial divide-and-conquering. And this is your honeymoon we're talking about! For many couples, the honeymoon is one of the most enjoyable, memorable aspects of their wedding. How many times do you get the opportunity—and, indeed, are encouraged—to drop everything, leave the real world behind for a while, and indulge yourselves in a custom-made fantasy just for the two of you? While you're enjoying it, you'll be thanking yourselves for the smart up-front planning you do now.

How Much Will It Cost?

The average *total expense* newlyweds are paying for a week-long honeymoon is between $3,000 and $4,000. This includes all costs, from travel and lodging to meals and purchases. Now, of course, you're no average couple: you're you. So how does that $3,000 to $4,000 figure apply? It really depends on your destination and preferences. Shorter trips will obviously be less expensive than longer ones, and driving is cheaper than flying. Some destinations are just more pricey, and some couple's priorities might have a higher price tag than those of others. Plan to spend more or less than the average depending on your own situation.

Things to Consider

Sit down together and decide how much you think you can spend overall, based on your situation (including the burden of your wedding budget). Include family contributions as well. Set this figure aside. For each destination you're considering, list all your possible expenses. Some of these will be estimates until you get more solid numbers from your travel agent or from collecting prices on your own. Consider everything: travel expenses, lodging, meals, activities you might try, entertainment, alcohol, and so forth.

Prioritize your categories, and choose where to cut back and where to splurge. If you're the kind of couple who cares less where they are as long as they're in a luxurious hotel, your adjustments will be different than those couples happy to crash in little more than a sleeping bag so long as they're in the right country or town.

How Long Will Your Honeymoon Be?

Based on the considerations above, think about the cost for each destination you're considering. Some will cost more than others. The duration of your honeymoon will depend on how much it costs relative to how much you have available for the trip overall, so keep this in mind when you're narrowing down your choices. Do you want to settle on your second destination choice if it means you can spend two weeks on your honeymoon instead of just one? Before making the final choice, talk it over with a travel agent or use the e-Resources we'll provide in the next section to collect some solid pricing information.

Money-Saving Ideas

Give yourself more getaway bang for your buck with the following suggestions to consider while budgeting your trip.

Go somewhere you can drive. You'll save the potentially expensive plane tickets and won't have to worry about a rental car, giving you more to spend on meals, activities, and lodging.

Use a family member or friend's timeshare or vacation house. It can be their wedding gift to you.

Buy a honeymoon package instead of purchasing hotel, airfare, and meals separately. Such all-inclusive deals are a great way to save money, but make sure you compare any such offers with á la carte pricing. And it should make sense with respect to your plans: if you're planning on taking off frequently on your own to explore, or eating a lot of meals away from the resort, then a package with included tours or meal plans isn't going to save you anything.

Use a credit card with airline miles as a spending reward, and put all your wedding costs through it. Pay the bill off every month to avoid finance charges, and at the end of it all use your miles towards your honeymoon tickets.

<TIP>

Delaying Gratification

If there's just no way you think you can afford the honeymoon you truly want right after your wedding, postpone it for a set length of time to give yourselves a chance to scrape up some extra travel funds. Just make sure that you take at least a few days off after the big day; you're going to need the rest and will appreciate the time alone after all that planning. It's essential at that point to unwind and just enjoy one another's company. And remember that the postponement should be a set length of time, not just an abstract "when we get around to it", or it will likely drift off into the abyss of woulda-coulda-shoulda's that never happen.

</TIP>

Be sure to check smaller, surrounding airports when deciding where to fly out of. San Jose or Oakland might be cheaper than San Francisco, for example. Check Milwaukee along with Chicago, or Baltimore along with D.C.

Make a list of all the little things you'll be needing: sunscreen, lip balm, insect spray, film, and so forth. It's a lot cheaper to buy it at home than at most resort locations.

Let everyone know you're honeymooners and ask if you qualify for specials.

Set up a honeymoon gift registry if your wedding website offers one, which allows guests to make donations towards your trip. Or use services like www.honeyluna.com and www.thehoneymoon.com, free online registries that do the same thing. In Chapter 15, we went over gift registries like these in more detail.

When you arrive, leave the real world behind and don't worry about making expensive long distance phone calls. Hit up a cybercafe and send everyone an email letting them know you're okay, then leave it at that.

If you're traveling internationally, do your money exchange at your destination, not at home. You'll get a better exchange rate there.

Hit restaurants and shops that aren't in the tourist areas. They'll be more authentic, and you'll pay less.

Get It Booked

Your honeymoon should be booked no later than five months before your wedding so you can focus on planning for the big day itself. Good resorts and hotels book up early, and you want to take advantage of the lower travel prices that booking early affords you.

Using a Travel Agent

You may want to use the services of a travel agent to locate a destination for you. You'll discuss your honeymoon vision with the agent, explain your preferences, and let her research the options for you. After searching affiliated airlines and hotels, your agent will call you back with some possibilities. The service is free (travel agents are paid commissions by airlines and hotels), and you may prefer this method of destination booking. A good travel agent will be able to give you the advantage of first-hand experience at the location, or at the very least have enough industry wisdom to know a good deal from a bad one.

Keep in mind, however, that not all travel agents are created equal. While some are well traveled, know all sorts of great tips and have priceless connections, others simply sit at a desk and do the equivalent of searching the e-Resources we'll cover next. In this case, you'd be better off searching yourselves, spending more time to investigate each option and keeping the control in your own hands.

Since the advantage of using a travel agent is only an advantage if you have an especially good one, you'd be well advised to get a recommendation. Ask well traveled friends and family which agent they use, if any. Or try contacting the American Society of Travel Agents for a referral in your area (www.astanet.com).

Online Travel, Hotel, and Rental Car Booking

These days, online travel websites and resources abound. You can find great deals at bargain prices, and build a complete travel itinerary with airfare, hotel, and rental car, then print out detailed maps to all the spots you want to hit.

SideStep.com

Don't miss this one. SideStep takes the hassle and time out of going from one online travel website to another by searching a ton of them and presenting the results together. At the time of this writing, SideStep claims to provide results from 585 domestic and international airlines, more than 90,000 hotels, and over 2,800 car locations. The search includes websites like Orbitz (www.orbitz.com), Hotels.com, and more. When you find a result in SideStep that you like, it sends you to the website it found the deal so you can view the details or book it.

Other Popular Travel Websites

Travel websites that you'll want to add to your search arsenal are Travelocity (www.travelocity.com), Expedia (www.expedia.com), Orbitz (www.orbitz.com), and Priceline (www.priceline.com). They each offer great ways to look up hotels, airfare, vacation packages, and most also offer online articles on destinations and honeymoon options.

Beverly Clark Travel Club (www.beverlyclarktravel.com)

Beverly Clark's Travel Club offers a travel agent service that will help customize your honeymoon. Give them a try if you're considering the travel agent approach. Check out the "Specials" link on the bottom of the main page to see a list of current honeymoon package deals and what's included for each.

Travel Packages vs. Á La Carte

Whether you purchase from a travel agent or web site, you can opt for a travel package "deal" that combines hotel, airfare, and more in one up-front discounted price. While they're easy to book and usually cost less than purchasing the different components separately, just make sure you know exactly what you're getting. You might get a great plane ticket for a good airline, at just the right times with no stops, but may be disappointed with your hotel room. Or vice versa. The bottom line: do your research. Check the flight times and number of stops in the travel itinerary. Call the hotel directly for more details on the amenities provided, included activities or meals, and to find out what class of room you'd have. See if you'd be able to upgrade anything, and if so whether you'd still be saving money versus purchasing the individual items separately.

Tips and Suggestions for a Great Honeymoon Getaway

Keep the following in mind when booking, preparing for, and enjoying your romantic getaway celebration.

Booking

When you purchase your airfare, try to get e-tickets; you don't have to worry about these getting lost or stolen. To be on the safe side, bring along a printout of the confirmation and itinerary as a backup.

Booking a cruise? Make sure you call in to get the specifics on your cabin. Ask about the cabin size, whether the bed is double or bunk, and whether yours is an outside room (you'll have a porthole window in this case...it's not much, but if you're a tad claustrophobic, it could make a big difference). Oh, and don't forget the Dramamine or other anti-seasickness measures.

Cruise ship gift shops usually discount their items on the way home, so buy your gifts on the way back.

Brides, use your maiden name for your airfare reservations. Your plane ticket needs to match your ID and passport. There will be plenty of time to deal with name changes when you get back (we mentioned the process in Chapter 23). For hotel reservations, you can go ahead and use your married name.

Preparation

Call a couple days before your wedding to confirm your lodging reservations, airfare, and rental car availability.

Make sure your luggage is labeled with your name, mailing address, and a phone number (preferably for a mobile phone you have on you). It's also a good idea to have a list of your luggage contents, which can be helpful in the event you need to claim a loss.

Rather than hopping on the plane immediately after your wedding, get your rest and book a honeymoon suite at or near the reception area to spend your first night.

If you're using film cameras, keep the film in a carry-on bag, as the scanning equipment that's used to inspect checked luggage can ruin it. While you're at it, make sure *all* important or valuable items are in your carry-on: jewelry, medicine, cash, your itinerary, phone numbers, and anything you might need en-route. While it's rare that airlines lose luggage, it does happen. Put a day's worth of essential toiletries and a change of clothes in your carry-on just in case.

Prepare ahead of time. Look up attractions, shows, shopping areas, restaurants, and so forth before you leave; use online map services like Google Earth (earth.google.com) or MapQuest

<TIP>

Don't Forget the Essentials

• Identification (passport, driver's license)

• Birth control

• Printed travel itinerary and all confirmation numbers

• Camera and film or large enough memory card(s)

• Batteries

• First-aid: antibacterial ointment, band-aids, wipes, anti-itch ointment

• Prescription meds, allergy pills, upset stomach remedies, antacid

• Sunblock, lotion

• Insect repellant

• Extra glasses or contact lenses

• Emergency phone numbers

• Emergency credit card

• Cash

• Toothbrush and toothpaste

• Pen and notebook (travel journal)

• If you want to send postcards, bring an address list

• Mobile phone (if your plan covers your destination)

</TIP>

(www.mapquest.com) to find cool places to hit and print out maps and directions. Get a guidebook on the area you're traveling to, and check out the online travel guides discussed in the previous e-Resource.

While You're There

It's every honeymooning couple's nightmare: you arrive at your hotel or resort and find that they don't have your room available. Bring proof of your confirmation (a computer print-out or receipt) or have them give your travel agent a call. Upon being presented with proof of confirmation they're obliged to accommodate you, either by upgrading your room or arranging for comparable lodging at another hotel, along with transportation there.

If your room isn't what you booked (it doesn't have that great ocean view you paid the extra buck for, or there are two full beds instead of one king), ask right away to speak to the manager and request your room be moved. Be firm but polite, and you should be accommodated fairly quickly.

Take lots of pictures! Make sure you're prepared with plenty of film, or an extra memory card or two, and don't forget your charger or spare batteries. Enlarge the best ones when you get back, add them to your wedding albums, and post them in a honeymoon album on your wedding website.

Bring back memories for all the senses: in addition to photos, collect things that will remind you of your getaway in more ways than just visually. Bring back regional taste souvenirs: chocolates or a great bottle of red wine from France, Rompope from Mexico, coconut syrup from Hawaii. Purchase regional music you've heard. Make a list of the songs that remind you of your trip, and buy a CD of the steel drum band that played during your first dinner.

Keep a day-to-day journal to record your thoughts and experiences. It will keep your honeymoon trip alive like nothing else!

e-Resource

Your Website's Honeymoon Page

Your guests will all love to know what your honeymoon destination is, what it looks like, and why you picked it. So why not let them in on it? Everyone knows your wedding website is the hot spot for all things regarding the two of you. Let your insiders know what the plans are after the big day by posting info about your getaway destination on a separate honeymoon page. Your guests will be thrilled to get the scoop on your spot, and it will make them feel that much more a part of your wedding. If you have access to a cybercafe while on your honeymoon, you can even hop on the web once or twice and post some quick notes on how things are in paradise. Feel free to make it a running travel blog.

Let your guests in on your honeymoon destination with the help of your wedding website. You can include photos and information on the spot, along with anecdotes on why you selected it.

<TIP>

Wish You Were Here

Sending postcards is a traditional way of giving those back at home a little glimpse of paradise. Depending on where you're at, though, postcards can take a while to get home; you might even make it back before they do. Take it to the next level with your wedding website! If you have access to a hotel computer or cybercafe (most hotels and resort destinations these days have a way online), you can drop everyone a word at the speed of the Net. Sending an email is another option, but your website makes it easier and a lot more slick. Post notes on your honeymoon page and make it a travel blog so everyone can visit your website and get the scoop. You can even upload photos from your digital camera and show them how the good life is, as you're enjoying it!

</TIP>

Considerations Worksheet: Honeymoon Budget

☐ Passport $ _____

☐ Medical Exam, Inoculations $ _____

☐ Honeymoon Clothing Purchases $ _____

☐ Honeymoon Trousseau $ _____

☐ Toiletries $ _____

☐ Camera, Batteries, Film/Media $ _____

☐ Maps/Guides/Travel Magazines $ _____

☐ _____ $ _____

☐ _____ $ _____

☐ Transportation Tickets $ _____

☐ Shuttle / Cab $ _____

☐ Rental Car $ _____

☐ Public Transportation $ _____

☐ _____ $ _____

☐ Accommodations $ _____

☐ Room Service $ _____

☐ _____ $ _____

☐ Meals $ _____

☐ Snacks $ _____

☐ _____ $ _____

☐ Entertainment $ _____

☐ Pampering $ _____

☐ Souvenirs and Gifts $ _____

☐ Postcards and Stamps $ _____

☐ _____ $ _____

☐ All-Inclusive Package $ _____

Total Estimated Honeymoon Budget $ _____

Considerations Worksheet: Honeymoon

Honeymoon Budget: $ _____

Destination

☐ Foreign
☐ Domestic
☐ Seaside
☐ Urban
☐ Nature
☐ Warm-Weather
☐ Cold-Weather
☐ _____

Destination Style

☐ Rest-and-Relaxation
☐ Action-Packed Adventure
☐ Touring and Exploring
☐ Cultural / Historic
☐ Big City Night Life
☐ Sports and Activities Filled
☐ Cruise
☐ Combination

Departure

☐ Directly from Wedding
☐ Following Day
☐ Later Date

Duration

☐ _____Days
☐ _____Weeks

Accommodations

☐ Secluded Resort
☐ All-Inclusive Resort
☐ Deluxe Resort
☐ Cruise or Train
☐ Pay as You Go
☐ Combination

Notes:
_____
_____
_____
_____
_____
_____
_____
_____
_____
_____
_____
_____
_____
_____
_____

Checklist: Packing Suggestions

Use the following list to help from missing any of those easy-to-forget items.

Essentials

- ☐ Identification (passport, visas, driver's license)
- ☐ Marriage License (if needed)
- ☐ Travel Itinerary
- ☐ Confirmation Numbers (hotel, car rentals)
- ☐ Birth Control
- ☐ Inoculations Certificate (if needed)
- ☐ Prescription Meds, Allergy and Cold Pills
- ☐ Aspirin, Antacid and Diarrhea Meds
- ☐ First Aid Kit
- ☐ Insect Repellent, Anti-itch Ointment
- ☐ Cash, Travelers' Checks
- ☐ Emergency Credit Card
- ☐ Emergency Phone Numbers (address book)

- ☐ Camera, Extra Film or Media
- ☐ Extra Batteries or Charger
- ☐ Reading Material
- ☐ Toothbrush, Toothpaste
- ☐ Chapstick, Breath Mints
- ☐ Sunblock, Dry Skin Lotion
- ☐ Sunglasses, Reading Glasses or Contact Lenses
- ☐ Eye Drops, Lens Solution and Case
- ☐ Mobile Phone and Charger (if in signal area)
- ☐ Pen and Notebook (travel journal)
- ☐ ompact Umbrella
- ☐ Dirty Laundry Bags
- ☐

Bride

- ☐ Casual Tops:
- ☐ Casual Pants:
- ☐ Shorts:
- ☐ Athletic Clothes:
- ☐ Skirts / Dresses:
- ☐ Dress Tops:
- ☐ Dress Pants:
- ☐ Evening Dress:
- ☐ Jackets/ Coats:
- ☐ Sweater:
- ☐ Shoes (dress, walking):
- ☐ Sneakers:
- ☐ Sandals:
- ☐ Swimwear, Cover-up:
- ☐ Underwear:
- ☐ Bras:
- ☐ Socks and Hosiery:
- ☐ Lingerie and Robe:
- ☐ Toiletries:
- ☐ Purse:
- ☐ Gloves/Scarf:
- ☐ Jewelry:

Groom

- ☐ Casual Shirts:
- ☐ Casual Pants:
- ☐ Shorts:
- ☐ Athletic Clothes:
- ☐ Tie(s):
- ☐ Dress Shirts:
- ☐ Dress Pants:
- ☐ Suit:
- ☐ Jackets/Coats:
- ☐ Sweater:
- ☐ Shoes (dress, walking):
- ☐ Sneakers:
- ☐ Sandals:
- ☐ Swimwear:
- ☐ Underwear:
- ☐ T-Shirts:
- ☐ Socks (Dress, Sport):
- ☐ Pajamas and Robe:
- ☐ Toiletries:
- ☐ Backpack:
- ☐ Gloves/Scarf:
- ☐ Watch:

Contact Sheet: Honeymoon Accommodations

Wedding Night Hotel:

Address:

Recommended By:

Email:

Phone:

Fax:

Website:

Amenities Description:

Staple Business Card

Confirmation No.:	Date Booked:	Date Confirmed:
Rate: $	Arrival Date:	Departure Date:

Honeymoon Hotel:

Address:

Recommended By:

Email:

Phone:

Fax:

Website:

Amenities Description:

Confirmation No.:	Date Booked:	Date Confirmed:
Rate: $	Arrival Date:	Departure Date:

Notes:

List of e-Resources

List of Worksheets

Index

About the Authors

Silicon Valley natives and technology professionals Crystal and Jason Melendez were motivated during their own wedding planning adventure to research the many convenient but often unknown ways that today's technology can assist an engaged couple. In addition to co-founding and developing WedShare.com, which has grown to be a top wedding website service provider and a leader in online planning tools, the newlyweds-turned-business partners are active members of the wedding industry and passionate about showing other couples how to plan and pull off their big day with minimal cost, hassle, and stress. Crystal and Jason live in San Jose, California where they continue their writing and development.

e-Plan Your Wedding Order Form

YES! I want to e-Plan my wedding and save as much time and money as possible. Check out the latest version of this cutting-edge comprehensive guide as well as other upcoming titles from Mediasoft Press on our website.

Order:

On the Web – www.eplanyourwedding.com, www.mediasoftpress.com

By Email – orders@mediasoftpress.com

By Phone – 800-592-9151 (toll free)

By Fax – 408-404-5226

By Mail – Mediasoft Press, P.O. Box 610487, San Jose, CA 95161-0487 USA

Please send me the following books, CDs or kits:

_____

_____

_____

Please send me more FREE information on:

☐ Other Books   ☐ Wedding Consulting   ☐ Author Seminars

Name:

Address:

City: State: Zip:

Phone: Email:

Priority Shipping:

Domestic – $4 for the first book or CD and $1 for each additional copy.

International – $9 for the first book or CD and $5 for each additional copy.

Payment:

☐ Visa   ☐ Mastercard   ☐ Check

Card Number: Exp:

Discount Replacements:

Is your copy of this book out-of-date, worn, or would you like to replace it with a brand new copy for a friend? Whether or not you ordered your book from us, send us just $14 (plus shipping) and the front cover—and we'll send you the brand new, completely updated edition!